Curriculum and Instruction for Becoming a Teacher

Forrest W. Parkay
Washington State University

PEARSON

*A*B

Boston • New York • San Francisco
Mexico City • Montreal • Toronto • London • Madrid • Munich • Paris
Hong Kong • Singapore • Tokyo • Cape Town • Sydney

Executive Editor and Publisher: Stephen D. Dragin
Editorial Assistant: Meaghan Minnick
Marketing Manager: Tara Kelly
Production Editor: Annette Joseph
Editorial Production Service: Modern Graphics, Inc.
Composition Buyer: Linda Cox
Manufacturing Buyer: Andrew Turso
Electronic Composition: Modern Graphics, Inc.
Interior Design: Glenna Collett
Photo Researcher: Po Yee Oster
Cover Administrator: Kristina Mose-Libon

For related titles and support materials, visit our online catalog at www.ablongman.com.

Between the time website information is gathered and then published, it is not unusual for some sites to have closed. Also, the transcription of URLs can result in typographical errors. The publisher would appreciate notification where these errors occur so that they may be corrected in subsequent editions.

Library of Congress Cataloging-in-Publication Data
Parkay, Forrest W.
  Curriculum and instruction for becoming a teacher / Forrest W. Parkay.
    p. cm.
  Includes bibliographical references and index.
  ISBN 0-205-42425-2
    1. Teachers—Training of—United States. 2. Curriculum planning—United States. I. Title.

LB1715.P24 2006
370′.71′1—dc22

                                                                                    2005050908

Printed in the United States of America
10 9 8 7 6 5 4 3 2 1   RRD-IN   09   08   07   06   05

Photo Credits: Page 2, Jose Luis Pelaez/CORBIS; 9, Comstock Royalty Free Photo; 12, Bill Aaron/ PhotoEdit; 19, Grantpix/ Photo Researchers; 31, 46, Will Hart/PhotoEdit; 52, Ellen Senisi/The Image Works; 64, T. Lindfors Photography; 79, Frank Siteman; 90, Will Hart; 93, CORBIS; 94 top left, Goodman/Photo Researchers; 94 top right, Hermine Dreyfuss; 94 bottom left, Forsyth; 94 bottom right, Byron/Photo Researchers; 104, Bonnie Kamin/PhotoEdit; 115, Mark Harmel/Getty Images; 128, Bob Daemmrich/PhotoEdit; 134, Bob Daemmrich/The Image Works; 143, Bob Daemmrich/PhotoEdit; 153, Tony Freeman/PhotoEdit; 168, Frank Siteman; 176, Bachmann/PhotoEdit; 194, 202, A. Ramey/PhotoEdit; 214, David Young-Wolff/PhotoEdit; 225, Andrew Halbrooke/The Image Works; 233, Michael Newman/PhotoEdit; 244, David Young-Wolff/ PhotoEdit; 248, Chip Henderson/ IndexStock Imagery.

Brief Contents

Contents

Preface

Teaching is one of the world's most important professions—and one of the most challenging. With continuing calls for higher standards, greater teacher accountability, and legislation such as the No Child Left Behind Act of 2001, becoming a teacher requires more professionalism and expertise than ever.

To facilitate your journey toward becoming a successful teacher, *Curriculum and Instruction for Becoming a Teacher* explains what it takes to create an effective, learning-oriented classroom. The book focuses on two critical elements of teaching—*what* is taught (the curriculum) and *how* it is taught (instruction). For example, you will learn about the importance of creating a multicultural curriculum to meet the needs and backgrounds of all students. You will also learn how to address the needs of learners at different developmental stages and with different abilities and disabilities, and you will learn about the latest approaches for assessing student learning. Because technology continues to have a profound influence on teaching, you will learn how teachers are using educational technologies to increase student learning. Lastly, you will learn how to plan for a successful first year of teaching.

Several features of the book are designed to give you a solid understanding of how to create a positive, learning-oriented classroom. For example, a Teachers' Voices feature in each chapter presents a short, first-person article written by a teacher to illustrate how teachers apply chapter content to actual classroom situations. The features will provide you with firsthand insights into real-world challenges teachers face and practical solutions for meeting those challenges.

To help you get the most out of your teacher education program, each chapter of this book includes a feature titled Relevant Standards. This feature illustrates how chapter content relates to standards developed by four professional associations: the Interstate New Teacher Assessment and Support Consortium (INTASC), the National Council for Accreditation of Teacher Education (NCATE), the Praxis Series: Professional Assessments for Beginning Teachers, and the National Board for Professional Teaching Standards (NBPTS).

Each chapter also includes a Case for Reflection designed to give you an opportunity to reflect on the contemporary issues teachers must deal with on a daily basis. The cases focus on controversial trends and issues that have aroused public opinion and have attracted media attention.

A Technology in Teaching feature in each chapter illustrates how educational technology is related to chapter content. This feature also provides current examples of how educational technologies are influencing schools and the profession of teaching.

Curriculum and Instruction for Becoming a Teacher also includes many learning aids to help you prepare for a rewarding future in teaching. Guiding Questions at the beginning of each chapter present the questions posed in the main headings within each chapter. Realistic opening scenarios present decision-making or problem-solving situations teachers frequently confront. At the end of each chapter, Reflective Application Activities (Discussion Questions, Professional Journal, Online Assignments, and Observations and Interviews) present further opportunities to apply chapter content.

The book also includes a Professional Portfolio feature that will enable you to document your professional growth over time. These features present guidelines for creating portfolio entries that you can use when you begin teaching, or you may wish to use selected portfolio entries during the process of applying for your first teaching position. As a further study aid, Key Terms and Concepts are bold-faced in the text and listed with page cross-references at the ends of chapters. A Glossary at the end of the book can help you quickly locate the definitions of key terms and concepts and the text pages on which they appear.

Acknowledgments

Many members of the Allyn and Bacon team provided the author with expert guidance and support during the writing of *Curriculum and Instruction for Becoming a Teacher*. The author benefited from the consistent encouragement and excellent suggestions provided by Steve Dragin, Executive Editor and Publisher. His extensive understanding of textbook publishing was invaluable in conceptualizing the book. In addition, Meaghan Minnick, Editorial Assistant, provided helpful feedback on the manuscript and steadfast support and encouragement.

The author also appreciates the support of his friends and colleagues while writing this book. In particular, Phyllis Erdman, Chair of the Department of Educational Leadership and Counseling Psychology at Washington State University; Gail Furman, Coordinator of the Educational Leadership Program Area; Len Foster, Coordinator of the Higher Education Program Area; and Eric J. Anctil, Assistant Professor of Educational Leadership, provided invaluable ideas and much-appreciated encouragement and support.

In addition, the author gives a sincere thanks to students (many of them now teachers and school administrators) in the classes he has taught at Washington State University. Conversations with them over the years have been thought provoking and professionally rewarding. And, for demonstrating the power of professional inquiry, he owes a profound debt to a great teacher, mentor, and friend, Herbert A. Thelen, Professor Emeritus, University of Chicago.

Lastly, the author would like to thank Wu Mei for her friendship, spiritual support, and encouragement during the writing of this book. Ni shi diyige, ye shi zuihou yige, wode yiqie.

Forrest W. Parkay

Curriculum and Instruction for Becoming a Teacher

1 Learning *What* to Teach and *How* to Teach It

Accomplished teaching involves making difficult and principled choices, exercising careful judgment and honoring the complex nature of the educational mission.

—National Board for Professional Teaching Standards,
What Teachers Should Know and Be Able to Do

It's your first day of teaching. You enter the classroom full of anticipation. As the students come into the room, chatting easily with one another, you think about how they feel comfortable, used to the routine. You, however, are anxious, not sure of what to expect.

For a week, you've spent an hour or two a day going over your plans for the first day with your students. You are amazed at the amount of time you've spent preparing for the first day, and you wonder how much time experienced teachers spend preparing for class. Last night, you woke up twice, and each time you mentally rehearsed what you would do during that first day.

Now you are finding out what it is like to be a "real teacher." "Can I adjust to the challenges of teaching?" you wonder. You got good grades in your teacher education courses, but you know that putting research and theory into practice is not easy. Right now, it's hard to imagine that you will ever feel as comfortable as your students do in the classroom.

Despite feeling anxious, you know that you are well prepared. You definitely know the material you are going to teach. Thinking about how well prepared you are gives you confidence. I *am* a "real teacher," you think, just as the bell rings, signaling the start of class. Now you begin to teach.

"Good morning, class. My name is . . ."

The next several hours seem to fly by. Already, it is afternoon, and the dismissal bell has just rung. As students file out of your room, you take stock of the first day. It's hard to remember everything that happened. Some things went well, you think, others not so well.

For the most part, students seemed to be interested and on task during the day. At other times, however, you could "feel" their resistance. Some students talked with their neighbors. Others stared out the window. Others yawned openly, as if to say "I am bored. Why don't we do something interesting?"

Though you had a definite plan for the day, you realize that teaching involves a lot more than just following a plan. Being a "good" teacher involves a lot. It's more than showing students "who's the boss." It's more than being a subject-matter expert. It's knowing *what* to teach and *how* to teach it.

Guiding Questions

1. **What knowledge do you need to teach?**
2. **What can you learn from observing in classrooms?**
3. **How can you gain practical experience for becoming a teacher?**

4. **What is taught in schools?**

5. **How is the school curriculum developed?**

6. **How can you develop a multicultural classroom and curriculum?**

A s the opening scenario for this chapter suggests, becoming a "real teacher" involves more than following a plan for teaching. Successful teaching involves knowing both *what* to teach and *how* to teach it. *Curriculum and Instruction for Becoming a Teacher* focuses on both of these important elements of teaching—*what* is taught (the curriculum) and *how* it is taught (instruction).

Curriculum and instruction are not separate elements of teaching; they are connected, as the following figure suggests. They are both part of teaching; each influences the other. When a teacher decides to include certain content in the curriculum, that decision means that some methods of instruction will be better suited than others to teach that content to students. Conversely, a particular instructional method (e.g., cooperative learning) may be more effective at presenting certain types of content than others. Effective teachers know that they must develop knowledge and skills in both areas—from planning the *what* of the curriculum to planning the *how* of instruction.

Curriculum
(What)   **Instruction**
                                                                        (How)

Within the broad areas of curriculum and instruction, this book will help you to answer questions such as the following: What content or curriculum will your students find meaningful and interesting? What content will they need to know? How can you develop style of teaching that motivates students to learn that content? What knowledge and skills will you need to develop an effective teaching style?

The willingness and ability to reflect on questions like these is the hallmark of a professional teacher. As a teacher, you will never arrive at *the* answers for these questions; you will realize that the answers change continually. With each new group of students at the start of a school year, you will need to formulate new answers to these questions. Indeed, you will formulate new answers with each new day in the classroom.

Teaching is not easy. Teaching is a complex act—one that requires thoughtfulness, insight into the motivations of others, and good judgment. You will come to understand that *how* you teach students is just as important as *what* they are taught, as the following comment by a teacher suggests:

Before becoming a teacher, I imagined that I would teach my students, they would take a test, and I would evaluate my teaching based on their test scores. Actually, that cycle happens very little. It is a part of teaching, but relating to kids, being able to encourage them, being able to laugh with them matters more and more as I develop my teaching style. Encouragement, respect, and trust—those things really make a difference. I am really interested in my subject, mathematics, but I am learning that what matters most to students and to me is becoming excited about learning. When I feel that excitement from the kids . . . that's what makes teaching great.

To facilitate your journey toward becoming successful as a teacher, *Curriculum and Instruction for Becoming a Teacher* explains what it takes to create a successful, learning-oriented classroom. Chapter 1 is divided into two parts: the first part examines the knowledge and skills required for successful teaching and explains how to acquire that knowledge and those skills. The second part explains how school curricula are developed and why today's teachers must create a multicultural curriculum to meet the needs and backgrounds of all students.

The remainder of the book is organized in the following manner. Chapter 2 examines the dynamics of classroom life and how to create a positive learning environment. Chapter 3 explains how to address the needs of learners at different developmental stages and with different abilities and disabilities. Chapter 4 describes the latest approaches for assessing student learning. Chapter 5 provides an up-to-date overview of how teachers are using educational technologies to increase student learning. Lastly, Chapter 6 explains how to plan for a successful induction into teaching and how to become involved in professional collaboration to ensure your continued professional growth.

To ensure that all students are taught by teachers who possess the knowledge and skills covered in *Curriculum and Instruction for Becoming a Teacher*, several professional associations and state departments of education have developed standards reflecting that knowledge and those skills. Most likely, your teacher education program uses one or more of these sets of standards to evaluate your progress toward becoming an effective teacher.

The professional standards that have had the greatest impact on teacher education programs nationally (as well as on teachers' ongoing professional growth and development) are those developed by the **Interstate New Teacher Assessment and Support Consortium (INTASC)**, the **National Council for Accreditation of Teacher Education (NCATE)**, the **Praxis Series: Professional Assessments for Beginning Teachers**, and the **National Board for Professional Teaching Standards (NBPTS)**.

To help you get the most out of this book, each chapter includes a feature titled *Relevant Standards* that illustrates how a professional standard developed by each of these four groups is related to chapter content. Figure 1.1 presents an overview of the standards developed by each group. Which of these sets of standards have influenced the teacher education program in which you are enrolled? Does your state have a set of professional standards that also applies to your teacher education program?

Figure 1.1 Professional standards for becoming a teacher.

INTASC Standards

A consortium of more than thirty states that has developed standards and an assessment process for initial teacher certification. INTASC model core standards are based on ten principles evident in effective teaching regardless of subject or grade level. The principles are based on the realization that effective teachers integrate *content knowledge* with *pedagogical understanding* to assure that all students learn (INTASC 1993).

1. Knowledge of Subject Matter
2. Knowledge of Human Development and Learning
3. Adapting Instruction for Individual Needs
4. Multiple Instructional Strategies
5. Classroom Motivation and Management
6. Communication Skills
7. Instructional Planning Skills
8. Assessment of Student Learning
9. Professional Commitment and Responsibility
10. Partnerships

NCATE Standards

Standards for the accreditation of colleges and universities with teacher preparation programs. Currently, fewer than half of the 1,300 institutions that prepare teachers are accredited by NCATE. Although NCATE standards primarily apply to teacher education programs, not to teacher education students per se, NCATE believes that "the new professional teacher who graduates from a professional accredited school, college, or department of education should be able to" do the following (NCATE 2002):

- Help all prekindergarten through twelfth grade (P–12) students learn
- Teach to P–12 student standards set by specialized professional associations and the states
- Explain instructional choices based on research-derived knowledge and best practice
- Apply effective methods of teaching students who are at different developmental stages, have different learning styles, and come from diverse backgrounds
- Reflect on practice, act on feedback, and integrate technology into instruction effectively

What knowledge, skills, and dispositions does society expect teachers to possess?

NBPTS Standards

A board that issues professional certificates to teachers who possess extensive professional knowledge and the ability to perform at a high level. Certification candidates submit a portfolio including videotapes of classroom interactions and samples of student work plus the teacher's reflective comments. Trained NBPTS evaluators who teach in the same field as the candidate judge all elements of the assessments. NBPTS has developed five "core propositions" on which voluntary national teacher certification is based (NBPTS 1994):

1. Teachers are committed to students and their learning.
2. Teachers know the subjects they teach and how to teach those subjects to students.
3. Teachers are responsible for managing and monitoring student learning.
4. Teachers think systematically about their practice and learn from experience.
5. Teachers are members of learning communities.

Praxis Series

Based on knowledge and skills states commonly require of beginning teachers, the Praxis Series assesses individual development as it corresponds to three steps in becoming a teacher. These three areas of assessment are Academic Skills Assessments: entering a teacher education program (Praxis I); Subject Assessments: licensure for entering the profession (Praxis II); and Classroom Performance Assessments: the first year of teaching (Praxis III). Praxis III involves the assessment of actual teaching skills in four areas (Danielson 1996):

1. *Planning and Preparation*
- Demonstrating knowledge of content and pedagogy
- Demonstrating knowledge of students
- Selecting instructional goals
- Demonstrating knowledge of resources
- Designing coherent instruction
2. *The Classroom Environment*
- Creating an environment of respect and rapport
- Establishing a culture for learning
- Managing classroom procedures
- Managing student behavior
- Organizing physical space
3. *Instruction*
- Communicating clearly and accurately
- Using questioning and discussion techniques
- Engaging students in learning
- Providing feedback to students
- Demonstrating flexibility and responsiveness
4. *Professional Responsibilities*
- Reflecting on teaching
- Maintaining accurate records
- Communicating with families
- Contributing to the school and district
- Growing and developing professionally

What Knowledge Do You Need to Teach?

Just as people hold different expectations for schools and teachers, there are different views on the knowledge teachers need in order to teach well. The complexities of teaching make it difficult to describe in exact detail the **knowledge base** on which teaching as a profession rests. This difficulty results, in part, because there is no universally accepted definition of what good teaching is. Educational researchers are still learning *what* good teachers know and *how* they use that knowledge.

To make sense out of the complexities of teaching, you must have three kinds of knowledge—knowledge of yourself and your students, knowledge of subject, and knowledge of educational theory and research. The following sections examine these three forms of essential knowledge.

Self-Knowledge

Effective teachers understand themselves, and they are sensitive to students' needs. Naturally, you should understand your students as much as possible. However, what is the connection between self-knowledge and the ability to promote student learning? If you understand your own needs (and are able to satisfy those needs), you will be in a better position to help students learn. As Arthur Jersild (1955), who studied the connection between the teacher's personal insight and professional effectiveness, pointed out, a teacher's self-understanding and self-acceptance help students to know and accept themselves.

Your self-evaluations as a teacher will be influenced by the emotions you may experience while teaching—emotions such as anxiety or loneliness, for example. As the opening scenario for this chapter suggests, anxiety is a common emotion to experience when teaching for the first time.

Three "realities" of teaching can result in anxiety: (1) the never-ending nature of teaching (i.e., a teacher's work is never completed), (2) the often unpredictable results of teaching (e.g., some students learn the material, whereas others may not), and (3) the difficulty of knowing for sure that student learning resulted from the teacher's teaching (e.g., students may have actually learned the material on their own, in spite of what the teacher did). Unlike architects, lawyers, and doctors, teachers can seldom stand back and admire their work. If a student learns a lot, that success rightfully belongs to the student.

Teachers must be able to tolerate ambiguities and to reduce their anxiety about being observably effective. If not, a teacher "can feel that one is 'wrong,' 'missing something,' a 'bad fit' with students and with teaching itself. One can feel that one's circumstances are unfair, that one is giving but not receiving. One can feel helpless, not knowing what to do, not even knowing how to get the frustration out of mind let alone how to resolve it in practice" (Hansen 1995, 60).

As a teacher, you may experience loneliness or isolation, because most of your time will be spent with children and youth, not adults. Though today's teachers have more opportunities to collaborate with their colleagues, you will be behind the classroom door most of the day. Alone in the classroom, you will have to deal with the complexities of teaching and try to meet the diverse needs of students.

Most teachers would like more interaction with their colleagues, especially time to observe one another. Without opportunities to receive feedback from your peers, you will be deprived of an important catalyst for professional growth. As Elliot Eisner puts it: "The result of professional isolation is the difficulty that teachers encounter in learning what they themselves do in their own classrooms when they teach. [How] can a teacher learn that he or she is talking too much, not providing sufficient time for student reflection, raising low-order questions, or is simply boring students? Teachers unaware of such features of their own performance are in no position to change them" (1998, 160–161).

In addition, observing how a colleague responds to the challenges of teaching will enable you to reflect on how you meet those same challenges. For example, a fourth-grade teacher came to the following insight as a result of observing his teaching partner: "Being a teacher is so much more than an extensive repertoire of strategies and techniques. [To] be a teacher is to find a way to live within an environment filled with dilemmas" (Hole 1998, 419).

Knowledge of Students

Knowledge of students is also important. Student characteristics, such as students' aptitudes, talents, learning styles, stage of development, and their readiness to learn new material, are among the essential knowledge teachers must have. The importance of this knowledge is evident in comments made by an intern at a middle school: "To teach a kid well you have to know a kid well. . . . Teaching middle school takes a special breed of teachers who understand the unique abilities and inabilities . . . [of] those undergoing their own metamorphosis into teenagers" (Henry et al. 1995, 124–125). As a teacher, you will gain this kind of knowledge through study, observation, and interactions with students.

Without considerable understanding of children and youth, teachers' efforts to help students learn and grow can be inappropriate and, in some cases, counterproductive. Your expectations of students will directly affect their achievement. What opportunities have you already had to acquire knowledge about learners—working as a camp counselor; working with service clubs such as Girl Scouts or Boy Scouts, 4-H, Campfire, or youth groups; volunteering at a child care center; or tutoring young children in reading or mathematics, for example?

Knowledge of Subject

Those who have the title *teacher* are assumed to have extensive knowledge. People who are not teachers expect a teacher to have knowledge far beyond their own. Without a doubt, teachers who have extensive knowledge of their subjects are better equipped to facilitate student learning.

However, knowledge of subject matter does not translate into an understanding of *how* to share that knowledge with students—a point illustrated in a case study

What kinds of basic knowledge and skills do teachers need to do their jobs well? Why is it important that you stay in touch with student culture?

conducted by a team of researchers at the National Center for Research on Teacher Learning. The case focused on "Mary," an undergraduate literature major enrolled in a teacher education program at a major university. By any standard, Mary was a subject-matter expert—she had been the valedictorian of a large, urban high school; she had received straight A's in the literature courses she had taken; and she had a sophisticated understanding of literature, especially poetry. However, the case study revealed that Mary had little understanding of classroom activities that would show her students *how* to read with sophistication and concluded that "some prospective teachers may come to teacher education unaware of how they have learned the processes they use and that render them expert. Unaided by their disciplines in locating the underpinnings of their expertise, these skilled, talented, and desirable recruits may easily become, ironically, those who can *do* but who cannot *teach*" (Holt-Reynolds 1999, 43).

As the National Board for Professional Teaching Standards (2002) puts it, extensive knowledge of subject matter "entails more than being able to recite lists of dates, multiplication tables, or rules of grammar. [Accomplished] teachers possess what is sometimes called '**pedagogical content knowledge**.' Such understanding is the joint product of wisdom about teaching, learning, students and content. It includes knowledge of the most appropriate ways to present the subject matter to students through analogies, metaphors, experiments, demonstrations and illustrations" (10–11). This chapter's Relevant Standards feature stresses the need for teachers to have a broad and deep understanding of the subject(s) they teach, as well as an understanding of *how* to teach those subjects.

Relevant Standards

Understanding of Subject

As the following standards indicate, highly accomplished teachers understand not only *what* they teach, they also understand *how* to teach it. Their extensive knowledge of subject matter enables them to teach it to students in multiple ways. For example, an elementary science teacher might tell students that our solar system is made up of nine planets that orbit the sun. Students, however, might have difficulty understanding why the planets stay in their orbits. A knowledgeable teacher would tell students that the sun's gravitational pull holds the planets in their orbits, just as the planets' gravitational pull keeps their moons in orbit around them. The teacher might go on to explain that, in the same way, objects on the earth are pulled toward the earth's center by gravitational force.

- "Teacher candidates have in-depth knowledge of the subject matter that they plan to teach as described in professional, state, and institutional standards. They demonstrate their knowledge through inquiry, critical analysis, and synthesis of the subject." (National Council for Accreditation of Teacher Education [NCATE], 2002, p. 14. Standard 1: Candidate Knowledge, Skills, and Dispositions, "target" level of knowledge.)

- "Teachers appreciate how knowledge in their subjects is created, organized, and linked to other disciplines. . . . Teachers command specialized knowledge of how to convey a subject to students. . . . Teachers generate multiple paths to knowledge." (National Board for Professional Teaching Standards [NBPTS], 2002, pp. 10–11. "Supporting statements" for Proposition #2: "Teachers know the subjects they teach and how to teach those subjects to students.")

- "The teacher can represent and use differing viewpoints, theories, 'ways of knowing' and methods of inquiry in his/her teaching of subject matter concepts." (Interstate New Teacher Assessment and Support Consortium [INTASC], 1992, p. 15. "Performance" statement for Principle #1: "The teacher understands the central concepts, tools of inquiry, and structures of the discipline(s) he or she teaches and can create learning experiences that make these aspects of subject matter meaningful for students.")

- "Teacher displays extensive content knowledge, with evidence of continuing pursuit of such knowledge." (Praxis Series, "distinguished" level of performance for Domain 1: Planning and Preparation, Component 1a: Demonstrating Knowledge of Content and Pedagogy.) (Danielson 1996, p. 112)

Knowledge of How to Use Educational Theory and Research

Theories about learners and learning will guide your decision making as a teacher. Not only will you know that a certain strategy works, you will also know *why* it works. Because you realize the importance of theories, you will have a greater range of available options for problem solving than teachers who do not have a repertoire of theories. Your ultimate goal as a professional is to learn how to apply theoretical knowledge to the practical problems of teaching. To illustrate how actual teachers do this, *Curriculum and Instruction for Becoming a Teacher* includes a feature titled

Teachers' Voices: Putting Research and Theory into Practice. This feature presents teacher-authored accounts showing how teachers have "put research and theory into practice."

One example of how research can be used to promote student learning is based on the work of Barak Rosenshine. Drawing from his own and others' research on cognitive processing, studies of teachers whose students have higher achievement gains than those of other teachers, and research on cognitive strategies, Rosenshine (1995, 267) recommends six teaching strategies:

1. Present new material in small steps so that the working memory does not become overloaded.
2. Help students develop an organization for the new material.
3. Guide student practice by (a) supporting students during initial practice and (b) providing for extensive student processing.
4. When teaching higher-level tasks, support students by providing them with cognitive strategies.
5. Help students to use cognitive strategies by providing them with procedural prompts (e.g., questions students ask themselves while learning new material— "who," "what," "why," "when," etc.) and modeling the use of procedural prompts.
6. Provide for extensive student practice.

Research on student learning such as Rosenshine's is not intended to set forth in cookbook fashion exactly what you should do to increase student learning. Instead, it may be helpful to think of educational research as providing you with general guidelines for practice. For example, Rosenshine, Meister, and Chapman (1996) point out that despite extensive research on the effectiveness of procedural prompts (giving students verbal feedback to guide their learning), "at the present time, developing procedural prompts appears to be an art. [It] is difficult to derive any prescriptions on how to develop effective procedural prompts for cognitive strategies in reading, writing, and subject matter domains" (198). Finally, noted educational psychologist Lee Cronbach (quoted in Eisner 1998) may have put it best when he said "[educational research] is to help practitioners use their heads" (112).

Teachers' Craft Knowledge

In addition to the three forms of professional knowledge discussed in the preceding sections, many people believe that a knowledge base for teaching should consist not only of what educational researchers have learned about teaching, but also what teachers themselves "know" about teaching—often called *teachers' craft knowledge* or *practitioner knowledge* (Hiebert, Gallimore, and Stigler, 2002; Kennedy, 1999; Leinhardt, 1990). When you enter the classroom, you will develop **teachers' craft knowledge** in response to specific problems of practice.

Technology in Teaching

What knowledge do teachers need in the area of technology?

To prepare teachers to use new educational technologies, many teacher education programs and state departments of education have developed technology competency guidelines for classroom teachers. For example, California teachers participate in the Technology Proficiency for California Teachers (CTAP) project. CTAP has prepared the "Professional Profiles" and "Performance Indicators" on the next page to guide teachers' professional development as they learn to use technology "to further classroom management, communication, lesson design and student performance." How many of these competencies do you possess, and what steps can you take to acquire those you do not have?

The following teacher describes how he developed "craft knowledge" related to motivating students and evaluating their efforts to learn.

> At the beginning of the school year, I explain my grading system to students. For most assignments, students also receive a grade for effort and participation. So, all completed in-class work and homework, even if it has errors, can receive a grade of 100. Partially completed assignments are graded based on the percentage of the assignment completed. Tests, of course, are graded based on the percentage correct. Projects and similar work are graded holistically, and part of the grade is based on my judgment about the level of effort and participation.
>
> When students understand my grading system, they are definitely more willing to make an effort to learn. They are not worried about receiving an "F," or receiving negative comments from me.
>
> I developed my grading system when I began teaching inner-city high school students, many of whom had given up trying to complete their work because they usually failed. I realized that if I gave "credit" for effort and participation, the positive effects of being rewarded for that might change students' thinking about learning. They would become more positive and realize that "I can succeed if I try." This approach works best for students who are more self-motivated or have parents or guardian to motivate them. However, nonmotivated students often realize that they, too, can learn.

Knowledge of How to Use Educational Technology   An important form of craft knowledge you will develop is how to use educational technologies. This Technology in Teaching

Professional Profile	**Performance Indicators**
• Identifies, selects, and uses digital communication tools appropriately. • Uses digital tools to communicate with students, parents, and community members to enhance management and learning.	• Evidence of the use of a variety of communication tools based on resources available (i.e., telephone, e-mail, fax, listserv, or Web page). • Evidence of the management of information using technology to increase communication (i.e., Web pages, voice mail, homework hotlines, etc.).
• Supports student learning through collaboration with parents, subject matter experts, educators, and others using digital tools. • Participates in professional growth activities that utilize digital communication tools.	• Evidence of sustained communication with parents, students, and/or colleagues (i.e., mailing lists, video conferencing, online staff development, shared network holders, etc.). • Student projects that utilize digital tools to interact with subject matter experts. • Lesson/activity plans designed collaboratively using appropriate communication tools as a medium (i.e., e-mail, listserv, shared network folders, mailing lists, videoconferences, etc.).
• Uses digital communication tools to work with educators and subject matter experts to design classroom activities to support student learning. • Seeks out and draws upon the expertise of others to support the learning process and technology enhanced curriculum.	• Student work that exemplifies evidence of active collaboration with outside experts. • Interdisciplinary lessons and cross grade level projects.
• Provides leadership by participating in school-wide decision making and learning activities that support learning through the use of technology. • Actively contributes to the development or updating of site- or district-based technology plans. • Explores new technologies and recommends innovative educational applications appropriate to the curricular needs of the students and site.	• Participation in grade level or department activities to develop a school site technology plan. • Pursues continuing education (i.e., educational technology, conference attendance, curriculum integration, online courses, workshops). • Evidence of active participation in the site or district decision-making process regarding the use and acquisition of technology (i.e., grade level, technology committee, technology planning, etc.).

Source: California Department of Education, Technology Proficiency for California Teachers (CTAP). Retrieved at www.fcoe.k12.ca.us/techprof/professional_profiles.htm# Communication%20and%20Collaboration, August 14, 2004.

feature describes the "performance indicators" California teachers must demonstrate in the use of technology. Each day, thousands of teachers and students routinely use desktop and laptop computers with built-in modems, faxes, and CD-ROM players; camcorders; optical scanners; speech and music synthesizers; laser printers; digital cameras; and LCD projection panels. In addition, they use sophisticated software for e-mail, word processing, desktop publishing, presentation graphics,

Figure 1.2 Essential knowledge and skills for the professional teacher.

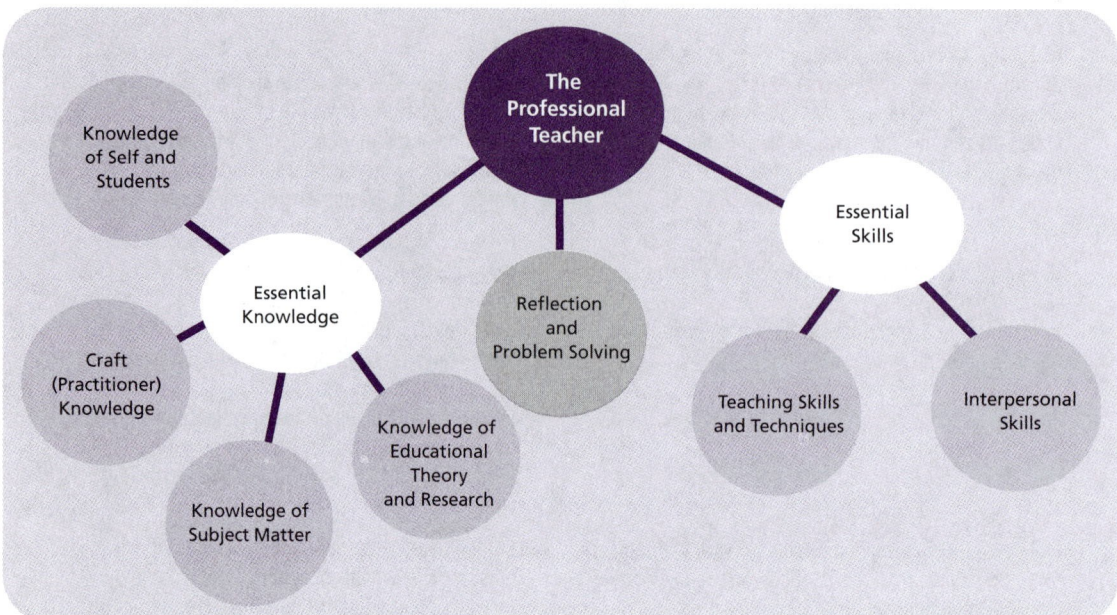

spreadsheets, databases, and multimedia applications. As mentioned earlier, Chapter 5 describes how teachers are using educational technologies to increase student learning.

Reflection and Problem Solving   The preceding discussion of essential knowledge for teaching highlights the fact that teaching is complex and demanding. As you use your knowledge to meet the challenges of teaching, you will be guided by **reflection** and a **problem-solving orientation**. As Figure 1.2 shows, reflection and problem solving will enable you to determine how to use knowledge of self and students (including cultural differences), craft knowledge, knowledge of subject matter, and knowledge of educational theory and research to create optimum conditions for student learning. The figure also illustrates how you will use reflection and problem solving to decide which *essential skills* to use and how you will use them.

What Can You Learn from Observing in Classrooms?

Classroom observations are an excellent way to develop knowledge about teaching. Most teacher education programs require that students participate in **field experiences** that include classroom observations. Students report that these experiences help them to make a final decision about becoming a teacher. Most become more enthusiastic about teaching and more motivated to acquire the essential knowledge and skills; however, a few decide that teaching is not for them.

Recognizing the value of observations, many teacher education programs are increasing the amount of field experiences and placing those experiences earlier in students' programs. For example, at Washington State University (WSU), students preparing to become elementary teachers complete one week of classroom observations as part of their first education course. Later in their program, WSU students complete two 45-hour blocks of observations in K–8 classrooms and a five-week advanced practicum (or field experience) that requires several hours of classroom observation each week.

Technology and Classroom Observations

Currently, many universities and school districts are cooperating on the use of two-way interactive compressed video technology to enable preservice teachers on campus to observe live coverage in school classrooms off campus. Compressed video can be transmitted over existing telephone lines or the Internet in a relatively inexpensive, unobtrusive, and time-efficient way. **Distance learning**—the use of technology, such as video transmissions, that enables students to receive instruction at multiple, often remote sites—now enables teacher education programs to use the power of models for learning how to teach. For example, distance learning enables students at Texas A&M University and the University of Memphis to observe inner-city classrooms and afterwards to discuss their observations with the teachers. One of the designers of the interactive video program at Memphis comments on its benefits: "Previously everyone visited different schools and saw very different things. [This] shared clinical experience will lead to a more focused discussion of teaching methods" (University of Memphis 1994/95, 2).

Focused Observations

Observations are more meaningful if they are focused and conducted with a clear purpose in mind. An observer may focus on students (the entire group or selected students), the teacher, teacher–student interactions, how the lesson is structured, or the overall classroom environment or climate. More specifically, for example, observers may note differences between the ways boys and girls or members of different ethnic groups communicate and behave in the classroom. They may focus on student interests and ability levels, student responses to a particular teaching strategy, or question–response patterns during a class discussion.

Observations may also be guided by questions related to specific areas. For instance, because beginning teachers are frequently frustrated by their inability to motivate students, asking questions related to motivation can make an observation more meaningful and instructive. Figure 1.3 presents a helpful set of focused questions on motivation. Similar questions can be generated for other focus areas, such as classroom management, student involvement, questioning skills, evaluation, and teacher–student rapport.

Figure 1.3 Focused questions on motivation.

Directions: As you observe, note the ways that students are motivated intrinsically (from within) and extrinsically (from factors outside themselves).

Intrinsic Motivation	Extrinsic Motivation
What things seem to interest students at this age?	How do teachers show their approval to students?
Which activities and assignments seem to give them a sense of pride?	What phrases do teachers use in their praise?
When do they seem to be confused? Bored? Frustrated?	What types of rewards do teachers give (e.g., grades, points, tangible rewards)?
What topics do they talk about with enthusiasm?	What reward programs do you notice (e.g., points accumulated toward free time)?
In class discussions, when are they most alert and participating most actively?	What warnings do teachers give?
What seems to please, amuse, entertain, or excite them?	What punishments are given to students?
What do they joke about? What do they find humorous?	How do teachers arouse concern in their students?
What do they report as being their favorite subjects? Favorite assignments?	How do students motivate other students?
What do they report as being their least favorite subjects and assignments?	What forms of peer pressure do you observe?
How do they respond to personalized lessons (e.g., using their names in exercises)?	How do teachers promote enthusiasm for an assignment?
How do they respond to activity-oriented lessons (e.g., fieldwork, project periods)?	How do teachers promote class spirit?
How do they respond to assignments calling for presentations to groups outside the classroom (e.g., parents, another class, the chamber of commerce)?	How do teachers catch their students' interest in the first few minutes of a lesson?
	Which type of question draws more answers—recall or open-ended?
	How do teachers involve quiet students in class discussions?
How do they respond to being given a choice in assignments?	How do teachers involve inactive students in their work?
	In what ways do teachers give recognition to students' accomplishments?

Observation Instruments

A wide range of methods can be used to conduct classroom observations, ranging from informal, qualitative descriptions to formal, quantitative checklists. With reform efforts to improve education in the United States has come the development of instruments to facilitate the evaluation of teacher performance, a task now widely required of school administrators. Students preparing to teach can benefit by using these evaluative instruments in their observations. An example is the Formative Observation Data Instrument that is part of the North Carolina Teacher Performance Appraisal System (see Appendix 1.1).

How Can You Gain Practical Experience for Becoming a Teacher?

Your teacher education program is designed to give you opportunities to experience, to the extent possible, the real world of the teacher. Through field experiences and carefully structured experiential activities, you will be given limited exposure to various aspects of teaching, from curriculum development to classroom management. Observing, tutoring, instructing small groups, analyzing video cases, operating instructional media, performing student teaching, and completing various noninstructional tasks are among the most common activities.

Classroom Experiences

Opportunities to put theory into practice *before* student teaching are important. Thus, many teacher education programs enable students to participate in microteaching, teaching simulations, analyses of video cases, field-based practica and clinical experiences, and classroom aide programs.

Microteaching Introduced in the 1960s, **microteaching** quickly became popular and now is widely used. When microteaching, students teach short lessons to a small group of students (five to ten). Microteaching gives students opportunities to practice specific teaching skills, such as positive reinforcement. Often the microteaching is videotaped for later analysis and critique.

As originally developed, microteaching includes the following six steps:

1. Identify a specific teaching skill to learn about and practice.
2. Read about the skill in one of several pamphlets.
3. Observe a master teacher demonstrate the skill in a short movie or on videotape.
4. Prepare a three- to five-minute lesson to demonstrate the skill.
5. Teach the lesson, which is videotaped, to a small group of peers.
6. Critique, along with the instructor and student peers, the videotaped lesson.

Simulations Simulations provide opportunities for vicarious practice of a wide range of teaching skills. In **teaching simulations**, students analyze teaching situations that are written, filmed, or videotaped. Students usually are given background information about a hypothetical school or classroom and the pupils they must prepare to teach. After this orientation, students role-play the student teacher or teacher who is confronted with a problem situation. Students then discuss the appropriateness of different solutions, developing their problem-solving skills and their understanding of the teacher's role as a decision maker in a complex setting.

Some teacher education programs are experimenting with computer-based simulations that enable students to hone their classroom planning and decision-making skills. Students at Nova Southwestern University in Florida, for example, learn to diagnose learning disabilities among children and youth by analyzing computer-simulated cases (Brown 1994). Computer simulations are also being used for teacher professional development. For example, a three-dimensional virtual reality (VR) simulation model proved more effective than a workshop method for training kindergarten teachers to understand children's needs and perceptions (Katz 1999), and a computer-based simulation has been used to train school personnel in crisis management (Degnan and Bozeman 2001).

Although progress is being made in the development of VR technology, "it is not possible to say how great the potential may actually be in the realm of teacher education" (Brown 1999, 318). Current simulations are limited to specific skills, such as classroom management or tutoring highly motivated individuals. As VR technology improves, however, one day we may see simulations of classrooms that show a variety of students with differing needs as learners.

Video Cases Teacher education students who view, analyze, and then write about video cases have an additional opportunity to appreciate the ambiguities and complexities of real-life classrooms, learning that "there are no clear-cut, simple answers to the complex issues teachers face" (Wasserman 1994, 606). Viewing authentic video cases enables students to see how "teaching tradeoffs and dilemmas emerge in the video 'text' as do the strategies teachers use, the frustrations they experience, the brilliant and less-brilliant decisions they make" (Grant, Richard, and Parkay 1996, 5).

Practica A **practicum** is a short-term field-based experience (usually about two weeks long) that allows teacher education students to spend time observing and assisting in classrooms. Though practica vary in length and purpose, students are often able to begin instructional work with individuals or small groups. For example, a cooperating teacher may allow a practicum student to tutor a small group of students, read a story to the whole class, conduct a spelling lesson, monitor recess, help students with their homework, or teach students a song or game.

Classroom Aides Serving as a teacher's aide is another popular means of providing field experience before student teaching. A teacher aide's role depends on the unique needs of the school and its students. Generally, aides work under the supervision of a certified teacher and perform duties that support the teacher's instruction. By helping teachers in the classroom, college students learn about class schedules, record-keeping procedures, and students' performance levels, while having ample opportunity for observations. In exchange, the classroom teacher receives much-needed assistance.

Student Teaching The most extensive and significant field experience in your teacher preparation program will be student teaching. "Student teaching provide[s] student teachers with realistic evaluations of their strengths and weaknesses as prospective teachers and help[s] them to develop competencies in classroom management" (Wentz 2001, 73).

What strategies can you use to make your student teaching experiences truly valuable to you in becoming a teacher? In what sense will you remain a student teacher throughout your career?

States require students to have a five-week to semester-long student teaching experience in the schools before certifying them as teachers. The nature of student teaching varies considerably among teacher education programs. Some programs even pay student teachers during the student teaching experience. Most likely, you will be assigned to a cooperating (or master) teacher in the school, and a university supervisor will make periodic visits to observe you.

Student teaching will be a time of responsibility. As one student teacher put it, "I don't want to mess up [my students'] education!" It will also be an opportunity for growth and a chance to master critical skills. The following Teachers' Voices feature illustrates the invaluable lesson a sixth-grade teacher learned during his student teaching experience. The feature also points out that he now shares what he learned with beginning teachers.

During your student teaching assignment, you will probably spend about half of your time teaching, with the remaining time devoted to observing and participating in classroom activities. The amount of time actually spent teaching, however, is not as important as your willingness to reflect carefully on your experiences. Two excellent ways to promote reflection during your student teaching experience are journal writing and maintaining a reflective teaching log.

Teachers' *Voices*   Putting Research and Theory into Practice

A Classroom Exchange

Dennis Donoghue

On my last day of student teaching sixth graders, I called one of my students a rotten little _____. Maybe I did it because I knew I'd never see the kid again, or because he had driven me crazy for eight weeks. I should not have said it—I knew that much—but I couldn't help myself. The words just came out: you rotten little _____.

. . . On my last day, the students presented me with a polished wooden apple inscribed with my name and the name of the school. Miss Hanson [the cooperating teacher] gave me a coffee mug and a thank-you card scented with Shalimar. At 2:15 the kids filed past me, following Miss Hanson to their buses. Jimmy drifted from the end of the line.

"You're the worst student teacher we've ever had," he said, "and since we've had them since the first grade, that's saying something."

"You rotten little _____," I said.

. . . Now, twenty-five years later, the young teachers on my team ask me how I am able to choose my words so carefully in the midst of a confrontation with one of our sixth graders. They want to know what to say and how to say it, afraid that in the heat of the moment they'll utter something they'll regret. They want to know my secret.

I tell them nothing beats experience, then suggest strategies that work for me. I do not tell them I once called a student a rotten little _____ and then denied it. But I do tell them that they should adhere to a standard of conduct, for what seems intolerable one day won't be the next. Once hurtful words are spoken, I warn them, those words cannot be taken back. The words I spoke to Jimmy will stay with me always, and chances are they're still with him too. It seems as if I'd etched them in stone, those four words which slipped so easily from my tongue on that spring day many years ago.

Questions

1. Donoghue learned that a teacher should never direct "hurtful words" toward a student, regardless of the student's behavior toward the teacher. What strategies can teachers use to avoid unprofessional behavior when responding to students who misbehave in a very hostile, provocative manner over a long period of time?
2. How should Donoghue have responded to Jimmy's comment? How would you have responded?
3. What are some reasons why a student might misbehave like Jimmy?

Dennis Donoghue teaches sixth grade in Salisbury, Massachusetts. He has written articles for several magazines, including *Teacher Magazine.* The preceding is excerpted from his article in *Am I Teaching Yet? Stores from the Teacher-Training Trenches,* Molly Hoekstra (Ed.), (Portsmouth, NH: Heinemann, 2002), pp. 120–124.

Student Teaching Journal   Many supervisors require student teachers to keep a journal of their experiences. A student teaching journal enables students to understand reflective teaching and to begin critiquing the decisions they make while teaching. The following two entries—the first written by a student teacher in a fourth-grade classroom, the second by a student teacher in a high school English class—illustrate how a student teaching journal can help student teachers develop strategies for dealing with the realities of teaching.

Entry #1 Today I taught a lesson on the geography of the Northeast, and the kids seemed so bored. I called on individuals to read the social studies text, and then I explained it. Some of them really struggled with the text. Mr. H. said I was spoon-feeding them too much. So tomorrow I am going to put them into groups and let them answer questions together rather than give them the answers. This ought to involve the students in the learning a bit more and enable some of the better readers to help out those who have difficulty, without the whole class watching. I feel bad when I see those glazed looks on their faces. I need to learn how to be more interesting (Pitton 1998, 120).

Entry #2 I had good feedback on small groups in their responses to questions on *Of Mice and Men.* They were to find a paragraph that might indicate theme and find two examples of foreshadowing. We found five!

The short story unit was awful during fourth hour. The kids just didn't respond. I quickly revamped my approach for the next hour. Fifth hour did seem to go better. (Mostly though, I think it was just that I was more prepared, having had one class to try things out.) I can see how experience really helps. Now that I've tried the story "The Tiger or the Lady," I would use the same material, but I would know *how* to use it more effectively! (Pitton 1998, 143).

Unstructured, open-ended journal entries such as these enable student teachers to reflect on the student teaching experience.

Reflective Teaching Logs   To promote more analytical reflections, some supervisors ask student teachers to use a structured form of journal writing, the **reflective teaching log**. In a reflective teaching log, the student briefly describes the daily classroom activities, selects a single episode to analyze, explains the reason for selecting the episode, and discusses what was learned from the analysis and how that might be applied in the future.

To illustrate a reflective teaching log, a partial entry for one episode follows. The entry shows how a college student can disagree with a supervising teacher's response to a classroom situation.

Log for December 1—Erin Tompkins
Sequence of Events
1. Arrival—end of eighth period
2. Ninth period—helped Sharad study science
3. After-school program—worked on science with Ricki, P.K., and Tom
4. Late bus duty with Ms. Soto
5. Departure

Episode
I was helping Ricki and P.K. fill out a table about the location and function of the different cell parts. P.K. asked me a question and two other students laughed at him. I began to answer his question when Ms. Soto came over to the table where we were working and yelled at P.K. She said, "P.K. I don't need you distracting other students who are trying to get their work done." He started to tell her what he asked me and she said, "I don't care. You can leave the room if you don't knock it off. Just do your work and be quiet or you're out!" She then apologized to me and went back to helping another student.

Analysis

I was very frustrated after this episode. This is the first time I've seen Ms. Soto raise her voice with a student and accuse him of causing problems when he was getting his work done and other students were being disruptive. P.K. had asked me a legitimate question; the other students who laughed at him were the problem. I was frustrated because Ricki and P.K. were working hard and asking me good questions. I was annoyed that P.K. was being reprimanded for asking a question that was relevant to the topic we were working on. I also felt helpless because I wanted to tell Ms. Soto that it wasn't P.K. who was the problem. I didn't feel it was my place to correct her in front of her students and kept quiet. I decided that my saying something would only make things worse because it would encourage P.K. to continue arguing with Ms. Soto and he would be in more trouble (Posner 2000, 137–138).

Though student teaching will be the capstone experience of your teacher education program, the experience should be regarded as an *initial* rather than a terminal learning opportunity—your first chance to engage in reflection and self-evaluation for a prolonged period.

Experiences in Multicultural Settings

The enrollment of students from diverse cultural backgrounds in the United States will continue to increase dramatically during the twenty-first century. As this trend continues, teacher education students must develop an understanding of children and youth from different backgrounds. Students in Washington State University's teacher education program, for example, must document how they have met the following state requirement for teacher certification: "All candidates for teacher certification must demonstrate in their field experience their ability to work effectively with students of various backgrounds including (1) students from racial and or ethnic populations other than the candidate's, and (2) students with exceptional needs (i.e., those with handicapping conditions and the highly capable)."

As a teacher you can be assured that you will teach students from backgrounds that differ from your own—including students from the more than one hundred racial and ethnic groups in the United States and students who are poor, gifted, or have disabilities. You will be challenged to reach out to all students and teach them that they are persons of worth who *can* learn. You will also be challenged to be sensitive to differences among students while at the same time treating all equally and fairly. To prepare for these realities of teaching, you should make every effort to gain experiences in multicultural settings.

Substitute Teaching

On completion of your teacher education program and prior to securing a full-time teaching job, you may choose to gain additional practical experience by substitute teaching. If you are unable to locate a full-time position, you may decide to substitute full time, knowing that many districts prefer to hire from their pool of substitutes when full-time positions become available.

Substitute teachers replace regular teachers who are absent due to illness, family responsibilities, personal reasons, or professional workshops and conferences. Each day, approximately 270,000 substitutes are employed in schools across the United States, and one full year of a student's K–12 education is taught by substitute teachers (Substitute Teaching Institute 2002).

Qualifications for substitutes vary from state to state and district to district. An area with a critical need for subs will often relax its requirements to provide class-room coverage. In many districts, it is possible to substitute teach without regular certification. Some districts have less stringent qualifications for short-term, day-to-day substitutes and more stringent ones for long-term, full-time substitutes. Figure 1.4 presents several advantages and disadvantages of substitute teaching.

In many districts, the application process for substitutes is the same as that for full-time applicants; in others, the process may be more brief. Often, substitutes are not limited to working in their area of certification; however, schools try to avoid making out-of-field assignments. If you decide to substitute teach, contact the schools in your area to learn about the qualifications and procedures for hiring substitutes.

Despite the significant role substitutes play in the day-to-day operation of schools, "research tells us that they receive very little support, no specialized train-ing, and are rarely evaluated. . . . In short, the substitute will be expected to show up to each class on time, maintain order, take roll, carry out the lesson, and leave a note for the regular teacher about the classes and events of the day without

Figure 1.4   *Advantages and disadvantages of substitute teaching.*

Advantages and Disadvantages of Substitute Teaching

Advantages
- Gain experience without all the nightly work and preparation
- Compare and contrast different schools and their environments
- Be better prepared for interviews by meeting administrators and teachers
- Teach and learn a variety of material
- Get to know people—network
- See job postings and hear about possible vacancies
- Gain confidence in your abilities to teach
- Practice classroom management techniques
- Learn about school and district politics—get the "inside scoop"
- Choose which days to work—flexible schedule

Disadvantages
- Pay is not as good as full-time teaching
- No benefits such as medical coverage, retirement plans, or sick days
- Lack of organized representation to improve wages or working conditions
- May receive a cool reception in some schools
- Must adapt quickly to different school philosophies
- Lack of continuity—may be teaching whole language one day; phonetics the next

Source: John F. Snyder, "The Alternative of Substitute Teaching." In *1999 Job Search Handbook for Educators.* Evanston, IL: American Associa-tion for Employment in Education, p. 38.

support, encouragement, or acknowledgment" (St. Michel 1995, 6–7). While working conditions such as these are certainly challenging, substitute teaching can be a rewarding, professionally fulfilling experience.

What Is Taught in Schools?

As mentioned at the beginning of this chapter, *what* is taught to students is just as important as *how* they are taught. To develop a positive, learning-oriented classroom, you will need to learn how to develop a meaningful, relevant curriculum for your students. In addition, you will need to understand that there are actually different types of curricula that students experience. Each type makes an important contribution to students' growth and development.

Think back to your experiences as a student at the elementary, middle, junior, and secondary schools you attended. What things did you learn? The curriculum you experienced certainly included reading, computation, penmanship, spelling, geography, and history. In addition to these topics, though, did you learn something about cooperation, competition, stress, football, video games, computers, popularity, and the opposite sex? Or, perhaps, did you learn to love chemistry and to hate English grammar?

The countless things you learned in school made up the curriculum that you experienced. Curriculum theorists and researchers have suggested several different definitions for **curriculum**; no one definition is universally accepted. Here are some definitions in current use.

1. A course of study, derived from the Latin *currere*, meaning "to run a course"
2. Course content, the information or knowledge that students are to learn
3. Planned learning experiences
4. Intended learning outcomes, the *results* of instruction as distinguished from the *means* (activities, materials, etc.) of instruction
5. All the experiences that students have while at school

No one of these five is in any sense the "right" definition. How we define *curriculum* depends on our purposes and the situation in which we find ourselves. If, for example, we were advising a high school student on the courses he or she needed to take in order to prepare for college, our operational definition of curriculum would most likely be "a course of study." However, if we were interviewing sixth-grade students for their views on the K–6 elementary school they had just graduated from, we would probably want to view curriculum as "all the experiences that students have while at school." The following is a definition that encompasses both perspectives: *Curriculum refers to the experiences, both planned and unplanned, that enhance (and sometimes impede) the education and growth of students.*

Kinds of Curricula

Elliot Eisner, a noted educational researcher, has said that "schools teach much more—and much less—than they intend to teach. Although much of what is taught is explicit and public, a great deal is not" (2002, 87). For this reason, you should understand the four curricula that all students experience. The more you understand these curricula and how they influence students, the better you will be able to develop educational programs that do, in fact, educate.

Explicit Curriculum The explicit, or overt, curriculum refers to what a school intends to teach students. This curriculum is made up of several components: (1) the goals, aims, and learning objectives the school has for all students; (2) the actual courses that make up each student's course of study; and (3) the specific knowledge, skills, and attitudes that teachers want students to acquire. If we asked a principal to describe the educational program at his or her school, our question would refer to the explicit curriculum. Similarly, if we asked a teacher to describe what he or she wished to accomplish with a particular class, the teacher would describe the explicit curriculum.

In short, the **explicit curriculum** represents the publicly announced expectations the school has for its students. These expectations range from learning how to read, write, and compute to learning to appreciate music, art, and cultures other than one's own. In most instances, the explicit curriculum takes the form of written plans or guides for the education of students. Examples of such written documents are course descriptions, curriculum guides that set forth the goals and learning objectives for a school or district, texts and other commercially prepared learning materials, and teachers' lesson plans. Through the instructional program of a school, then, these curricular materials are brought to life.

Hidden Curriculum The hidden, or implicit, curriculum refers to the behaviors, attitudes, and knowledge the culture of the school unintentionally teaches students (Parkay and Hass 2000). What students learn via the **hidden curriculum** can be positive or negative, depending on their day-to-day experiences at school. For example, from teachers who are knowledgeable, well organized, and personable, students are likely to develop positive habits and abilities—cooperating with others, taking responsibility, planning ahead, and forgoing immediate gratification to obtain long-range goals. However, from teachers who are ill prepared, apathetic, or aloof, students may acquire habits and attitudes that are negative and that discourage personal growth and development—a dislike for learning, the ability to deceive or defy adult authority figures, or a tendency to procrastinate.

In the following excerpts from letters to their former teachers, four students describe the hidden curricula they experienced in school. In examples 1 and 2, the hidden curricula "taught" students to be more confident in their ability to learn. In examples 3 and 4, the hidden curricula undermined the students' confidence and desire to learn.

Example #1
I was in your grade 10 English class. I sure felt safe to take a risk in your class. I actually tried hard, knowing I might fail, but felt safe enough to do so (Paul, Christensen, and Falk 2000, 23).

Example #2
I was in your grade 9 class and you praised me for my creative writing. Until that time, I had never thought of myself as a very creative person but your faith in me spurred me on to choose English as my major at the university (Paul, Christensen, and Falk 2000, 23).

Example #3
The teacher just put [material] on the board and if you don't know how, the teacher get angry. I try to get help but when I come after school, they gotta go somewhere and can't help you . . . like when I ask somebody to help me, just because some other kid won't need help, then they think others won't either; some kids are smarter (Wilson and Corbett 2001, 38).

Example #4
I was in your 11th grade biology class. I loved science and biology until I took your class. You gave me a great disdain for the subject. Your teaching methods bored the class to tears. We read each chapter out loud at the beginning of the week and spent the rest of the week working quietly on the questions at the end of the chapter along with the endless dittos you passed out. We never discussed anything and you never taught us anything. We were graded on how well we could come up with the answers you thought were right and heaven forbid if we did not head our paper using the "correct" format. I think the only thing I learned in your class was conformity (Colucci 2000, 38).

As a result of the hidden curriculum of schools, students learn more than their teachers imagine. Although teachers cannot directly control what students learn through the hidden curriculum, they can increase the likelihood that what it teaches will be positive. By allowing students to help determine the content of the explicit curriculum, by inviting them to help establish classroom rules, and by providing them with challenges appropriate for their stage of development, you can ensure that the outcomes of the hidden curriculum in your classroom will be largely positive.

Null Curriculum Discussing a curriculum that cannot be observed directly is like talking about dark matter or black holes, unseen phenomena in the universe whose existence must be inferred because their incredible denseness and gravitational fields do not allow light to escape. In much the same way, we can consider the curriculum that we *do not* find in the schools; it may be as important as what we *do* find. Elliot Eisner has labeled the intellectual processes and content that schools do not teach "the **null curriculum**—the options students are not afforded, the perspectives they may never know about, much less be able to use, the concepts and skills that are not a part of their intellectual repertoire" (2002, 106–107).

For example, the kind of thinking that schools foster among students is largely based on manipulations of words and numbers. Thinking that is imaginative, subjective, and poetic is stressed only incidentally. Also, students are seldom taught anthropology, sociology, psychology, law, economics, filmmaking, or architecture.

Eisner points out that "certain subject matters have been traditionally taught in schools not because of a careful analysis of the range of other alternatives that could be offered but rather because they have traditionally been taught. We teach what we teach largely out of habit, and in the process neglect areas of study that could prove to be exceedingly useful to students" (2002, 103).

Extracurricular/Cocurricular Programs   This curriculum includes school-sponsored activities—music, drama, special interest clubs, sports, student government, and honor societies, to name a few—that students may pursue in addition to their studies in academic subject areas. When such activities are perceived as additions to the academic curriculum, they are termed *extracurricular*. When these activities are seen as having important educational goals—and not merely as extras added to the academic curriculum—they are termed *cocurricular*. To reflect the fact that these two labels are commonly used for the same activities, this book uses the term *extracurricular/cocurricular* activities.

Though **extracurricular/cocurricular programs** are most extensive on the secondary level, many schools at the elementary, middle, and junior high levels also provide students with a broad assortment of extracurricular/cocurricular activities. For students who choose to participate, such activities provide an opportunity to use social and academic skills in many different contexts.

Research shows that the larger a school is, the less likely it is that a student will take part in extracurricular/cocurricular activities. At the same time, those who do participate tend to have higher self-concepts than those who do not (Coladarci and Cobb 1996). The actual effects that extracurricular/cocurricular activities have on students' development, however, are not entirely clear.

Students who participate in extracurricular/cocurricular activities tend to receive higher grades than nonparticipants and are more frequently identified as gifted (Gerber 1996; Jordan and Nettles 1999; Modi, Konstantopoulos, and Hedges 1998). However, it is not known whether participation influences achievement, or whether achievement influences participation. Nevertheless, participation has a positive influence on the decision to remain in school (Mahoney and Cairns 1997), educational aspirations (Modi, Konstantopoulos, and Hedges 1998), and the occupation one aspires to and eventually attains (Brown, Kohrs, and Lanzarro 1991; Holland and Andre 1987). Furthermore, students themselves tend to identify extracurricular/cocurricular activities as a high point in their school careers.

It is also clear that students who might benefit the most from participating in extracurricular/cocurricular activities—those below the norm in academic achievement and students at risk—tend not to participate. In addition, students from low socioeconomic backgrounds participate less often (National Center for Education Statistics 1995).

Curriculum Content

The nation's schools teach what the larger society believes young people should learn. For example, Table 1.1 on page 28, based on a survey by Public Agenda, shows several content areas that the public believes are "absolutely essential." The public believes that the basics of reading, writing, and mathematics plus the

Table 1.1 **What content is essential for the curriculum?**				
	Absolutely Essential	**Important, But Not Essential**	**Not that Important**	**Don't Know**
Basic reading, writing, and math skills	92%	8%	<0.5%	1%
Good work habits such as being responsible, on time, and disciplined	83%	15%	1%	1%
The value of hard work	78%	20%	1%	1%
Values such as honesty and tolerance of others	74%	23%	2%	1%
Computer skills and media technology	80%	18%	1%	1%

Note: Does not total 100% due to rounding. Methodology: telephone survey of 800 adults.

Source: Adapted from Public Agenda, *Education: A Nation Divided?* New York: Public Agenda, 1999.

development of good work habits should be the heart of the curriculum. Additional support for these curriculum goals comes from employers and college professors who deal with students after they graduate from high school. For example, when asked whether public school graduates have the skills needed to succeed "in the work world" or "in college," only 32 percent of employers surveyed and 39 percent of professors believe students have the skills (Public Agenda 1999). The following comments by two parents who participated in an earlier Public Agenda survey typify the concern many people have about the position of the basic skills in the school curriculum:

> *Education is becoming more about social issues as opposed to reading, writing, and arithmetic. Some of it's fine, but I think schools need to stay with the basics. . . . You can't get by in the business world on social issues if you can't add and subtract.*
>
> *They all talk all the time about this "whole child educational process." . . . It's not your business to make a "whole child." Your business is to teach these students how to read, how to write, and give them the basic skills to balance their checkbook. It's not to make new Emersons out of them (Johnson and Immerwahr 1994, 13).*

How Is the School Curriculum Developed?

Although there is no easy-to-follow set of procedures you can use to develop a curriculum, Ralph Tyler has provided four fundamental questions that must be answered in developing any curriculum or plan of instruction. These four questions, known as the **Tyler rationale** (see Figure 1.5), are as follows (Tyler 1949, 1):

Figure 1.5   The Tyler rationale for curriculum development.

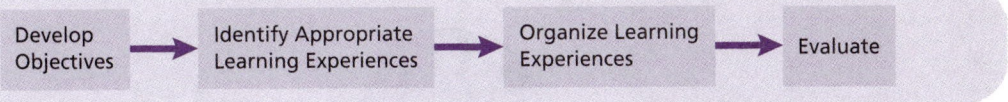

Develop Objectives → Identify Appropriate Learning Experiences → Organize Learning Experiences → Evaluate

1. What educational purposes should the school seek to attain?
2. What educational experiences can be provided that are likely to attain these purposes?
3. How can these educational experiences be effectively organized?
4. How can we determine whether these purposes are being attained?

Some educators believe that the Tyler rationale underestimates the complexities of curriculum development because it advocates a straightforward, step-by-step process that is difficult to follow in the "real" classroom. Nevertheless, Tyler's classic work has been used by a great number of school systems to bring some degree of order and focus to the curriculum development process.

The Focus of Curriculum Planning

In discussing curriculum development, it is helpful to clarify the focus of curriculum planning. Figure 1.6 illustrates two dimensions of this planning process: the target and the time orientation. The target of curriculum planning may be at the macro or the micro level.

At the macro level, decisions about the content of the curriculum apply to large groups of students. The national goals for education and state-level curriculum guidelines are examples of macro-level curricular decisions. At the micro level, curriculum decisions are made that apply to groups of students in a particular school or classroom. To some extent, you will be a micro-level curriculum developer—that is, you will make numerous decisions about the curricular experiences you provide students in your classroom.

Another dimension of curriculum planning is the time orientation—does the planning focus on the present or the future? In addition to national goals and state-level curriculum guidelines, the semester-long or monthly plans or unit plans that teachers make are examples of future-oriented curriculum planning. Present-oriented curriculum planning usually occurs at the classroom level and is influenced by the unique needs of specific groups of students. The daily or weekly curriculum decisions and lesson plans that teachers make are examples of present-oriented curriculum planning.

Student-Centered versus Subject-Centered Curricula

A key concern in curriculum development is whether greater emphasis should be given to the requirements of the subject area or to the needs of the students. It is

Figure 1.6 Two dimensions of curriculum planning.

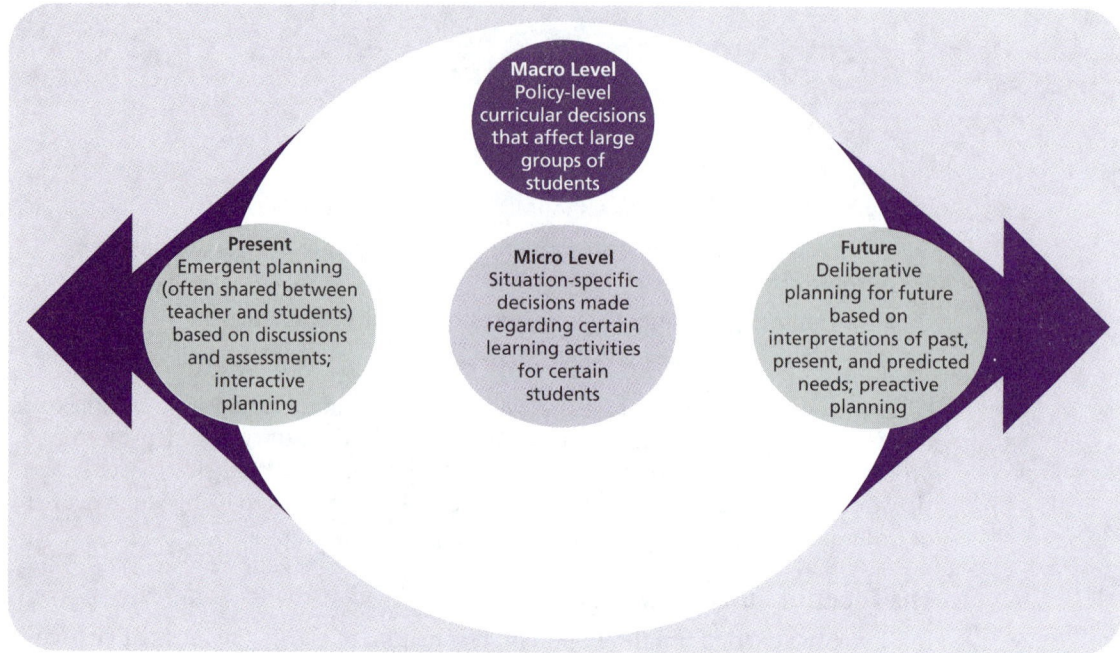

helpful to imagine where a school curriculum might be placed on the following continuum,

Student-Centered Curriculum ⟷ **Subject-Centered Curriculum**

Although no course is entirely subject- or student-centered, curricula vary considerably in the degree to which they emphasize one or the other. The **subject-centered curriculum** places primary emphasis on the logical order of the discipline students are to study. The teacher of such a curriculum is a subject-matter expert and is primarily concerned with helping students understand the facts, laws, and principles of the discipline. Subject-centered curricula are more typical of high school education.

Some teachers develop curricula that reflect greater concern for students and their needs. Though teachers of the **student-centered curriculum** also teach content, they emphasize the growth and development of students. This emphasis is generally more typical of elementary school curricula.

The Integrated Curriculum

To provide students with more meaningful learning experiences, you may decide to use an integrated approach to developing your curriculum. Used most frequently with elementary-age students, the **integrated curriculum** draws from several dif-

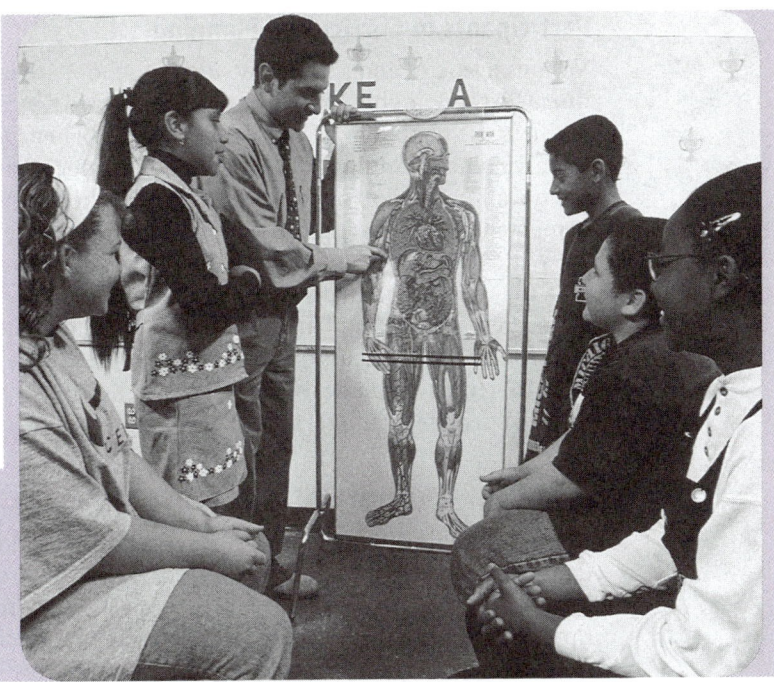

Is the curriculum this teacher is presenting primarily a subject-centered or student-centered curriculum? In what ways might the curriculum be both subject-centered and student-centered?

ferent subject areas and focuses on a theme or concept rather than on a single subject. Early childhood education expert Suzanne Krogh (2000, 340) suggests that an integrated approach based on thematic "webs" is a more "natural" way for children to learn:

> [Children] do not naturally learn through isolating specific subjects. These have been determined by adult definition. Children's natural learning is more likely to take place across a theme of interest: building a fort, exploring a sandbox, interacting with the first snow of winter. Teachers can create a good deal of their curriculum by building webs made up of these themes of interest. Done with knowledge and care, a web can be created that incorporates most, or even all, of the required and desired curriculum.

According to a national survey of elementary teachers' views on the integrated curriculum, 89 percent believed that integration was the "most effective" way to present the curriculum. As one teacher who was surveyed said, "I'm not interested in presenting isolated facts which children seem to memorize and forget. I want to help students put each lesson in perspective" (Boyer 1995, 83). In *The Basic School: A Community for Learning*, the late Ernest Boyer suggested that the elementary school curriculum should be integrated according to eight themes or "core commonalities": The Life Cycle, The Use of Symbols, Membership in Groups, A Sense of Time and Space, Response to the Aesthetic, Connections to Nature, Producing and Consuming, and Living with Purpose (Boyer 1995).

Participants in Curriculum Planning

Various agencies and people outside the school are involved in curriculum planning. Textbook publishers, for example, influence what is taught because many teachers use textbooks as curriculum guides. The federal government contributes to curriculum planning by setting national education goals, and state departments of education develop both broad aims for school curricula and specific minimum competencies for students to master.

Within a given school, the curriculum-planning team and the classroom teacher plan the curriculum that students actually experience. As a teacher you will draw from a reservoir of curriculum plans prepared by others; thus you, too, will play a vital role in the curriculum-planning process. Whenever you make decisions about what material to include in your teaching, how to sequence content, and how much time to spend teaching certain material, you are planning the curriculum.

How Can You Develop a Multicultural Classroom and Curriculum?

Effective teaching in today's classrooms requires the ability to communicate with students from diverse cultural backgrounds. Professional teachers see cultural diversity as an asset to be preserved and valued, not a liability. To provide equal educational opportunity to all students means that teachers and schools promote the full development of students as individuals, without regard for race, ethnicity, gender, sexual orientation, socioeconomic status, abilities or disabilities. More specifically, teachers fulfill this important obligation by continually evaluating the appropriateness of the curriculum each student experiences. Understanding the concept of multicultural education will enable you to develop a curriculum that is appropriate for all students.

Multicultural education is committed to providing all students with equal opportunities to learn in school. Multicultural education is based on the fact that students do not learn in a vacuum—their culture predisposes them to learn in certain ways. And finally, multicultural education recognizes that current school practices have provided, and continue to provide, some students with greater opportunities for learning than students who belong to other groups.

As multiculturalism has become more pervasive in U.S. schools, controversy over the need for multicultural education and its purposes has emerged. Carl Grant has identified as "myths" the following six arguments against multicultural education: "(1) It is both divisive and so conceptually weak that it does little to eliminate structural inequalities; (2) it is unnecessary because the United States is a melting pot; (3) multiculturalism—and by extension multicultural education—and political correctness are the same thing; (4) multicultural education rejects the notion of a common culture; (5) multicultural education is a 'minority thing'; and (6) multicultural education will impede learning the basic skills" (1994, 5). Though multicultural education is being challenged by those who promote these beliefs, public dialogue and debate about how schools can more effectively address diversity is healthy—an indicator that our society is making real progress toward creating a culture that incorporates the values of diverse groups.

Dimensions of Multicultural Education

According to James A. Banks, "Multicultural education is a complex and multidimensional concept" (2001, 5). More specifically, Banks suggests that multicultural education may be conceptualized as consisting of five dimensions: (1) content integration, (2) knowledge construction, (3) prejudice reduction, (4) an equity pedagogy, and (5) an empowering school culture (see Figure 1.7).

Figure 1.7   Banks's dimensions of multicultural education.

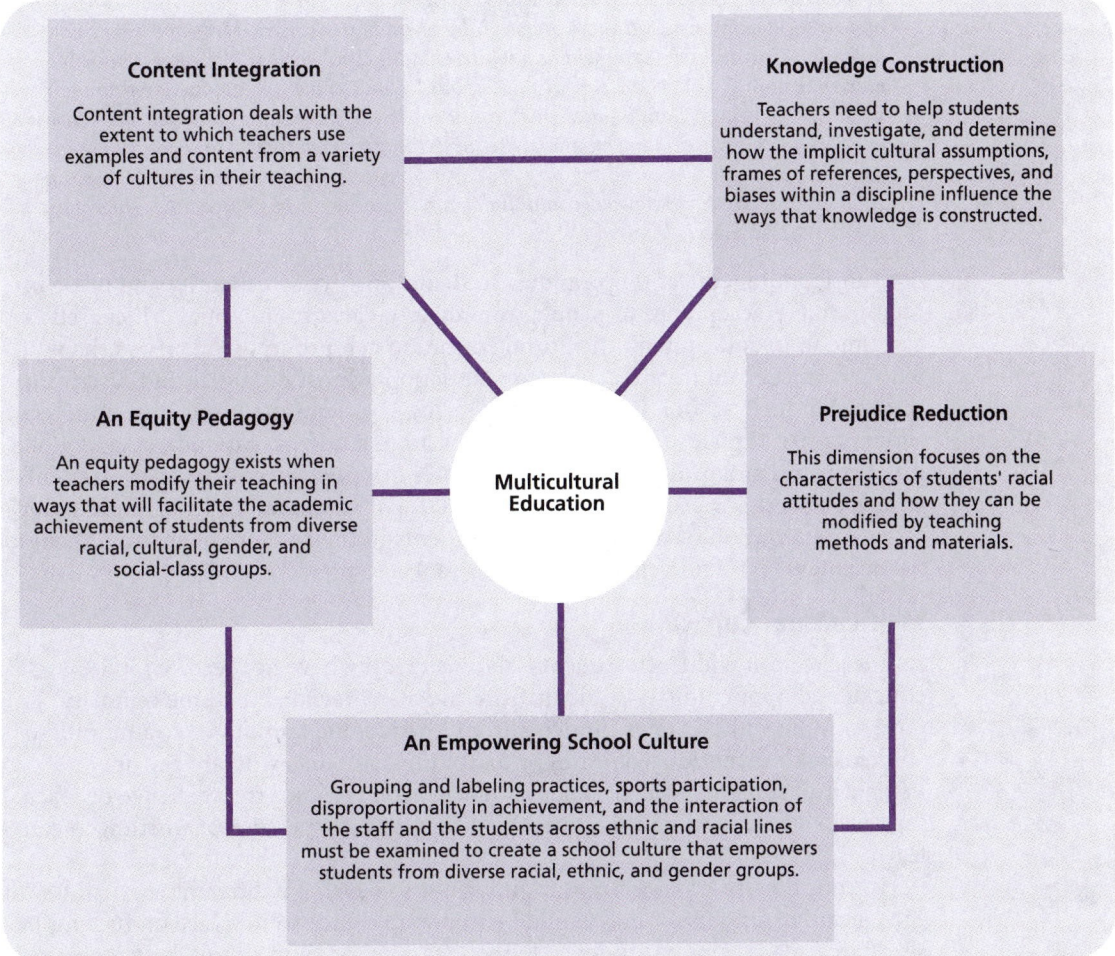

Content Integration

Content integration deals with the extent to which teachers use examples and content from a variety of cultures in their teaching.

Knowledge Construction

Teachers need to help students understand, investigate, and determine how the implicit cultural assumptions, frames of references, perspectives, and biases within a discipline influence the ways that knowledge is constructed.

An Equity Pedagogy

An equity pedagogy exists when teachers modify their teaching in ways that will facilitate the academic achievement of students from diverse racial, cultural, gender, and social-class groups.

Multicultural Education

Prejudice Reduction

This dimension focuses on the characteristics of students' racial attitudes and how they can be modified by teaching methods and materials.

An Empowering School Culture

Grouping and labeling practices, sports participation, disproportionality in achievement, and the interaction of the staff and the students across ethnic and racial lines must be examined to create a school culture that empowers students from diverse racial, ethnic, and gender groups.

Source: From James A. Banks and Cherry A. McGee Banks, *Multicultural Education: Issues and Perspectives,* 3d ed. Boston: Allyn & Bacon, 1997, p. 24. Copyright © 1997 by Allyn & Bacon. Reprinted by permission.

As you progress through your teacher education program and eventually begin to prepare curriculum materials and instructional strategies for your multicultural classroom, remember that integrating content from a variety of cultural groups is just one dimension of multicultural education. Multicultural education is not "something that is done at a certain time slot in the school day where children eat with chopsticks or listen to Peruvian music. . . . [It is] something that is infused throughout the school culture and practiced daily" (Henry 1996, 108). In the following comments, a teacher explains how she developed an understanding of multicultural education:

> My first teaching assignment was in a very low socioeconomic area of Seattle in the late 1990s. Most of my students were African American, Latino and Hispanic Americans, and Asian Americans . . . a very diverse group of students. At first, I was apprehensive about how I would relate to them as a white, middle-class teacher. I was not confident about my ability. I knew the subject matter, but I didn't know if I could relate it to their lives. Now, however, I am a much more confident in the classroom. I have learned a lot about their cultures and how to make the subject matter meaningful to them. I have good rapport with them, and, so, they are eager to learn what I have to offer. I like seeing students grow in their knowledge and understanding of my subject area, and I like learning about their lives.

Multicultural education promotes students' positive self-identity and pride in their heritage, acceptance of people from diverse backgrounds, and critical self-assessment. In addition, multicultural education can prompt students, perhaps with guidance from their teachers, to take action against prejudice and discrimination within their school. Indeed, as Joel Spring says, "multicultural education should create a spirit of tolerance and activism in students. An understanding of other cultures and of differing cultural frames of reference will . . . spark students to actively work for social justice" (1998, 163). For example, students might reduce the marginalization of minority-group students in their school by inviting them to participate in extracurricular and after-school activities.

Multicultural Curricula

As a teacher you will teach students who historically have not received full educational opportunity—students from the many racial and ethnic minority groups in the United States, students from low-income families or communities, students with exceptional abilities or disabilities, students who are gay or lesbian, and students who are male or female. You will face the challenge of reaching out to all students and teaching them that they are persons of worth who can learn.

In your diverse classroom, your aim is not to develop a different curriculum for each group of students—that would be impossible and would place undue emphasis on differences among students. Rather, your curriculum should help increase students' awareness and appreciation of the rich diversity in U.S. culture.

A **multicultural curriculum** addresses the needs and backgrounds of all students regardless of their cultural identity. As Banks suggests, the multicultural curriculum "enable[s] students to derive valid generalizations and theories about the characteristics of ethnic groups and to learn how they are alike and different, in both their past and present experiences. . . . [It] focus[es] on a range of groups that *differ* in their racial characteristics, cultural experiences, languages, histories, values, and current problems" (2003, 16). Teachers who provide multicultural education recognize the importance of asking questions such as those posed by Valerie Ooka Pang: "Why is a child's home language important to keep? What strengths does culture give children? What impact does culture have on learning? What does racism, sexism, or classism look like in schools?" (1994, 292).

In developing a multicultural curriculum, you should be sensitive to how your instructional materials and strategies can be made more inclusive so that they reflect cultural perspectives, or "voices," that previously have been silent or marginalized in discussions about what should be taught in schools and how it should be taught. "Non-dominant groups representing diversity in the school whose voices traditionally have not been heard include those defined by race, language, gender, sexual orientation, alternative family structures, social class, disability, bilingualism, and those with alien or refugee status" (Henry 1996, 108). Effective teachers attend to these previously unheard voices not as an act of tokenism but with a genuine desire to make the curriculum more inclusive and to "create space for alternative voices, not just on the periphery but in the center" (Singer 1994, 286).

Multicultural Instructional Materials and Strategies

To create classrooms that are truly multicultural, effective teachers select instructional materials that are sensitive, accurately portray the contributions of ethnic groups, and reflect diverse points of view. They also recognize that "[s]ome of the books and other materials on ethnic groups published each year are insensitive, inaccurate, and written from mainstream and insensitive perspectives and points of view" (Banks 2003, 111). Some guidelines for selecting multicultural instructional materials follow:

- Books and other materials should accurately portray the perspectives, attitudes, and feelings of ethnic groups.
- Fictional works should have strong ethnic characters.
- Books should describe settings and experiences with which all students can identify and yet should accurately reflect ethnic cultures and lifestyles.
- The protagonists in books with ethnic themes should have ethnic characteristics but should face conflicts and problems universal to all cultures and groups.
- The illustrations in books should be accurate, ethnically sensitive, and technically well done.
- Ethnic materials should not contain racist concepts, clichés, phrases, or words.
- Factual materials should be historically accurate.
- Multiethnic resources and basal textbooks should discuss major events and documents related to ethnic history (Banks 2003, 127).

Materials and Strategies for Gender-Fair Classrooms   Gender is also an important dimension of multicultural education. Clearly, as a teacher you must encourage girls and boys to develop to the full extent of their capabilities. You must provide them an education that is free from **gender bias**—subtle favoritism or discrimination on the basis of gender.

Following is a list of basic guidelines for creating a **gender-fair classroom**. Adherence to these guidelines will help you "address the inequities institutionalized in the organizational structure of schools, the curriculum selected to be taught, the learning strategies employed, and their ongoing instructional and informal interactions with students" (Stanford 1992, 88).

- Become aware of differences in interactions with girls and boys.
- Promote boys' achievement in reading and writing and girls' achievement in mathematics and science.
- Reduce young children's self-imposed sexism.
- Teach about sexism and sex role stereotyping.
- Foster an atmosphere of collaboration between girls and boys.

Materials and Strategies for Multilingual Classrooms   In today's diverse classrooms, teachers must be able to meet the needs of **language-minority students**—students whose first language is not English. These needs are best met by teachers who speak their native language as well as English. However, this is often not possible, and monolingual teachers will find increasing numbers of limited English proficiency (LEP) students in their classrooms.

As a teacher in a multilingual setting, one of your goals would be to help language-minority students become proficient in English. Another goal would be for them to become **bicultural**, that is, able to function effectively in two or more linguistic and cultural groups. To help you achieve this goal, see Appendix 1.2, "Creating Classroom Environments That Support Second-Language Learners," and Appendix 1.3, "Strategies for Enhancing the Learning and Literacy of Second-Language Learners" at the end of this chapter. Developed by bilingual/ESL education expert Gisela Ernst and her colleagues, these strategies can be used whether or not a teacher is bilingual.

Teaching in a Diverse Society

It is not easy to learn how to be an effective teacher of students from diverse backgrounds. Without a doubt, learning to be effective depends on being open and willing to learn about other groups. Yvonne Wilson, a first-grade teacher in Talmoon, Minnesota, and an Ojibwe Indian, points out that a teacher's willingness to learn about other cultures is very important to students and their parents:

People in the community know if you are trying to understand their culture. Students also see it. Becoming involved—going to a powwow or participating in other cultural events—shows people that here is a teacher who is trying to learn about our culture.

Case for Reflection

Teaching in a Multilingual Setting

You are a first-year teacher at a school in a large city in the Northeast. The school is located in a working-class neighborhood that is ethnically and racially diverse. The school's enrollment is approximately 35 percent Anglo-European American (approximately half of whom have parents who immigrated to the United States from Russia); 40 percent African American, 15 percent Latino and Hispanic, and 10 percent Asian American.

It is the first day of school, and students are just now entering your classroom. There is a lot of talking, joking, and good-natured horseplay. As students enter the room, you realize that many of the students are speaking languages other than English. You listen carefully and are able to identify Russian, Spanish, and Chinese among the languages being spoken.

This year, you have set up your classroom for cooperative learning. Five octagonal tables are distributed evenly around the room. Students at each table will make up a "team." Though students will work in teams, you plan to de-emphasize competition among the teams.

As the students select tables at which to sit, you notice that they are clustering themselves according to linguistic background. After taking their seats, most of the students continue to talk with the other students at their table. The Russian-speaking students are seated at one table; the Spanish-speaking students at another; the Chinese-speaking students at another; and students who are speaking English are seated at the remaining two tables.

"Welcome to my class," you begin. "We are going to have a great year together!"

The students gradually quiet down and give you their attention. You continue with a brief overview of what students will learn in your class that year. Following the overview, you ask each student to introduce him- or herself to the class.

As students introduce themselves, you are thinking about how students have obviously used linguistic background as a criterion for choosing a table at which to sit. Your preference is for students to choose work tables for the year. Assigning tables might minimize the tendency of students to cluster by linguistic background, you realize. However, that would work against the democratic classroom climate you hope to create. Also, your hunch is that interaction among students would still reflect linguistic backgrounds, regardless of assigned seats.

You are well aware that during the next few days you will set the tone for the new school year. What can you do during that time to encourage students to interact as much as possible with students from linguistic backgrounds other than their own? What can you do throughout the school year to encourage cohesiveness in your diverse classroom?

Questions

1. In the preceding case, your students have divided themselves into groups according to linguistic background. Assuming they are allowed to form small groups on their own, what other criteria might students use to determine group membership?
2. Why do you think students prefer to work with classmates with the same linguistic background?
3. With reference to the grade level and subject area for which you are preparing to teach, what instructional activities would encourage students to see themselves as *one* cohesive group, rather than several small groups formed according to linguistic background or other criteria, such as race, ethnicity, gender, ability, or socioeconomic status?

Participating wholeheartedly in cross-cultural experiences such as Wilson describes will help you to grow in the eight areas outlined in Figure 1.8 as being essential for successful teaching in a diverse society. Your growth in these eight areas will require more than reading about different cultural groups and/or learn-

Figure 1.8 Essential knowledge and skills for successful teaching in a diverse society.

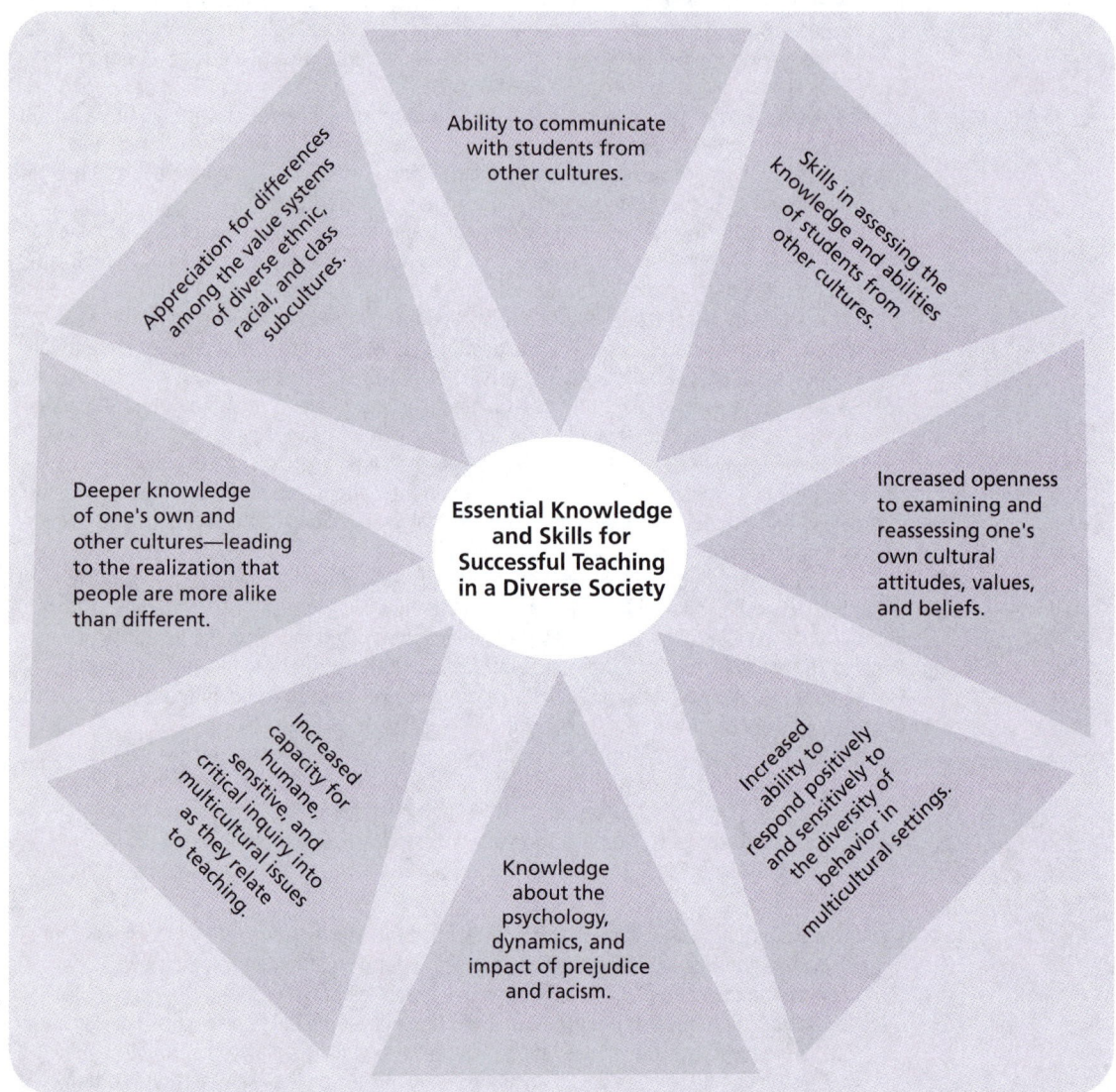

Source: Adapted from Forrest W. Parkay and Henry T. Fillmer, "Improving Teachers' Attitudes toward Minority-Group Students: An Experiential Approach to Multicultural Inservice," *New Horizons Journal of Education,* November 1984, pp. 178–179.

ing about strategies and materials for teaching in diverse settings. You must actively seek out experiences in diverse settings. These experiences will bring to life what you have learned. Most importantly, you will understand on a feeling level what you have learned on a cognitive level.

Summary

What Knowledge Do You Need to Teach?

- Professional teachers reflect on their classroom experiences.
- Teachers need three kinds of knowledge: knowledge of self and students, knowledge of subject, and knowledge of how to use educational theory and research.
- Teachers' self-knowledge influences their ability to understand students.
- The ambiguities of teaching can cause teachers to experience anxiety.
- Elementary teachers can experience loneliness because they are isolated from adults; secondary teachers can experience loneliness because of departmentalization.
- Teachers must know their students' aptitudes, talents, learning styles, stage of development, and readiness to learn new material.
- Teachers must understand their subjects deeply so that they can modify instructional strategies based on students' perception of content.
- Knowledge of educational theory enables professional teachers to know why certain strategies work.
- Educational research provides teachers with general guidelines for practice.
- Teachers also use craft knowledge, what they "know" about teaching as a result of reflecting on their classroom experiences.
- An important form of craft knowledge for today's teachers is knowledge of how to use educational technology.

What Can You Learn from Observing in Classrooms?

- The opportunity to observe in classrooms helps some students make the final decision as to whether to become a teacher.
- Many teacher education programs are providing students with more and earlier opportunities to observe in classrooms.
- Distance-learning classrooms, using compressed video, link teacher education programs to schools off campus.
- Observations can focus on a particular aspect of classroom life or be guided by a set of questions related to a specific area, such as how the teacher motivates students.
- Observation instruments range from informal, qualitative descriptions to formal, quantitative checklists.

How Can You Gain Practical Experience for Becoming a Teacher?

- Teacher education students can gain practical experience through focused classroom observations, microteaching, teaching simulations, analyses of video cases, field-based practical and clinical experiences, and classroom aide programs.
- In microteaching, students practice specific skills by teaching brief lessons that are later analyzed.
- Computer simulations and virtual reality—as well as written, videotaped, and audiotaped cases—are being used for teaching simulations.
- Journal writing and reflective teaching logs increase the benefits of the student teaching experience.

- To prepare to teach students from diverse backgrounds, teacher education students should actively seek field experiences in multicultural settings.
- Substitute teaching provides additional practical experience after completing a teacher education program.

What Is Taught in Schools?

- There are many different definitions for the term *curriculum*. A general definition is that *curriculum* refers to the experiences, both planned and unplanned, that either enhance or impede the education and growth of students.
- All students experience four types of curricula. In addition to learning what teachers intend to teach (the explicit curriculum), students learn from the hidden curriculum, the null curriculum, and extracurricular/cocurricular programs.
- Curriculum content reflects what the larger society believes young people should learn.
- The public believes that the school curriculum should give primary emphasis to the "basics" of reading, writing, and mathematics and the development of good work habits.

How Is the School Curriculum Developed?

- Curricula are based on the needs and interests of students and also reflect a variety of professional, commercial, local, state, national, and international pressures.

- Teachers must be prepared to assume important roles in the curriculum development process, especially in developing student-centered and integrated curricula.

How Can You Develop a Multicultural Classroom and Curriculum?

- Five dimensions of multicultural education have been suggested: content integration, knowledge construction, prejudice reduction, an equity pedagogy, and an empowering school culture.
- A multicultural curriculum addresses the needs and backgrounds of all students—regardless of their cultural identity—and expands students' appreciation for diversity. Effective multicultural materials and instructional strategies include the contributions of ethnic groups and reflect diverse points of view or "voices" that previously may have been silenced or marginalized in society.
- Both boys and girls experience inequities in the classroom; teachers, however, can provide both sexes with an education free of *gender bias* by creating gender-fair classrooms and curricula.
- Today's teachers will find an increasing number of language-minority students—students whose first language is not English—in their classrooms.

Key Terms and Concepts

Reflective Application Activities

Discussion Questions

1. What does self-knowledge mean to you? Why is self-knowledge important in teaching? What steps can you take to achieve greater self-knowledge?
2. Which of the field experiences discussed in this chapter, other than student teaching, is the most important?

Professional Journal

1. Reflect on the 12,000 or so hours that you have spent in classrooms on the K–12 levels. What did the hidden curricula in these classes teach you about yourself?
2. On the basis of your field experiences to date and the information in Chapter 1, ask yourself these questions and respond in your journal: Do I have the aptitude to become a good teacher? Am I willing to acquire the essential knowledge and skills teachers need? Do I really want to become a teacher?

Online Assignments

1. Visit the home pages of three or more of the following research publications on the Web. These journals focus on educational research, learning theories, student and teacher attitudes and behaviors, and the effectiveness of teaching methods. Some journals emphasize the implications of educational psychology theory and research for educational policy and applications to teaching practice. Note the kinds of studies and research topics each selected journal reports. How might articles in these journals help you as an education major? As a classroom teacher? As a teaching professional?

   American Educational Research Journal
   Cognition and Instruction
   Contemporary Educational Psychology
   Educational Psychologist
   Educational Psychology Review
   Educational Researcher
   Journal of Educational Psychology
   Journal of Teaching and Teacher Education
   Review of Educational Research
   Review of Research in Education
   Social Psychology of Education

2. Conduct an online keyword search for sources of information on one or more of the following topics from Chapter 1.

   multicultural education
   language-minority students
   distance learning
   integrated curriculum

Observations and Interviews

1. Spend a half-day at a school at the level at which you plan to teach. Take note of your impressions regarding that school's hidden curriculum. If possible, chat briefly with administrators, teachers, and students. Share your observations with others in your education class.
2. Observe students outside the classroom during a school day and record your impressions of the hidden curriculum. For each topic you list, think how it could be made a desirable and effective part of the explicit curriculum. Share your observations and ideas with others in your class.

Professional Portfolio

Survey the Internet to begin locating and creating bookmarks or favorites for websites, schools, networks, and teacher discussion groups that you could use to help develop a subject-area curriculum for your students.

Appendix 1.1
Formative Observation
Data Instrument

Teacher Name: _____ Date: _____ Period/Time: _____ Evaluator: _____ Signature: _____

FORMATIVE OBSERVATION DATA INSTRUMENT

Instructions: Use this sheet to record the events that occur during the classroom observation. Be sure to code each instance of a TPAI practice as follows: appropriate use of practice (); strong or positive use of practice (+); weak or negative use of practice (−).

Function/Practice	*Time*	*Comments*
I. Instructional Time 1.1 Materials ready 1.2 Class started quickly 1.3 Time-on-task for learning		
II. Student Behavior 2.1 Rules—Administrative matters 2.2 Rules—Verbal participation 2.3 Rules—Movement 2.4 Frequently monitors behavior 2.5 Stops inappropriate behavior 2.6 Reflective practice—Student behavior		
III. Instructional Presentation 3.1 Links to prior learning. 3.2 Understands content; makes it meaningful 3.3 Speaks fluently 3.4 Relevant examples 3.5 High rate of success on tasks 3.6 Brisk pace 3.7 Effective, smooth transitions 3.8 Assignment clear 3.9 Adapts instruction to diverse learners 3.10 Develops critical thinking, problem solving, and performance skills 3.11 Uses technology to support instruction 3.12 Students engaged, responsible for learning		
IV. Instructional Monitoring 4.1 Maintains deadlines, standards 4.2 Circulates to check students' performance 4.3 Uses varied work products to check progress		

Source: Public Schools of North Carolina, State Board of Education.

Function/Practice	Time	Comments
4.4 Questions clear, one at a time 4.5 Uses responses to adjust teaching V. Instructional Feedback 5.1 Feedback on in-class work 5.2 Prompt feedback on out-of-class work 5.3 Affirms correct response quickly 5.4 Sustaining feedback after incorrect response 5.5 Fosters active inquiry supportive interaction VI. Facilitating Instruction 6.1 Aligned instructional plans 6.2 Uses diagnostic information, assessment 6.3 Maintains accurate records 6.4 Appropriate instructional activities 6.5 Available resources support program VII. Communicating in Educational Environment 7.1 Treats all students fairly 7.2 Participates in development of school vision 7.3 Relationships with colleagues, parents, community VIII. Performing Non-Instructional Duties 8.1 Carries out non-instructional duties 8.2 Adheres to laws, policies, rules, and regulations 8.3 Plan for professional development 8.4 Reflective practitioner		

Appendix 1.2
Creating Classroom Environments that Support Second-Language Learners

Classroom Environment and Attitude

1. Relax and enjoy. Language is more caught than taught. Your relaxed, receptive, interested concern will be the magical ingredient for enhancing the teaching and learning process.

2. Provide a warm, encouraging environment in which help is readily available to LEP students.

3. Books that are sensitive to the adjustments of the new student can be shared with the class (e.g., *Crow Boy* by Yashima; *I Hate English* by Levine; *What Does the Rooster Say, Yoshio?* by Battles).

4. Fill the room with meaningful, relevant print. These are springboards for discussion and rudiments of second-language literacy.

5. Label as many objects in the classroom as possible and invite your students to provide labels in their own language.

6. Increase possibilities for success by using a satisfactory/unsatisfactory option for grading until students are able to successfully complete classroom assignments.

7. Try to avoid anglicizing your students' names. Sometimes their names are the only connection they have with their native language, culture, and country.

Cross-cultural Communication and Understanding

1. Become informed about the different cultures and languages represented in your classroom. This can be done by designing activities wherein your students become the "experts" by sharing part of their culture with the class.

2. If you find a student's behavior to be unusual or disconcerting, you might ask students or parents to clarify its meaning (e.g., Native-American and Asian-American students avoid eye contact with authority figures out of respect). This could prevent misunderstandings further down the road.

3. Try to talk individually with your students as much as possible. This lets them know you are interested in them as individuals, not just as students.

4. Avoid forcing students to speak and allow a wait time for students to answer.

5. LEP students need instruction to be clear and interesting. By using exaggerated facial expressions, a slower speech rate, abundance of gestures, and enunciating clearly you can reach more students. Many times our expressions and gestures can help students understand what we are saying when our words do not.

6. Try to incorporate tutors who speak students' native languages.

7. Start by asking questions (backed by visual aids) that can be answered with yes or no. Then move, little by little, to questions requiring slightly longer answers.

Source: Gisela Ernst, Margaret Castle, and Lauren C. Frostad, "Teaching in Multilingual/Multicultural Settings: Strategies for Supporting Second-Language Learners," *Curriculum in Context* (Fall/Winter 1992): 14–15. Used by permission of the authors and the publisher.

Appendix 1.3
Strategies for Enhancing the Learning and Literacy of Second-Language Learners

Instructional Techniques and Strategies

1. Whenever possible, try to use a variety of formats that go beyond the traditional lecture format. This will enable you to target different learning styles in your classroom.

2. Organize, when possible, cooperative-learning activities. Small groups give second-language learners a chance to use their second-language skills in a nonthreatening environment.

3. The use of videos, films, drama/role plays, manipulatives (great for math), pictures, artifacts, posters, music, nursery rhymes, games, filmstrips, maps, charts, and fieldtrips can enhance teaching and learning.

4. Your school ESL specialist is a wonderful source of knowledge and information about what to do and what materials to use with your LEP students.

Encourage students to indicate when they are confused or do not understand. Students may feel more comfortable indicating understanding rather than acknowledging confusion.

When testing we need to be sensitive to students' cultural background. Culturally biased tests are a major hurdle for second-language learners. Standardized tests can be a common culprit. Misinterpreting terms, directions, or situational cues can cause your students' test performance to drop drastically.

When planning lessons or assignments, think about the following questions: What background knowledge do students have? Will the assignment use academic language or critical thinking skills unfamiliar to your students?

Restate, rephrase, summarize, and review frequently.

Literacy and Oral Language Development

1. Keep in mind specialized vocabulary that is content specific. Each content area has specific terminology that can confuse most second-language learners. Math, for example, has several terms for the function of addition (e.g., add, plus, combine, sum, increased by).

2. Whenever possible define key terms in several ways.

3. Make use of pictionaries.

4. Encourage the use of bilingual dictionaries, materials, and content-area books in students' first language. They can help students understand new concepts both in their native language and in English.

5. Consult your media specialist for books appropriate for students' reading/comprehension level.

Source: Gisela Ernst, Margaret Castle, and Lauren C. Frostad, "Teaching in Multilingual/Multicultural Settings: Strategies for Supporting Second-Language Learners," *Curriculum in Context* (Fall/Winter 1992): 14–45. Used by permission of the authors and the publisher.

2 Creating a Community of Learners

My teacher for fifth and sixth grade . . . was the sweetest person in the world. You didn't have somebody telling you, "You have to do this." You could make your way around the room at your own pace. If you liked to read, you could spend a little bit more time reading. Or if you liked math, you could do that. It was more like I was doing this on my own. It made you feel more independent and it gave you more confidence in yourself.

—Kathy Title, graduate of Central Park East Elementary School in Harlem, quoted in Bensman, *Central Park East and Its Graduates*, 2000

Jacqui Fisher crouches beside a tow-headed first grader and points to his hands. "If we have eight boys and eight girls, how many hands and feet do they have?"

The student looks at Fisher, looks at his hands, and then gets up and prances around the long, narrow table where his fellow students sit. He points to each student and announces "Two there, and um, two there, and um . . ."

It's five hours into a nonstop day in Miss Fisher's first-grade class at Edison Elementary School in Tacoma, Washington. Fisher has been here since early morning and, with the exception of a brief lunch break, shepherds students through reading, writing, and a host of other academic tasks without pause. She is always on, always engaged, always moving. Her students never stop needing her attention. Fisher must be commanding yet gentle, energetic yet well paced, creative yet simple. . . .

The clock crawls to 2:45 P.M. in Miss Fisher's classroom. Students put away pencils and paper, homework folders, and books. They stand beside their desks, set their chairs on top, gather their backpacks and coats, and line up at the door.

Miss Fisher leads them in songs as they await the day's ending bell. Voices rise. Enthusiasm is far more important than pitch.

"My mother is a baker, a baker, a baker . . ."

For a moment, all is youthful optimism. Odds are, most of their mothers are not the kind of professional bakers the song describes, but struggling servants to minimum-wage service jobs. If they can find work at all.

But because of [teachers like] Jacqui Fisher, some of these first-graders may become bakers, engineers, or writers (Olson 2004, 33–34, 37).

Guiding Questions

1. How does the culture of the classroom develop?

2. How will you establish a positive learning environment?

3. What are the keys to successful classroom management?

4. What methods do effective teachers use?

5. What characterizes effective teaching?

The opening scenario for this chapter profiles Jacqui Fisher, a successful teacher at a school in a low-income area of Tacoma, Washington. More than 70 percent of students at her school are eligible to receive free or low-cost breakfast and lunch. Few of the students live with both of their parents. Fisher learned to be an effective teacher at her "high needs" school through her participation in the CO-TEACH (Collaboration for Teacher Education Accountable to Children with High Needs) program at Washington State University (WSU).

CO-TEACH is a collaborative partnership involving WSU, four community colleges, and 13 Washington State school districts. CO-TEACH focuses on preparing teachers of learners with diverse backgrounds and needs. The program includes a variety of supportive experiences, including mentoring, for new teachers in high-needs schools.

Through her experiences in CO-TEACH, Fisher learned how to organize her classroom to create a positive learning environment—a community of learners. Sensitivity to the elements that combine to create such an environment is the hallmark of a professional, reflective teacher.

For teacher education students, such as yourself, making the transition between the study of teaching and actual teaching can be a challenge. However, if you understand how "the classroom learning environment develops gradually in response to the teacher's communication of expectations, modeling of behavior, and approach to classroom management" (Good and Brophy 2003, 112), you will be to make the transition smoothly. This chapter, then, focuses on creating an authentic community of learners.

What Determines the Culture of the Classroom?

A community of learners has a strong positive culture. One definition of *culture* is the way of life common to a group of people. In much the same way, each classroom develops its own culture, or way of life. **Classroom culture** is determined by the manner in which teachers and students participate in common activities.

The activities that teachers and students engage in are influenced by several factors. As a teacher, you will make countless decisions that will shape the physical and social milieus of your classroom. From seating arrangement, to classroom rules and procedures, to the content and relevance of the curriculum, you will have a strong influence on the culture that emerges in your classroom. You will have many methodological choices to make—when to shift from one activity to another, when to use discussion rather than lecture, or whether to make one requirement rather than another, for example.

Classroom Climate

One dimension of classroom culture is the **classroom climate**—the atmosphere or quality of life in a classroom. The climate of your classroom will be determined by how you interact with your students and "by the manner and degree to which you exercise authority, show warmth and support, encourage competitiveness or cooperation, and allow for independent judgment and choice" (Borich 2000, 346–347).

In a study of how teachers responded to the stress of working at a challenging, high-needs school on Chicago's South Side, the author found that three types of teachers ("Burnouts," "Altruists," "Technicians") created three distinctly different classroom climates. Their classroom climates are described in the following:

> In general, the classroom climate of the Burnouts emphasized the necessity of adhering to teacher-determined rules and revealed tension or conflict between teacher and students. Burnouts . . . experienced high levels of frustration and anxiety related to their work, [and] they were frequently very scathing in their evaluations of students' abilities and the overall [school] milieu.
>
> The classroom climate of the Altruists was characterized by warm, supportive teacher–student interactions and the absence of tension and conflict. Altruists expressed accepting and caring attitudes toward their students and concern for their intellectual and emotional development.
>
> The classroom climate created by the Technicians also revealed little or no conflict between teacher and student, but here the emphasis was on productivity and achievement rather than on authentic teacher–student relationships. [Technicians] stressed the importance of having students cover and master predetermined course materials, and they expressed their belief that well-prepared, hard-working teachers *could* succeed (Parkay 1983, 82–83).

In addition to promoting learning, the climate of your classroom should convince students that you care about them and believe they can learn, are sensitive to their differing needs and abilities, have knowledge of subject matter, and maintain effective classroom discipline. Figure 2.1 shows how important these dimensions of teaching are to a group of roughly two thousand students and the "grades" they would give their teachers for each dimension.

The climate of your classroom will be complex and multidimensional; its character will be determined by a wide array of variables, many of which will be beyond your control. However, many classroom variables will be within your control. You can take specific steps to a create classroom climate with the following eight characteristics:

- A productive, task-oriented focus
- Group cohesiveness
- Open, warm relationships between teacher and students
- Cooperative, respectful interactions among students
- Low levels of tension, anxiety, and conflict
- Humor
- High expectations
- Frequent opportunities for student input regarding classroom activities

Figure 2.1 Most important aspects of teaching and their ratings.

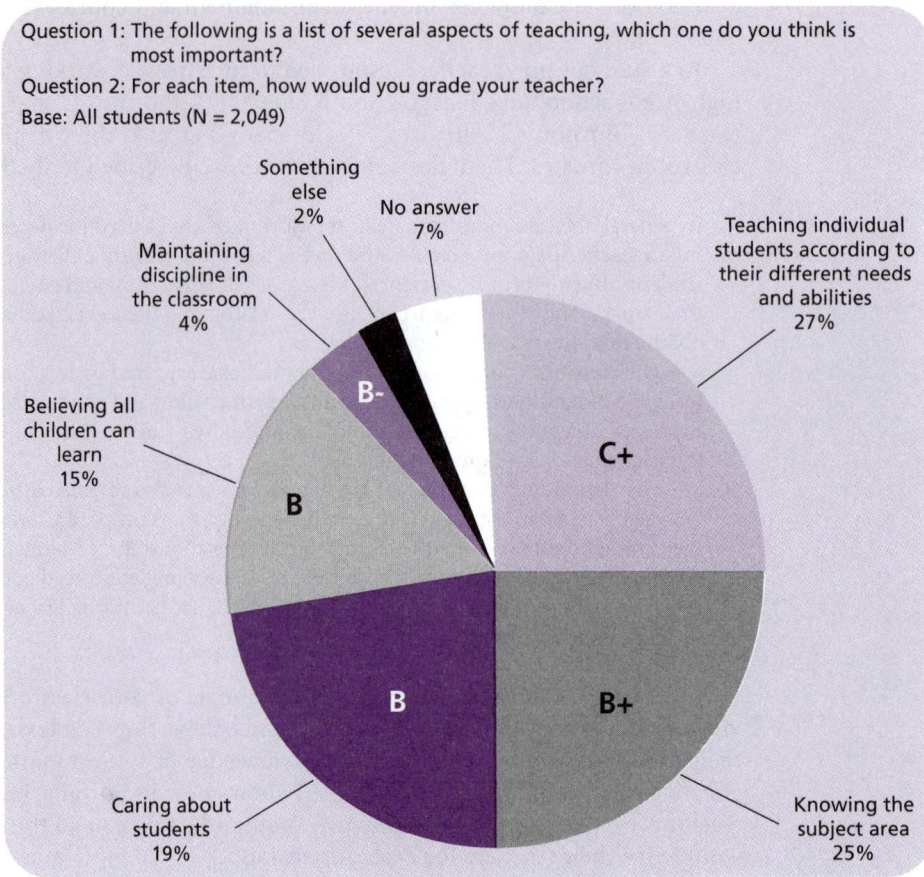

Question 1: The following is a list of several aspects of teaching, which one do you think is most important?
Question 2: For each item, how would you grade your teacher?
Base: All students (N = 2,049)

Source: The MetLife Survey of the American Teacher 2001: Key Elements of Quality Schools. New York: Harris Interactive, Inc., 2001.

The degree to which these dimensions of classroom climate will be present within your classroom will be influenced by your communication style and how you treat students. As the following reflections by a student teacher indicate, creating a classroom climate characterized by these eight dimensions is not easy, because a teacher must make moment-to-moment judgments about what actions will enhance students' motivation to learn.

The next day, as I was going over the instructions for a science experiment I noticed Sheila and Devon leaning over and whispering. I immediately stopped my presentation and said, "Sheila and Devon, you need to turn around in your seats and stop whispering while I am talking." Both girls rolled their eyes and slowly turned their bodies around in their seats. Neither of them made eye contact with me as I continued the lesson. Although the class was now quiet, I felt uncomfortable myself. As the students gathered the science materials they needed to carry out the experiment in their cooperative learning groups, I noticed that Theresa was passing a note to Sheila. Trying to hide my anger and frustration, I said, "Theresa, you need to get rid of that note now. You can come up and put it in the wastebasket. It is time to be working on science, not note passing." Although singling out the girls worked in the short term, to tell the truth I did not feel comfortable dealing with the situation as I did.

I didn't want to feel as if I was spending half the time handling misbehavior, but that's just what I was doing. I had learned in school to reach for student strengths, so I am trying to practice the strategy of giving the students a better attitude about themselves through praise. I explained to them that by correcting their behavior I was just trying to create a climate in which they could learn. I am trying to be a supportive teacher who still corrects misbehavior—always with the goal of redirecting students toward meaningful classroom work.

That same afternoon, I began to gather the students together for literature circles. I had four groups reading different novels. Today I was planning to have the students discuss their reactions to the first chapter and make predictions about the rest of the book. For the first five minutes or so, the groups were very productive, and I felt a surge of hope that all would go well. Just then, I noticed Devon lean back in her chair to pass a note to Theresa, who was in a different group. I wanted to shout across the room at them, but I kept my calm and tried to figure out what I should do now (Rand and Shelton-Colangelo 1999, 10–11).

How would you describe this classroom climate using the eight dimensions listed earlier? What changes in the student teacher's behavior could transform the overall climate?

Although how you regard and treat your students will influence your classroom climate, the instructional decisions you make will also influence it. For example, a teacher's instructional decisions can result in three types of relationships among members of the class: cooperative, or positive, interdependence; competitive, or negative, interdependence; and individualistic, or no, interdependence (Johnson and Johnson 1999). A group project to measure classroom furniture would promote *cooperative interdependence*. A race to be the first student to measure the furniture would call for *competitive interdependence*. And, having a student measure the furniture independently would be an example of *no interdependence*. Obviously, you should use strategies that foster all three forms of interactions, depending on your instructional goals. In most cases, though, your primary emphasis will be on furthering cooperative interdependence.

Life in Classrooms

The culture of the classroom is largely determined by the interactions between the teacher and students. The quality of daily life in classrooms reveals to students how the teacher feels about them. Teachers who empathize with students, genuinely respect them, and expect them to learn are more likely to develop a classroom

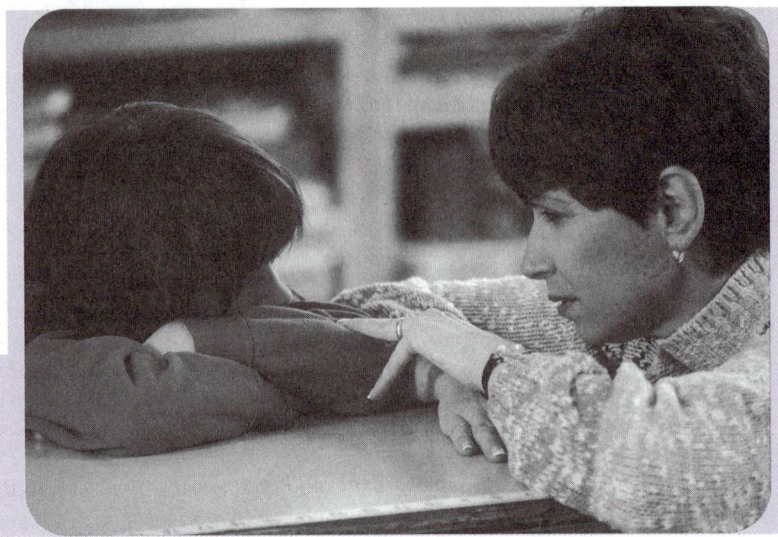

What words might describe the interaction between this teacher and student? What do you think the teacher is saying to her student?

climate free of management problems. In classrooms with positive group dynamics, teachers and students work toward a common goal—learning. In classrooms with negative interactions, the energy of teachers and students may be channeled into conflict rather than into learning.

There is no precise formula to guarantee success in the classroom; however, educational psychologist Anita Woolfolk (2001, 419–421) suggests four "necessary conditions" to increase student learning through positive interactions:

1. The classroom must be relatively organized and free from constant interruptions and disruptions.
2. The teacher must be a patient, supportive person who never embarrasses students for mistakes.
3. The work must be challenging but reasonable.
4. The learning tasks must be authentic.

Communication Skills Successful teachers possess effective communication skills. They express themselves verbally and nonverbally (and in writing) in a manner that is clear, concise, and interesting. They "are able to communicate clearly and directly to their students without wandering, speaking above students' levels of comprehension, or using speech patterns that impair the clarity of what is being presented" (Borich 2000, 8). In addition, they are good listeners. Their students feel that not only are they heard, they are understood.

Figure 2.2   Characteristics of groups at four stages of development.

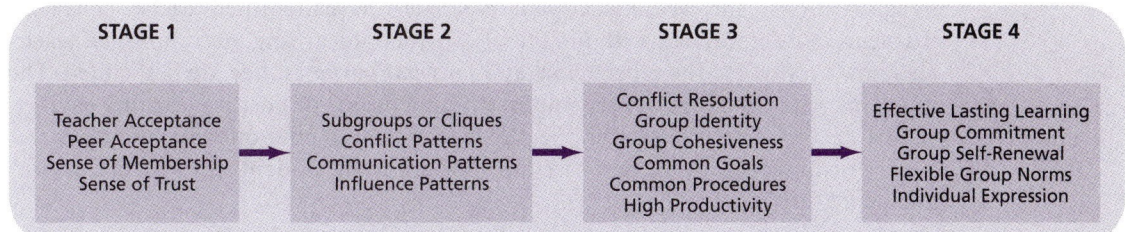

Effective teachers relish the interactive, spontaneous dimensions of classroom discourse. They respond appropriately to events that would undermine the efforts of less effective teachers: a student's misbehavior, interruptions over the PA system, arguments between students, interruptions by other teachers, or a resistant group of students on the first day of class after a holiday.

Interactions Among Students   In addition to engaging in positive, success-oriented interactions with their students, effective teachers foster positive, cooperative inter-actions among students. As a result, students feel supported by their peers and free to devote their attention to learning. The climate of such a classroom is "mature" and "self-renewing" (Schmuck and Schmuck 2001). Typically, the classroom cli-mate has evolved through four stages of group development (see Figure 2.2).

During Stage 1, students are on their best behavior. Teachers can use this "hon-eymoon period" to their advantage. They can discuss classroom rules and proce-dures, outline learning goals, and clarify expectations. During Stage 2, teachers can encourage student participation and communication, while discouraging the for-mation of cliques.

Groups that have reached Stage 2 then move into Stage 3, which may last for the remainder of the school year. In Stage 3, the group sets clear goals, shares tasks, and agrees on deadlines. A fully evolved group reaches Stage 4. In this stage, group members accept responsibility for the quality of life in the group, and they contin-uously strive to improve it.

Teachers who effectively facilitate group processes in their classrooms recognize that students as well as teachers exert leadership in the classroom. Accomplished teachers identify student leaders and are able to influence these students to use their leadership abilities to help the entire group to reach its goals.

How Can You Create a Positive Learning Environment?

A positive classroom culture and positive classroom dynamics are essential for a good learning environment. Developing and then maintaining such an environment is a complex challenge. No single set of strategies will ensure success in all situations. However, educational researchers have identified teacher behaviors that tend to be associated with high levels of student learning. Accomplished teachers know how to use these behaviors and *for what purposes* they are best suited. The following sections address three important dimensions of positive learning environments: the caring classroom, the physical classroom environment, and classroom organization, including procedures for grouping students for instruction and managing time.

The Caring Classroom

At this point in your journey to become a teacher, you may doubt your ability to create a positive learning environment. You may feel anxious about your ability to orchestrate the complex dynamics of classroom life so that you and your students become a cohesive, productive, and mutually supportive group. In your quest to develop these abilities, remember that an authentic spirit of caring is at the heart of a positive learning environment. "[C]*aring pedagogy* can . . . create or restore self confidence needed for participating in the positive learning opportunities in the classroom. It can also help form the moral foundation of responsible citizenship, productive community membership and leadership, and lifelong engagement in learning" (italics added) (Paul and Colucci 2000, 45).

How can you establish a **caring classroom**? First, you can demonstrate caring through your efforts to help all students learn to their fullest potential. You can learn as much as you can about your students' abilities and what motivates them to do their best. You should actually become *a student of your students*—as a tenth-grade student states: An effective teacher "[gets] to know all students well" (Harris Interactive, Inc. 2001). You can also support student learning by encouraging and conveying appropriate (neither too high nor too low) expectations.

In addition, you should recognize that how you speak and listen to students determines the extent to which they believe that you care about them. In a synthesis of research on classroom environments that enhance students' learning, Herbert Walberg and Rebecca Greenberg (1997, 46) found that "students learn more when their classes are satisfying, challenging, and friendly and they have a voice in decision making. [When] classes are unfriendly, cliquish, and fragmented, they leave students feeling rejected and therefore impede learning." Table 2.1, based on Walberg and Greenberg's work, presents fifteen dimensions of classroom life and how each influences students' learning at the junior and senior high levels.

Although students learn best in caring classrooms, Nel Noddings has suggested that students also must learn to care for others. Toward this end, she recommends reorganizing the school curriculum around "themes of care" and suggests that "all students should be engaged in a general education that guides them in caring for self, intimate others, global others, plants, animals, the environment, objects and instruments, and ideas" (2002, 99).

Table 2.1 Fifteen dimensions of classroom environment

Dimension	Learning		Percent Positive Influence on Description
Satisfaction	100%	(17)	Students enjoy classroom work and find it satisfying.
Challenge	87	(16)	Students find the work difficult and challenging.
Cohesiveness	86	(17)	Students know one another well and are helpful and friendly toward one another.
Physical Environment	85	(15)	Adequate books, equipment, space, and lighting are available.
Democracy	85	(14)	Students share equally in making decisions that affect the entire class.
Goal Direction	73	(15)	Learning goals are clear.
Competition	67	(9)	Competition among students is minimized.
Formality	65	(17)	Class is informal, with few formal rules to guide behavior.
Speed	54	(14)	Students have sufficient time to finish their work.
Diversity	31	(14)	Students' interests differ and are provided for.
Apathy	14	(15)	Students don't care about what the class does.
Favoritism	10	(13)	All students do not enjoy the same privileges; the teacher has favorites.
Cliquishness	8	(13)	Certain students work only with close friends and refuse to interact with others.
Disorganization	6	(17)	Activities are disorganized and confusing, rather than well organized and efficient.
Friction	0	(17)	Tension and quarreling among students characterize the classroom.

Note: Percent indicates the percentage of research studies that reported a positive influence on learning for that dimension; number in parentheses indicates number of research studies that investigated that dimension.

Source: Adapted from Herbert J. Walberg and Rebecca C. Greenberg, "Using the Learning Environment Inventory," *Educational Leadership*, May 1997, p. 47.

The Physical Environment of the Classroom

When you become a teacher, the physical environment of your school will probably be similar to that of the schools you attended. However, with the help of your students, it is possible that you can improve your surroundings. Fresh air; plants; clean, painted walls; displays of students' work; a comfortable reading or resource area; and a few prints or posters help to create a positive learning environment. Seating arrangements and the placement of other classroom furniture also do much to shape the culture of the classroom. Although seating by rows may be very appropriate for whole-group instruction or examinations, other arrangements may be more beneficial for other activities. For example, you can enhance small-group activities by moving desks into small clusters in different parts of the room. Figure 2.3 on page 56 shows the arrangement of a classroom at an exemplary elementary school. The room is designed to encourage students to learn through discovery at learning centers located around the room.

Figure 2.3   Learning centers in an elementary classroom.

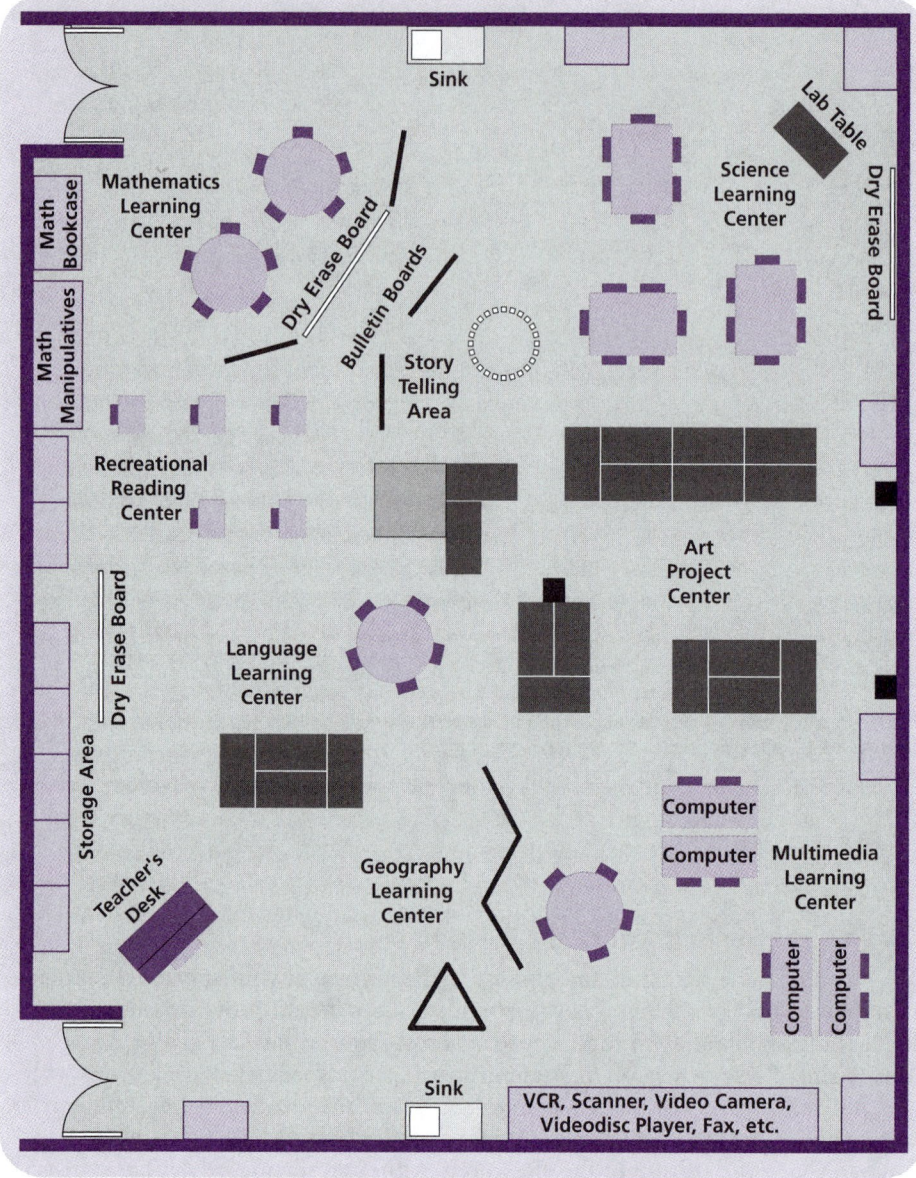

However you design your classroom, be certain that seating arrangements do not reduce the opportunity of some students to learn. For example, students in some classrooms receive more attention if they are seated in the "action zone," the middle front-row seats and seats on the middle aisle. Teachers often stand near this area and unknowingly give students seated there more opportunities to speak.

Classroom Organization

A critical factor in creating a positive learning environment is **classroom organization**—how students are grouped for instruction, how learning tasks are structured, and how other resources are used. The following sections focus on these aspects of classroom organization.

Grouping Students by Ability   Two common approaches for grouping students on the basis of shared characteristics are between-class ability grouping, often called tracking, and within-class ability grouping. Students who attend schools where **between-class ability grouping** is practiced are assigned to classes on the basis of ability or achievement (usually determined by scores on standardized tests). Another form of between-class ability grouping, especially at the high school level, is based on students' goals after graduation. Many high schools, for example, have a college preparatory track, a vocational track, and a business education track.

Research suggests that, for the most part, between-class ability grouping does not contribute to greater achievement (Good and Brophy 2003). Supporters nevertheless claim that teachers are better able to meet the needs of students in homogeneous groupings. Among the alternatives to between-class ability grouping are heterogeneous (or mixed-ability) grouping, regrouping by subject area, the Joplin Plan (regrouping students for reading instruction by ability across grade levels), and cooperative learning.

Within-class ability grouping often is used for instruction in reading and mathematics within a class, where a teacher instructs students in homogeneous, small groups. Within-class grouping is used widely in elementary classrooms. You may recall learning to read in a small group with a name such as the Eagles, the Redbirds, or the Mustangs. Like tracking, within-class ability grouping can heighten preexisting differences in achievement between groups of students, especially if teachers give high-achieving groups more attention. Also, once students are grouped, they tend not to be regrouped, even when differences in achievement are reduced.

At best, evidence to support student groupings is mixed. Whether students are grouped on the basis of ability, curricular interests, or disabling condition, there is a danger that some group labels can evoke negative expectations, causing teachers to "underteach" certain students, and their peers to isolate or reject them. The most serious consequence, of course, is that students so labeled are taught to feel inadequate, inferior, and limited in their options for growth.

Grouping Students for Cooperative Learning   Cooperative learning is an approach to teaching in which students work in small groups, or teams, sharing the work and helping one another complete assignments. Student-Team-Learning, for example, is a cooperative approach teachers use to increase the basic skills achievement of at-risk students. In cooperative learning arrangements, students are motivated to learn in small groups through rewards that are made available to the group as a whole and to individual members of the group. **Cooperative learning** includes the following key elements:

- Small groups (four to six students) work together on learning activities.
- Assignments require that students help one another while working on a group project.
- In competitive arrangements, groups may compete against one another.
- Group members contribute to group goals according to their talents, interests, and abilities.

In addition, cooperative learning is an instructional method that can strengthen students' interpersonal skills. When students from different racial, ethnic, and cultural backgrounds and mainstreamed special-needs students all contribute to a common group goal, friendships increase and group members tend to view one another as more equal in status and worth. The contribution that cooperative learning can make to the culture of the classroom is supported by research that indicates that, under cooperative learning arrangements, "African American, Mexican American, and White students develop more positive racial attitudes and choose more friends from outside racial groups" (Banks 2002, 47). In addition, cooperative learning has "a positive effect on the academic achievement of students of color" (Banks 2002, 47).

Cooperative learning also enables students to learn a variety of roles and responsibilities, as the following comments by a fifth-grade science teacher indicate:

> *I have the class divided into groups of five students and each group works as a team. The job duties are as follows: principal investigator (PI), materials manager (MM), reader, recorder, and reporter. The PI is the leader of the group and helps mediate when problems occur. The PI is the only student who can come to me with questions during the actual procedure. This rule enables me to monitor the groups and also teaches the group to work independently.*
>
> *Students change job duties within their group [for] each activity and every six weeks students change groups. This plan gives each student the experience of working with different classmates as well as learning the responsibility of group participation through performing the different job duties.*

Delivering Instruction The delivery of instruction is a key element in creating positive learning environments. What the teacher does and what students do have powerful influences on learning and on the quality of classroom life. A common activity in elementary schools consists of students doing seatwork on their own or listening to their teachers and participating in whole-class recitations. In addition, students participate in reading groups, games, and discussions; take tests; check work; view films; give reports; help clean up the classroom; and go on field trips.

As a teacher, you must answer the question, "What activity will enable me to accomplish my instructional goals?" You should also realize that learning activities should meet *students'* goals. Activities in your classroom must be meaningful and authentic for students. Authentic learning tasks enable students to see the connections between classroom learning and the world beyond the classroom—both now and in the future.

To understand how **authentic learning tasks** can motivate students to learn, reflect on your own school experiences. Do you recall memorizing facts only because they would appear on a test? Did you ever wonder why a teacher asked you to complete a learning task? Did you ever feel that a teacher asked you to do "busy-work"? What kinds of learning tasks motivated you the most?

Herbert A. Thelen contends that authentic learning activities represent "the first criterion all educational activity must meet" (1981, 86). According to Thelen, an activity is authentic for a person if he or she "feels emotionally 'involved' and mentally stimulated . . . is aware of choices and enjoys the challenge of making decisions," and feels he or she "has something to bring to the activity and that its outcome will be important" (1981, 86).

A comprehensive nationwide study of successfully restructured schools reported that "authentic pedagogy" helps students to (1) "construct knowledge" through the use of higher-order thinking, (2) acquire "deep knowledge" (relatively complex understandings of subject matter), (3) engage in "substantive conversations" with teachers and peers, and (4) make connections between substantive knowledge and the world beyond the classroom (Newmann and Wehlage 1995; Newmann et al. 1996). In addition, as Figure 2.4 on page 60 shows, high authentic pedagogy classes boost achievement for students at all grade levels.

How Time Is Used   How teachers use time affects student learning. **Allocated time** is the time teachers allocate for instruction in various areas of the curriculum. Teachers vary widely in their instructional use of time. Educational researchers Tom Good and Jere Brophy report, for example, that "some students [may receive] as much as four times more instructional time in a given subject than other students in the same grade" (2003, 29).

Researchers have shown that **time on task**—the amount of time students are actively engaged in learning activities—is directly related to learning. As anyone who has ever daydreamed while appearing to pay attention can confirm, time on task is difficult to measure. In response to this difficulty, researchers have introduced the concept of **academic learning time**—the amount of time a student spends working on academic tasks with a high level of success (80 percent or higher). Not surprisingly, learning time, like allocated time, varies greatly from classroom to classroom. For example, Figure 2.5 on page 61 shows how the more than one thousand hours most states mandate for instruction at the elementary level actually result in about three hundred hours during which students are truly engaged in meaningful, appropriate tasks.

An additional concept that is proving useful in understanding teachers' use of time in the classroom is known as **opportunity to learn (OTL)**. OTL is based on the premise that teachers should use time to provide all students with challenging content through appropriate instruction. Many states are developing OTL standards for how teachers should use time in the classroom.

Figure 2.4 Level of authentic student performance for students who experience low, average, and high authentic pedagogy in restructuring elementary, middle, and high schools.

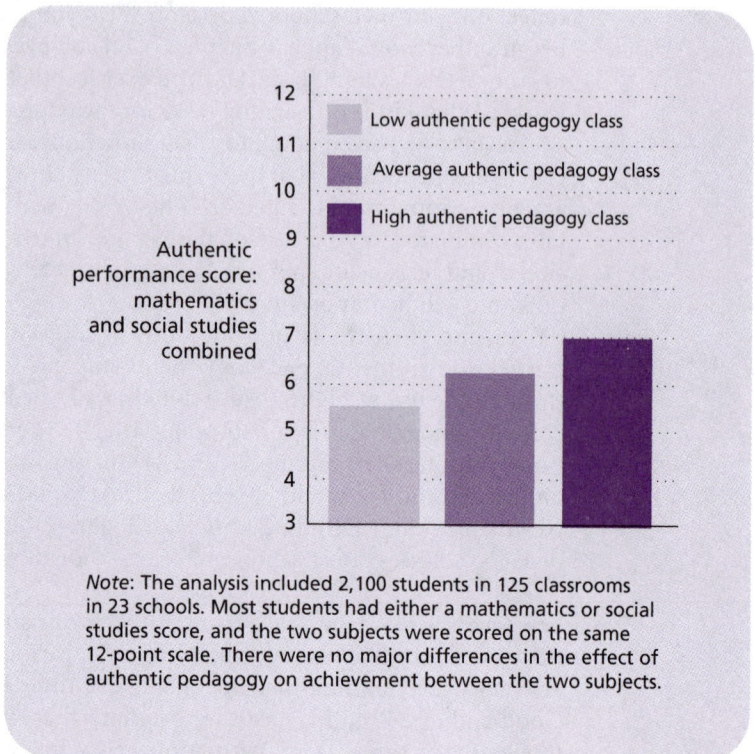

Note: The analysis included 2,100 students in 125 classrooms in 23 schools. Most students had either a mathematics or social studies score, and the two subjects were scored on the same 12-point scale. There were no major differences in the effect of authentic pedagogy on achievement between the two subjects.

Source: Fred M. Newmann and Gary G. Wehlage, *Successful School Restructuring: A Report to the Public and Educators by the Center on Organization and Restructuring of Schools.* University of Wisconsin-Madison: Center on Organization and Restructuring of Schools, 1995, pp. 21, 55.

In the Teachers' Voices feature on page 62, Claudia Meek, a third-grade teacher in California, points out that state- and district-mandated testing and the time needed to prepare students for testing reduce the amount of instructional time available to teachers. During a one-year period, approximately thirty-two hours of her class time were devoted to testing. That same year, two hundred sixty-two hours were devoted to fund-raising, disaster preparedness, socialization, holidays, assemblies, regular interruptions, and miscellaneous time losses. Taken together, more than one-third of Meek's classroom time was devoted to these activities. Her observations are based on large-scale research study conducted by the National Center for Education Statistics and an analysis of data collected from her own classroom.

Figure 2.5 How much time is there, anyway?

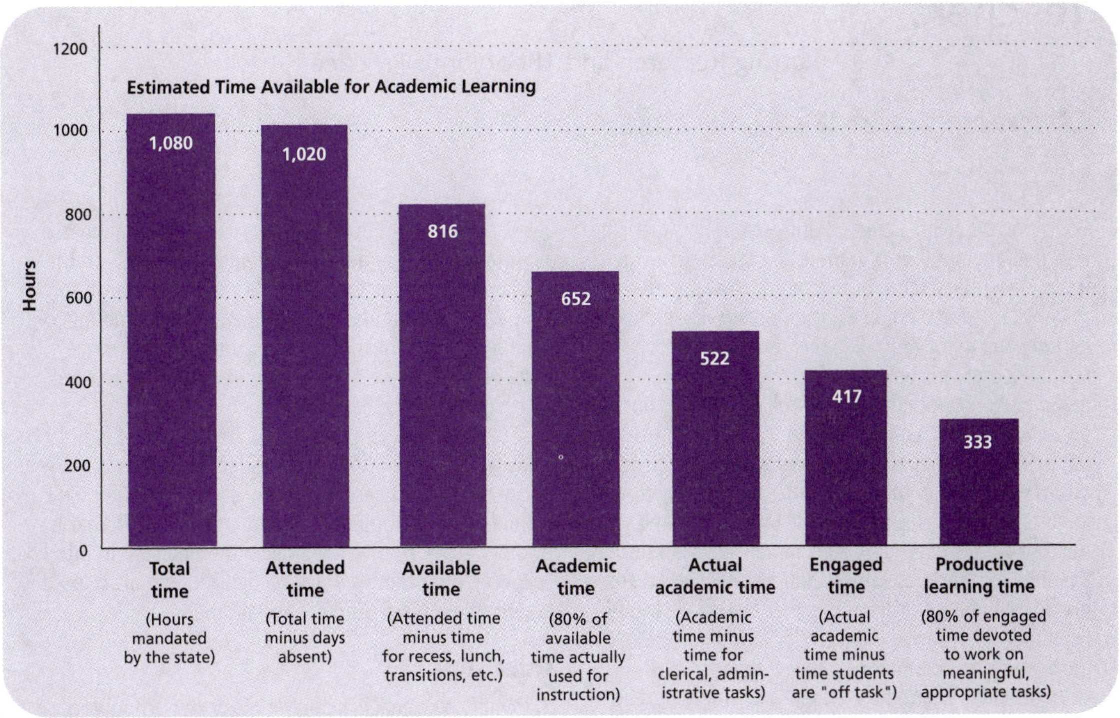

Source: From Carol Simon Weinstein and Andrew J. Migano, Jr. *Elementary Classroom Management: Lessons from Research and Practice,* 2nd ed. New York: McGraw-Hill, p. 142. Copyright © 1997 by McGraw-Hill Companies. Adapted with permission of The McGraw-Hill Companies.

To increase the time available for active learning, many high schools have implemented block scheduling arrangements. **Block scheduling** uses longer blocks of time each class period, with fewer periods each day. Longer blocks of time allow more in-depth coverage of subject matter and lead to deeper understanding and higher-level applications. Block scheduling also gives teachers more time to present complex concepts and students more time to practice applying those concepts to authentic problems.

What Are the Keys to Successful Classroom Management?

For most new teachers, classroom management is a primary concern. How can you prevent discipline problems from arising and keep students productively engaged in learning activities? Effective **classroom management** cannot be reduced to a cookbook recipe. However, there are definite steps you can take to create an effective learning environment in your classroom.

Teachers' *Voices* Putting Research and Theory into Practice

Classroom Crisis: It's About Time

Claudia Meek

Education guidelines created at the state level can suggest that any number of minutes be spent on academics in elementary school classrooms. However, the California Department of Education assigns *only eight minutes a day* for housekeeping tasks in the classroom. Please! This time is to include collecting assigned homework, taking the roll, discussing upcoming school events, collecting money and notes from parents, writing behavior referrals, settling classroom disputes, dealing with health issues, responding to intercom calls or classroom visits by parents, and . . . need I go on? In addition, zero minutes are allotted by the state for electives, which theoretically should complement all the other functions that take place in public school classrooms. From this brief look inside a third-grade classroom, one can see that the state-recommended academic minutes are simply bureaucratic fictions.

Furthermore, schools are free to arrange for any number of assemblies and fund-raisers. The social services we provide to children are enormously important. Assemblies that cover drug awareness and divorce issues, for example, help children and families in ways that perhaps no other social institution can. But these extensive social services take time away from teaching the academic curriculum.

The public and the politicians can also demand high test scores, and solid academic standards are the backbone of public education. But the current extensive academic standards require enormous amounts of time to teach. Which of our classroom social service activities should we eliminate to free the time needed to cover these standards?

The numbers don't add up. In reality, there is not enough classroom time to shoulder the academic, social service, and assessment missions that the public schools have accumulated. What can be done? That is another story. But we have taken the first step in our recovery program: we have recognized and articulated a serious problem. And it's about time.

Questions

1. What can a teacher do if at his or her school too much instructional time is being devoted to other activities?
2. What are the arguments for and against using classroom time to prepare students to take state- and district-mandated tests?

Claudia Meek teaches third grade at Bautista Creek Elementary School in Hemet, California. The preceding is excerpted from her article in the April 2003 *Phi Delta Kappan*, pp. 592–595.

First, it is important to understand that classroom management refers to how teachers structure their learning environments to prevent, or minimize, behavior problems; *discipline* refers to the methods teachers use *after* students misbehave. *Classroom management* is prevention oriented, whereas *discipline* is control oriented.

Second, it is important to recognize that "the key to good management is use of techniques that elicit student cooperation and involvement in activities and thus *prevent* problems from emerging in the first place" (Good and Brophy 2003, 112).

In addition, sound classroom management techniques are based on the guidelines for creating an effective learning environment presented earlier in this chapter—in other words, (1) creating a caring classroom, (2) organizing the physical classroom environment, (3) grouping students for instruction, (4) providing authentic learning tasks, and (5) structuring the use of time to maximize students' learning. Positive leadership and preventive planning thus are central to effective classroom management.

Recommendations for Classroom Management

In his work with schools and teachers, the author has gathered recommendations for classroom management during the first day of school from experienced elementary through secondary teachers in urban, suburban, and rural schools. Their recommendations fall into three categories: planning, managing, and following up.

Planning   Without exception, experienced teachers stress the importance of planning. As the following teachers put it:

> *An important part of preparation is having the room and all your materials ready. Ask yourself, "Where do I want students to sit?" "Do I have all the supplies I need?" You should be one hundred percent prepared on the first day.*
> —High school mathematics teacher

> *From the start, plan to get students involved. On the first day there are a lot of clerical, paperwork-type things that need to be done—distributing books, lockers, fee receipts, etc. Before taking care of those things, give students a short assignment or some task. With their attention focused, they're less likely to fool around. They'll know that in your class they're expected to work.*
> —Middle school science teacher

> *It really helps on the first day to have plenty of material to cover and things to do. I'd recommend taking the material you plan to cover that day and doubling it. It's better to have too much than to run out. What you don't use the first day, you use the next. It takes a while to get a feeling for how fast the kids are going to go.*
> —Third-grade teacher

Managing   Experienced teachers are unanimous in pointing out the importance of establishing effective management practices on the first day. Two of their recommendations follow.

> *From the beginning, it's important to do what you're there to do—that's teach. Teach the class something, maybe review material they learned last year. That lets them know that you're in charge, you expect them to learn. They'll look to you for direction—as long as you give it to them, you're fine.*
> —Junior high language arts teacher

From this photo, what can you tell about the teacher's proficiency in planning and preparation, structuring the classroom environment, and instruction?

The first day is a good time to go over rules and procedures for the year. But don't overdo it. Be very clear and specific about your expectations for classroom behavior.

—Sixth-grade teacher

Following Up   Two experienced teachers stressed the importance of following up on procedures established during the first day:

What you want to establish on the first day is a businesslike atmosphere. But you have to keep that going beyond the first day. Don't let up. Don't get lazy. Remember, there are 179 days left.

—High school mathematics teacher

What I've found very helpful is to get in touch with all my kids' parents right after the first day. I tell them a bit about how I run my class, what we're going to do that year, and how pleased I am to have their child in my room. I keep it upbeat, very positive.

We're going to have a great year! It takes time to do that—everyone's so busy at the start of the year—but it's worth it. It pays off during the rest of the year.

—First-grade teacher

The Democratic Classroom

Teachers who allow students to participate in making decisions about the physical classroom environment, classroom rules and procedures, modifications to the curriculum, and options for learning activities also have fewer discipline problems. Students in democratic classrooms have both more power and more responsibility than students in conventional classrooms. If students are to live in a democracy, they must learn to manage freedom responsibly; thus, teachers model democracy by giving their students some choices and some control over classroom activities.

William Glasser, well-known psychiatrist and author of *Quality School* (1998a), *The Quality School Teacher* (1998b), *Choice Theory* (1998c), and (with Karen Dotson) *Choice Theory in the Classroom* (1998), recommends that teachers develop "quality" classrooms based on democratic principles. According to Glasser, many teachers struggle with classroom management because their actions are guided by stimulus-response theory. They try to coerce students through rewards or punishment, or what many teachers term "logical consequences." Instead, Glasser believes teachers should establish "quality" environments in the classroom by following *choice theory*. Choice theory recognizes that human beings make choices that enable them to create "quality worlds" that satisfy four needs: the need to belong, the need for power, the need for freedom, and the need for fun.

From a **choice theory** perspective, misbehavior in the classroom arises when students' learning experiences do not enable them to create quality worlds for themselves. Therefore, teachers "must give up bossing and turn to 'leading' " (Glasser 1997, 600). We follow leaders, Glasser says, because we believe they are concerned about our welfare. To persuade students to do quality schoolwork, teachers must do four things: establish warm, noncoercive relationships with students; teach students meaningful skills rather than ask them to memorize information; enable them to experience satisfaction and excitement by working in small teams; and move from teacher evaluation to student self-evaluation.

Preventive Planning

What other strategies can you use to prevent discipline problems from occurring? The key to successful classroom management is excellent planning and an understanding of life in classrooms. In addition, if you master the essential teaching skills you will have fewer discipline problems. Your students will recognize that you are prepared, well organized, and have a sense of purpose. You will be confident of your ability to teach all students, and your task-oriented manner will tend to discourage misbehavior. This chapter's Relevant Standards feature stresses the connection between preventive planning and a positive classroom climate.

Relevant Standards

Creating a Positive Learning Environment

As the following standards indicate, highly accomplished teachers plan carefully for instruction. They understand the relationship between careful planning and a smooth running, task-oriented classroom environment.

- "[Teacher candidates] are able to create learning environments encouraging positive social interaction, active engagement in learning, and self-motivation." (National Council for Accreditation of Teacher Education [NCATE], 2002, 14. Supporting statement for Standard 1: Candidate Knowledge, Skills, and Dispositions.)

- "Accomplished teachers have developed systems for overseeing their classrooms so that students and teacher alike can focus on learning, not on controlling disruptive behavior. Discipline and management techniques vary, and no one system has been proven most effective. Hence, proficient teachers consider the desired learning results, their knowledge of their students and the social context, and their own prior experience in selecting management strategies." (National Board for Professional Teaching Standards [NBPTS], 2002, 14. "Supporting statements" for Proposition #3: "Teachers are responsible for managing and monitoring student learning.")

- "The teacher understands the principles of effective classroom management and can use a range of strategies to promote positive relationships, cooperation, and purposeful learning in the classroom." (Interstate New Teacher Assessment and Support Consortium [INTASC], 1992, 22. "Knowledge" statement for Principle #5: "The teacher uses an understanding of individual and group motivation and behavior to create a learning environment that encourages positive social interaction, active engagement in learning, and self-motivation.")

- "Monitoring by teacher is subtle and preventive. Students monitor their own and their peers' behavior, correcting one another respectfully." (Praxis Series, "distinguished" level of performance for Domain 2: The Classroom Environment, Component 2d: Managing Student Behavior.) (Danielson 1996, 87)

In a seminal study of how teachers prevent discipline problems, Jacob Kounin looked at two sets of teachers: those who managed their classrooms smoothly and productively with few disruptions and those who seemed to be plagued with discipline problems and chaotic working conditions. He found that the teachers who managed their classrooms successfully had certain teaching behaviors in common: (1) they displayed the proverbial eyes-in-the-back-of-the-head, a quality of alertness Kounin termed *withitness*; (2) they used individual students and classroom events as examples to communicate to the class their expectations for student conduct—Kounin's *ripple effect*; (3) they supervised several situations at once effectively; and (4) they were adept at making smooth transitions (Kounin 1970). In addition to the principles of effective classroom management that Kounin found, two key elements of preventive planning are establishing rules and procedures and organizing and planning for instruction.

Establishing Rules and Procedures   Successful classroom managers have carefully planned rules and procedures, which they teach early in the year using clear explanations, examples, and practice (Evertson, Emmer, and Worsham 2003; Good and Brophy 2003). Your classroom rules should be clear, concise, reasonable, and few in number. For example, five general rules for elementary-age students might include: (1) be polite and helpful; (2) respect other people's property; (3) listen quietly while others are speaking; (4) do not hit, shove, or hurt others; and (5) obey all school rules. Rules for the secondary level might stipulate the following: (1) bring all needed materials to class; (2) be in your seat and ready to work when the bell rings; (3) respect and be polite to everyone; (4) respect other people's property; (5) listen and stay seated while someone else is speaking; and (6) obey all school rules (Evertson, Emmer, and Worsham 2003).

It is important to enforce classroom rules consistently and fairly. "Consistency is a key reason why some rules are effective while others are not. Rules that are not enforced or that are not applied evenly and consistently over time result in a loss of prestige and respect for the person who has created the rules and has the responsibility for carrying them out" (Borich 2000, 354).

Procedures—the routines your students will follow as they participate in learning activities—also are essential for smooth classroom functioning and minimizing opportunities for misbehavior. How will homework be collected? How will supplies be distributed? How will housekeeping chores be completed? How will attendance be taken? How do students obtain permission to leave the classroom? Part of developing classroom rules and procedures is to decide what to do when students do not follow them. Students must be made aware of the consequences for failing to follow rules or procedures. For example, consequences for breaking rules can range from an expression of teacher disapproval to penalties such as loss of privileges, detention after school, disciplinary conference with a parent or guardian, or temporary separation from the group.

Organizing and Planning for Instruction   Organizing instructional time, materials, and activities so that classes run smoothly will enable you to keep your students engaged in learning, thereby reducing the need for discipline. Time spent planning authentic learning activities appropriate to students' needs, interests, and abilities will enable you to enjoy the satisfaction that comes from having a well-managed classroom.

In the following, a remedial algebra teacher in an urban school tells how organization and planning helped her effectively teach a class of twenty-seven students, grades 9 through 12, who enrolled in the class "for a myriad of reasons, [including] absenteeism, learning disabilities, failure in college prep classes, unwillingness to do required work in college prep classes, personal problems, nonconformity, and a need for credits":

I am consistently rewarded by the creative thinking and quickness of these students when they are asked to do something other than listen to my thinking, take notes, and copy examples from the board. I have learned that planning meaningful activities, choosing engaging tasks, organizing small groups and pair problem-solving experiences, valuing thinking, and carefully assessing understanding promote an improved classroom atmosphere where learning is the objective for everyone (Schifter 1996, 75–76).

Effective Responses to Student Behavior

When students do misbehave, effective teachers draw from a repertoire of problem-solving strategies. These strategies are based on their experience and common sense, their knowledge of students and the teaching-learning process, and their knowledge of human psychology. There are many structured approaches to classroom management; some are based on psychological theories of human motivation and behavior, whereas others reflect various philosophical views regarding the purposes of education. None of these approaches, however, is appropriate for all situations or for all teachers or for all students. The usefulness of a given method depends, in part, on the teacher's individual personality and leadership style and ability to analyze the complex dynamics of classroom life. In addition, what works should not be the only criterion for evaluating structured or "packaged" approaches to discipline; what they teach students about their self-worth, acting responsibly, and solving problems is also important (Curwin and Mendler 1988, 1989).

Severity of Misbehavior   Your response to student misbehavior will depend, in part, on whether an infraction is mild, moderate, or severe and whether it is occurring for the first time or is part of a pattern of chronic misbehaviors. For example, a student who throws a wad of paper at another student might receive a warning for the first infraction. Another student who repeatedly throws objects at other students might receive an after-school detention. Definitions of the severity of misbehavior vary from school to school and from state to state. Table 2.2 presents one classification of examples of mild, moderate, and severe misbehaviors and several alternative responses.

Constructive Assertiveness   The effectiveness of your responses to students' misbehavior will depend, in part, on your ability to use "constructive assertiveness" (Evertson, Emmer, and Worsham 2003). Constructive assertiveness "lies on a continuum of social response between aggressive, overbearing pushiness and timid, ineffectual, or submissive responses that allow some students to trample on the teacher's and other students' rights. Assertiveness skills allow you to communicate to students that you are serious about teaching and about maintaining a classroom in which everyone's rights are respected" (Evertson, Emmer, and Worsham, 2003, 152). Communication based on constructive assertiveness is neither hostile, sarcastic, defensive, nor vindictive; it is clear, firm, and concise.

Evertson and colleagues (2003) suggest that constructive assertiveness has three basic elements:

- A clear statement of the problem or concern
- Body language that is unambiguous (e.g., eye contact with student, erect posture, facial expressions that match the content and tone of corrective statements)
- Firm, unwavering insistence on appropriate behavior

Table 2.2 Mild, moderate, and severe misbehaviors and some alternative responses

Misbehaviors	Alternative Responses
Mild misbehaviors	**Mild responses**
Minor defacing of school property or property of others	Warning
Acting out (horseplaying or scuffling)	Feedback to student
Talking back	Time out
Talking without raising hand	Change of seat assignment
Getting out of seat	Withdrawal of privileges
Disrupting others	After-school detention
Sleeping in class	Telephone/note to parents
Tardiness	
Throwing objects	
Exhibiting inappropriate familiarity (kissing, hugging)	
Gambling	
Eating in class	
Moderate misbehaviors	**Moderate responses**
Unauthorized leaving of class	Detention
Abusive conduct toward others	Behavior contract
Noncompliant	Withdrawal of privileges
Smoking or using tobacco in class	Telephone/note to parents
Cutting class	Parent conference
Cheating, plagiarizing, or lying	In-school suspension
Using profanity, vulgar language, or obscene gestures	Restitution of damages
Fighting	Alternative school service (e.g., clean up, tutoring)
Severe misbehaviors	**Severe responses**
Defacing or damaging school property or property of others	Detention
Theft, possession, or sale of another's property	Telephone/note to parents
Truancy	Parent conference
Being under the influence of alcohol or narcotics	In-school suspension
Selling, giving, or delivering to another person alcohol, narcotics, or weapons	Removal from school or alternative school placement
Teacher assault or verbal abuse	
Incorrigible conduct, noncompliance	

Source: Gary Borich, *Effective Teaching Methods,* 4th ed. Upper Saddle River, NJ: Merrill, 2000, p. 386. © 2000. Reprinted by permission of Prentice-Hall, Inc., Upper Saddle River, NJ.

Case for Reflection

Motivating Students

As a third-year teacher, you are participating in your school's teacher mentoring program. You have been assigned to mentor Charlene, a first-year social studies teacher. Today you are observing Charlene conduct a discussion with her fourth-period world history class of thirty-one ninth graders. Charlene has told you that she is having trouble motivating some of her students. After your observation, she would like you to make some recommendations for motivating students.

During your observation, two of Charlene's students tell her that they see little value in studying world history. Charlene then makes the following comments to her students.

CHARLENE: (somewhat shaken) I guess I'm a bit surprised at what some of you are saying! Let me ask the entire class a question. How many of you feel there is some value in studying history? (Only about one third of the students raise their hand. Others hesitate as though deciding.) This is such an important issue that I think we need to spend the next class meeting discussing it. All of you come prepared with your arguments, and we'll sort of debate both sides of the issue and then see how people feel (Greenwood, Fillmer, and Parkay 2002, 191).

Questions

1. What recommendations will you give Charlene to motivate her students to learn?
2. What are the advantages of allowing students to express their true feelings about the subject matter they are expected to learn in an open debate in the classroom? What are the disadvantages?
3. When Charlene learned that only about one-third of her students saw any value in studying history, how might she have responded differently?

Lee Cantor developed an approach to discipline based on teacher assertiveness. The approach calls on teachers to establish firm, clear guidelines for student behavior and to follow through with consequences for misbehavior. Cantor comments on how he arrived at the ideas behind assertive discipline: "I found that, above all, the master teachers were assertive; that is, they *taught* students how to behave. They established clear rules for the classroom, they communicated those rules to the students, and they taught students how to follow them" (1989, 58). **Assertive discipline** requires teachers to do the following:

1. Make clear that they will not tolerate anyone preventing them from teaching, stopping learning, or doing anything else that is not in the best interest of the class, the individual, or the teacher.

2. Instruct students clearly and in specific terms about what behaviors are desired and what behaviors are not tolerated.

3. Plan positive and negative consequences for predetermined acceptable or unacceptable behaviors.

4. Plan positive reinforcement for compliance. Reinforcement includes verbal acknowledgment, notes, free time for talking, and, of course, tokens that can be exchanged for appropriate rewards.

5. Plan a sequence of steps to punish noncompliance. These range from writing a youngster's name on the board to sending the student to the principal's office (MacNaughton and Johns 1991, 53).

Teacher Problem Solving   If your efforts to get a student to stop misbehaving are unsuccessful, a problem-solving conference with the student is warranted. A problem-solving conference may give you additional understanding of the situation, thus paving the way for a solution. A conference also helps you and the student under-stand the other's perceptions better and begin to build a more positive relationship.

The goal of a problem-solving conference is for the student to accept responsibility for his or her behavior and make a commitment to change it. Although there is no "right way" to conduct a problem-solving conference, Glasser's choice theory lends itself to a conferencing procedure that is flexible and appropriate for most situations. Students will usually make good choices (i.e., behave in an acceptable manner) if they experience success and know that teachers care about them. The following steps are designed to help misbehaving students see that the choices they make may not lead to the results they want.

1. Have the misbehaving student evaluate and take responsibility for his or her behavior. Often, a good first step is for the teacher to ask "What are you doing?" and then "Is it helping you?"

2. Have the student make a plan for a more acceptable way of behaving. If necessary, the student and the teacher brainstorm solutions. Agreement is reached on how the student will behave in the future and the consequences for failure to follow through.

3. Require the student to make a commitment to follow the plan.

4. Don't accept excuses for failure to follow the plan.

5. Don't use punishment or react to a misbehaving student in a punitive manner. Instead, point out to the student that there are logical consequences for failure to follow the plan.

6. Don't give up on the student. If necessary, remind the student of his or her commitment to desirable behavior. Periodically ask "How are things going?"

Developing Your Own Approach to Classroom Management   There is no single "right" strategy for successful classroom management. No approach is effective with all students at all times. How you respond to misbehavior in your classroom will depend on your personality, your value system, and your beliefs about children and will range along a continuum from the "minimum power" of giving students non-verbal cues to the "maximum power" of physical intervention.

Classroom management expert Charles Wolfgang points out that teachers usually present one of three "philosophies" (or attitudes) to students who misbehave:

1. The *relationship-listening* "philosophy" involves the use of minimum power. This reflects a view that the student has the capabilities to change his or her own behavior, and that if the student is misbehaving, it is because of inner emotional turmoil, flooded behavior, or feelings of inner inadequacy.

2. The *confronting-contracting* "philosophy" is one of "I am the adult. I know misbehavior when I see it and will confront the student to stop this behavior. I will grant the student the power to decide how he or she will change, and encourage and contract with the student to live up a mutual agreement for behavioral change."

3. The *rules and consequences* "philosophy" is one that communicates an attitude of "This is the rule and behavior that I want and I will set out assertively to get this action" (Wolfgang 2001, 4–5).

See Appendix 2.1, "Beliefs on Discipline Inventory," so you can determine which "philosophy of discipline" best fits your personality.

In your journey toward becoming a professional teacher, you will develop a repertoire of strategies for classroom management; then, when you encounter a discipline problem in the classroom, you can analyze the situation and respond with an effective strategy. The ability to do so will give you confidence, like the following beginning teacher:

> *I went into the classroom with some confidence and left with lots of confidence. I felt good about what was going on. I established a comfortable rapport with the kids and was more relaxed. Each week I grew more confident. When you first go in you are not sure how you'll do. When you know you are doing OK, your confidence improves.*

What Teaching Methods Do Effective Teachers Use?

Beliefs about teaching and learning, about students, and about what knowledge is worth knowing will influence the methods you use. In addition, variables such as your teaching style, learners' characteristics, the culture of the school and surrounding community, and the resources available will influence the methods you use. All of these components will contribute to the "model" of teaching you will use in the classroom. A model of teaching provides the teacher with "rules of thumb" to follow to create a positive learning environment. As Bruce Joyce, Marsha Weil, and Emily Calhoun point out in *Models of Teaching* (2004, 7), "models of teaching are really models of *learning*. As we help students acquire information, ideas, skills, values, ways of thinking, and means of expressing themselves, we are also teaching them how to learn." Table 2.3 on page 74 presents brief descriptions of four widely used models of teaching.

Effective teachers use a repertoire of teaching models and assessment strategies, depending upon their situations and the goals and objectives they wish to attain. Your teaching strategies in the classroom will most likely be eclectic, that is, a combination of several models and assessment techniques. Also, as you gain classroom experience and acquire new skills and understanding, your personal model of teaching will evolve, enabling you to respond appropriately to a wider range of teaching situations.

Methods Based on Learning New Behaviors

Many teachers use instructional methods that have emerged from our greater understanding of how people acquire or change their behaviors. **Direct instruction**, for example, is a systematic instructional method that focuses on the transmission of knowledge and skills from the teacher (and the curriculum) to the student. Direct instruction is organized on the basis of observable learning behaviors and the actual products of learning. Generally, direct instruction is most appropriate for step-by-step knowledge acquisition and basic skill development but not for teaching less structured, higher-order skills such as writing, the analysis of social issues, and problem solving.

Extensive research was conducted in the 1970s and 1980s on the effectiveness of direct instruction (Gagné, 1974, 1977; Good and Grouws 1979; Rosenshine 1988; Rosenshine and Stevens 1986). The following eight steps are a synthesis of research on direct instruction and may be used with students ranging in age from elementary to senior high school.

1. Orient students to the lesson by telling them what they will learn.
2. Review previously learned skills and concepts related to the new material.
3. Present new material, using examples and demonstrations.
4. Assess students' understanding by asking questions; correct misunderstandings.
5. Allow students to practice new skills or apply new information.
6. Provide feedback and corrections as students practice.
7. Include newly learned material in homework.
8. Review material periodically.

Table 2.3 Four instructional models

	Goals and Rationale	Methods
Cooperative Learning	Students can be motivated to learn by working cooperatively in small groups if rewards are made available to the group as a whole and to individual members of the group.	• Small groups (four to six students) work together on learning activities. • Assignments require that students help one another while working on a group project. • In competitive arrangements, groups may compete against one another. • Group members contribute to group goals according to their talents, interests, and abilities.
Theory into Practice	Teachers make decisions in three primary areas: content to be taught, how students will learn, and the behaviors the teacher will use in the classroom. The effectiveness of teaching is related to the quality of decisions the teacher makes in these areas.	The teacher follows seven steps in the classroom: 1. Orients students to material to be learned 2. Tells students what they will learn and why it is important 3. Presents new material that consists of knowledge, skills or processes students are to learn 4. Models what students are expected to do 5. Checks for student understanding 6. Gives students opportunity for practice under the teacher's guidance 7. Makes assignments that give students opportunity to practice what they have learned on their own
Behavior Modification	Teachers can shape student learning by using various forms of enforcement. Human behavior is learned, and behaviors that are positively reinforced (rewarded) tend to increase and those that are not reinforced tend to decrease.	• Teacher begins by presenting stimulus in the form of new material. • The behavior of students is observed by the teacher. • Appropriate behaviors are reinforced by the teacher as quickly as possible.
Nondirective Teaching	Learning can be facilitated if teachers focus on personal development of students and create opportunities for students to increase their self-understanding and self-concepts. The key to effective teaching is the teacher's ability to understand students and to involve them in a teaching-learning partnership.	• Teacher acts as a facilitator of learning. • Teacher creates learning environments that support personal growth and development. • Teacher acts in the role of a counselor who helps students to understand themselves, clarify their goals, and accept responsibility for their behavior.

A direct instruction method called **mastery learning** is based on two assumptions about learning: (1) virtually all students can learn material if given enough time and taught appropriately and (2) students learn best when they participate in a structured, systematic program of learning that enables them to progress in small, sequenced steps (Bloom 1981; Carroll 1963). The following five steps present the mastery learning cycle:

1. Set objectives and standards for mastery.
2. Teach content directly to students.
3. Provide corrective feedback to students on their learning.
4. Provide additional time and help in correcting errors.
5. Follow a cycle of teaching, testing, reteaching, and retesting.

In mastery learning, students take diagnostic tests and then are guided to do corrective exercises or activities to improve their learning. These may take the form of programmed instruction, workbooks, computer drill and practice, or educational games. After the corrective lessons, students are given another test and are more likely to achieve mastery.

Methods Based on Child Development

As you have no doubt learned in your teacher education program, children move through stages of cognitive, psychosocial, and moral development. Effective instruction includes methods that are developmentally appropriate, meet students' diverse learning needs, and recognize the importance of learning that occurs in social contexts. For example, one way that students reach higher levels of development is to observe and then imitate their parents, teachers, and peers, who act as models. As Woolfolk points out:

> Modeling has long been used, of course, to teach dance, sports, and crafts, as well as skills in subjects such as home economics, chemistry, and shop. Modeling can also be applied deliberately in the classroom to teach mental skills and to broaden horizons—to teach new ways of thinking. Teachers serve as models for a vast range of behaviors, from pronouncing vocabulary words, to reacting to the seizure of an epileptic student, to being enthusiastic about learning (2001, 327).

Effective teachers also use **modeling** by "thinking out loud" and following three basic steps of "mental modeling" (Duffy and Roehler 1989):

1. Showing students the reasoning involved
2. Making students conscious of the reasoning involved
3. Focusing students on applying the reasoning

In this way, teachers can help students become aware of their learning processes and enhance their ability to learn.

Since the mid-1980s, several educational researchers have examined how learners *construct* understanding of new material. "Constructivist views of learning, therefore, focus on how learners make sense of new information—how they construct meaning based on what they already know" (Parkay and Hass 2000, 168). Teachers with this constructivist view of learning focus on students' thinking about the material being learned and, through carefully orchestrated cues, prompts, and questions, help students arrive at a deeper understanding of the material. The common elements of **constructivist teaching** include the following:

- The teacher elicits students' prior knowledge of the material and uses this as the starting point for instruction.
- The teacher not only presents material to students, but he or she also responds to students' efforts to learn the material. While teaching, the teacher must *learn about students' learning*.
- Students not only absorb information, but they also actively use that information to construct meaning.
- The teacher creates a social milieu within the classroom, a community of learners, that allows students to reflect and talk with one another as they construct meaning and solve problems.

Constructivist teachers provide students with support, or "scaffolding," as they learn new material. By observing the child and listening carefully to what he or she says, the teacher provides **scaffolding** in the form of clues, encouragement, suggestions, or other assistance to guide students' learning efforts. The teacher varies the amount of support given on the basis of the student's understanding. If the student understands little, the teacher gives more support. The teacher gives progressively less support as the student's understanding becomes more evident. Overall, the teacher provides just enough scaffolding to enable the student to "discover" the material on his or her own.

The concept of scaffolding is based on the work of L. S. Vygotsky (1896–1934), a well-known Soviet psychologist. Vygotsky (1978, 1986) coined the term *zone of proximal development* to refer to the point at which students need assistance in order to continue learning. The effective teacher is sensitive to the student's zone of development and ensures that instruction neither exceeds the student's current level of understanding nor underestimates the student's ability.

Methods Based on the Thinking Process

Some teaching methods are derived from the mental processes involved in learning, thinking, remembering, problem solving, and creativity. **Information processing**, for example, is a branch of cognitive science concerned with how people use their long- and short-term memory to access information and solve problems. The computer is often used as an analogy for information-processing views of learning:

Like the computer, the human mind takes in information, performs operations on it to change its form and content, stores the information, retrieves it when needed, and generates responses to it. Thus, processing involves gathering and representing information, or encoding; holding information, or storage; and getting at the information when needed, or retrieval. The whole system is guided by control processes that determine how and when information will flow through the system (Woolfolk 2001, 243).

Although several systematic approaches to instruction are based on information processing—teaching students how to memorize, think inductively or deductively, acquire concepts, or use the scientific method, for example—they all focus on how people acquire and use information. Table 2.4 presents general teaching guidelines based on ideas from information processing.

Inquiry Learning and Discovery Learning   In **inquiry learning** and **discovery learning**, students are given opportunities to inquire into subjects so that they "discover" knowledge for themselves. When teachers ask students to go beyond information in a text to make inferences, draw conclusions, or form generalizations and when teachers do not answer students' questions, preferring instead to have students develop their own answers, they are using methods based on inquiry and discovery learning. These methods are best suited for teaching concepts, relationships, and theoretical abstractions and for having students formulate and test hypotheses.

Inquiry learning and discovery learning approaches frequently use a *research-share-perform* cycle. During the *research* phase, students generate their own questions and hypotheses about a topic. They reflect on their prior experiences and knowledge and formulate a main question for inquiry. Research is carried out in small groups that focus on specific parts of the larger research question. During the *share* phase, knowledge is developed during a dialogue between students and the teacher and among students themselves. The usefulness of the knowledge is

---

Table 2.4 Using information processing ideas in the classroom

- Make sure you have the students' attention. For example, begin a lesson by asking a question that stimulates interest in the topic.
- Help students separate essential from nonessential details and focus on the most important information as it relates to instructional objectives.
- Help students make connections between new information and what they already know.
- Provide for repetition and review of information and the practice of skills.
- Present material in a clear, organized, concrete way. For example, give students a brief outline to follow and summarize lessons.
- Focus on meaning, not memorization.

Source: Adapted from Anita E. Woolfolk, *Educational Psychology*, 7th ed. Boston: Allyn and Bacon, 1998, pp. 265–266.

evaluated by the group, which, ideally, functions as a *learning community*. During the *perform* phase, students integrate and synthesize their shared knowledge by making presentations to the public.

The following example shows how inquiry and discovery learning in a first-grade classroom fostered a high level of student involvement and thinking.

> *The children are gathered around a table on which a candle and jar have been placed. The teacher, Jackie Wiseman, lights the candle and, after it has burned brightly for a minute or two, covers it carefully with the jar. The candle grows dim, flickers, and goes out. Then she produces another candle and a larger jar, and the exercise is repeated. The candle goes out, but more slowly. Jackie produces two more candles and jars of different sizes, and the children light the candles, place the jars over them, and the flames slowly go out. "Now we're going to develop some ideas about what has just happened," she says. "I want you to ask me questions about those candles and jars and what you just observed" (Joyce, Weil, and Calhoun 2004, 3).*

Contextual Teaching and Learning   One form of inquiry learning and/or discovery learning that is being implemented in Washington State is known as **contextual teaching and learning (CTL)**. CTL is an approach to teaching based on the theory that students learn best in a concrete manner. They learn best when they are involved in hands-on activities and have opportunities for personal discovery within the context of relationships that are familiar to them. In a CTL environment, students construct, apply, and demonstrate knowledge in relevant contexts. They learn material that is meaningful, relevant, and vital to their futures.

Actually, CTL is not new. CTL is derived from the ideas of the great educational philosopher John Dewey (1859–1952). In *Democracy and Education* (1916), Dewey observed that "the great waste in school comes from . . . the isolation of the school—its isolation from life." During the 1970s, contextual teaching and learning was referred to as *experiential learning* or *applied learning*.

In CTL classrooms, "it is the major task of the teacher to broaden students' perceptions so that meaning becomes visible and the purpose of learning immediately understandable. This is is not an add-on or something nice to do. It is fundamental if students are to be able to connect knowing with doing" (Parnell 2000).

Education professors from Washington State University and other colleges and universities in Washington State collaborated with K–12 teachers and school districts to create the Consortium for Contextual Teaching and Learning. The Consortium created a "Contextual Education Academy" to develop exemplary CTL strategies and activities. Projects included second-graders learning about paleontology through a simulated dinosaur dig, high school special education students refurbishing public housing apartments in Spokane, Washington, and service learning projects addressing citizenship and social policy issues.

Methods Based on Peer-Mediated Instruction

Student peer groups can be a deterrent to academic performance (Steinberg et al. 1996), but they can also motivate students to excel. Because school learning occurs in a social setting, **peer-mediated instruction** provides teachers with options for increasing students' learning. Cooperative learning, described earlier in this chapter, is an example of peer-mediated instruction.

Another example of cooperative learning is **group investigation**, in which the teacher's role is to create an environment that allows students to determine what they will study and how. Students are presented with a situation to which they "react and discover basic conflicts among their attitudes, ideas, and modes of perception. On the basis of this information, they identify the problem to be investigated, analyze the roles required to solve it, organize themselves to take these roles, act, report, and evaluate these results" (Thelen 1960, 82).

The teacher's role in group investigation is multifaceted; he or she is an organizer, guide, resource person, counselor, and evaluator. The method is very effective in increasing student achievement (Sharan and Sharan 1989/90, 17–21), positive attitudes toward learning, and the cohesiveness of the classroom group. The model also allows students to inquire into problems that interest them and enables each student to make a meaningful, authentic contribution to the group's effort based on his or her experiences, interests, knowledge, and skills.

Other common forms of peer-mediated instruction include peer tutoring and cross-age tutoring. In **peer-tutoring** arrangements, students are tutored by other pupils in the same class or the same grade. **Cross-age tutoring** involves, for example, sixth-grade students tutoring second-grade students in reading. Research clearly shows that with proper orientation and training, cross-age tutoring can

What form of tutoring is taking place in this photo? What are some advantages of this form of tutoring? What is required for it to be effective?

Technology in Teaching

How do effective teachers use technology to enhance instruction?

Effective teachers recognize that educational technologies should be used to enhance students' inquiry, reflection, and problem solving rather than merely "grafted" onto existing practices. They also recognize that "schools need not be technology rich to be 'information age.' Rather, the phrase 'information age' signals that the schools focus on developing students' critical habits of mind with regard to ideas and evidence—the ability to use their minds well" (Brunner and Tally 1999, 32).

The following excerpt describes how two teachers—members of an interdisciplinary team of teachers at the Marin School of the Arts and Technology Charter High School (MSAT), a charter high school in Novato, California—have students work on project-based learning activities. Project-based learning, described more fully in Chapter 4, is designed to promote students' higher-order thinking. Working individually and in groups, students conducted original research, created models, and presented their findings to an audience of other students, teachers, family, and friends. After reading the following excerpt, identify several ways in which you will use technology as a tool to promote inquiry, reflection, and problem solving among your students.

> In science class, Adrianna (the teacher) introduced her class to the various components of a watershed. From there, students designed projects that addressed the aspect of the watershed they found most interesting. A bonus for her students, Adrianna has extensive field experience—she spent six months in the Congo studying fruit dispersal by birds—and enjoys the opportunity to take lessons outside of the traditional classroom. Still, she acknowledges that project-based learning requires her to work beyond her typical comfort zone. "I am constantly going back and forth, thinking [science] needs to be more hands on and more authentically project based," she explains, "but also wondering what I will have to give up in terms of the standards." Her passion for science

and for protecting the local watershed enables her to work through these questions, though, and to find a balance between hands-on learning and standards-based instruction.

As the project progressed, it became clear that students were connecting their lessons in science, English, and media studies. "A lot of the writing skills that I was teaching carried over into their writing for scripts and for their presentations," said Justin (a member of Adrianna's interdisciplinary team). . . .

The Project Comes to an End.   There was excitement in the audience as parents, friends, teachers, and classmates found their seats. A group of students stood proudly at the front of the room with a scale model of a section of the local watershed—including trees, a rock formation, and a waterfall—as a backdrop. As the lights dimmed, all attention shifted to the presenters, and a student took the microphone and began to share all he had learned about the local watershed. His presentation was followed by those of his fellow researchers, each with new insights and facts to share.

Speaking to the audience that evening MSAT principal Bob Lenz talked about the value of projects and of student presentations: "How the students present is not only a reflection of their own learning; it's also a reflection of our teaching. It raises the stakes in a very powerful way."

Despite the high stakes and the inevitable bumps along the way, the presentations demonstrated the power of the projects to change how students learn and how teachers teach—and how others can benefit as well. At the conclusion of each researcher's presentation, the audience applauded, acknowledging the students and congratulating the teachers.

"It felt like a celebration," said Justin, "a fitting end to all of the hard work" (Furger and Shaffner 2004).

greatly benefit both "teacher" and learner (Henriques 1997; Schneider and Barone 1997; Utay and Utay 1997; Zukowski 1997). Pilot programs pairing students at risk of dropping out of school with younger children and with special-needs students have proved especially successful. The preceding Technology in Teaching feature describes how teachers can use technology to promote peer-mediated instruction and group investigation.

What Are Some Characteristics of Effective Teaching?

The *outcomes* of effective teaching are relatively easy to list: (1) students acquire an understanding of the subject at hand; (2) they can apply what they have learned to new situations; and (3) they have a desire to continue learning. However, if we wish to identify the *characteristics* of effective teaching, we find ourselves confronted with a more difficult task.

What do effective teachers do when they are teaching? How do they communicate with students? How do they manage classroom activities? What models of teaching do they use? As the previous discussions of classroom cultures, learning environments, classroom management, and teaching methods suggest, answers to questions such as these are not easy to formulate. However, the International Academy of Education publication titled, simply, *Teaching* presents the set of general principles of instruction shown in Table 2.5 on page 82. The principles are based on extensive research on classroom teaching and learning. Although the principles may appear deceptively simple when stated in plain English, they require a high degree of skill and understanding to put into practice in actual classrooms. In addition to using these general principles, effective teachers have clearly stated goals to guide their decision making in the classroom.

Establishing Goals

One characteristic of effective teachers is that they focus on the outcomes—the results or consequences of their teaching. Regardless of the instructional method used, with clear goals to provide guidance teachers can make good decisions about classroom activities to select or develop.

Goals are general statements of purpose that guide schools and teachers as they develop instructional programs. **Instructional goals** can be derived from the curriculum or content being taught; or they can be derived from various educational philosophies. Goals range from very broad statements of purpose that apply to a large number of students to those that apply to students in a particular classroom.

In addition, effective teachers evaluate their teaching by how well students master certain objectives. **Learning objectives** are specific, measurable outcomes of learning that students are to demonstrate. For example, "Students will identify the structural elements of cells and explain their functions" might be a specific objective toward a larger goal of "understanding biological concepts and principles."

Successful teachers also realize that the quality of their teaching depends on what students *can do*, not only on what they *know*. To evaluate their effectiveness in this area, teachers assess students' mastery of performance tasks in which they

Table 2.5 Principles of Effective Teaching

1. **Supportive classroom environment**: Students learn best within cohesive and caring learning communities.
2. **Opportunity to learn**: Students learn more when most of the available time is allocated to curriculum-related activities and the classroom management system emphasizes maintaining their engagement in those activities.
3. **Curriculum alignment**: All components of the curriculum are aligned to create a cohesive program for accomplishing instructional purposes and goals.
4. **Establishing learning opportunities**: Teachers can prepare students for learning by providing an initial structure to clarify intended outcomes and cue desired learning strategies.
5. **Coherent content**: To facilitate meaningful learning and retention, content is explained clearly and developed with emphasis on its structure and connections.
6. **Thoughtful discourse**: Questions are planned to engage students in sustained discourse structured around powerful ideas.
7. **Practice and application activities**: Students need sufficient opportunities to practice and apply what they are learning and to receive improvement-oriented feedback.
8. **Scaffolding students' task engagement**: The teacher provides whatever assistance students need to enable them to engage in learning activities productively.
9. **Strategic teaching**: The teacher models and instructs students in learning and self-regulation activities.
10. **Cooperative learning**: Students often benefit from working in pairs or small groups to construct understandings or help one another master skills.
11. **Goal-oriented assessment**: The teacher uses a variety of formal and informal assessment methods to monitor progress toward learning goals.
12. **Achievement expectations**: The teacher establishes and follows through on appropriate expectations for learning outcomes.

Source: Brophy, J. (1999). *Teaching–Educational Practice Series-1*. Brussels, Belgium: International Academy of Education, pp. 366–367.

apply their learning to a new problem. Figure 2.6 illustrates two different approaches to lesson planning that take into account targeted goals, objectives, and performance tasks.

Examples of Effective Teachers

This chapter concludes with comments by several effective teachers in which they describe strategies that help them create communities of learners. As you read the teachers' comments, identify how each has put into practice many of the concepts discussed in this chapter. In addition, reflect on the degree to which that teacher's approach would "fit" your personality and value system.

Laurie Robben, Fourth-Grade Teacher, Greenwich, Connecticut

I am extremely proud of the positive rapport that I have with my students. One way that I instill mutual respect is through classroom meetings. Every Friday, I set aside at least fifteen minutes for a class meeting. We all sit together on the floor, including myself, to show that no one's ideas are more important than another's.

Figure 2.6 Two approaches to planning lessons.

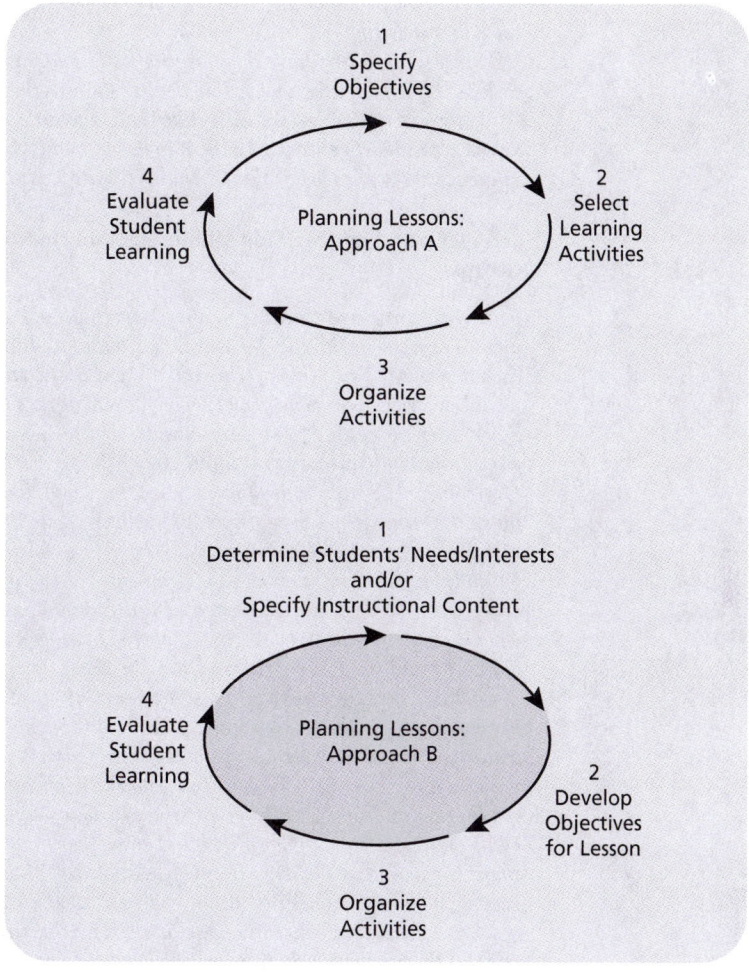

Classroom meetings provide a time for students to share their feelings openly about their school experience, and issues can be positive or negative. An important rule is that if someone wants to say something negative about a particular student, the class is not allowed to talk about that conversation outside the confines of our meeting. This is to prevent a student from being badgered.

One example is Alex, a nine-year-old who desperately wants peer attention but resorts to behaving like a clown. In a recent meeting, students told him they were not comfortable with his clowning and wished that he would stop. I asked the class to share times when they enjoyed being with Alex, and they encouraged him to practice those behaviors more frequently. At the end of the meeting, Alex asked his peers, "Could you help me be better and tell me when I'm bugging you?" We talked about how to tell Alex.

The class concluded that a person is more likely to respond if you ask nicely ("Alex, this is an example of something that bugs me. Please stop."). Improvement has been apparent since that meeting.

Since we regularly have class meetings, the students will give me updates on past issues, such as "Lunch is better now. Adam doesn't show us the food in his mouth anymore!"

Class meetings show the class that I care about them outside of the traditional academic areas. It also encourages them to listen to one another. And it allows me to use peer influence to encourage behavioral changes. We all win! (Burden and Byrd 1999, 120).

Terri Jenkins, Eighth-Grade Middle School Language Arts Teacher, Hephzibah, Georgia

Four years ago, I was teaching in an inner-city school with 99 percent minority enrollment. From the beginning, I was convinced that all these children could learn. My goal each day was to provide material and present in such a way that ensured every student would experience some degree of success. I will never forget one particular series of lessons.

We began reading "The Graduation" by Maya Angelou, which recounts her own graduation and valedictory address. We then learned the Negro spiritual, "We Shall Overcome." The story and song were inspirational, but they weren't enough. I wanted to make the entire experience personal. I told the class that one day someone sitting in that very classroom would be responsible for giving a valedictory address at his or her own graduation, and that their next assignment was to prepare a speech and present it in class. The speeches were wonderful as I introduced each and every one of them as the valedictorian of that year. As they spoke, I could hear a new determination in their voices; I could see a new pride in their posture.

Three weeks ago, there was a soft tap on my classroom door and a welcomed face appeared. Immediately I recognized Carol, one of those students who had given her valedictory address in my eighth-grade classroom almost five years ago. After a big smile and a warm hug, she quietly spoke. "I just had to come by and personally invite you to my graduation on June 5. I'll be giving the valedictory address, and I want you to be there." With that, an irrepressible smile burst across her face. After much earned congratulations, she looked at the tears in my eyes and said, "I did it just for you." Carol had become a believer in her dreams, a believer in herself.

Self-esteem and belief in oneself are essential. I firmly believe that self-esteem must be built through real achievement. I still strive to provide lessons designed to maximize student success and ensure achievement, and I continually verbalize my own convictions that they all can be winners. I make every effort to personalize success in the classroom. I realize that I cannot assure success for every student in my classroom, but I now know that I truly can make a difference (Burden and Byrd 1999).

Kathlee C. Reilly, Tenth- and Twelfth-Grade English teacher, Scarsdale, New York

When I first introduced thinking skills to my students, I announced that we were going to use a metaphor as a way to "look inside" the texts we were studying. We started with an exercise on metaphors that we live by, then easily moved into a search for metaphors in the texts we studied. Most interesting, I think, were student responses to my questions about specific metaphors to describe our classroom. They immediately mentioned the placement of my desk in the back of the room, and they told me confidently that ours was a "student-centered classroom." They extended this metaphor when they noted my selection of seminar tables instead of desks to encourage collaboration. They also noted the way I sat in different places among them, not in front of them.

Many other classroom elements served as metaphors for my students. For example, they saw the quotations hanging on the walls as metaphors for my expectations. They were particularly drawn to an Annie Dillard passage: "Why are we reading—if not in hopes of beauty laid bare and life's darkest mysteries probed?" They also pointed to Hannah Arendt's words: "Welcome to a place of excellence . . . where we come together to be the best we can be." Other elements suggested some serious work that would remain after they left the classroom: individual portfolios, dialectic notebooks along the window shelves, and favorite childhood drawings that prompted an early writing assignment. . . .

Teaching for thinking simply means that teachers strive to develop classroom conditions conducive to student thinking. Teachers pose problems and raise questions, and then follow up by introducing dilemmas, paradoxes, and discrepancies for students to resolve. Teachers also structure the classroom environment for thinking: They value thinking, make time for it, support it, and assess student growth in it. Teaching for thinking assumes a classroom atmosphere that balances trust, risk taking, and originality. I am confident this environment can be created anywhere because it is established through the behavior of a teacher who models respect for intelligence and establishes the clear, convincing expectation that all students can become better thinkers. In this kind of classroom you find an almost palpable sense of community that stems from collaboration and open investigation of ideas (Reilly 2000, 98–100).

Summary

How Does the Culture of the Classroom Develop?

- From seating arrangements, to classroom rules and procedures, to the content and relevance of the curriculum, teachers make many decisions that influence the culture of the classroom.

- Classroom climate refers to the atmosphere or quality of life in a classroom. The climates established by high-performing teachers are characterized by a productive, task-oriented focus; group cohesiveness; open, warm relationships between teacher and students; cooperative, respectful interactions among students; low levels of tension, anxiety, and conflict; humor; high expectations; and frequent opportunities for student input regarding classroom activities.

How Will You Establish a Positive Learning Environment?

- An important element of a positive learning environment is a caring classroom climate. Teachers show care for students by providing support, structure, and appropriate expectations.

- The physical environment of a classroom—seating arrangements and the placement of other classroom furniture, for example—can make a positive contribution to students' learning.

- Classroom organization, how students are grouped for instruction and how time is used, is an important element of the effective learning environment. Among the patterns for organizing classrooms are grouping students by ability, grouping students for cooperative learning, using activity formats based on authentic learning tasks, and using time to maximize students' learning.

What Are the Keys to Successful Classroom Management?

- The key to successful classroom management is preventing problems before they occur. Teachers who prevent problems foster effective, harmonious interpersonal interactions; understand how their leadership style influences students; and facilitate the development of the classroom group so that it becomes more cohesive and supportive.

- Teachers who establish a democratic classroom climate that allows students to participate in making decisions about the classroom environment, rules and procedures, curriculum materials, and learning activities have fewer discipline problems.

- When management problems occur, effective teachers use a repertoire of problem-solving skills based on experience, common sense, and understanding of the teaching–learning process. Regardless of the management strategy used, effective teachers base their response to problems on three elements of "constructive assertiveness": a clear statement of the problem or concern; unambiguous body language; and a firm, unwavering insistence on appropriate behavior.

What Methods Do Effective Teachers Use?

- Although it is difficult to identify all the skills teachers need, research indicates that effective teachers use a repertoire of models of teaching based on students' learning behaviors, child development, the thinking process, and peer mediation.

- Direct instruction and mastery learning are based on the view that learning is the acquisition of new behaviors.

- Modeling, constructivism, and scaffolding are based primarily on an understanding of how students construct meaning as they learn new material.

- Information processing, inquiry learning, discovery learning, and contextual teaching and learning (CTL) are based on our understanding of the cognitive processes involved in learning.

- Peer-mediated instruction, which views learning as taking place in social situations, includes cooperative learning, group investigation, and peer- and cross-age tutoring.

What Characterizes Effective Teaching?

- Effective teaching focuses on outcomes—the results or consequences of teaching. Outcomes include clear goals, objectives, and performance tasks that students are to master.

Key Terms and Concepts

academic learning time, 59
allocated time, 59
assertive discipline, 70
authentic learning tasks, 59
between-class ability grouping, 57
block scheduling, 61
caring classroom, 54
choice theory, 65
classroom climate, 48
classroom culture, 48
classroom management, 61

classroom organization, 57
constructivist teaching, 76
contextual teaching and learning (CTL), 78
cooperative learning, 58
cross-age tutoring, 79
direct instruction, 73
discovery learning, 77
group investigation, 79
information processing, 76
inquiry learning, 77

instructional goals, 81
learning objectives, 81
mastery learning, 75
modeling, 75
opportunity to learn (OTL), 59
peer-mediated instruction, 79
peer-tutoring, 79
scaffolding, 76
time on task, 59
within-class ability grouping, 57

Reflective Application Activities

Discussion Questions

1. Have you had any experiences with between-class ability grouping or within-class ability grouping? What do you think about each form of student grouping?

2. The process of group development might be compared with the stages that occur in the preparation and performance of a play. Between casting and opening night the participants gradually become an effective, cohesive team. What other activities might be compared to the process of group development?

Professional Journal

1. Recall the teachers and classmates you had during your school career. Select one class and analyze its group proc-esses in terms of the stages of group development discussed in this chapter. At what stage of development was the group near the end of the school year? What conditions facilitated or impeded the development of this group?

2. Describe the "ideal" physical classroom environment for you. How would the seating arrangement facilitate the attainment of your instructional goals and objectives? How would you involve students in arranging the classroom?

Online Assignments

1. Survey the Internet to begin locating and creating bookmarks or favorites for websites and teacher discussion groups that focus on classroom management.

2. Visit the home pages of three or more of the following research publications on the Internet. These journals frequently have articles that focus on the effectiveness of different teaching methods. Read one of these articles that focuses on a teaching method of interest to you. What does the article say about the effectiveness of that method? What are the implications for the methods you will use as a teacher?

   American Educational Research Journal
   Cognition and Instruction
   Contemporary Educational Psychology
   Educational Psychologist
   Educational Psychology Review
   Educational Researcher
   Journal of Educational Psychology
   Review of Research in Education
   Journal of Teaching and Teacher Education
   Review of Educational Research

Observations and Interviews

1. Observe a few teachers at the level for which you are preparing to teach. To what extent does each teacher use the "general principles of instruction" presented in Table 2.5 on page 82?

2. For each of the teachers observed in #1 above, what teaching methods do they use as part of their instructional repertoire?

Professional Portfolio

Prepare a poster depicting a classroom arrangement appropriate for the subject area and grade level for which you are preparing to teach. The poster should indicate the seating arrangement and location of other classroom furniture. In addition, make a list of classroom rules that will be posted in the room. You may wish to organize the rules according to the following categories.

- Rules related to academic work
- Rules related to classroom conduct
- Rules that must be communicated on your first teaching day
- Rules that can be communicated later

Lastly, prepare a flow chart depicting routine activities for a typical day. This chart could include procedures for the following:

- Handling attendance, tardy slips, and excuses
- Distributing materials
- Turning in homework
- Doing seatwork or various in-class assignments
- Forming small groups for cooperative learning activities
- Returning materials and supplies at the end of class

Appendix 2.1
Beliefs on Discipline Inventory

This inventory is designed for teachers to assess their own beliefs on classroom discipline. It enables teachers to assess to what extent they believe in the Human Relations-Listening; Confronting-Contracting; and/or Rules/Rewards-Punishment approach to discipline. Our hypothesis is that teachers believe and act according to all three approaches of discipline, yet usually one predominates in their beliefs and actions.

FORCED CHOICES

Instructions: Select either A or B. You may not completely agree with either choice, but choose the one that is closer to how you feel.

1. I believe that:
   A. Although children think, the decisions they make are not yet fully rational and moral.
   B. Students' inner emotions and decision-making processes must always be considered legitimate and valid.

2. Generally in my class:
   A. I assign students to specific areas or seats in the classroom.
   B. My seating (or work area) assignments are open to negotiation.

3. I believe that:
   A. No matter how limited the students' opportunities may be, students should still be given the responsibility to choose and make decisions.
   B. Teachers need to realize that, in addition to their effect on students during school hours, students are greatly influenced by their own families, the neighborhoods where they live, their peers, and television.

4. When the high noise level in a classroom bothers me, I will more likely:
   A. Discuss my discomfort with the students and attempt to come to a compromise about noise levels during activity periods.
   B. Allow the activity to continue as long as the noise is not disturbing or upsetting any student.

5. If a student breaks a classmate's portable tape player that the classmate brought to school, I, the teacher, will more likely:
   A. Scold both students, one for disrespecting other people's property, and the other for breaking a rule that prohibits bringing radios and tape players to school.
   B. Avoid interfering in something that the students (and possibly their parents) need to resolve themselves.

6. If students unanimously agree that a classroom rule is unjust and should be removed, but I, the teacher, disagree with them, then:
   A. The rule should probably be removed and replaced by a rule made by the students.
   B. The students and I should jointly decide on a fair rule.

7. When a student does not join in a group activity:
   A. The teacher should explain the value of the activity to the student and encourage the student to participate.
   B. The teacher should attempt to identify the student's reasons for not joining and should create opportunities that respond to those reasons.

8. During the first week of class, I will more likely:
   A. Let the students interact freely and let them initiate any rule making.
   B. Announce the classroom rules and inform students how the rules will be fairly enforced.

9. I believe that:
   A. The students' creativity and self-expression should be encouraged and nurtured as much as possible.
   B. Limits on destructive behaviors need to be set without denying students their sense of choice and decision.

10. If a student interrupts my lesson by talking to a neighbor, I will more likely:
   A. Move the first student away from the others and continue the lesson because time should not be wasted on account of one individual.
   B. Tell students how angry I feel and conduct a dialogue about how the first student would feel about being interrupted.

11. I believe that:
   A. A good educator is firm but fair in taking disciplinary action on violators of school rules.
   B. A good educator discusses several alternative disciplinary actions with the student who violates a school rule.

12. When one of the more conscientious students does not complete an assignment on time:
   A. I will assume the student has a legitimate reason and will turn in the assignment when he or she completes it.
   B. I will tell the student that she or he is expected to turn in the assignment when it is due, and then, with the student, we will decide on the next steps.

SCORING KEY INTERPRETATION

Circle your responses on the following table and tally the totals in each table:

Table I *(high control)*		*Table II* *(low control)*		*Table III* *(medium control)*	
2A	1A	4B	1B	2B	4A
3B	5A	6A	5B	3A	6B
7A	8B	9A	8A	7B	9B
11A	10A	12A	10B	11B	12B

Total number of responses in Table I _____ (Interventionist; high control)
Total number of responses in Table II _____ (Non-Interventionist; low control)
Total number of responses in Table III _____ (Interactionalist; medium control)

A high percentage of responses in Table I represents a leaning toward the Rules/Rewards-Punishment approach (Interventionists) to discipline; in Table II, toward the Human Relations-Listening approach (Noninterventionists); and in Table III, toward the Confronting-Contracting approach (Interactionalists) to discipline.

By examining which table contains the largest number of responses, you can identify the approach to discipline that dominates your beliefs. The table with the second largest total of responses represents your second most prominent belief. The table with the fewest total responses represents the discipline approach that you least believe in.

If you have an equal number of responses in each table (or close to equal), this may indicate your approach to discipline is eclectic rather than clearly identified with any one of the discipline models.

This brief summary is not definitive. However, it ought to give you a general picture of how strongly you believe in each of these three discipline approaches.

3 Meeting the Needs of All Learners

I was . . . *fortunate that I chose theoretical physics, because it is all in the mind. So my disability has not been a serious handicap.*

—Stephen W. Hawking
A Brief History of Time: From the Big Bang to Black Holes

It's early Monday morning, and you have just finished setting up the last of three multimedia learning centers in your classroom. Each center has a computer with a high-speed Internet connection, a printer, a scanner, and a desktop video camera. As you walk back to your desk, you imagine how things will go when your students arrive in twenty minutes. Everything should go well, you think, with the possible exception of Alecia. Since the first day of school, she's withdrawn on some days, and then very disruptive on others. Her teacher last year described her as "very peculiar" and "rather obnoxious."

Last week, Alecia seemed especially angry. She was belligerent and noncompliant for the entire week. For the most part, Alecia does what she wants, when she wants. As far as you know, she has no close friends; she teases the other kids constantly and occasionally gets into fights with other girls.

Alecia and her twin brother, Herb, live with their mother in a housing project in a poor section of the city. Their mother divorced her second husband three years ago, after she learned that he had been sexually abusing Alecia. Since then, Alecia's mother has been struggling to make ends meet with her job at the post office. You've heard that Alecia, her mother, and her brother have been receiving counseling services from the local mental health clinic.

Alicia's school records indicate that other teachers have had trouble with her in the past. Academically, she's below her classmates in all subjects except physical education and art. Comments from two of her previous teachers suggest that Alecia has a flair for artwork. Last year, she was diagnosed with attention deficit hyperactivity disorder (ADHD).

Ms. Chavez, the school psychologist, and Mr. Tamashiro, the school's inclusion facilitator, have been working with you on developing an individualized education program (IEP) for Alecia. In fact, before school on Monday, you're meeting with Mr. Tamashiro to discuss how to involve Alecia in the small groups that will be working at the multimedia learning centers. You're anxious to get his suggestions, and you're confident that with his help and Ms. Chavez's, you can meet Alecia's learning needs.

Guiding Questions

1. How do students' needs change as they develop?
2. How do students vary in intelligence?
3. How do students vary in ability and disability?
4. What are special education, mainstreaming, and inclusion?
5. How can you teach all learners in your inclusive classroom?

As the preceding scenario about Alecia suggests, when you become a teacher you must understand and appreciate students' unique learning and developmental needs. You must be willing to learn about students' abilities and disabilities and to explore the special issues and concerns of students at three broad developmental levels—childhood, early adolescence, and late adolescence. Learning about the intellectual and psychological growth of students at the age level you plan to teach is essential, as the following comment by a student suggests:

> To me what makes a good teacher is someone who understands the students. If the teacher knows how the students are thinking, you can teach a class more easily. I mean, if you see the kids are dead, common sense will tell you you better change your strategy, you know? If all these kids are looking at you like a bunch of zombies, common sense will tell you you're doing something wrong (Michie 1999, 143–44).

Understanding how students' interests, questions, and problems will change throughout their school years will better equip you to serve them in the present. This chapter examines how students' needs change as they develop and how their needs reflect various intelligences, abilities, and disabilities.

How Do Students' Needs Change as They Develop?

Development refers to the predictable changes that all human beings undergo as they progress through the life span—from conception to death. Although developmental changes "appear in orderly ways and remain for a reasonably long period of time" (Woolfolk 2001, 24), it is important to remember that students develop at different rates. Within a given classroom, for example, some students will be larger and physically more mature than others; some will be socially more sophisticated; and some will be able to think at a higher level of abstraction. This chapter's Relevant Standards feature stresses the importance of understanding how students' needs change as they develop.

As humans progress through different **stages of development**, they mature and learn to perform the tasks that are a necessary part of daily living. There are several different types of human development. For example, as children develop physically, their bodies undergo numerous changes. As they develop cognitively, their mental capabilities expand so that they can use language and other symbol systems to solve problems. As they develop socially, they learn to interact more effectively with other people—as individuals and in groups. And, as they develop morally, their actions come to reflect a greater appreciation of principles such as equity, justice, fairness, and altruism.

Because no two students progress through the stages of cognitive, social, and moral development in quite the same way, teachers need perspectives on these three types of development that are flexible, dynamic, and, above all, useful. By becoming familiar with models of cognitive, social, and moral development, teach-

Relevant Standards

Knowledge of Students' Developmental Stages

As the following standards indicate, highly accomplished teachers plan carefully for instruction. They understand the relationship between careful planning and a smoothly running, task-oriented classroom environment.

- "[Teacher candidates] know the ways children and adolescents learn and develop, including their cognitive and affective development and the relationship of these to learning." (National Council for Accreditation of Teacher Education [NCATE], 2002, 19. Supporting statement for Standard 1: Candidate Knowledge, Skills, and Dispositions.)

- "Accomplished teachers understand how students develop and learn. They incorporate the prevailing theories of cognition and intelligence in their practice." (National Board for Professional Teaching Standards [NBPTS], 2002, 3. "Supporting statements" for Proposition #1: "Teachers are committed to students and their learning.")

- "The teacher is aware of expected developmental progressions and ranges of individual variation within each domain (physical, social, emotional, moral and cognitive), can identify levels of readiness in learning, and understands how development in any one domain may affect performance in others." (Interstate New Teacher Assessment and Support Consortium [INTASC], 1992, 16. "Knowledge" statement for Principle #2: "The teacher understands how children learn and develop, and can provide learning opportunities that support their intellectual, social and personal development".)

- "Teacher displays knowledge of typical developmental characteristics of age group, exceptions to the patterns, and the extent to which each student follows patterns." (Praxis Series, "distinguished" level of performance for Domain 1: Planning and Preparation, Component 1b: Demonstrating Knowledge of Students.) (Danielson 1996, 67)

ers at all levels, from preschool through college, can better serve their students. Three such models are Piaget's theory of **cognitive development**, Erikson's stages of **psychosocial development**, and Kohlberg's stages of **moral reasoning**.

Jean Piaget
(1896–1980)

Piaget's Model of Cognitive Development

Jean Piaget (1896–1980), the noted Swiss biologist and epistemologist, made extensive observational studies of how children develop. He concluded that children reason differently from adults and even have different perceptions of the world. Piaget surmised that children learn through actively interacting with their environments, much as scientists do, and proposed that a child's thinking progresses through a sequence of four cognitive stages (see Figure 3.1 on page 94). According to Piaget's theory of cognitive development, the rate of progress through the four stages varies from individual to individual.

During the school years, students move through the **preoperational stage**, the **concrete operations stage**, and the **formal operations stage**; yet, because of

Figure 3.1   Piaget's stages of cognitive growth.

1. Sensorimotor Intelligence (birth to 2 years):
Behavior is primarily sensory and motor. The child does not yet "think" conceptually; however, "cognitive" development can be observed.

2. Preoperational Thought (2–7 years):
Development of language and rapid conceptual development are evident. Children begin to use symbols to think of objects and people outside of their immediate environment. Fantasy and imaginative play are natural modes of thinking.

3. Concrete Operations (7–11 years):
Children develop ability to use logical thought to solve concrete problems. Basic concepts of objects, number, time, space, and causality are explored and mastered. Through use of concrete objects to manipulate, children are able to draw conclusions.

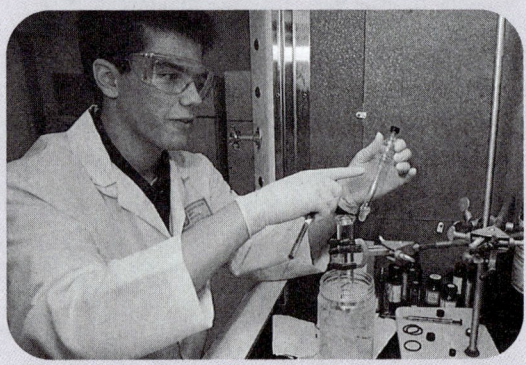

4. Formal Operations (11–15 years):
Cognitive abilities reach their highest level of development. Children can make predictions, think about hypothetical situations, think about thinking, and appreciate the structure of language as well as use it to communicate. Sarcasm, puns, argumentation, and slang are aspects of adolescents' speech that reflect their ability to think abstractly about language.

individual interaction with the total environment, each student's perceptions and learning will be unique. According to Piaget,

> The principal goal of education is to create [learners] who are capable of doing new things, not simply repeating what other generations have done—[learners] who are

creative, inventive, and discoverers. [We] need pupils who are active, who learn early to find out by themselves, partly by their own spontaneous activity and partly through material we set up for them; who learn early to tell what is verifiable and what is simply the first idea to come to them (quoted in Ripple and Rockcastle 1964, 5).

Figure 3.2 presents guidelines for teaching children at the preoperational stage, the concrete operations stage, and the formal operations stage.

Figure 3.2   Guidelines for teaching school-age children at Piaget's stages of cognitive growth.

Guidelines for Teaching School-Age Children at Piaget's Stages of Cognitive Growth

Teaching the Child at the Preoperational Stage

1. Use concrete props and visual aids whenever possible.
2. Make instruction relatively short, using actions as well as words.
3. Don't expect the students to be consistent in their ability to see the world from someone else's point of view.
4. Be sensitive to the possibility that students may have different meanings for the same word or different words for the same meaning. Students may also expect everyone to understand words they have invented.
5. Give children a great deal of hands-on practice with the skills that serve as building blocks for more complex skills such as reading comprehension.
6. Provide a wide range of experiences in order to build a foundation for concept learning and language.

Teaching the Child at the Concrete-Operational Stage

1. Continue to use concrete props and visual aids, especially when dealing with sophisticated material.
2. Continue to give students a chance to manipulate and test objects.
3. Make sure presentation and readings are brief and well organized.
4. Use familiar examples to explain more complex ideas.
5. Give opportunities to classify and group objects and ideas on increasingly complex levels.
6. Present problems that require logical, analytical thinking.

Teaching the Child at the Formal Operations Stage

1. Continue to use concrete-operational teaching strategies and materials.
2. Give students the opportunity to explore many hypothetical questions.
3. Give students opportunities to solve problems and reason scientifically.
4. Whenever possible, teach broad concepts, not just facts, using materials and ideas relevant to the students' lives.

Source: Excerpted from Anita E. Woolfolk, *Educational Psychology,* 7th ed. Boston: Allyn and Bacon, 1998, pp. 33, 36, 39. Copyright © 1998 by Allyn and Bacon. Reprinted by permission.

Erikson's Model of Psychosocial Development

Erik Erikson's model of psychosocial development delineates eight stages, from infancy to old age (see Table 3.1). For each stage, a **psychosocial crisis** is central in the individual's emotional and social growth. Erikson expresses these crises in polar terms; for instance, in the first stage, that of infancy, the psychosocial crisis is trust versus mistrust. Erikson explains that the major psychosocial task for the infant is to develop a sense of trust in the world but not to give up totally a sense of distrust. In the tension between the poles of trust and mistrust, a greater pull toward the more positive pole is considered healthy and is accompanied by a virtue. In this case, if trust prevails, the virtue is hope. Shortly before his death in 1994 at the age of 91, Erikson postulated a ninth stage in the human life cycle,

Table 3.1 Erikson's eight stages of psychosocial development

Stage	Psychosocial Crisis	Approximate Age	Important Event	Description
1. Infancy	Basic trust versus basic mistrust	Birth to 12–18 months	Feeding	The infant must form a first loving, trusting relationship with the caregiver or develop a sense of mistrust.
2. Early childhood	Autonomy versus shame/doubt	18 months to 3 years	Toilet training	The child's energies are directed toward the development of physical skills, including walking, grasping, controlling the sphincter.
3. Play age	Initiative versus guilt	3 to 6 years	Independence	The child learns control but may develop shame and doubt if not handled well.
4. School age	Industry versus inferiority	6 to 12 years	School	The child continues to become more assertive and to take more initiative but may be too forceful, which can lead to guilt feelings.
5. Adolescence	Identity versus role confusion	Adolescence	Peer relationships	The child must deal with demands to learn new skills or risk a sense of inferiority, failure, and incompetence.
6. Young adult	Intimacy versus isolation	Young adulthood	Love relationships	The teenager must achieve identity in occupation, gender roles, politics, and religion.
7. Adulthood	Generativity versus stagnation	Middle adulthood	Parenting/mentoring	The young adult must develop intimate relationships or suffer feelings of isolation. Each adult must find some way to satisfy and support the next generation.
8. Mature love	Ego integrity versus despair	Late adulthood	Reflection on and acceptance of one's life	The culmination is a sense of acceptance of oneself as one is and a sense of fulfillment.

Source: Adapted from Lester A. Lefton and Linda Brannon, *Psychology,* 7th ed. Boston: Allyn and Bacon, 2003. Copyright © 2003. Reprinted by permission.

gerotranscendence, during which some people mentally transcend the reality of their deteriorating bodies and faculties. In the final chapter of an extended version of Erikson's *The Life Cycle Completed*, first published in 1982, his wife and lifelong colleague, Joan M. Erikson (1901–1997), described the challenge of the ninth stage:

> Despair, which haunts the eighth stage, is a close companion in the ninth, because it is almost impossible to know what emergencies and losses of physical ability are imminent. As independence and control are challenged, self-esteem and confidence weaken. Hope and trust, which once provided firm support, are no longer the sturdy props of former days. To face down despair with faith and appropriate humility is perhaps the wisest course (1997, 105–106).

When we examine the issues and concerns of students in childhood and early and late adolescence later in this chapter, we will return to Erikson's model of psychosocial development. To learn more about this major theory of human development, you may wish to read Erikson's first book, *Childhood and Society* (1963).

Kohlberg's Model of Moral Development

According to Lawrence Kohlberg (1927–1987), the reasoning process people use to decide what is right and wrong evolves through three levels of development. Within each level, Kohlberg has identified two stages. Table 3.2 on page 98 shows that at Level I, the preconventional level, the individual decides what is right on the basis of personal needs and rules developed by others. At Level II, the conventional level, moral decisions reflect a desire for the approval of others and a willingness to conform to the expectations of family, community, and country. At Level III, the postconventional level, the individual has developed values and principles that are based on rational, personal choices that can be separated from conventional values.

Kohlberg suggests that "over 50 percent of late adolescents and adults are capable of full formal reasoning [i.e., they can use their intelligence to reason abstractly, form hypotheses, and test these hypotheses against reality], but only 10 percent of these adults display principled (Stages 5 and 6) moral reasoning" (2000, 138–139). In addition, Kohlberg found that maturity of moral judgment is not highly related to IQ or verbal intelligence.

Some individuals have criticized Kohlberg's model as being too systematic and sequential. They argue that it is limited because it focuses on moral reasoning rather than actual behavior and biased because it tends to look at moral development from a male perspective (Bracey 1993). Carol Gilligan, for example, suggests that male moral reasoning tends to address the rights of the individual, whereas female moral reasoning addresses the individual's responsibility to other people. In her book, *In a Different Voice: Psychological Theory and Women's Development* (1993), Gilligan refers to women's principal moral voice as the "ethics of care," which emphasizes care of others over the more male-oriented "ethics of justice." Thus, when confronted with a moral dilemma, females tend to suggest solutions based more on altruism and self-sacrifice than on rights and rules (Gilligan 1993).

Table 3.2 Kohlberg's theory of moral reasoning

I. Preconventional Level of Moral Reasoning

Child is responsive to cultural rules and labels of good and bad, right or wrong, but interprets these in terms of consequences of action (punishment, reward, exchanges of favors).

Stage 1: Punishment-and-obedience orientation
Physical consequences of action determine its goodness or badness.
Avoidance of punishment and deference to power are valued.

Stage 2: The instrumental-relativist orientation
Right action consists of that which satisfies one's own needs and occasionally the needs of others. Reciprocity is a matter of "You scratch my back and I'll scratch yours."

II. Conventional Level of Moral Reasoning

Maintaining the expectations of the individual's family, group, or nation is perceived as valuable, regardless of consequences.

Stage 3: The interpersonal concordance or "good boy-nice girl" orientation
Good behavior is that which pleases or helps others and is approved by them.

Stage 4: The "law and order" orientation
Orientation toward fixed rules and the maintenance of the social order. Right behavior consists of doing one's duty and showing respect for authority.

III. Postconventional, Autonomous, or Principled Level of Moral Reasoning

Effort to define moral principles that have validity and application apart from the authority of groups.

Stage 5: The social-contract, legalistic orientation
Right action defined in terms of rights and standards that have been agreed on by the whole society. This is the "official" morality of the American government and Constitution.

Stage 6: The universal-ethical-principle orientation
Right is defined by conscience in accord with self-chosen ethical principles appealing to logic and universality.

Sources: Adapted from Lawrence Kohlberg, "The Cognitive-Developmental Approach to Moral Education," Forrest W. Parkay and Glen Hass (eds.), in *Curriculum Planning: A Contemporary Approach,* 7th ed. Boston: Allyn and Bacon, 2000, p. 137. The original version appeared in *Journal of Philosophy, 70*(18), 1973, pp. 631–632.

The question remains, can moral reasoning be taught? Can teachers help students develop so that they live according to principles of equity, justice, caring, and empathy? Kohlberg suggests the following three conditions that can help children internalize moral principles:

1. Exposure to the next higher stage of reasoning
2. Exposure to situations posing problems and contradictions for the child's current moral structure, leading to dissatisfaction with his [her] current level

3. An atmosphere of interchange and dialogue combining the first two conditions, in which conflicting moral views are compared in an open manner (Kohlberg 2000, 144)

One approach to teaching values and moral reasoning is known as **character education**, a movement that stresses the development of students' "good character." In remarks at the opening of the 2002 White House Conference on Character and Community, President George W. Bush stressed the importance of building character in our nation's schools:

> We've got to do more than just teach our children skills and knowledge. We also want to make sure they're kind and decent, compassionate and responsible, honest and self-disciplined. Our children must learn to make a living, but even more, they must learn how to live . . . [as] Martin Luther King, Jr. said: "Intelligence is not enough. Intelligence plus character, that is the goal of true education" (White House press release, June 19, 2002).

There is no single way for teachers to develop students' character; however, in comments made shortly after the shooting deaths of fourteen students and a teacher at Columbine High School in Colorado, well-known sociologist and organizer of several White House conferences on character education Amitai Etzioni (1999) said, "What schools should help youngsters develop—if schools are going to help lower the likelihood of more Columbines—are two crucial behavior characteristics: the capacity to channel impulses into prosocial outlets, and empathy with others." In addition, Figure 3.3 on page 100 illustrates twelve strategies Thomas Lickona suggests teachers can use to create moral classroom communities.

Many schools, such as the Hyde Schools in Bath, Maine, and Woodstock, Connecticut, emphasize specific moral values in their curricula. The character-based educational program at the Hyde Schools focuses on five words: *curiosity, courage, concern, leadership*, and *integrity* (Gauld and Gauld 2002). Kennedy Middle School in Eugene, Oregon, implemented the "Second Step" program, described by a teacher as "a schoolwide curriculum that teaches students skills such as how to communicate, problem-solve, and work together in a community. They learn the importance of responsibility and honesty . . . [and] a large section at the beginning of each unit emphasizes empathy" (DeRoche and Williams 2001, 163).

Maslow's Hierarchy of Needs

Students' developmental levels also vary according to how well their biological and psychological needs have been satisfied. Psychologist Abraham Maslow (1908–1970) formulated a model of a **hierarchy of needs** (see Figure 3.4 on page 101) that suggests that people are motivated by basic needs for survival and safety first. When these basic needs have been met sufficiently, people naturally seek to satisfy higher needs, the highest of which is self-actualization—the desire to use one's talents, abilities, and potentialities to the fullest. Students whose needs for safety have been fairly well satisfied will discover strong needs for friendship, affection, and

Figure 3.3 A comprehensive approach to values and character education.

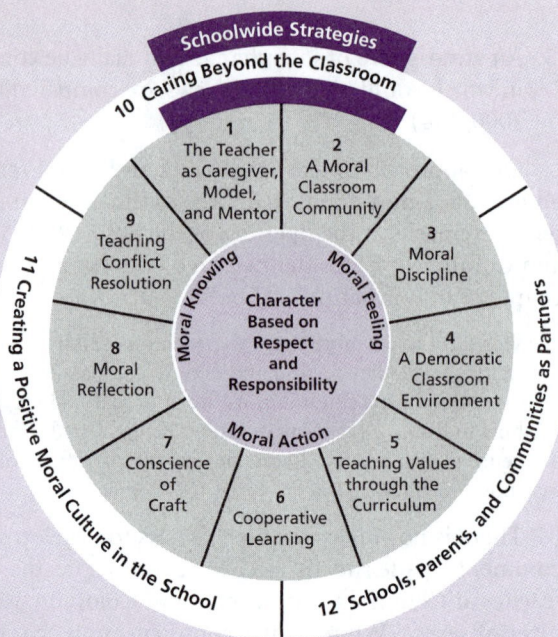

1. *Act as caregiver, model, and mentor,* treating students with love and respect, setting a good example, supporting positive social behavior, and correcting hurtful actions through one-on-one guidance and whole-class discussion.

2. *Create a moral community,* helping students know one another as persons, respect and care about one another, and feel valued membership in, and responsibility to, the group.

3. *Practice moral discipline,* using the creation and enforcement of rules as opportunities to foster moral reasoning, voluntary compliance with rules, and a respect for others.

4. *Create a democratic classroom environment,* involving students in decision making and the responsibility for making the classroom a good place to be and learn.

5. *Teach values through the curriculum,* using the ethically rich content of academic subjects (such as literature, history, and science) as vehicles for teaching values and examining moral questions.

6. *Use cooperative learning* to develop students' appreciation of others, perspective taking, and the ability to work with others toward common goals.

7. *Develop the "conscience of craft"* by fostering students' appreciation of learning, capacity for hard work, commitment to excellence, and sense of work as affecting the lives of others.

8. *Encourage moral reflection* through reading, research, essay writing, journal keeping, discussion, and debate.

9. *Teach conflict resolution,* so that students acquire the essential moral skills of solving conflicts fairly and without force.

10. *Foster caring beyond the classroom,* using positive role models to inspire altruistic behavior and providing opportunities at every grade level to perform school and community service.

11. *Create a positive moral culture in the school,* developing a schoolwide ethos that supports and amplifies the values taught in classrooms.

12. *Recruit parents and the community as partners in character education,* letting parents know that the school considers them their child's first and most important moral teacher.

Source: Thomas Lickona, *Educating for Character: How Our Schools Can Teach.* New York: Bantam Books, 1991, p. 69. Copyright © 1991 by Thomas Likona. Used by permission of Bantam Books, a division of Random House, Inc.

Figure 3.4 Maslow's hierarchy of needs. Note: The four lower-level needs are called deficiency needs because the motivation to satisfy them decreases when they are met. On the other hand, when being (growth) needs are met, motivation to fulfill them increases.

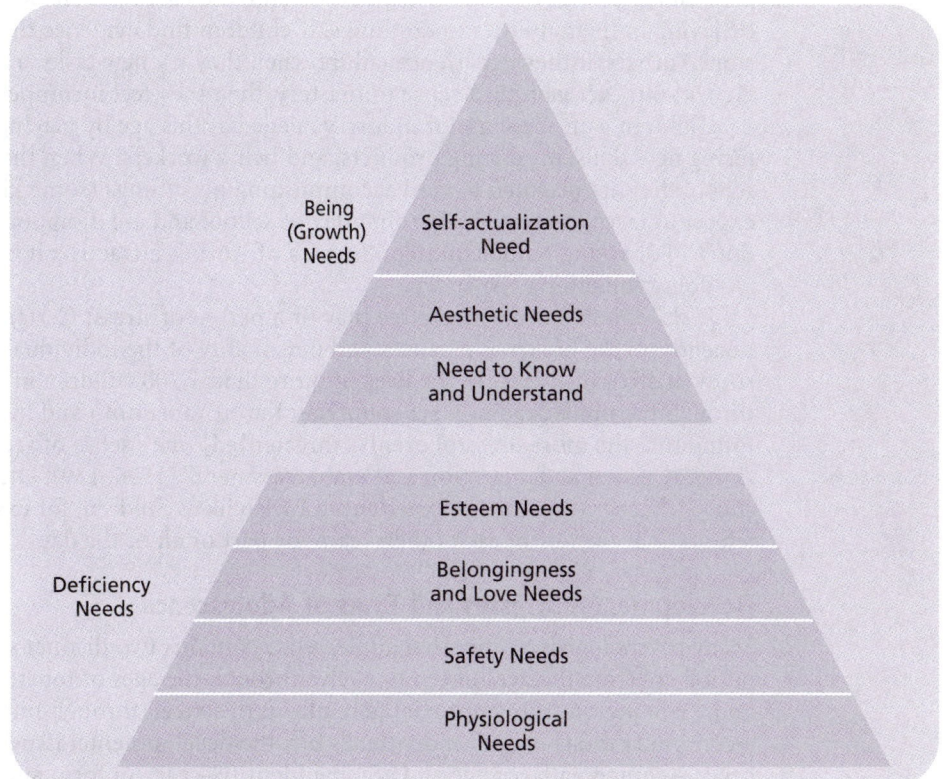

Sources: Based on Abraham H. Maslow, *Toward a Psychology of Being,* 3rd ed. New York: John Wiley & Sons, 1999; and *Motivation and Personality,* 3rd ed. Boston: Addison-Wesley Publishing Company, 1987.

love, for example. If efforts to satisfy the various needs are thwarted, the result can be maladjustment and interruption or delay in the individual's full and healthy development.

This model has particular relevance for teachers because students differ markedly in terms of where they are on Maslow's hierarchy of needs. Many families lack the resources to provide adequately for children's basic needs. Children from families that are concerned with day-to-day survival may not receive the support that could help them succeed in school. They come to school tired and hungry and may have trouble paying attention in class. Others may be well fed and clothed but feel unsafe, alien, or unloved; they may seek to protect themselves by withdrawing emotionally from activities around them.

Developmental Stresses and Tasks of Childhood

During Erikson's school-age stage, children strive for a sense of industry and struggle against feelings of inferiority. If successful, they gain the virtue of competence, believing in their abilities to do things. If children find evidence that they are inferior to others, if they experience failure when they try new tasks, and if they struggle without ever gaining a sense of mastery, then they feel incompetent.

Children gain the sense of industry needed at this age by playing seriously, mastering new skills, producing products, and being workers. When they first go to school they are oriented toward accomplishing new things (some kindergartners expect to learn to read on their first day of school and are disappointed when they don't). For young schoolchildren, the idea of work is attractive; it means that they are doing something grown-up.

Is childhood a time of carefree play or a period of stress? Certainly the answer depends on the life circumstances and personality of the individual child. In a study of stressful events in the lives of more than 1,700 children in the second through the ninth grades in six countries, Karou Yamamoto and his associates found that the most stressful events "threaten[ed] one's sense of security and occasion[ed] personal denigration and embarrassment" (1996, 139). Other studies have shown that serious stress is experienced by latchkey children, for example, who are left on their own or in each others' care for part or all of the day.

Developmental Stresses and Tasks of Adolescence

Many psychologists believe that adolescence contains two distinct stages: an early period covering the ages of ten to twelve through the ages of fourteen to sixteen, and a late period from approximately fifteen to sixteen through nineteen. Although a continuity exists in each individual's life, the developmental issues of adolescence—coping with change and seeking identity—vary in form and importance as individuals progress through the transition from childhood to adulthood.

In the following Teachers' Voices feature, a sixth-grade teacher describes how he developed a "walkabout program" based on the Australian Aborigine trial of manhood that provides students with developmental opportunities for self-discovery and challenge. The program is designed around five "challenge areas" of personal development: adventure, creativity, logical inquiry, practical skills, and service.

In Erik Erikson's model of the eight stages of human development, identity versus role diffusion is the psychosocial crisis for the adolescent years. Although the quest for identity is a key psychosocial issue for both early and late adolescence, many believe that Erikson's identity-versus-role diffusion stage fits best for early adolescence. During this time, young adolescents, using their new thinking abilities, begin integrating a clearer sense of personal identity. Erikson's role diffusion refers to the variety of roles that adolescents have available to them.

According to Erikson's developmental theory, when adolescents identify themselves with a peer group, with a school, or with a cause, their sense of fidelity—the "virtue" of this stage—is clear and strong. At this stage adolescents are loyal and

Teachers' *Voices* Putting Research and Theory into Practice

Walkabout in Sixth Grade

Richard Isenberg

The term *walkabout*—originating in the Australian Aborigine trial of manhood—is probably more familiar to Americans today than at any time in the past. However, the idea that self-discovery and challenge are important parts of the passage into adulthood is ancient. The beauty of the ancient tradition of the walkabout is that it creates an opportunity for growth as young people move from childhood to adulthood. Those on walkabout are challenged to use all their skills, apply their knowledge to real problems, and see tangible results. The experience also includes time to be introspective and to assimilate what has been learned through the trial itself. When the walkabout is completed, the sojourners return to a new adult life with great pride in their accomplishments. These are worthy goals for any educational setting, but they are especially appropriate for early adolescents.

My first exposure to the idea of walkabout as an educational program was . . . when I attended a presentation by the Center for Educational Services and Research in Yorktown Heights, New York. I was intrigued enough to gather the literature that was available at that time. And I was surprised to discover numerous programs evolving throughout the country. While there was considerable variety, they all shared core principles of walkabout in that they were student-centered, activity-oriented, and focused on authentic life skills. However, I was disappointed to discover that most of them were designed as alternative high school programs for high-risk students. I did not see any reason why the basic principles of walkabout needed to

be limited to older students. So, while it took some years to find myself in the right situation to launch a program, in 1986 I began to offer the challenge of walkabout to my sixth-grade students.

Sixth grade seemed like an ideal time to introduce the walkabout concept. Children of eleven or twelve years of age are undergoing rapid physical and emotional change. They are typically given more freedom and independence as well as additional responsibilities at home, in school, and in the community. In my school system in Vermont, students are preparing to make a significant instructional leap from small rural elementary schools into the larger consolidated high school. Most important, many students are eager to become more independent and to expand their opportunities to govern their own learning. Walkabout can channel these natural energies in productive ways.

Questions

1. Why does Isenberg state that "sixth grade seemed like an ideal time to introduce the walkabout concept"? What developmental tasks are students focusing on at that time?
2. Isenberg's walkabout program focuses on five "challenge areas." What "challenge areas" might be appropriate for students at other stages of development?

Richard Isenberg teaches sixth grade in Cornwall, Vermont. The preceding is excerpted from his article in the March 1997 *Phi Delta Kappan*, pp. 513–516.

committed, sometimes to people or ideas that may dismay or alarm their parents, sometimes to high ideals and dreams.

In late adolescence, the quest for identity shifts from relying on others to self-reliance. Young people continue to work on strengthening their sense of identity in late adolescence, but as they do so they draw less on the reactions of their peers

What needs must this child satisfy for healthy development? What childhood stresses does she face? What developmental tasks must she accomplish in her psychosocial development? What needs, stresses, and developmental tasks will affect this child as an adolescent? Why is information about development important to teachers?

and more on their own regard for what matters. Although late adolescents possess an array of interests, talents, and goals in life, they share a desire to achieve independence. More like adults than children, late adolescents are anxious to use newly acquired strengths, skills, and knowledge to achieve their own purposes, whether through marriage, parenthood, full-time employment, education beyond high school, a career, or military service.

The vulnerability of today's adolescents is dramatically evident in the results of a survey of one thousand schools and one million students based on forty "developmental assets" (positive relationships, opportunities, skills, and values) adolescents need to become healthy, mature adults: "[O]n average, youth have less than half of the 40 assets they need to grow up healthy, caring, and responsible. . . . [T]his statistic remains relatively consistent among urban, rural, and suburban communities" (Search Institute 2002). Moreover, a Public Agenda poll "found that a solid majority of American adults—two thirds—spontaneously describe adolescents in starkly negative terms: wild, rude, irresponsible. Half give those descriptions even to younger children" (Scales 2001, 64). The list of alarming concerns in adolescence includes academic failure and retention, accidents, anorexia, assaultive behavior, criminal activity, cultism, depression, discipline problems, dropouts, drug abuse, homicides, incest, prostitution, runaways, school absenteeism, suicide, teenage pregnancy, vandalism, and the contraction of sexually transmitted diseases.

As a teacher, what can you do to help children and adolescents develop to their full potential? To help prevent the problems that place them at risk, an energetic, creative, and multifaceted approach is necessary. Figure 3.5 presents several strategies for helping students develop competence, positive self-concepts, and high esteem and for intervening to prevent or address problems that place them at risk.

How Do Students Vary in Intelligence?

In addition to developmental differences, students differ in terms of their intellectual capacity. Unfortunately, test scores, and sometimes intelligence quotient (IQ) scores, are treated as accurate measurements of students' intellectual ability because of their convenience and long-time use. What is intelligence and how has it been redefined to account for the many ways in which it is expressed?

Though many definitions of intelligence have been proposed, the term has yet to be completely defined. One view is that **intelligence** is the ability to learn. As David Wechsler, the developer of the most widely used intelligence scales for children and adults, said: "Intelligence, operationally defined, is the aggregate or global capacity to act purposefully, to think rationally, and to deal effectively with the

Figure 3.5 What teachers can do to help children and adolescents develop.

1. **Provide opportunities and encouragement for students to develop competence.**

   - Provide a learning environment in which students can risk making mistakes.
   - Assign work that students can perform successfully and still be challenged.
   - Have realistic but high expectations for students.
   - Express belief in students' ability to succeed.
   - Encourage industry by letting students work on goals or projects of their choosing.
   - Provide opportunities for students to take special responsibility.
   - Assign older students to work with younger ones.
   - Reward industry and competence.

2. **Promote the development of positive self-concept and high self-esteem.**

   - Give praise more than criticism.
   - Take students and their work seriously.
   - Respect students' dignity.
   - Plan individual and group activities that boost morale.
   - Provide opportunities for students to interact and work cooperatively.
   - Teach and model acceptance of human diversity and individuality.
   - Develop systems for the recognition and reward of individual and group achievement.
   - Support students' efforts to achieve and appropriately express independence.

3. **Intervene to prevent or address problems that place students at risk.**

   - Provide a safe and structured learning environment where students feel secure.
   - Practice effective leadership and classroom management.
   - Provide opportunities to discuss preferences, values, morals, goals, and consequences.
   - Teach and model critical thinking, decision making, and problem solving.
   - Teach and model prosocial attitudes and behaviors and conflict resolution strategies.
   - Provide information on subjects of special concern to students and parents.
   - Cultivate family involvement.
   - Collaborate, consult, network, and refer on behalf of students.

environment" (1958, 7). Other definitions of intelligence that have been proposed are the following:

- Goal-directed adaptive behavior
- Ability to solve novel problems
- Ability to acquire and think with new conceptual systems
- Problem-solving ability
- Planning and other metacognitive skills
- Memory access speed
- What people think intelligence is
- What IQ tests measure
- The ability to learn from bad teaching (Woolfolk 2001, 108)

Intelligence Testing

The intelligence tests that we now use can be traced to the 1905 Metrical Scale of Intelligence designed by French psychologists Alfred Binet and Theodore Simon, who were part of a Paris-based commission that wanted a way to identify children who would need special help with their learning. Binet revised the scale in 1908, which was adapted for American children in 1916 by Lewis Terman, a psychologist at Stanford University. Terman's test was, in turn, further adapted, especially by the U.S. Army, which transformed it into a paper-and-pencil test that could be administered to large groups. The use of such intelligence tests has continued throughout the years. Approximately 67 percent of the population have an IQ between 85 and 115—the range of normal intelligence.

Individual intelligence tests are presently valued by psychologists and those in the field of special education because they can be helpful in diagnosing a student's strengths and weaknesses. However, group intelligence tests given for the purpose of classifying students into like-score groups have received an increasing amount of criticism.

The most significant and dramatic criticism of group IQ tests has been that test items and tasks are culturally biased, drawn mostly from white middle-class experience. Thus the tests are more assessments of how informed students are about features in a specific class or culture than of how intelligent they are in general. This complaint became a formal, legal challenge when, on the basis of their IQ test scores, a group of African American children were put into special classes for mentally retarded children. Their parents brought the complaint to the courts in 1971 and persisted with it all the way to the federal appellate court, where a decision was eventually made in their favor in 1984. In that well-known case, *Larry P. v. Riles* (1984), the court decided that IQ tests were discriminatory and culturally biased. However, in another case, *PASE v. Hannon* (1980), an Illinois district court ruled that when IQ tests were used in conjunction with other forms of assessment, such as teacher observation, they were not discriminatory for placement purposes. Although the criticism continues, a number of psychometricians are seeking other solutions by attempting to design culture-free intelligence tests.

Multiple Intelligences

Many theorists believe that intelligence is a basic ability that enables one to perform mental operations in the following areas: logical reasoning, spatial reasoning, number ability, and verbal meaning. However, other theorists believe "that conventional notions of intelligence are incomplete and hence inadequate. [One's] ability to achieve success depends on capitalizing on one's strengths and correcting or compensating for one's weaknesses through a balance of analytical, creative, and practical abilities" (Sternberg 2002, 447–448). For example, Howard Gardner believes that human beings possess at least eight separate forms of intelligence; "each intelligence reflects the potential to solve problems or to fashion products that are valued in one or more cultural settings. [Each] features its own distinctive form of mental representation" (1999, 71–72). Drawing on the theories of others and research findings on savants, prodigies, and other exceptional individuals, Gardner originally suggested in *Frames of Mind* (1983) that human beings possessed seven human intelligences: logical-mathematical, linguistic, musical, spatial, bodily-kinesthetic, interpersonal, and intrapersonal. In the mid-1990s, he identified an eighth intelligence, that of the naturalist; and in his book *The Disciplined Mind*, he suggests that "it is possible that human beings also exhibit a ninth, existential intelligence—the proclivity to pose (and ponder) questions about life, death, and ultimate realities" (1999, 72). According to Gardner, every person possesses the eight intelligences (see Figure 3.6 on page 108), yet each person has his or her particular blend of the intelligences.

Gardner's theory of **multiple intelligences** is valuable for teachers. As Robert Slavin suggests, "Teachers must avoid thinking about children as smart or not smart because there are many ways to be smart (2000, 130). Some students are talented in terms of their interpersonal relations and exhibit natural leadership abilities. Others seem to have a high degree of what some researchers have termed *emotional intelligence*—awareness of and ability to manage their feelings (Salovey and Feldman-Barrett 2002; Salovey, Mayer, and Caruso 2002; Salovey and Sluyter 1997). Differences in musical, athletic, and mechanical abilities can be recognized by even the minimally informed observer. Because these intelligences are not tested or highlighted, they may go unnoticed and possibly wasted.

However, keep in mind Gardner's "reflections" fourteen years after the publication of *Frames of Mind*:

> MI [multiple intelligences] may be appealing, but it is not for the faint-hearted, nor for those in search of a quick fix. After initial experimentation with the ideas and practices of MI, practitioners realize that MI is not an end in itself. To say that one has an MI classroom or an MI school is not meaningful—one has to ask "MI for what?" (1997, 20).

Figure 3.6 The eight intelligences.

The Eight Intelligences

Linguistic intelligence allows individuals to communicate and make sense of the world through language. Poets exemplify this intelligence in its mature form. Students who enjoy playing with rhymes, who pun, who always have a story to tell, who quickly acquire other languages—including sign language— all exhibit linguistic intelligence.

Musical intelligence allows people to create, communicate, and understand meanings made out of sound. While composers and instrumentalists clearly exhibit this intelligence, so do the students who seem particularly attracted by the birds singing outside the classroom window or who constantly tap out intricate rhythms on the desk with their pencils.

Logical-mathematical intelligence enables individuals to use and appreciate abstract relations. Scientists, mathematicians, and philosophers all rely on this intelligence. So do the students who "live" baseball statistics or who carefully analyze the components of problems—either personal or school-related—before systematically testing solutions.

Spatial intelligence makes it possible for people to perceive visual or spatial information, to transform this information, and to recreate visual images from memory. Well-developed spatial capacities are needed for the work of architects, sculptors, and engineers. The students who turn first to the graphs, charts, and pictures in their textbooks, who like to "web" their ideas before writing a paper, and who fill the blank space around their notes with intricate patterns are also using their spatial intelligence.

Bodily-kinesthetic intelligence allows individuals to use all or part of the body to create products or solve problems. Athletes, surgeons, dancers, choreographers, and craftspeople all use bodily-kinesthetic intelligence. The capacity is also evident in students who relish gym class and school dances, who prefer to carry out class projects by making models rather than writing reports, and who toss crumpled paper with frequency and accuracy into wastebaskets across the room.

Interpersonal intelligence enables individuals to recognize and make distinctions about others' feelings and intentions. Teachers, parents, politicians, psychologists, and salespeople rely on interpersonal intelligence. Students exhibit this intelligence when they thrive on small-group work, when they notice and react to the moods of their friends and classmates, and when they tactfully convince the teacher of their need for extra time to complete the homework assignment.

Intrapersonal intelligence helps individuals to distinguish among their own feelings, to build accurate mental models of themselves, and to draw on these models to make decisions about their lives. Although it is difficult to assess who has this capacity and to what degree, evidence can be sought in students' uses of their other intelligences—how well they seem to be capitalizing on their strengths, how cognizant they are of their weaknesses, and how thoughful they are about the decisions and choices they make.

Naturalist intelligence allows people to distinguish among, classify, and use features of the environment. Farmers, gardeners, botanists, geologists, florists, and archaeologists all exhibit this intelligence, as do students who can name and describe the features of every make of car around them.

Source: Project SUMIT (Schools Using Multiple Intelligence Theory), "Theory of Multiple Intelligences."

Learning Styles

Students vary greatly in regard to **learning styles**, the approaches to learning that work best for them. These differences have also been called *learning style preferences* or *cognitive styles* (Woolfolk 2001). The National Task Force on Learning Style and Brain Behavior suggests that there is a "consistent pattern of behavior and performance by which an individual approaches educational experiences. It is the composite of characteristic cognitive, affective, and physiological behaviors that serve as relatively stable indicators of how a learner perceives, interacts with, and responds to the learning environment."

Students' learning styles are determined by a combination of hereditary and environmental influences. Some more quickly learn things they hear; others learn faster when they see material in writing. Some need a lot of structure; others learn best when they can be independent and follow their desires. Some learn best in formal settings; others learn best in informal, relaxed environments. Some need almost total silence to concentrate; others learn well in noisy, active environments. Some are intuitive learners; others prefer to learn by following logical, sequential steps.

There is no one "correct" view of learning styles to guide you in your daily decision making as a teacher. Culture-based differences in learning styles are subtle, variable, and difficult to describe (Zhang and Sternberg 2001); and learning styles change as the individual matures. Moreover, critics maintain that there is little evidence to support the validity of dozens of conceptual models for learning styles and accompanying assessment instruments. Nevertheless, you should be aware of the concept of learning styles and realize that any given classroom activity may be more effective for some students than for others. Knowledge of your own and your students' learning styles will help you to individualize instruction and motivate your students.

Learning with Style   An example of how one school modified its educational programs is Libertyville High School in Libertyville, Illinois. All Libertyville freshmen take a five-week course called Learning with Style during the second half of their lunch period. At the beginning of the course, students complete the "Learning Preference Inventory" (Hanson & Silver, 2000) to help the students and their teachers understand their personal learning styles.

During the course, students learn about different approaches to learning, and they begin to reflect on their own learning behaviors. With the help of teachers, guidance counselors, and parents, each student develops a set of skills and learning strategies that matches his or her interests.

Students also learn about the strengths and weaknesses of each style. Students develop "personal growth plans" and explore careers that fit their learning styles. Students map out their high school careers, meeting regularly with their guidance counselors to discuss and revise their goals in light of new learning and experiences.

All teachers at the high school are trained in learning styles. They work closely with the teacher of the Learning with Style course and the guidance counselors.

Parents are also encouraged to attend an adult version the Learning with Style course at night. Parents then help their children and the school make the best decisions about the child's education and future career.

During the adult Learning with Style course, the teacher reviews student profiles and explains to parents how their children learn, what they need to be successful, and what areas may need special attention. Parents learn about how a student's learning style can influence decisions about college, vocation, and becoming a lifelong learner. The teacher of the Learning with Style course sums up how knowledge of students' learning styles can help teachers establish authentic learning communities in their classrooms: "It keeps the learning environment fresh by helping us to remember that every student has unique interests, talents, and needs and that as an educational institution, we really can treat all our students to the personalized learning program they need and deserve" (Strong, Silver, and Perini 2001, 92–93).

How Do Students Vary in Ability and Disability?

Students also differ according to their special needs and talents. Some enter the world with exceptional abilities or disabilities; others encounter life experiences that change their capabilities significantly, and still others struggle with conditions that medical scientists have yet to understand. Where possible, all children and youth with exceptionalities are given a public education in the United States.

Exceptional Learners

Children "who require special education and related services if they are to realize their full human potential" (Hallahan and Kauffman 2003, 7) are referred to as **exceptional learners**. They are taught by special education teachers and by regular teachers into whose classrooms they have been integrated or *included*. Among the many exceptional children that teachers may encounter in the classroom are students who have physical, mental, or emotional disabilities and students who are gifted or talented.

Special-needs students are often referred to synonymously as *handicapped* or *disabled*. However, it is important for teachers to understand the following distinction between a disability and a handicap:

> A disability . . . results from a loss of physical functioning (e.g., loss of sight, hearing, or mobility) or from difficulty in learning and social adjustment that significantly interferes with normal growth and development. A handicap is a limitation imposed on the individual by environmental demands and is related to the individual's ability to adapt or adjust to those demands (Hardman, Drew, and Egan 2003, 3).

For example, Stephen W. Hawking, the gifted physicist who provided the epigraph for this chapter, has amyotrophic lateral sclerosis (also known as Lou Gehrig's disease), which requires him to use a wheelchair for mobility and a speech synthesizer to communicate. If Hawking had to enter a building accessible only by stairs or if a computer virus infected his speech synthesizer program, his disability would then become a handicap.

In addition, as a teacher you should know that current language use emphasizes the concept of "people first." In other words, a disabling condition should not be used as an adjective to describe a person. Thus, you should say "a child with a visual impairment," not a "blind child" or even a "visually impaired child."

You should also realize that the definitions for disabilities are generalized, open to change, and significantly influenced by the current cultural perception of normality. For example, the American Association on Mental Retardation (AAMR) has changed its definition of mental retardation seven times since 1950 to reflect shifting views of people with cognitive disabilities.

Cautions about labeling should also apply to gifted and talented students. Unfortunately, people commonly have a negative view of gifted and talented youngsters. Like many ethnic groups, gifted students are "different" and thus have been the target of many myths and stereotypes. However, a landmark study of 1,528 gifted males and females begun by Lewis Terman (Terman, Baldwin, and Bronson 1925; Terman and Oden 1947, 1959) in 1926 and to continue until 2010 has "exploded the myth that high-IQ individuals [are] brainy but physically and socially inept. In fact, Terman found that children with outstanding IQs were larger, stronger, and better coordinated than other children and became better adjusted and more emotionally stable adults" (Slavin 2003, 429).

Students with Disabilities

Table 3.3 on page 112 shows that the percentage of all students participating in federally supported education programs for **students with disabilities** increased from 8.33 percent in 1976–77 to 13.22 percent in 1999–2000. Nearly 6.2 million students participated in these programs in 2000 (National Center for Education Statistics 2001).

Various tests and other forms of assessment are used to identify persons in various categories of disability. The following brief definitional characteristics are based on the Individuals with Disabilities Education Act (IDEA) and definitions used by professional organizations dedicated to meeting the needs of persons in each category.

1. *Specific learning disabilities (LD)*—Learning is significantly hindered by difficulty in listening, speaking, reading, writing, reasoning, or computing
2. *Speech or language impairments*—Significant difficulty in communicating with others as a result of speech or language disorders
3. *Mental retardation*—Significant limitations in cognitive ability
4. *Serious emotional disturbance (SED)*—Social and/or emotional maladjustment that significantly reduces the ability to learn
5. *Hearing impairments*—Permanent or fluctuating mild to profound hearing loss in one or both ears

| Table 3.3 | Children 0 to 21 years old served in federally supported programs for the disabled, by type of disability: 1976–77 to 1999–2000* |

Number served as a percent of total enrollment**

Type of Disability	1976–77	1988–89	1997–98	1998–99	1999–2000
Specific learning disabilities	1.80	4.94	5.91	5.99	6.05
Speech or language impairments	2.94	2.41	2.29	2.29	2.30
Mental retardation	2.16	1.40	1.28	1.28	1.28
Serious emotional disturbance	0.64	0.94	0.98	0.99	1.00
Hearing impairments	0.20	0.14	0.15	0.15	0.15
Orthopedic impairments	0.20	0.14	0.15	0.15	0.15
Other health impairments	0.32	0.11	0.41	0.47	0.54
Visual impairments	0.09	0.06	0.05	0.06	0.06
Multiple disabilities	–	0.21	0.23	0.23	0.24
Deaf-blindness	–	****	****	****	****
Autism and traumatic brain injury	–	–	0.12	0.14	0.17
Developmental delay	–	–	0.01	0.03	0.04
Preschool disabled***	0.44	0.89	1.22	1.22	1.24
Infants and toddlers	–	0.08	–	–	–
All disabilities	8.33	11.26	12.80	13.01	13.22

–Data not available
*Data reported in this table for years prior to 1993–94 include children ages 0–21 served under Chapter 1 of the Elementary and Secondary Education Act. Data reported in this table for years after 1993–94 reflects children ages 3–21 served under IDEA, Part B.
**Based on the enrollment in public schools, K–12, including a relatively small number of PreK students.
***Includes preschool children 3–5 years served under Chapter I and IDEA, Part B.
****Less than .005 percent.
Note: Counts are based on reports from the fifty states and District of Columbia only (i.e., figures from outlying areas are not included). Increases since 1987–88 are due in part to new legislation enacted fall 1986, which mandates public school special education services for all children with disabilities ages 3 through 5. Some data have been revised from previously published figures. Detail may not sum to totals due to rounding.

Sources: U.S. Department of Education, Office of Special Education and Rehabilitative Services, *Annual Report to Congress on the Implementation of the Individuals with Disabilities Act,* various years, and unpublished tabulations; and National Center for Education Statistics, Common Core of Data survey. (This table was prepared April 2001.)

6. *Orthopedic impairments*—Physically disabling conditions that affect locomotion or motor functions

7. *Other health impairments*—Limited strength, vitality, or alertness caused by chronic or acute health problems

8. *Visual impairments*—Vision loss that significantly inhibits learning

9. *Multiple disabilities*—Two or more interrelated disabilities

10. *Deaf-blindness*—Vision and hearing disability that severely limits communication

11. *Autism and other*—Significantly impaired communication, learning, and reciprocal social interactions

Of the six million children in special education, half are identified as having a specific learning disability (President's Commission on Excellence in Special Education 2002). Since the term **learning disability (LD)** was first introduced in the early 1960s, there has been no universally accepted definition. The National Joint Committee on Learning Disabilities (1997) states that

> Learning disabilities is a general term that refers to a heterogeneous group of disorders manifested by significant difficulties in the acquisition and use of listening, speaking, reading, writing, reasoning, or mathematical skills. These disorders are intrinsic to the individual, presumed to be due to central nervous system dysfunction, and may occur across the life span. Problems in self-regulatory behaviors, social perception, and social interaction may exist with learning disabilities but do not, by themselves, constitute a learning disability.

Imagine that you are concerned about two of your new students—Mary and Bill. Mary has an adequate vocabulary and doesn't hesitate to express herself, but her achievement in reading and mathematics doesn't add up to what you believe she can do. Often, when you give the class instructions, Mary seems to get confused about what to do. In working with her one-on-one, you've noticed that she often reverses letters and numbers the way much younger children do—she sees a *b* for a *d* or a *6* for a *9*. Mary may have a learning disability that makes it difficult for her to take in, organize, remember, or express information. Like Mary, students with learning disabilities often show a significant difference between their estimated intelligence and their actual achievement in the classroom.

Bill presents you with a different set of challenges. He is obviously bright, but he frequently seems to be "out of sync" with classroom activities. He gets frustrated when he has to wait for his turn. He sometimes blurts out answers before you've even asked a question. He can't seem to stop wiggling his toes and tapping his pencil, and he often comes to school without his backpack and homework. Bill may have **attention deficit hyperactivity disorder (ADHD)**, one of the most commonly diagnosed disabilities among children. Students with ADHD have difficulty remaining still so they can concentrate. Students with an **attention deficit disorder (ADD)** have difficulty focusing their attention long enough to learn well. Children with ADD/ADHD do not qualify for special education unless they also have another disability in a federally defined category.

Treatment for students with ADD/ADHD includes behavior modification and medication. Since the early 1980s, Ritalin has become the most commonly prescribed drug for ADD/ADHD, and more than one million American children are currently estimated to take Ritalin to increase their impulse control and attention span.

By being alert for students who exhibit several of the following academic and behavioral characteristics, you can help in the early identification of students with learning disabilities so they can receive the instructional adaptations or special education services they need.

- Significant discrepancy between potential and achievement
- Inability to solve problems
- Substantial delay in academic achievement
- Lack of involvement in learning tasks
- Poor language and/or cognitive development
- Lack of basic reading and decoding skills
- Lack of attention during lectures or class discussion, distractible
- Excessive movement, hyperactive
- Impulsivity
- Poor motor coordination and spatial relation skills
- Poor motivation
- Overreliance on teacher and peers for class assignments (Smith 2001, 139)

Students Who Are Gifted and Talented

Gifted and talented students, those who have demonstrated a high level of attainment in intellectual ability, academic achievement, creativity, or visual and performing arts, are evenly distributed across all ethnic and cultural groups and socioeconomic classes. Although you might think it is easy to meet the needs of **gifted and talented** students, you will find that this is not always the case. "Students with special gifts or talents often challenge the system of school, and they can be verbally caustic. Their superior abilities and unusual or advanced interests demand teachers who are highly intelligent, creative, and motivated" (Hallahan and Kauffman 2000, 497). The ability of such students to challenge the system is reflected in a recent U.S. Department of Education study that found that gifted and talented elementary schoolchildren have mastered 35 to 50 percent of the grade curriculum in five basic subject areas *before* starting the school year.

Giftedness may take many different forms; Joseph S. Renzulli (1998), Director of the National Research Center on the Gifted and Talented at the University of Connecticut, for example, suggests two kinds of giftedness: "schoolhouse giftedness [which] might also be called test-taking or lesson-learning giftedness" and "creative-productive giftedness." The trend during the last few decades has been to broaden our view of what characterizes giftedness.

Drawing from the work of Renzulli and his colleagues, Woolfolk defines *giftedness* "as a combination of three basic characteristics: above-average general ability, a high level of creativity, and a high level of task commitment or motiva-

Gifted and talented students benefit from enriched learning experiences and individualized plans that give them the opportunity to grow at an accelerated rate. What are some forms of enrichment you will offer your students?

tion to achieve in certain areas. Truly gifted children are not the students who simply learn quickly with little effort. The work of gifted students is original, extremely advanced for their age, and potentially of lasting importance" (Woolfolk 2001, 123).

Variations in criteria used to identify gifted and talented students are especially evident in the reported incidence of giftedness from state to state; for example, North Dakota identifies only 1.0 percent of its students as gifted and talented, whereas Wisconsin identifies 15.0 percent (National Center for Education Statistics 1999, 67). Depending on the criteria used, estimates of the number of gifted and talented students range from 3 to 5 percent of the total population.

Strategies for teaching students who are gifted and talented begin with effective teachers. Educational psychologist Anita Woolfolk suggests that "teaching methods for gifted students should encourage abstract thinking (formal-operational thought), creativity, and independence, not just the learning of greater quantities of facts. In working with gifted and talented students, a teacher must be imaginative, flexible, and unthreatened by the capabilities of these students. The teacher must ask, What does this child need most? What is she or he ready to learn? Who can help me to challenge them?" (2001, 126).

Effective teachers of the gifted and talented tend to have many of the same characteristics as their students (Davis and Rimm 1998; Piirto 1999). In fact,

Feldhusen (1997) suggests that teachers of gifted students should be gifted themselves and should possess the following characteristics:

- Be highly intelligent
- Have cultural and intellectual interests
- Strive for excellence and high achievement
- Be enthusiastic about talent
- Relate well to talented people
- Have broad general knowledge

Several innovative approaches exist for meeting the educational needs of gifted students.

Acceleration   Accelerated programs for intellectually precocious students have proven successful. For example, an analysis of 314 studies of the academic, psychological, and social effects of acceleration practices at the elementary and secondary levels found "generally positive academic effects for most forms of acceleration" and no negative effects on socialization or psychological adjustment (Rogers 1991). In addition, the analysis identified the following acceleration options as the most beneficial at different grade levels:

- *Elementary school*—Early entrance, grade-skipping, nongraded classes, and curriculum compacting (modifying the curriculum to present it at a faster pace).
- *Junior high school*—Grade-skipping, grade telescoping (shortening the amount of time to complete a grade level), concurrent enrollment in a high school or college, subject acceleration, and curriculum compacting.
- *Senior high school*—Concurrent enrollment, subject acceleration, advanced placement (AP) classes, mentorships, credit by examination, and early admission to college.

One example of acceleration is a suburban Chicago alternative school where high-potential at-risk students work at their own pace in high-tech classrooms. They engage in "integrative accelerative learning," which offers advanced curricula and encourages individual creativity, positive reinforcement, and relaxation. At the National Research Center on Gifted and Talented Education, teachers in experimental classrooms practice thematic "curriculum compacting," which encourages brighter students to forge ahead in the regular curriculum while all students work to their strengths and less able students still get the time and attention they need. Also, many colleges and universities now participate in accelerated programs whereby gifted youth who have outgrown the high school curriculum may enroll in college courses.

Case for
Reflection

Meeting the Needs of Gifted Students

You are concerned about the poor performance of Paul, a student in your eighth-period high school class. Paul is undeniably bright. When he was ten, he had an IQ of 145 on the Stanford-Binet. Last year, when he was sixteen, he scored 142. Paul's father is a physician, and his mother is a professor. Both parents clearly value learning and are willing to give Paul any needed encouragement and help.

Throughout elementary school, Paul had an outstanding record. His teachers reported that he was brilliant and very meticulous in completing his assignments. He entered high school amid expectations by his parents and teachers that he would continue his outstanding performance. However, during his first two years of high school, Paul never seemed to live up to his promise. Now, halfway through his junior year, Paul is failing English and geometry. Paul seems to be well adjusted to the social side of school. He has a lot of friends and says he likes school.

Today, you are meeting with Paul to find out why he is failing two of his classes. You begin the conversation with a few comments about last night's basketball game and mention that you saw Paul at the game.

After those comments, you change the focus of the conversation. "So, Paul, tell me about English and geometry. It looks like you may not pass those courses."

"I just don't like to study," Paul says, sliding down in his chair as he tries to convey a nonchalant attitude. "Besides, studying doesn't get you anywhere around here."

"What do you mean, 'doesn't get you anywhere around here?' " you ask.

"When I first got here, kids would say I was 'frantic,' you know. 'Cause I'd finish all my work in class. I felt funny about it, 'cause here I am trying to do all my work to try and get an 'A.' I'm really working, and they're always putting me down 'cause I try. Well, I just got tired of that."

Questions

1. Several innovative approaches for meeting the needs of gifted and talented students are presented in this chapter. Which of these approaches might best meet Paul's educational needs?
2. Why do you think Paul's classmates were critical of his efforts to be a good student? Can teachers do anything to minimize the criticism gifted and talented students may receive from their peers?
3. In light of what Paul says about his experiences at the high school, how might you motivate him to work up to his potential in his English and geometry classes?

Self-Directed or Independent Study For some time, self-directed or independent study has been recognized as an appropriate way for teachers to maintain the interest of gifted students in their classes. Gifted students usually have the academic backgrounds and motivation to do well without constant supervision and the threat or reward of grades.

Individual Education Programs   Since the passage of PL 94-142 and the mandating of Individual Education Programs (IEPs) for special education students, IEPs have been promoted as an appropriate means for educating gifted students. Most IEPs for gifted students involve various enrichment experiences, self-directed study, and special, concentrated instruction given to individuals or small groups in pull-out programs. For example, at Columbia Teachers College in New York, economically disadvantaged students identified as gifted participate in Project Synergy, which pairs students with mentors who nurture their talents and guide them through advanced academic content.

Alternative or Magnet Schools   Several large-city school systems have developed magnet schools organized around specific disciplines, such as science, mathematics, fine arts, basic skills, and so on. The excellent programs at these schools are designed to attract superior students from all parts of the district. Many of these schools offer outstanding programs for gifted and talented youth. Gary Davis and Sylvia Rimm, experts in education for the gifted and talented, say that such schools "are indeed relevant, and they do meet students' needs" (1998, 137).

What Are Special Education, Mainstreaming, and Inclusion?

Prior to the twentieth century, children with disabilities were usually segregated from regular classrooms and taught by teachers in state-run and private schools. Today, an array of programs and services in general and special education classrooms is aimed at developing the potential of exceptional students. Three critical concepts to promote the growth, talents, and productivity of exceptional students are special education, mainstreaming, and inclusion.

Special education refers to "specially designed instruction that meets the unusual needs of an exceptional student" (Hallahan and Kauffman 2003, 13). Teachers who are trained in special education become familiar with special materials, techniques, and equipment and facilities for students with disabilities. For example, children with visual impairment may require reading materials in large print or Braille; students with hearing impairment may require hearing aids and/or instruction in sign language; those with physical disabilities may need special equipment; those with emotional disturbances may need smaller and more highly structured classes; and children with special gifts or talents may require access to working professionals. "Related services—special transportation, psychological assessment, physical and occupational therapy, medical treatment, and counseling—may be necessary if special education is to be effective" (Hallahan and Kauffman 2003, 13).

Special Education Laws

Until 1975, the needs of students with disabilities were primarily met through self-contained special education classes within regular schools. That year, however, Congress passed the **Education for All Handicapped Children Act (Public Law 94-142)**. This act guaranteed to all children with disabilities a free and appropriate public education. The law, which applied to every teacher and every school in the country, outlined extensive procedures to ensure that exceptional students between the ages of three and eighteen were granted due process in regard to identification, placement, and educational services received. As a result of PL 94-142, the participation of students with disabilities in all classrooms and school programs became routine.

In 1990, PL 94-142 was replaced by the **Individuals with Disabilities Education Act (IDEA)**. IDEA included the major provisions of PL 94-142 and extended the availability of a free, appropriate education to youth with disabilities between the ages of three and twenty-one years of age. IDEA, which is one of the most important and far-reaching pieces of educational legislation ever passed in this country, has several provisions with which all teachers should be familiar. In 1997, the **Amendments to the Individuals with Disabilities Education Act (IDEA 97)** were passed. IDEA 97, which went beyond IDEA's focus on public school *access* for students with disabilities to emphasize educational *outcomes*, modified eligibility requirements, IEP guidelines, public and private placements, student discipline guidelines, and procedural safeguards.

Least Restrictive Environment   IDEA requires that all children with disabilities be educated in the **least restrictive environment**. In other words, a student must be mainstreamed into a general education classroom whenever such integration is feasible and appropriate and the child would receive educational benefit from such placement. Figure 3.7 on page 120 shows the educational service options for students with disabilities, from the least restrictive to the most restrictive. Among students with high-incidence disabilities (those with a child count over 100,000), students with speech or language impairments and specific learning disabilities are served in the regular classroom for most of the school day. Students with emotional disturbance, mental retardation, and multiple disabilities typically receive services outside the regular classroom for more than 60 percent of the school day (President's Commission on Excellence in Special Education 2002).

Individualized Education Plan   Every child with a disability is to have a written **individualized education plan (IEP)** that meets the child's needs and specifies educational goals, methods for achieving those goals, and the number and quality of special educational services to be provided. The IEP must be reviewed annually by five parties: (1) a parent or guardian, (2) the child, (3) a teacher, (4) a professional who has recently evaluated the child, and (5) others, usually the principal or a special-education resource person from the school district.

Related Services   IDEA 97 ensures that students with disabilities receive any related services, including "transportation, and such developmental, corrective, and other supportive services as may be required to assist a child with a disability to benefit from special education" (Amendments to IDEA 97).

Figure 3.7   Educational service options for students with disabilities.

Level	Educational Delivery System	Professional Responsibility
Most inclusive **I**	Student placed in general classroom; no additional or specialized assistance	*Greatest number of pupils*
II	Student placed in general classroom; consultative specialist provides assistance to classroom teacher	General education has primary responsibility for student's educational program. Special education is support service designed to facilitate student's success in educational mainstream.
III	Student placed in general classroom for majority of school day; attends special education resource room for specialized instruction in areas of need	
IV	Student placed in special education class for majority of school day; attends general class in subject areas consonant with capabilities	
V	Student placed in full-time special education class in general education school	Special education has primary resonsibility for student's educational program.
VI	Student placed in separate school for children with special needs	
VII	*Most restrictive* Student educated through homebound or hospital instructional program	*Least number of pupils*

Source: Michael L. Hardman, Clifford J. Drew, and M. Winston Egan, *Human Exceptionality: Society, School, and Family,* 7th ed., p. 29. Boston: Allyn and Bacon. Copyright © 2002 by Allyn and Bacon. Reprinted by permission.

Confidentiality of Records   IDEA also ensures that records on a child are kept confidential. Parental permission is required before any official may look at a child's records. Moreover, parents can amend a child's records if they feel information in it is misleading, inaccurate, or violates the child's rights.

Due Process   IDEA gives parents the right to disagree with an IEP or an evaluation of their child's abilities. If a disagreement arises, it is settled through an impartial due process hearing presided over by an officer appointed by the state. At the hearing, parents may be represented by a lawyer, give evidence, and cross-examine, and are entitled to receive a transcript of the hearing and a written decision on the case. If either the parents or the school district disagree with the outcome, the case may then be taken to the civil courts.

Meeting the Mainstreaming Challenge

To help teachers satisfy the provisions of IDEA, school districts across the nation have developed in-service programs designed to acquaint classroom teachers with the unique needs of students with disabilities. In addition, colleges and universities with preservice programs for educators have added courses on teaching students with special educational needs.

The guidelines for IDEA suggest that schools must make a significant effort to include, or mainstream, *all* children in the classroom. However, it is not clear how far schools must go to meet this **mainstreaming** requirement. For example, should children with severe disabilities be included in general education classrooms if they are unable to do the academic work? Recent court cases have ruled that students with severe disabilities must be included if there is a potential benefit for the child, if the class would stimulate the child's language development, or if other students could act as appropriate role models for the child. In one case, the court ordered a school district to place a child with an IQ of 44 in a regular second-grade classroom and rejected as exaggerated the district's claim that the placement would be prohibitively expensive (*Board of Education, Sacramento City Unified School District v. Holland* 1992). In another case, the court rejected a school district's argument that inclusion of a child with a severe disability would be so disruptive as to significantly impair the learning of the other children (*Oberti v. Board of Education of the Borough of Clementon School District* 1992).

To meet the mainstreaming challenge, teachers must have knowledge of various disabilities and the teaching methods and materials appropriate for each. Because teachers with negative attitudes toward students with special needs can convey those feelings to all students in a class and thereby reduce the effectiveness of mainstreaming (Lewis and Doorlag 1999), general education teachers must have positive attitudes toward students receiving special education. An accepting, supportive climate can significantly enhance the self-confidence of students with disabilities.

In addition, Hallahan and Kauffman suggest that all teachers should be prepared to participate in the education of exceptional learners. Teachers should be willing to do the following:

1. Make maximum effort to accommodate individual students' needs.
2. Evaluate academic abilities and disabilities.
3. Refer [students] for evaluation [as appropriate].
4. Participate in eligibility conferences [for special education].
5. Participate in writing individualized education programs.
6. Communicate with parents or guardians.
7. Participate in due process hearings and negotiations.

8. Collaborate with other professionals in identifying and making maximum use of exceptional students' abilities (2003, 19–20).

The Debate over Inclusion

Whereas mainstreaming refers to the application of the least restrictive environment clause of PL 94-142, **inclusion** goes beyond mainstreaming to integrate all students with disabilities into general education classes and school life with the active support of special educators and other specialists and service providers, as well as **assistive technology** and adaptive software. Advocates of inclusion believe that "if students cannot meet traditional academic expectations, then those expectations should be changed. They reject the mainstreaming assumption that settings dictate the type and intensity of services and propose instead the concept of inclusion" (Friend and Bursuck 2002, 4).

Full inclusion goes even further and "represents the belief or philosophy that students with disabilities should be fully integrated into general education classrooms and schools and that their instruction should be based on the abilities, not their disabilities" (Friend and Bursuck 2002, 4). According to the full-inclusion approach, if a child needs support services, these are brought *to the child*; the child does not have to participate in a pull-out program to receive support services. Advocates of full inclusion maintain that pull-out programs stigmatize participating students because they are separated from their general-education classmates, and pull-out programs discourage collaboration between general and special education teachers. Those who oppose full inclusion maintain that classroom teachers, who may be burdened with large class sizes and be assigned to schools with inadequate support services, often lack the training and instructional materials to meet the needs of all exceptional students.

In addition, some parents of children with disabilities believe that full inclusion could mean the elimination of special education as we know it along with the range of services currently guaranteed by federal special education laws. Full inclusion, they reason, would make them depend upon individual states, not the federal government, to meet their children's needs. Moreover, some parents believe that special education classes provide their children with important benefits.

How do classroom teachers feel about inclusion? Lin Chang, an eighth-grade teacher, addresses the concerns general education teachers may have about the availability of resources to help them be successful in inclusive classrooms.

> *At first I was worried that it would all be my responsibility. But after meeting with the special education teacher, I realized that we would work together and I would have additional resources if I needed them (Vaughn, Bos, and Schumm 1997, 18).*

In addition, the following comments by Octavio Gonzalez, a ninth-grade English teacher who has three students with disabilities in two of his five sections of

English, express the satisfaction that teachers can experience in inclusive classrooms:

> *At first I was nervous about having students with disabilities in my class. One of the students has a learning disability, one student has serious motor problems and is in a wheelchair, and the third student has vision problems. Now I have to say the adaptations I make to meet their special learning needs actually help all of the students in my class. I think that I am a better teacher because I think about accommodations now (Vaughn, Bos, and Schumm 1997, 18).*

The attitudes of the two teachers quoted above are confirmed in research on teachers' attitudes toward inclusion. Two studies, for example, found that teachers who had experience with inclusion and opportunities for professional development had more positive attitudes toward inclusion and more confidence in their ability to fulfill students' IEPs (Avramidis, Bayliss, and Burden 2000; Van Reusen, Shoho, and Barker 2000).

Equal Opportunity for Exceptional Learners

Like many groups in our society, exceptional learners have often not received the kind of education that most effectively meets their needs. Approximately 10 percent of the population aged three to twenty-one is classified as exceptional; that is, "they require special education because they are markedly different from most children in one or more of the following ways: They may have mental retardation, learning disabilities, emotional or behavioral disorders, physical disabilities, disorders of communication, autism, traumatic brain injury, impaired hearing, impaired sight, or special gifts or talents" (Hallahan and Kauffman 2003, 7).

Just as there are no easy answers for how you should meet the needs of students from diverse cultural backgrounds, there is no single strategy for you to follow to ensure that exceptional students in your classroom receive an appropriate education. The key, however, lies in not losing sight of the fact that "*the most important characteristics of exceptional children are their abilities*" (Hallahan and Kauffman 2003, 6).

To build on students' strengths, classroom teachers must work cooperatively and collaboratively with special education teachers, and students in special education programs must not become isolated from their peers. In addition, teachers must understand how some people can be perceived as "different" and presumed to be "handicapped" because of their appearance or physical condition. Evidence suggests, for example, that people who are short, obese, or unattractive are often victims of discrimination, as are people with conditions such as AIDS, cancer, multiple sclerosis, or epilepsy. Significantly, many individuals with clinically diagnosable and classifiable impairments or disabilities do not perceive themselves as *handicapped*. The term itself means permanently unable to be treated equally.

Officially labeling students has become a necessity with the passage of the laws that provide education and related services for exceptional students. The classification labels help determine which students qualify for the special services, educational programs, and individualized instruction provided by the laws, and they bring to educators' attention many exceptional children and youth whose educational needs could be overlooked, neglected, or inadequately served otherwise. Detrimental aspects include the fact that classification systems are imperfect and have arbitrary cutoff points that sometimes lead to injustices. Also, labels tend to evoke negative expectations, which can cause teachers to avoid and underteach these students and their peers to isolate or reject them, thereby stigmatizing individuals, sometimes permanently. The most serious detriment, however, is that students so labeled are taught to feel inadequate, inferior, and limited in terms of their options for growth.

How Can You Teach All Learners in Your Inclusive Classroom?

As a teacher, you will have a responsibility to address all students' developmental, individual, and exceptional learning needs. Although addressing the range of student differences in the inclusive classroom is challenging, it can also be very rewarding. Consider the comments of three teachers who reflect on their experiences teaching diverse learners:

> *This is a note I wrote on the bottom of her [final] report card: "Sara is a sweet, bright child. As much as she could be a challenge, she made me a better teacher by keeping me on my toes. I will truly, truly miss her!"*
>
> (Teacher of a student with Turner syndrome)

> *It was a gratifying year. I had no idea at the beginning that we would see the progress that we did. . . . Irina came back for a visit today. She ran right up to me and gave me a hug. A year ago, such an obvious display of emotion would have been unthinkable!*
>
> (Teacher of a student with an "attachment disorder" resulting from a lack of human contact during the years she spent in a Romanian orphanage)

> *On complex and difficult days, it sometimes feels like it would be a lot easier not to have children with special needs in my classroom. . . . But, you know, I really mourned having to give Daniel up at the end of the school year. There was a special connection I made with that child, and I wanted to be sure that his next teacher felt the same way.*
>
> (Teacher of a student with Down syndrome)
> (Kostelnik, Onaga, Rohde, Whiren 2002, 55, 92–93, 149).

It is beyond the scope of this book to present in-depth instructional strategies to address students' diverse learning needs. However, attention to three key areas will help you to create a truly inclusive classroom: collaborative consultation, partnerships with parents, and assistive technology for special learners.

Collaborative Consultation with Other Professionals

One approach to meeting the needs of all students is known as **collaborative consultation**, an approach in which a classroom teacher meets with one or more other professionals (a special educator, school psychologist, or resource teacher, for example) to focus on the learning needs of one or more students. The following first-year teacher describes how collaborative consultation enabled her to meet the needs of a special student.

> *I taught a Down's syndrome child who was very frustrated. I convened a meeting that included district experts, his parent, and a resource teacher, suggesting a change in educational strategy. All agreed to pilot the plan, and things have worked more smoothly ever since. It was a very rewarding experience (Sallie Mae Corporation 1995, 11).*

Collaborative consultation is based on mutuality and reciprocity (Hallahan and Kauffman 2003), and participants assume equal responsibility for meeting students' needs. Friend and Bursuck (2002, 95–96) make the following suggestions for working with a consultant: "prepare for meetings, be open to the consultant's suggestions, use the consultant's strategies systematically, and document the effectiveness of the ideas you try."

To meet the educational goals of a student's IEP, regular education teachers are part of an IEP team that includes special educators, other support personnel, and parents (see Figure 3.8 on page 126). The following special education professionals are among those who consult with and/or collaborate with regular education teachers:

- *Consulting teacher*—A special educator who provides technical assistance such as arranging the physical setting, helping to plan for instruction, or developing approaches for assessing students' learning
- *Resource-room teacher*—A special educator who provides instruction in a resource room for students with disabilities
- *School psychologist*—Consults with the general education teacher and arranges for the administration of appropriate psychological, educational, and behav-ioral assessment instruments; may observe a student's behavior in the classroom
- *Speech and language specialist*—Assesses students' communication abilities and works with general education teachers to develop educational programs for students with speech and/or language disorders
- *Physical therapist*—Provides physical therapy for students with physical disabilities
- *Occupational therapist*—Instructs students with disabilities to prepare them for everyday living and work-related activities

Working with Parents

In addition to working with education professionals to meet the learning needs of all students, you will need to develop good working relationships with parents. As the following comment by the mother of a daughter with Rett syndrome

Figure 3.8   Student's IEP team.

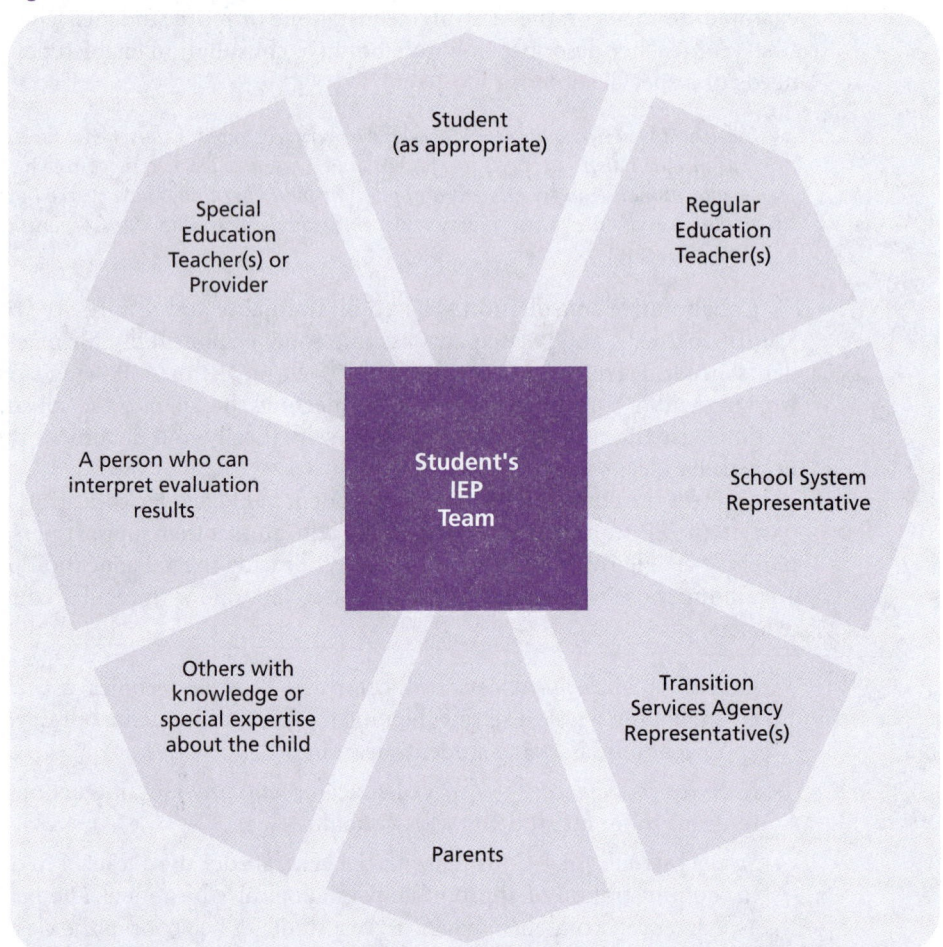

Source: Office of Special Education Programs and Rehabilitation Services, U.S. Department of Education, *A Guide to the Individualized Education Program,* July 2000, p. 9. Washington, DC: U.S. Department of Education.

makes clear, parents of children with disabilities expect their teachers to be committed to meeting the learning needs of their children: "My child will never be considered a poster child. She does not give professionals the satisfaction of making great progress, nor is she terribly social. But I need the same type of investment by professionals as any other parents of children with disabilities. The most important thing any educator can do for me is to love my Mary" (Howard et al. 2001, 123).

Parents of exceptional children can be a source of valuable information about the characteristics, abilities, and needs of their children; they can be helpful in securing necessary services for their children; and they can assist you by reviewing skills at home and praising their children for their learning. The power of partnerships with parents is evident, for instance, in three examples from the U.S. Department of Education's *Schools with IDEAs That Work* (1999), state-by-state descriptions of schools that work closely with parents to implement IDEA.

- *O'Loughlin Elementary School*—At this award-winning school in Hays, Kansas, parents pay for after school programs such as Young Astronauts and O'Loughlin Singers; and students lead the four parent-teacher conferences per year.
- *Sudduth Elementary School*—Because this rural school of approximately 1,000 students in Starkville, Mississippi, has limited fiscal and human resources, parent volunteers come and go throughout the day; during the first eight weeks of school one year, parents had 1,129 contacts with the school.
- *Mirror Lake Middle School*—At this school in Chugiak, Alaska, parents volunteer in the office, classroom, and other areas of the school; they frequently help teach lessons and serve as guest speakers in classrooms.

Assistive Technology for Special Learners

Each day, most people use assistive technology—that is, technology that extends or augments human ability. For example, within the last day have you done any of the following?

- Worn glasses or contact lenses?
- Used the speed-dial button on your cell phone?
- Used a remote to change channels on a TV?
- Entered a building that had an automatic door?
- Used an Internet search engine to locate information?

Such technologies are tools we use to help make certain tasks easier. Similarly, technological advances have increased the ability of teachers to create inclusive classrooms. It is now easier for exceptional students to learn and communicate. It is estimated that there are over 25,000 assistive technology devices designed to enhance the abilities of persons with disabilities (Edyburn 2003). Assistive technology is "anything that improves the functional performance of an individual with a disability" (Edyburn 2003, 2).

Assistive technologies enhance the learning of students with disabilities in many ways. For example, computer-based word processing and math tutorials can assist students with learning disabilities in acquiring literacy and computational skills. Students with hearing impairments can communicate with other students by using telecommunications equipment. Students with physical disabilities can operate computers through voice commands or with a single switch or key. The following are some recent developments in assistive technology:

1. Talking word processor
2. Speech synthesizer
3. Touch-sensitive computer screens
4. Computer screen image enlarger
5. Teletypewriter (TTY) (connects to telephone and types a spoken message to another TTY)
6. Customized computer keyboards
7. Ultrasonic head controls for computers
8. Voice-recognition computers
9. Television closed captioning
10. Kurzweil reading machine (scans print and reads it aloud)

In addition, assistive technology includes devices to enhance the mobility and everyday activities of people with disabilities (e.g., wheelchairs, lifts, adaptive driving controls, scooters, laser canes, feeders). The Technology in Teaching feature describes how word-prediction software can enhance the writing abilities of students with disabilities.

The IEP for this student with multiple disabilities provides for assistive technology, which enables him to create and respond to language.

Technology in Teaching

How can word-prediction software enhance the writing abilities of students with disabilities?

"What should I write?" "What words will best express what I want to say?" Although most people find these questions to be at least somewhat difficult to answer, students with disabilities may confront unique challenges when they write. Students with learning disabilities may not be able to retain ideas in their memory long enough to express them in writing; others may have difficulty with spelling; and students with motor disabilities may be challenged when forming letters with pen or pencil or making repetitive keystrokes on a word processor.

Students with disabilities that affect their ability to write can be assisted by word-prediction software that reduces the number of keystrokes needed to type words. When writing with word-prediction software, a student types the first letter of a word, and then a numbered list of words beginning with that letter appears on the computer screen. If the desired word is on the list, the student enters the number and the word is typed automatically. For example, assume a student wants to write the word *tonight* to complete the sentence "I will watch TV *tonight*." First, she enters a "t," and a list of common "t" words is shown in screen #1. Because the word *tonight* is not on this list, she types

an "o," and screen #2 appears. Because *tonight* is on this list, she types the number "3," and the word is entered automatically. Thus, the seven keystrokes needed to write *tonight* have been reduced to three.

The following list describes additional features of various word-prediction software programs.

- *Synthesized speech output*—human speech is artificially produced by a software program.
- *Prediction methods*—Some programs predict on the basis of spelling only; others consider earlier words in the sentence; for example, only nouns are listed after the word *a* or *an*.
- *List updating*—After "learning" a student's vocabulary, the word-prediction program tailors the word prediction lists to the student's usage. Some programs update automatically; others allow the user to decide when to update.
- *Prediction-window customizing*—The size, the screen location, and the amount of words in the word prediction window can be customized by the user.
- *Keyboard-sensitivity adjustment*—Keyboard sensitivity can be adjusted to prevent repetition if keys are not quickly released.

I will watch TV t

Word Prediction Window:

1 talk   2 that   3 the

4 this   5 them   6 they

Screen #1

I will watch TV to

Word Prediction Window:

1 today   2 tomorrow   3 tonight

4 topic   5 toward   6 town

Screen #2

Many technology-related special education resources and curriculum materials are available on the Internet. One of these sites, The National Center to Improve Practice in Special Education through Technology, Media, and Materials, also maintains discussion forums for teachers of students with disabilities. Clearly, the dazzling revolution in microelectronics will continue to yield new devices to enhance the learning of all students.

Summary

How Do Students' Needs Change as They Develop?

- People move through different stages of cognitive, psychosocial, and moral development throughout their life spans.

- Piaget maintains that children, who reason differently from adults, pass through four stages of cognitive development as they mature. Effective teachers are aware of the characteristics of school-age children's thinking during three of these stages: the preoperational stage, the concrete operations stage, and the formal operations stage.

- According to Erikson's model of psychosocial development, people pass through eight stages of emotional and social development throughout their lives. Each stage is characterized by a "crisis" with a positive and negative pole. Healthy development depends upon a satisfactory, positive resolution of each crisis.

- Kohlberg believes that moral development, the reasoning people use to decide between right and wrong, evolves through three levels. Evidence suggests that males may base their moral reasoning on rights and rules, and females on altruism and self-sacrifice. Many teachers and schools emphasize character education to "teach" moral reasoning and values.

- Maslow suggests that human growth and development depends on how well the individual's biological and psychological needs have been met. According to his hierarchy of needs model, people must satisfy their survival and safety needs before addressing "higher" needs such as self-actualization.

- Teachers must be aware of the developmental stresses and tasks students encounter during childhood and early and late adolescence.

How Do Students Vary in Intelligence?

- There are conflicting definitions of *intelligence*; they range from "what IQ tests measure" to "goal-directed adaptive behavior." Some theorists believe that intelligence is a single, basic ability, though recent research suggests that there are many forms of intelligence.

- According to Howard Gardner's theory of multiple intelligences, there are at least eight human intelligences.

- Students differ in their learning styles—the patterns of behavior they prefer to use while learning. Although there is conflict about the concept of learning styles, effective teachers are aware of differences among students regarding their preferences for learning activities.

How Do Students Vary in Ability and Disability?

- Some students are "exceptional" because they have abilities or disabilities that distinguish them from other students. Students with physical, cognitive, or emotional disabilities and students who are gifted and talented have unique learning needs.

- There is a lack of agreement regarding the definition of *learning disability (LD)*. Teachers can identify students with learning disabilities by noting difficulties they have acquiring and processing new information. Learning disabilities are the most common disability among students, with attention deficit hyperactivity disorder (ADHD) and attention deficit disorder (ADD) the most common learning disabilities.

- There are many forms of giftedness. Among the approaches used to meet the learning needs of gifted students are acceleration, self-directed or independent study, individual education programs, special or magnet schools, and weekend and summer programs.

What Are Special Education, Mainstreaming, and Inclusion?

- Special education includes a variety of educational services to meet the needs of exceptional students. Key provisions of the Individuals with Disabilities Education Act (IDEA) include least restrictive environment, individualized education program (IEP), confidentiality of records, and due process.

- *Mainstreaming* is the process of integrating students with disabilities into regular classrooms.

- *Inclusion* integrates all students with disabilities into regular classrooms, with the support of special education services as necessary. *Full inclusion* is the integration of students with disabilities in general education classrooms at all times regardless of the severity of the disability.

How Can You Teach All Learners in Your Inclusive Classroom?

- Though challenging, teachers have a responsibility to create inclusive classrooms that address the developmental, individual, and exceptional learning needs of all students.

- Through collaborative consultation, an arrangement whereby the regular classroom teacher collaborates with other education professionals, teachers can meet the needs of exceptional students. Collaborative consultation is based on mutuality and reciprocity, and all participants assume responsibility for meeting students' needs.

- By developing effective relationships with parents of exceptional students, teachers acquire valuable information and support.

- An array of assistive technologies and resources is available to help exceptional students learn and communicate in inclusive classrooms.

Key Terms and Concepts

Amendments to the Individuals with Disabilities Education Act (IDEA 97), 119
assistive technology, 122
attention deficit disorder (ADD), 113
attention deficit hyperactivity disorder (ADHD), 113
character education, 99
cognitive development, 93
collaborative consultation, 124
concrete operations stage, 93
Education for All Handicapped Children Act (Public Law 94-142), 119

exceptional learners, 110
formal operations stage, 93
full inclusion, 122
gifted and talented, 114
hierarchy of needs, 99
inclusion, 122
individualized education plan (IEP), 119
Individuals with Disabilities Education Act (IDEA), 119
intelligence, 105
learning disability (LD), 113

learning styles, 109
least restrictive environment, 119
mainstreaming, 121
moral reasoning, 93
multiple intelligences, 107
preoperational stage, 93
psychosocial crisis, 96
psychosocial development, 93
special education, 118
stages of development, 92
students with disabilities, 111

Reflective Application Activities

Discussion Questions

1. What are the characteristics of teachers who are successful teachers of students with disabilities? How can you acquire or further develop those characteristics yourself?

2. What are the benefits of IQ tests? The limitations? Should teachers know the IQs of their students? If so, how should teachers "use" that information?

Professional Journal

1. Describe your preferred learning environment. Where, when, and how do you learn best? Does certain lighting, food, or music seem to enhance your learning?

2. Think about how you acquire new information—do you prefer being analytical and abstract or commonsensical and concrete? Do you prefer thinking about things or doing things? Do you prefer to learn alone, in a small group, or in a large group? When given an assignment, do you prefer a lot of structure and details, or do you prefer more unstructured or open-ended assignments?

3. Relate Erikson's stages of psychosocial development to your own experiences as a child and as an adolescent. How did sources of stress, psychosocial crises, and your resolution of them affect your learning in school?

Online Assignments

1. Investigate sources of information on students with disabilities or exceptional learners at the ERIC Clearinghouse on Disabilities and Gifted Education. This website is main-tained by the Council for Exceptional Children (CEC) in Reston, Virginia. Then visit the National Information Center for Children and Youth with Disabilities website. This government clearinghouse answers questions about disability issues, refers you to disability organizations, provides fact sheets, and identifies relevant educational resources in your state.

2. "Observe" children online by locating chat rooms by and for children and youth. As an adult, you may not be allowed to participate, but in many cases you will be invited to visit (called "lurking" in Internet jargon). What educational interests, needs, and concerns do students share with one another? How might visiting students' sites be viewed as an extension of your field experiences as an education major or a student teacher? What teacher observation techniques and protocols could you use in this situation? What are some ethical concerns about this practice? How might any new knowledge of students gained in this way help make you a more effective teacher?

Observations and Interviews

1. Observe in a classroom that has exceptional students. What steps does the teacher take to meet the needs of these students? Interview the teacher to determine what he or she sees as the challenges and rewards of teaching exceptional students.

2. Visit a school at the level you plan to teach. Interview the counselor, asking questions about the problems that bring students to the counselor most often. If possible, shadow the school counselor for a day.

Professional Portfolio

For the grade level and content area you are preparing to teach, identify learning activities that address each of the eight multiple intelligences identified by Gardner. For example, you might plan activities such as the following. For one activity in each category, list the preparations you would need to make and/or the materials you would need to gather, and add this information to your portfolio.

Logical-Mathematical

- Design an experiment on. . .
- Describe the rules for a new board game called. . .

Linguistic

- Write a short story about. . .
- Write a biographical sketch of. . .

Musical

- Write song lyrics for. . .
- Locate music that sounds like. . .

Spatial

- Draw, paint, or sculpt a. . .
- Create an advertisement for. . .

Bodily-Kinesthetic

- Role-play a person who is. . .
- Do a dance that shows. . .

Intrapersonal

- Assess your ability to. . .
- Describe how you feel about. . .

Interpersonal

- Show one or more of your classmates how to. . .
- In a small group, construct a. . .

Naturalist

- Identify the trees found in. . .
- Classify the rocks found in. . .

4 Assessing Student Learning

*T*he typical teacher will spend one-quarter to one-third of his or her professional time involved in assessment-related activities. . . . without question, teachers need to know and understand the principles of sound assessment.

—Rick Stiggins, "New Assessment Beliefs for a New School Mission,"
Phi Delta Kappan, September 2004

You are a first-year teacher at a school in a city of about 500,000 people. Your state has an induction program that provides support for teachers during their first year of teaching. As part of this induction program, new teachers are required to observe in classrooms of other teachers during the year. Throughout the year you have observed two fifth- and sixth-grade social studies teachers—Mrs. Allen and Ms. Rodriguez. The following are excerpts from the notes you took during two recent observations. The excerpts describe how Mrs. Allen and Ms. Rodriguez typically assess student learning.

Mrs. Allen's Classroom

The task for [Mrs. Allen's] fifth-graders required them to copy a set of questions about famous explorers from a work sheet and to add the correct short-answer responses in the appropriate spots. The class spent thirty minutes on this exercise, which was part of a larger unit on exploration and which the teacher, Mrs. Allen, described as very consistent with the typical assessment.

During the four times that [I] observed Allen's hour-long classes, students read aloud from the textbook, a routine occasionally punctuated with Allen's asking them factual recall questions. During one class, students copied a chart from the board organizing the facts from the reading into categories. After finding more facts to fill up the chart, the students then completed a work sheet crossword puzzle built from the vocabulary words of the lesson.

Ms. Rodriguez's Classroom

As an assessment of their learning, Ms. Rodriguez had her class of fifth- and sixth-graders research and write a paper on ecology, an assignment that occupied forty hours of class time during the twelve-week grading period. Each student produced several drafts of the paper and met individually with the teacher several times to discuss the drafts. Before they began the project, students received eleven pages of written directions on how to research, organize, and write the paper, including a step-by-step checklist for completing the assignment, a sample outline, and sample bibliography entries. The paper counted for 75 percent of the student's grade for the twelve-week period (Marks, Newmann, and Gamoran, 1996, 59–60).

Guiding Questions

1. What is the role of assessment in teaching?
2. What methods can you use to assess student learning?
3. What are emerging trends in classroom assessment?
4. How can you develop high-quality classroom assessments?

Newspaper headlines and special reports on television frequently remind us that the public is concerned about declining test scores, the performance of U.S. students on international comparisons of achievement, and our nation's standing in a competitive global economy. Pressure to get "back to the basics" and drives by parents, citizen groups, and politicians to hold teachers accountable have led to a nationwide push to develop more effective ways to assess student learning.

Despite the increased emphasis on assessing student learning, it is difficult to determine what students really know as a result of being taught. As a veteran teacher of twenty-seven years noted: "How do we truly know when our students have sufficient knowledge, understanding, and the skills required to be successful with the learning? In short, how do we know that our students know?" (Tileston 2004, 13).

Clearly, the purpose of teaching is to develop within students an understanding of the world around them. However, our knowledge of human nature tells us that it is hard to determine precisely what another person does or does not understand. Though the aims of teaching may be specified in carefully worded standards, one of the realities of teaching, as the following junior high school teacher points out, is that some of what students learn may be hard to measure:

> There is no clear end result. . . . That frustrates me. I want so badly for my joy [of teaching] to be neatly tied up so that I can look at it admiringly. . . . I want so badly to see my successes—I don't know, give me certificates or badges or jelly beans. Then I can stack them up, count them, and rate myself as a teacher (Henry et al. 1995, 68–69).

Currently, there is a nationwide emphasis on high-stakes testing. That is, the tests have "high-stakes" consequences for students, teachers, and administrators. For example, students' performance on a test may determine if teachers at a school receive a merit pay increase. High-stakes tests are one way to hold teachers accountable for student learning.

However, the conventional wisdom among teachers is that they are often uncertain about just what their students have learned. We have enormous amounts of assessment data, but often little understanding of what lies behind a student's written response and little understanding of what the assessment experience really means to a student. As one educational researcher concludes: "The inaccessibility of data is similar both in science and in learning. We cannot directly 'see' subatomic particles, nor can we 'see' the inner-workings of the mind and emotions of the child. Both are inferential: both are subject to human interpretation" (Costa 1984, 202).

On the one hand, then, when you become a teacher you must be realistic about the challenges of assessing student learning; on the other, you must continuously work to become aware of the latest approaches to assessing students' learning. Figure 4.1 presents a set of guiding principles for teachers to follow in developing a student-centered approach to classroom assessment.

As the opening scenario for this chapter illustrates, teachers can use very different methods for assessing student learning. For example, what differences did you

Figure 4.1   The principles of sound assessment: A critical blend.

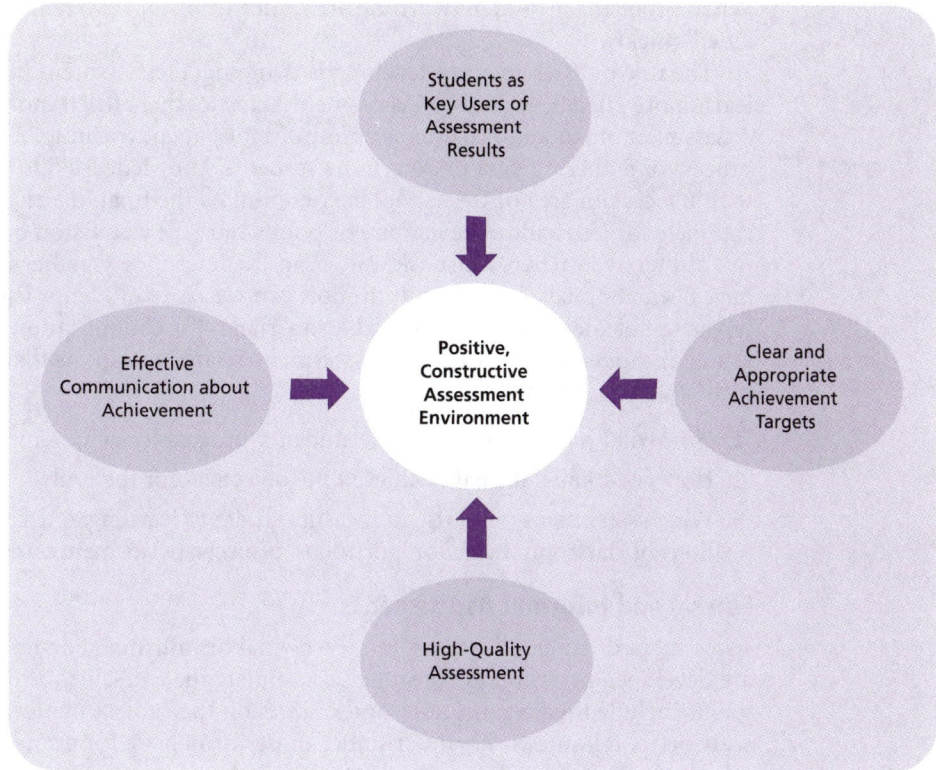

Source: Adapted from Richard J. Stiggins, *Student-Involved Classroom Assessment,* 3rd ed. Upper Saddle River, NJ: Merrill, 2000, p. 18.

notice between the assessment activities in Mrs. Allen's classroom and Ms. Rodriguez's classroom? What do you think Mrs. Allen's students thought about the learning tasks they were asked to complete? Ms. Rodriguez's students? When you were a fifth- or sixth-grade student, which teacher would you have preferred? Why?

What Is the Role of Assessment in Teaching?

During the 1980s and early 1990s, numerous studies were conducted to identify the characteristics of successful (or effective) schools. A common finding in these studies was that successful schools place primary emphasis on assessing student learning. The environment, or culture, of these schools emphasizes the achievement of academic excellence *for all students*. Toward this end, successful schools have definite procedures in place for making frequent, systematic assessments of student learning. In short, the learning of students at these schools is monitored closely. When problems in student learning are noticed, appropriate remediation is provided quickly.

The role of assessment in teaching is twofold: (1) assessment helps students learn more effectively, and (2) assessment helps teachers teach more effectively. Assessment of student learning is an important part of teaching. **Assessment** is the process of gathering data to determine students' knowledge, skills, and attitudes within a certain area of the school curriculum. As the final question in the Tyler rationale for curriculum development points out (see discussion of Tyler rationale in Chapter 1), teachers must ask "How can we determine whether [our] purposes have been attained." In other words, how can we assess students' learning? Similarly, the last element in the "Generic Lesson Plan for a Unit of Study" outline presented in Appendix 4.1 lists three assessment-related questions that all teachers must ask:

1. How will I measure and evaluate students' progress or achievement?
2. How will I know if I have achieved the objectives for the unit?
3. What assessments will I use to measure students' learning: quizzes, tests, observations of classroom behavior, portfolios, projects, performances, etc.?

Formal and Informal Assessments

Assessment of student learning may be formal or informal. **Formal assessments** are developed prior to having students complete the assessments. Formal assessments include final exams, tests, and quizzes on the subject matter studied; in-class seatwork and homework; and critiques of performances, for example, tryouts for a school play or athletic team.

Informal assessments occur during teaching, and they are made spontaneously. The teacher might, for example, note students' facial expressions to determine their level of understanding of the material taught, listen carefully to a student's explanation of how she solved a problem in mathematics; or ask questions to monitor students' level of understanding during a lecture. Teachers frequently make informal assessments of their students at the beginning of each school day or class session.

Informal assessments are less obvious to the classroom observer. In other words, during a classroom observation, an observer may not know just when a teacher is making informal assessments of student learning. Actually, professional teachers continuously assess students' responses to their teaching.

How Teachers Use Assessments

For most people, the term *classroom assessment* brings to mind a four-step process: (1) the teacher prepares a test (or selects a preexisting test) to cover material that has been taught, (2) students take the test, (3) the teacher corrects the test, and (4) the teacher assigns grades based on how well students performed on the test.

Classroom assessment, however, involves more—it provides information teachers use (1) to determine how well students are learning the material being taught; (2) to identify the type of feedback that will enhance student learning; (3) to develop strategies for improving their effectiveness as teachers; and (4) to determine if students have reached certain levels of performance. For example, the Teachers' Voices feature on page 140 illustrates how two teachers used assessments of students' learning to evaluate their effectiveness as teachers.

What Methods Can You Use to Assess Student Learning?

The assessment of student learning will enable you to make judgments about the performance of students and about your performance as a teacher. You will use assessment to evaluate your effectiveness because you recognize that how well students learn depends on how well you teach. Furthermore, you will realize that "assessment is more than a collection of techniques. It is a systematic process that plays a significant role in effective teaching" (Linn and Gronlund 2000, xiii).

Assessment has been defined as "the full range of procedures used to gain information about student learning (observations, ratings of performances or projects, paper-and-pencil tests) and the formation of value judgments concerning learning progress" (Linn and Gronlund 2000, 31). As a professional teacher, you will strive to become aware of the latest approaches to assessing student learning. You will understand the critical role that assessment plays in teaching and the importance of "establishing credible performance standards, communicating these standards to students, and providing feedback to students on their progress" (McMillan 2001, xiii). In addition, the classroom assessments you develop will reflect four "guiding principles": "(1) Students are the key assessment users, (2) Clear and appropriate targets are essential, (3) Accurate assessment is a must, (4) Sound assessments must be accomplished by effective communication" (Stiggins 2001, 17–23).

Quantitative and Qualitative Assessments

To assess student learning, you can use both quantitative and qualitative approaches. Quantitative approaches make use of measurement and evaluation techniques—such as teacher-made classroom tests composed of multiple-choice, true-false, matching, or essay items—or performance-based assessments. **Quantitative assessments** yield numerical scores that teachers use to evaluate student learning as well as the effectiveness of their teaching.

Qualitative approaches may include formal and informal observations of students' performance on various learning tasks, the manner with which they approach those learning tasks, or students' self-reports of their interests and attitudes. For example, teachers routinely assess students' work habits. *Work habits* is a term suggested by the Coalition of Essential Schools for various dispositions important for effective thinking and learning, including reading with curiosity; reflecting critically on one's own work; developing independence, clarity, and

Teachers' *Voices* Putting Research and Theory into Practice

Eric Learns to Read: Learning Styles at Work

June Hodgin and Caaren Wooliscroft

We have seen dramatic changes in many students in our inclusive classroom since we have employed learning styles strategies. In our class of twenty-two students (ten Hispanic, twelve Anglo), four students were identified as learning disabled and qualified for special education and another three had attention deficit disorders. The students' IQs ranged from 74 to 126.

We introduce learning styles to our students at the beginning of each school year. We expose them to a variety of learning styles elements (for example, working with the lights off, while listening to classical music, or with everyone sitting on the floor) and discuss how the different elements help or hinder learning ability. After reading stories about learning styles and explaining the Learning Styles Model, we hold class discussions.

Our students' scores on the Texas Assessment of Academic Skills (TAAS) during the three-year period from 1993 to 1996 demonstrate the effectiveness of reading styles and inclusion practices. During 1993–94, the year before we implemented reading styles and inclusion, only 50 percent of the regular student population passed the test, and none of the special education children passed. We saw dramatic improvements during the next two years as we implemented the reading styles strategies and inclusion practices. All the regular education students passed the test both years, with 25 percent of special education students passing in 1994–95, and 20 percent in 1995–96. In addition, student mastery of all test objectives increased from 11 percent in 1994, to 67 percent in 1995, to 80 percent in 1996.

We saw another indicator of success in the classroom climate. Our students worked together in heterogeneous small and large groups. Because we did not separate students by ability level, our students were not aware of any labels. The self-esteem, motivation, and attitude of all students improved because they did not feel stress, learning was fun and pleasurable, and it was easy to succeed. We had created a real community of learners.

Questions

1. For Hodgin and Wooliscroft, their students' scores on the TAAS demonstrated the effectiveness of reading styles and inclusion practices. What other types of assessments might they have used to determine the effectiveness of reading styles and inclusion practices?

2. Hodgin and Wolliscroft used their students' scores on the TAAS to reflect on their effectiveness as teachers. How might teachers misuse students' scores on state-mandated tests like the TAAS?

3. Hodgin and Wooliscroft state that "We had created a real community of learners." What are the characteristics of a community of learners?

June Hodgin is a consultant for the Special Education Department in Abilene, Texas; *Caaren N. Wooliscroft* is a third-grade teacher at Alta Vista Elementary School in Abilene. The preceding is excerpted from their article in the March 1997 *Educational Leadership*, pp. 43–45.

incisiveness of thought; willingness to work hard; an ability to manage time effectively; persistence; accuracy and precision; and working collaboratively. **Qualitative assessments** are more subjective than quantitative assessments. However, quantitative assessments are also subjective because teachers must *interpret the meaning* of the scores.

Classroom Assessment

To assess student learning, you will use measurement and evaluation techniques. **Measurement** is the gathering of quantitative data related to the knowledge and skills students have acquired. Measurement yields scores, rankings, or ratings that teachers can use to determine the degree to which students have attained specified standards. At some point in your teacher education program, you will be introduced to basic statistical methods for comparing the learning of students within a group and between groups of students.

Evaluation is a critical teaching skill. In your role as an evaluator, you will make judgments about the performance of students *and* about your own effectiveness as a teacher. **Evaluation** involves making judgments about or assigning a value to measurements the teacher makes of student learning. Successful teachers continually evaluate the effectiveness of their teaching because they recognize that how well students learn depends on how well they teach.

Formative Evaluation When teachers measure students' attainment of knowledge and skills for the purpose of making decisions about their teaching, they are engaging in **formative evaluation**. Teachers use the results of formative evaluations to make decisions about what learning activities are appropriate for students. For example, as an aid to planning for a new unit of instruction, you may assess students' understanding of a subject by having them take a short diagnostic test or quiz, complete homework or seatwork assignments, or participate in a group project.

As a teacher, you will also conduct informal formative evaluations while you are teaching. For example, you will pay close attention to what students say; you will use probing questions to gauge students' understanding of the subject; and you will note students' facial expressions and behavior. During these informal formative evaluations, you will not only assess students' understanding; you will also assess students' attitudes toward learning the subject. For example, in the following, a teacher makes some candid comments about his informal formative evaluations while teaching:

> I'd become dissatisfied with the closed Q & A style that my unthinking teaching had fallen into, and I would frequently be lazy in my acceptance of right answers and sometimes even tacit complicity with a class to make sure none of us had to work too hard. . . . They and I knew that if the Q & A wasn't going smoothly, I'd change the question, answer it myself, or only seek answers from the "brighter students." There must have been times (still are?) where an outside observer would see my lessons as a small discussion group surrounded by many sleepy onlookers (Black et al. 2004, 11).

Summative Evaluation When teachers use measurements of student learning to determine grades at the end of a unit, semester, or year and to decide whether students are ready to proceed to the next phase of their education, they are engaging in **summative evaluation**. Summative evaluations usually provide the teacher with an overview of student learning across a broad range of knowledge and skills. In contrast, formative evaluations are usually more focused and cover a narrower range of knowledge and skills. Teachers also use summative evaluations to make changes in their teaching that might be beneficial with the next group of students. Figure 4.2 illustrates the essential elements of effective classroom assessment and the questions that guide teachers' decision making in this important area of teaching.

Standardized Assessments

Standardized assessments (or standardized tests) are pencil-and-paper tests that are taken by large groups of students and scored in a uniform manner. The test items, the conditions under which students take the test, how the tests are scored, and how the scores are interpreted are "standardized" for all who take the test. This standardization enables educators to compare scores for different groups of students in different schools around the country. **Standardized assessments** are administered at the district, state, and national levels.

The first standardized test in the United States was administered by Horace Mann, Secretary of the Massachusetts State Board of Education, in the mid-1800s. Mann, who eventually came to be known as "father of the common school," wanted to classify students by ability and gather evidence for the effectiveness of the state school system. He hoped to use the results of the state test to further his educational reform efforts. Prior to the use of this standardized test, teachers conducted their own assessments at the individual classroom level.

Current examples of standardized tests are the Iowa Test of Basic Skills, the California Achievement Test, the Metropolitan Achievement Tests, the Stanford Achievement Test, the Scholastic Assessment Test (SAT), and the American College Test (ACT) Assessment. In addition, the federal government funds the National Assessment of Educational Progress (NAEP). The NAEP is periodically used to

Figure 4.2 Effective classroom assessment.

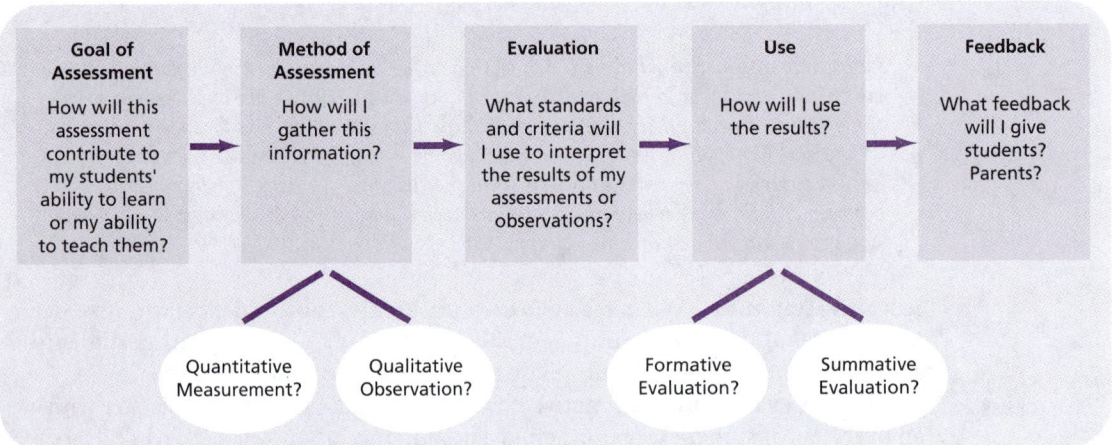

What might be some of the pressures felt by students and teachers as a result of the increased emphasis on testing?

sample student achievement around the country. On a biannual basis, the performance of national samples of nine-, thirteen-, and seventeen-year-olds is assessed. Educational policy makers then use the results—reported by geographic region, gender, and ethnic background—to guide their decision making. First administered in 1969, the NAEP has assessed student learning in all areas of the curriculum.

International Assessments   In 1991, the first **International Assessment of Educational Progress (IAEP)** was conducted, and the achievement of U.S. students was compared to that of students in more than thirty nations. The results indicated that the achievement levels of U.S. students were often below those of students from other countries. Subsequent IAEP comparisons have shown some improvement in the rankings of American students in mathematics and science. Figure 4.3(a), for example, which is based on the **Third International Mathematics and Science Study (TIMSS)** sponsored by the International Association for the Evaluation of Educational Achievement (1997a, 1997b), shows how the mathematics and science achievement levels of fourth-grade U.S. students compare with those of students from several other countries. However, as Figure 4.3(b) shows, the relative standing of U.S. students in these subject areas was significantly lower by the final year of secondary school. Gains in literacy, however, have been more significant; for example, *A First Look—Findings from the National Assessment of Educational Progress* (National Center for Education Statistics 1995) reported that U.S. fourth-graders ranked second in 1995 on a thirty-two-nation survey of reading skills.

Figure 4.3   Nation's average mathematics and science performance compared with the United States.

Nations' Average Mathematics and Science Performance Compared with the United States—Grade 4

MATHEMATICS

Nation	Average
Singapore	625
Korea	611
Japan	597
Hong Kong	587
(Netherlands)	577
(Czech Republic)	567
(Austria)	559
(Slovenia)	552
Ireland	550
(Hungary)	548
(Australia)	546
United States	545
Canada	532
(Israel)	531
(Latvia LSS)	525
Scotland	520
England	513
Cyprus	502
Norway	502
New Zealand	499
Greece	492
(Thailand)	490
Portugal	475
Iceland	474
Iran, Islamic Republic	429
(Kuwait)	400

International Average = 529

SCIENCE

Nation	Average
Korea	597
Japan	574
United States	565
(Austria)	565
(Australia)	562
(Netherlands)	557
Czech Republic	557
England	551
Canada	549
Singapore	547
(Slovenia)	546
Ireland	539
Scotland	536
Hong Kong	533
(Hungary)	532
New Zealand	531
Norway	530
(Latvia LSS)	512
(Israel)	505
Iceland	505
Greece	497
Portugal	480
Cyprus	475
(Thailand)	473
Iran, Islamic Republic	416
(Kuwait)	401

International Average = 524

(a)

Nations' Average Mathematics and Science General Knowledge Performance Compared with the United States—Final Year of Secondary School

MATHEMATICS

Nation	Average
(Netherlands)	560
Sweden	552
(Denmark)	547
Switzerland	540
(Iceland)	534
(Norway)	528
(France)	523
New Zealand	522
(Australia)	522
(Canada)	519
(Austria)	518
(Slovenia)	512
(Germany)	495
Hungary	483
(Italy)	476
(Russian Fed)	471
(Lithuania)	469
Czech Republic	466
(United States)	461
(Cyprus)	446
(South Africa)	356

International Average = 500

SCIENCE

Nation	Average
Sweden	559
(Netherlands)	558
(Iceland)	549
(Norway)	544
(Canada)	532
New Zealand	529
(Australia)	527
Switzerland	523
(Austria)	520
(Slovenia)	517
(Denmark)	509
(Germany)	497
(France)	487
Czech Republic	487
(Russian Fed)	481
(United States)	480
(Italy)	475
Hungary	471
(Lithuania)	461
(Cyprus)	448
(South Africa)	349

International Average = 500

(b)

Notes:
1) Nations not meeting international guidelines are shown in parentheses.
2) The international average is the average of the national averages of the 21 nations.

↑ Nations with average scores significantly higher than the U.S.

= Nations with average scores not significantly different from the U.S.

↓ Nations with average scores significantly lower than the U.S.

Source: National Center for Education Statistics. *Pursuing Excellence: A Study of U.S. Fourth-Grade Mathematics and Science Achievement in International Context,* Figures 1 & 2. Washington, DC, NCES, 1997.

Since the publication of *A Nation at Risk* (National Commission on Excellence in Education 1983), there has been an unbroken trend for the media and some observers of U.S. education to decry the perceived poor performance of U.S. students on international comparisons of achievement. A closer examination of international comparisons, however, reveals the seldom-reported fact that the United States' position in country-by-country rankings is based on *aggregate* achievement scores—in other words, achievement scores of all students are used to make the comparisons. Not taken into account is the United States' commitment to educating all students (not just the academically able or those from home environments that encourage education), the widely varying quality of U.S. schools, and differences in students' *opportunity to learn* the content covered in achievement tests. That is, when only the top students of each country are compared, the rankings of U.S. students improve dramatically. As David Berliner and Bruce Biddle point out in *The Manufactured Crisis: Myths, Fraud, and the Attack on America's Public Schools* (1995, 52), "If one actually looks at and thinks about the comparative evidence, [o]ne discovers that it does not confirm the myth of American educational failure. Indeed, it suggests that in many ways American education stands head and shoulders above education in other countries."

To illustrate their point, Berliner and Biddle summarize Ian Westbury's (1992) analysis of data from the International Association for the Evaluation of Educational Achievements' (IEA) Second International Mathematics Study, which purported to show that U.S. eighth-graders were significantly behind their Japanese peers in mathematics achievement. Westbury noted that Japanese eighth-grade students were *required* to take courses that covered algebra, whereas U.S. students typically take such courses a year or two later. When Westbury compared the achievement of U.S. and Japanese students who had taken prealgebra and algebra, the achievement of U.S. students matched or exceeded that of Japanese students (see Figure 4.4).

Berliner and Biddle (1995, 63) go on to offer the following cautions about interpreting cross-national studies of educational achievement:

- Few of these studies have yet focused on the unique values and strengths of American education.
- Many of the studies' results have obviously been affected by sampling biases and inconsistent methods for gathering data.
- Many, perhaps most, of the studies' results were generated by differences in curricula—in opportunities to learn—in the countries studied.
- Aggregate results for American schools are misleading because of the huge range of school quality in this country—ranging from marvelous to terrible.
- The press has managed to ignore most comparative studies in which the United States has done well.

Norm-Referenced Assessments   Some standardized assessments are norm-referenced—that is, students' scores are compared with scores of other students who are

Figure 4.4 Japanese and American achievement scores for students age thirteen—from The Second International Mathematics Study of the IEA.

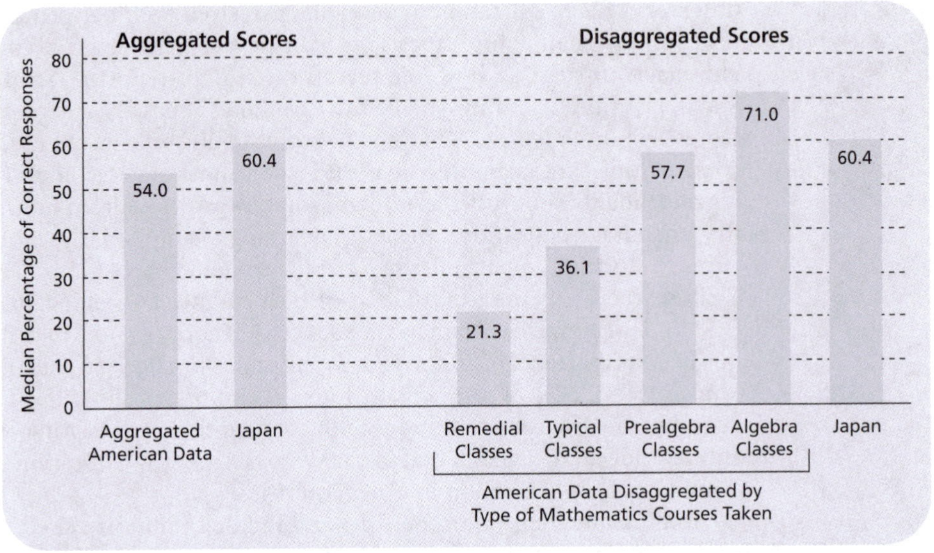

Source: Ian Westbury. "Comparing American and Japanese Achievement: Is the United States Really a Low-Achiever?" *Educational Researcher, 21*(5), 1992, pp. 18–24. Taken from David C. Berliner and Bruce J. Biddle, *The Manufactured Crisis: Myths, Fraud, and the Attack on America's Public Schools.* Reading, MA: Addison-Wesley Publishing Company, 1995, p. 57.

similar. The comparison group of students, called the *norm group*, is usually from the same age group and grade level. An individual student's score is then compared to the average, or mean, score for the total group. Norm-referenced tests are used to determine where a student is compared to the "typical" performance of other students at the same age and grade level. Thus, **norm-referenced assessments** enable teachers to rank students in terms of their achievement.

To understand the meaning of scores on a norm-referenced assessment, imagine that a student received a total of seventy-five points on a one hundred-point norm-referenced assessment. If the mean, or average, score for the comparison group of students was also seventy-five, the student would be at the fiftieth percentile. That is, 50 percent of the students in the comparison group scored higher, and 50 percent scored lower. However, if the mean score for the comparison group was ninety, the student might be in the thirtieth percentile. That is, 70 percent of students in the comparison group scored higher, and 30 percent scored lower.

The preceding example can also be used to illustrate why scores on norm-referenced tests should be interpreted carefully. Norm-referenced test scores can be misused. If the student scored in the thirtieth percentile, it would be a mistake to assume that score is evidence that the student is doing poorly. The student might not have done well on the material covered by the norm-referenced assessment; however, the student might be doing quite well in other areas not included in the test. Following are four examples of norm-referenced interpretations of students' performance:

1. Frank won the one-mile race.
2. On the test of basic skills, Susan's scores were near the average.
3. On the districtwide chemistry test, our school had the best scores.
4. On the test of physical fitness, Paul was in the ninetieth percentile.

Criterion-Referenced Assessments   Other standardized assessments are criterion referenced—that is, students' learning is compared with clearly defined criteria or standards, rather than with the performance of other students. **Criterion-referenced assessments** do not indicate what is "average" or "typical" for students from the same age group and grade level. Criterion-referenced assessments indicate what students know and can do within a specific subject area. Students' scores are not compared with the scores of other groups of students.

A teacher might use a criterion-referenced assessment to assess a student's ability to calculate the square root of a number, to write a well-organized paragraph, or to type sixty words per minute on a computer keyboard. In other words, the assessment is made with reference to an instructional objective, rather than the performance of other students on the assessment. Similarly, the student's score is interpreted without reference to how other students performed. Following are four examples of criterion-referenced interpretations of students' performance:

1. In the chemistry lab, Mary can correctly light a Bunsen burner.
2. Frank can identify each element on the periodic table.
3. Yiming can calculate the sine, cosine, and tangent of angles.
4. Using a map of the world, Karen can identify the countries that were involved in World War II.

What Are Emerging Trends in Classroom Assessment?

Declining test scores, international comparisons of student achievement, and calls to hold teachers more accountable for student learning have fueled a movement to assess student learning with an ever-increasing number of standardized tests. Test scores are frequently used to make "high-stakes" decisions about teacher accountability and the promotion of students to the next grade level.

The majority of the public supports testing in schools. According to the 2004 Phi Delta Kappa/Gallup Poll, 40 percent believe there is "about the right amount" of testing, whereas 22 percent believe there is "not enough" (Rose and Gallup 2004). However, the percentage believing that there is "too much" testing increased from 20 percent in 1997 to 32 percent in 2004. According to the 2004 poll, the public is almost evenly divided regarding the use of standardized test scores to judge the quality of teachers (49 percent favor, 47 percent oppose, and 4 percent "don't know") and to determine whether a student should receive a high school diploma (51 percent favor, 47 percent oppose, and 2 percent "don't know").

The drive for more testing has, in some cases, led to a lowering of standards. For example, some states have changed their assessment criteria to avoid the penalties that The No Child Left Behind Act of 2001 imposes on schools whose students score poorly on standardized tests. According to NCLB, states that fail to comply risk losing federal education money. Schools deemed failing several years in a row must offer tutoring to low-achieving students and, eventually, can be forced into complete reorganization. But the law leaves it up to the states to establish their own standards of success. The following states are among those that have modified their assessment criteria:

- Texas reduced the number of questions that students must answer correctly to pass the third-grade reading exam, from twenty-four out of thirty-six, to twenty.

- Michigan lowered the percentage of students who must pass statewide tests to certify a school as making adequate progress. For example, the percentage of high school students that must pass English tests has been reduced from 75 to 42 percent.

- Colorado changed the grading system used on its tests, combining students previously characterized on the basis of test scores as "partially proficient" with those called "proficient."

Although the push to assess student learning more frequently has led to some modifications in assessment criteria, new forms of assessment are being used more widely. Innovations in assessment are partly in response to criticisms of the fairness and objectivity of standardized tests, such as the Iowa Test of Basic Skills, the SAT, and the ACT. Educators and the public have criticized these tests not only for the class and gender bias in their content, but also for failing to measure accurately students' true knowledge, skills, and levels of achievement. For all of these reasons, educators are increasingly going beyond traditional pencil-and-paper tests, oral questioning, and formal and informal observations. In addition, they are using an array of new assessment tools—individual and small-group projects, portfolios of work, exhibitions, videotaped demonstrations of skills, and community-based activities, to name a few. The following Technology in Teaching feature illustrates how teachers can use educational software to assess students' problem-solving skills and higher-order thinking.

Increasingly, teachers are using alternative assessments—that is, "forms of assessment that require the active construction of meaning rather than the passive regurgitation of isolated facts" (McMillan 2001, 14). The following sections examine several forms of **alternative assessments**: authentic assessments, portfolio assessments, peer assessments, self-assessments, performance-based assessments, alternate assessments, and project-based learning.

Technology in Teaching

How can educational software be used to assess students' problem-solving skills?

Today's teachers can use an array of exciting educational software to assess students' problem-solving skills and higher-order thinking. For example, the *Astronomy Village: Investigating the Universe*, developed by the National Aeronautics and Space Administration (NASA) and available at a modest cost, promotes ninth- and tenth-grade students' learning within a virtual observatory community (see accompanying figure) that includes extensive multimedia resources and sophisticated exploration tools. The *Astronomy Village* requires that teams of three students select one of the following ten investigations, develop a plan, and carry it out.

- *Search for a Supernova*—Uses neutrino data to locate a supernova

- *Looking for a Stellar Nursery*—Views Omega nebula using different wavelengths
- *Variable Stars*—Identifying a Cepheid-variable star in another galaxy
- *Search for Nearby Stars*—Movement of stars' positions as Earth circles the Sun
- *Extragalactic Zoo*—Different galaxies and clusters
- *Wedges of the Universe*—Viewing depths of space in two wedges of sky
- *Search for a "Wobbler"*—Looking for stars that wobble in their motion
- *Search for Planetary Building Blocks*—Examines the Orion nebula for proplanetary disks
- *Search for Earth-Crossing Objects*—Looks for asteroids that cross Earth's path
- *Observatory Site Selection*—Selects a site for an observatory (Jonassen, Peck, and Wilson 1999, 94–95).

Included as part of the *Astronomy Village* are a star life-cycle simulator, an orbital simulator, and a three-dimensional star simulator. In addition, the student teams can use the program's digitized video clips, images from the Hubble space telescope and other instruments, audio clips of astronomers discussing their work, and book chapters, NASA publications, and articles from astronomy journals and magazines.

Authentic Assessment Authentic assessment (sometimes called *alternative assessment*) requires students to use higher-level thinking skills to perform, create, or solve a real-life problem, not just choose one of several designated responses, as on a multiple-choice test item. A teacher might use **authentic assessment** to evaluate the quality of individual or small-group projects, videotaped demonstrations of skills, or participation in community-based activities. In science, for example, students might design and conduct an experiment to solve a problem and then explain in writing how they solved the problem.

Authentic assessments require students to solve problems or to work on tasks that approximate as much as possible those they will encounter beyond the classroom. For example, authentic assessment might allow students to select projects on which they will be evaluated, such as writing a brochure, making a map, creating a recipe, writing and directing a play, critiquing a performance, inventing something useful, producing a video, creating a model, writing a children's book, and so on. In addition, authentic assessment encourages students to develop their own responses to problem situations by allowing them to decide what information is relevant and how that information should be organized and used.

When teachers use authentic assessment to determine what students have learned—and the depth to which they have learned—student achievement and attitudes toward learning improve. For example, a study of eleven pairs of K–12 science and math teachers found that when teachers assess student learning in real-life problem-solving situations, learning and attitudes toward school improve (Appalachia Educational Laboratory 1993). Similarly, a synthesis of research on successfully restructured schools (Newmann and Wehlage 1995) revealed that teachers in those schools emphasized authentic assessment. Their assessments focused on students' ability to think, to develop in-depth understanding, and to apply academic learning to important, realistic problems.

Portfolio Assessment   Professionals in the fine arts, architecture, photography, and advertising routinely compile portfolios to document their best work. They show their portfolios to prospective clients or employers. Periodically, the professional will update the portfolio contents to reflect his or her latest, and best, accomplishments.

Similarly, **portfolio assessment** is based on a collection of student work that "tell[s] a story of a learner's growth in proficiency, long-term achievement, and significant accomplishments in a given academic area" (Tombari and Borich 1999, 164). In short, a portfolio provides examples of important work undertaken by a student, and it represents that student's *best* work. For example, a high school physics student might include in a portfolio (1) a written report of a physics lab experiment illustrating how vector principles and Newton's laws explain the motion of objects in two dimensions, (2) photographs of that experiment in progress, (3) a certificate of merit received at a local science fair, and (4) an annotated list of Internet sites related to vector principles and Newton's laws.

For students, an important part of portfolio assessment is clarifying the criteria used to select the work to be included in the portfolio and then selecting, organizing, and presenting that work for the teacher to assess. The following purposes have been suggested for student portfolios:

- Growth monitoring, in which portfolio content is used to document student progress toward goals or improvement in proficiency

- Skill certification, in which the portfolio is used to establish which instructional goals the student has adequately accomplished
- Evidence of best work, in which the portfolio contains a student's exemplary work and presents the highest level of proficiency the student has achieved with each goal
- External assessment, in which the portfolio is used to establish student proficiency by agencies outside the classroom, such as the school, school district, or a state agency
- Communication with parents, in which a portfolio is taken home or maintained at home to convey how the child is performing at school (Oosterhof 2003, 186)

As students prepare portfolios, four general guidelines should be followed to maximize the learning that results from their involvement in the process of portfolio development:

1. Have students individualize their portfolios—that is, portfolios should focus on the attainment of instructional goals that are important and meaningful for the students.
2. Portfolios should focus on students' accomplishments, their best work—not on their mistakes or limitations.
3. Portfolios should be collaboratively evaluated by teacher and students.
4. Use students' portfolios to discuss their progress with parents, counselors, and other teachers.

Peer Assessment   Peer assessment occurs when students assess one another's work. Typically, peer assessment is done informally during a class session. At times, a student may be more open to accepting critical feedback from a peer than from the teacher. Also, a peer may use a manner of speaking typical of his of her age level (word choice, for example), and it may be easier for another student to understand the feedback. Lastly, as the following teacher indicates, **peer assessment** frees the teacher to observe the peer assessment process and to provide input when necessary:

> We regularly do peer marking—I find this very helpful indeed. A lot of misconceptions come to the fore, and we then discuss these as we are going over the homework. I then go over the peer marking and talk to pupils individually as I go round the room (Black et al. 2004, 14).

Self-Assessment   Self-assessment occurs when students assess their own work and their thought processes while completing that work. It has been suggested that "[self-assessment] is the most underused form of classroom assessment but has the most flexibility and power as a combined assessment and learning tool" (Tileston 2004, 99). When students assess their own work, they become more aware of the factors that promote, or hinder, their learning. Students may, for example, ask assessment questions such as the following: What have I learned as a result of this activity? What problems did I encounter during my learning? How will I overcome these problems in the future?

As a teacher, you should help your students develop skills of **self-assessment**, particularly low achieving students. As the following teacher indicates, once students develop self assessment skills, their learning can improve dramatically:

> *The kids are not skilled in what I am trying to get them to do. I think the process is more effective long term. If you invest time in it, it will pay off big dividends, this process of getting the students to be more independent in the way that they learn and to take the responsibility themselves (Black et al. 2004, 14).*

Some teachers have taught students how to assess their work with reference to a common "traffic light." Students label their work green, yellow, or red based on whether they have good, partial, or little understanding. Teachers then have the "greens" and the "yellows" meet in small groups to help one another, while the teacher meets with the "reds" to address their learning problems.

Performance-Based Assessment   Put simply, **performance-based assessment** is based on observation and judgment (Stiggins 2001). Performance-based assessment focuses on assessing students' mastery of learning objectives or outcomes. We observe a student perform a task or review a student-produced product, and we judge its quality. We could observe a student's science experiment and judge the quality of the thinking involved, or we could read a student's research report in history and judge the quality of argumentation and writing. Performance-based assessment is used to determine what students can *do* as well as what they *know*. In some cases, the teacher observes and then evaluates an actual performance or application of a skill; in others, the teacher evaluates a product created by the student.

State-Level Performance-Based Assessments   Many states have developed statewide performance-based curriculum goals. Washington State, for example, developed the Essential Academic Learning Requirements (EALRs), which includes mandatory assessments of students' performance at the elementary, middle, and high school levels. The EALRs are based on the following four goals, each of which includes several outcomes and essential learning requirements:

Goal 1. READ with comprehension, WRITE with skill, and COMMUNICATE effectively and responsibly in a variety of ways and settings.

Goal 2. KNOW and APPLY the core concepts and principles of mathematics, social, physical and life sciences; civics; history and geography; arts; and health and fitness.

Goal 3. THINK analytically, logically, and creatively, and INTEGRATE experiences and knowledge to form reasoned judgments and solve problems.

Goal 4. UNDERSTAND the importance of work and how performance, effort and decisions directly affect future career and educational opportunities (Commission on Student Learning 1993).

What type of assessment is taking place in this classroom?

The EALRs are intended to improve student achievement and raise academic standards. Instruments for measuring student achievement were developed for the fourth-, seventh-, and tenth-grade levels. "Benchmarks"—points in time used to measure students' progress—were developed for the three grade levels, predicated on the assumption that students would have mastered certain skills and knowledge upon completion of those grades. Participation in the fourth-grade assessment became mandatory for all schools in Washington as of spring 1998. Assessments for seventh- and tenth-grade students were voluntary until spring 2001.

Washington's assessment system has four major components: state-level assessments, classroom-based assessments, professional staff development, and a "context indicator" system. The state-level assessments allow students to select and/or create responses to demonstrate their skills, knowledge, and understanding for each of the EALRs. Unlike traditional norm-referenced assessments, none of the state assessments are timed, so students feel little pressure to rush through their work.

The second component of the system is classroom-based assessment. These assessments address learning requirements not easily measured by the state assessment (e.g., oral presentations or group discussion); offer teachers opportunities to gather evidence of learning that best fit the needs of individual students; and assist teachers in gathering valid evidence of student learning (Ensign, 1998).

The third component of the new assessment system is professional development. Ongoing, comprehensive training and support for teachers and administrators improves their understanding of the EALRs, the elements of sound assessment, and effective instructional techniques that enable students to achieve the state standards. Learning and Assessment Centers have been established in several locations across the state to further facilitate use of the assessment system (Ensign, 1998).

The last component is the "context indicator" system. The context indicators provide insight into why some students do not achieve to the desired level and identify factors that both inhibit and support students' learning. Context indicators may include such information as faculty experience and training, instructional strategies employed, condition of facilities and equipment, availability of appropriate instructional materials and technology, relevant characteristics of the students and the community, and school dropout and graduation rates (Ensign, 1998).

Performance-based assessment focuses on students' ability to apply knowledge, skills, and work habits through the performance of tasks they find meaningful and engaging. While traditional testing helps teachers answer the question, "Do students *know* content?", performance-based assessment helps answer the question, "How well can students *use* what they know?"

Students should find that performance tasks are interesting and relevant to the knowledge, skills, and work habits emphasized in the curriculum. If appropriate, students can help teachers construct performance-based assessments. For example, the author observed elementary level and high school level students helping their teachers construct the following two performance-based assessments, each of which required students to create graphs.

Example 1—Elementary Level

At various times during the school day, students observe and count, at fifteen-minute intervals, the number of cars and trucks that crossed an unlit intersection near their school. Students also gather the same information for a lit intersection near the school. Using data for both intersections, students construct graphs to illustrate the results. If the data suggest the need for a light at the unlit intersection, the graphs will be sent to the local police department.

As students work on various parts of this performance task, the teacher would observe students and make judgments about the quality of their work. Do the counts of cars and trucks appear to be accurate? Do the graphs illustrate the results clearly? Is the students' decision about the need for a traffic light supported by the data they have gathered?

Example 2—High School Level

Students go online to find data on traffic accidents in their state. Based on the data they locate, students prepare graphs that show, by driver's age, various types of accidents, fatalities, speed at the time of accident, and so on. Exemplary graphs will be displayed in the driver education classroom.

As with the elementary level example, the teacher would make judgments about the quality of the high school students' work. Naturally, these judgments would reflect the teacher's beliefs about the characteristics of exemplary student work at the high school level. Did students visit online sites that have extensive, accurate data on traffic accidents? Were students exhaustive in their online search? Do their graphs show a high degree of technical accuracy? Do the graphs "look professional"?

Alternate Assessments   **Alternate assessments** are designed to measure the performance of students who are unable to participate in traditional large-scale assessments used by districts and states. This approach to assessment emerged as a result of the reference to "alternate assessment" in the 1997 reauthorization of the Individuals with Disabilities Education Act (IDEA), which called for states to have alternate assessments in place by the year 2000. An alternate assessment is an alternative way of gathering data about what a student, regardless of the severity of his or her disability, knows and can do. Alternate strategies for collecting data might consist of observing the student during the school day, asking the student to perform a task and noting the level of performance, or interviewing parents or guardians about the student's activities outside of school.

The primary purpose for alternate assessments in state assessment systems is to provide information about how well a school, district, or state is doing in terms of enhancing the performance of *all* students. Gathering data through alternate assessments requires rethinking traditional assessment methods.

An alternate assessment is neither a traditional large-scale assessment nor an individualized diagnostic assessment. Alternate assessments can be administered to students who have a unique array of educational goals and experiences and who differ greatly in their ability to respond to stimuli, solve problems, and provide responses.

Most states are in the process of developing alternate assessments for students with severe disabilities. The National Center on Educational Outcomes at the University of Minnesota suggests six principles for developing inclusive assessment and accountability systems:

Principle 1. All students with disabilities are included in the assessment system.

Principle 2. Decisions about how students with disabilities participate in the assessment system are the result of clearly articulated participation, accommodation, and alternate assessment decision-making processes.

Principle 3. All students with disabilities are included when student scores are publicly reported, in the same frequency and format as all other students, whether they participate with or without accommodations, or in an alternate assessment.

Principle 4. The assessment performance of students with disabilities has the same impact on the final accountability index as the performance of other students, regardless of how the students participate in the assessment system (i.e., with or without accommodation, or in an alternate assessment).

Principle 5. There is improvement of both the assessment system and the accountability system over time, through the processes of formal monitoring, ongoing evaluation, and systematic training in the context of emerging research and best practice.

Principle 6. Every policy and practice reflects the belief that *all students* must be included in state and district assessment and accountability systems (Guenemoen, Thompson, Thurlow, and Lehr 2001).

The U.S. Department of Education decided in 2003 that the achievement of students with severe learning problems could be compared to the achievement of students without learning problems. The new ruling would enable more schools to demonstrate that they had made adequate yearly progress (AYP), a key requirement of The No Child Left Behind Act.

Prior to the Department of Education ruling, students who took alternate assessments could not be considered "proficient." In addition, many schools failed to make adequate yearly progress because their students with disabilities scored low on "regular" assessments or did not take the assessments. Thus, schools were "penalized" when they reported their yearly achievement scores for all students. Furthermore, schools that received federal aid for the poor but failed to make adequate yearly progress faced increasing sanctions from the government.

According to the new ruling, states can develop their own criteria to identify students with "significant cognitive disabilities." The federal government requires that standards for students with disabilities be tied to state academic standards, however. Identified students would be tested against standards appropriate for their intellectual development, and their scores counted as part of their school's overall academic performance.

Project-Based Learning (PBL) A growing body of research supports the use of **project-based learning** (PBL) as a way to engage students, cut absenteeism, boost cooperative learning skills, and improve test scores. In project-based learning, students work in teams to explore real-world problems and create presentations to share what they have learned. Compared with learning solely from textbooks, this approach has many benefits for students, including deeper knowledge of subject matter, increased self-direction and motivation, and improved research and problem-solving skills. Furthermore, as George Lucas, founder of the George Lucas Educational Foundation and Director of *Star Wars*, points out, project-based learning has benefits that go beyond academic learning: "[Project-based learning] promotes emotional intelligence, which is actually much more important in the real world than a high degree of intellectual intelligence, because what you're really doing is working with other people" (George Lucas Educational Foundation 2001).

A three-year 1997 study of two British secondary schools—one that used open-ended projects and one that used more traditional, direct instruction—found striking differences between the two schools with regard to students' understanding of mathematics and standardized achievement data. Students at the project-based school did better than those at the more traditional school both on math problems requiring analytical or conceptual thought and on those requiring memory of a rule or formula. Three times as many students at the project-based school received the top grade achievable on the national examination in math (George Lucas Educational Foundation 2001).

Project-based learning, which transforms teaching from *teachers telling* to *students doing*, includes five key elements:

1. Engaging learning experiences that involve students in complex, real-world projects through which they develop and apply skills and knowledge.

2. Recognizing that significant learning taps students' inherent drive to learn, their capability to do important work, and need to be taken seriously.

3. Learning for which general curricular outcomes can be identified up front, while specific outcomes of the students' learning are neither predetermined nor fully predictable.

4. Learning that requires students to draw from many information sources and disciplines in order to solve problems.

5. Experiences through which students learn to manage and allocate resources such as time and materials (Oaks, Grantman, Pedras 2001, 443).

These five key elements are reflected in the following examples of project-based learning:

- At Mountlake Terrace High School in Mountlake Terrace, Washington, teams of students in a high school geometry class design a state-of-the-art high school for the year 2050. The students create a site plan, make simple architectural drawings of rooms and a physical model, draw up a budget, and write a narrative report. They present their work to real architects, who judge the projects and "award" the contract.

- At Newsome Park Elementary School in Newport News, Virginia, second-graders curious about the number of medicines a classmate takes and her frequent trips to the doctor investigate—with the classmate's permission—the causes of cystic fibrosis. They invite experts to tell them about the disease, write up their research, use graphs and Microsoft PowerPoint to tell the story, sell pledges to a cystic fibrosis walkathon, and participate in the walkathon.

- At the Mott Hall School in New York City's Harlem, a fifth-grade project on kites involves using creative writing skills in poems and stories with kite themes. While designing their own kites on the computer and then making them by hand, students learn about electromagnetism and the principles of ratios and proportions. A casual remark by one student leads to an in-depth study of the role of kites in various cultural celebrations.

How Can You Develop High-Quality Classroom Assessments?

To develop high-quality classroom assessments, you should focus on what *you* do to ensure that assessments fairly and accurately measure students' knowledge, skills, and levels of achievement. You should use various criteria to grade the assignments students complete and the tests they take. Among the criteria you may consider are effort, neatness, correctness, how well students did compared with other students or with their own past performance, and how long students had been studying the topic. These criteria, of course, focus on what *students* do to demonstrate their learning. To assess student learning, you should be skilled in the following:

- Choosing and/or developing assessment methods appropriate for attaining instructional goals and objectives

- Administering, scoring, and interpreting the results of both externally produced and teacher-produced assessment methods
- Using assessment results when making decisions about individual students, planning teaching, developing curriculum, and school improvement
- Developing valid grading procedures based on high-quality assessment of student learning
- Communicating assessment results to students, parents, other nonteaching audiences, and other educators
- Recognizing unethical, illegal, and otherwise inappropriate assessment methods and uses of assessment information

This chapter's Relevant Standards feature stresses the need for teachers to be proficient in using various approaches to assessing student learning.

Validity and Reliability

Two important qualities of classroom assessments—whether teacher made or commercially prepared—are validity and reliability. Because high-quality assessments are directly related to teaching effectiveness, assessments must be valid and reliable. **Validity** refers to the extent to which assessments measure what they are supposed to measure. If assessments fail to do this, they are useless. Valid assessments, however, ensure that what students are asked to do is a direct reflection of stated standards, goals, expectations, and/or targeted learning outcomes. If assessments are valid, teachers can use that information to improve their teaching, and students can use that information to improve their learning.

Perhaps surprisingly, examples of assessments that lack sufficient validity can be found among state-mandated tests of student learning. For example, Beverly Falk observes that

> Numerous accountability systems use tests that have little relation to the standards they are supposed to evaluate. As recently as 1999, at least 25 states that claimed to be implementing new standards were still using old-style, norm-referenced tests to measure student progress. Although the rhetoric of new and lofty standards is used when discussing what the tests measure, their actual content includes few performance items, and their formats provide scant opportunities for students to demonstrate the higher-order thinking of the new standards (2002, 614).

Reliability refers to the degree to which an assessment provides results that are consistent over time. In other words, an entire test (or individual test item) is considered to be reliable if it yields similar results at different times and under different conditions. For example, imagine that Mr. Jones wants to assess his students' multiplication and division skills using whole numbers by giving them a forty-point quiz (twenty points for multiplication, twenty points for division). After scoring his students' quizzes, Mr. Jones is uncertain about whether he should begin teaching the more complex skills of multiplying and dividing using fractions. He decides to gather more information by giving another quiz three days later on the

Relevant Standards

Assessing Student Learning

As the following standards indicate, highly accomplished teachers use a variety of approaches for assessing student learning. These assessment strategies are linked to instructional objectives, and they are used to promote student learning rather than to determine what students do not understand.

- "Teacher candidates accurately assess and analyze student learning, make appropriate adjustments to instruction, monitor student learning, and have a positive effect on learning for all students." (National Council for Accreditation of Teacher Education [NCATE], 2002, 16. Standard 1: Candidate Knowledge, Skills, and Dispositions, "target" level of knowledge.)

- "Accomplished teachers can assess the progress of individual students as well as that of the class as a whole. They employ multiple methods for measuring student growth and understanding and can clearly explain student performance to parents." (National Board for Professional Teaching Standards [NBPTS], 2002, 4. "Supporting statements" for Proposition #3: Teachers are responsible for managing and monitoring student learning.")

- "The teacher appropriately uses a variety of formal and informal assessment techniques (e.g., obser-

vation, portfolios of student work, teacher-made tests, performance tasks, projects, student self-assessments, peer assessment, and standardized tests) to enhance her or his knowledge of learners, evaluate students' progress and performances, and modify teaching and learning strategies." (Interstate New Teacher Assessment and Support Consortium [INTASC], 1992, 29. "Performance" statement for Principle #8: "The teacher understands and uses formal and informal assessment strategies to evaluate and ensure the continuous intellectual, social and physical development of the learner".)

- "The [teacher's] approach to assessment is completely congruent with the instructional goals, both in content and process." (Praxis Series, "distinguished" level of performance for Domain 1: Planning and Preparation, Component 1f: Assessing Student Learning.) (Danielson 1996, 78)

same multiplication and division skills. The following table presents the scores several students received on both quizzes.

	Multiplication		Division	
Student	*Quiz #1*	*Quiz #2*	*Quiz #1*	*Quiz #2*
Carlos	20	18	17	9
Kim	14	13	13	17
Shawn	11	11	12	17
Nong	16	17	16	12
Mary	20	19	15	14

The items that assessed students' multiplication skills, Mr. Jones notes, are quite consistent (or reliable). On quiz #1 and #2, all five students received comparable scores, with Carlos and Mary receiving the highest scores on both quizzes, and Shawn and Kim receiving the lowest scores. The items that assessed students' division skills are less consistent (or reliable). On quiz #1, Carlos and Nong received the highest scores on the division items; Kim and Shawn received the highest scores on the items for quiz #2.

At this point, Mr. Jones must make a judgment about the reliability of the information he has gathered. Because the results for the multiplication items are fairly consistent and those for the division items fairly inconsistent, he decides to spend one more class session instructing students on division using whole numbers before he proceeds to teach multiplication and division using fractions.

Scoring Rubrics

Teachers also frequently have students conduct a self-assessment by using *rubrics* (guides for evaluating the performance of a learning task) and/or benchmarks to assess their work. When students are involved in self-assessment, they are also engaged in self-evaluation—that is, interpreting information from the assessment of their own work.

Rubrics are an important element of quality classroom assessments. Sometimes called *scoring guides*, **scoring rubrics** are rating scales that consist of preestablished performance criteria. As a teacher, you can use rubrics to differentiate between levels of student performance on a rating scale, and your students can even use them to guide their learning. Rubrics can be used to specify performance criteria for a variety of learning activities—writing an essay, conducting a science experiment, or delivering an informative speech.

Because students can benefit from seeing examples of excellent work appropriate to their grade and ability levels, you should collect "models" of exemplary performances and products by your students. Besides using a scoring rubric to learn about the specific elements that will be used to assess the quality of their work, students must see what quality looks (sounds, feels, smells, or tastes) like. Over time, you should collect sets of excellent work such as graphs, nonfiction writing, solutions to open-ended math problems, and designs for science experiments from students. Less than exemplary work may also be used in the process of teaching students how to use the rubrics.

Rubrics are typically used as scoring instruments when teachers evaluate student performances or products resulting from a performance task. There are two types of rubrics: holistic and analytic.

Holistic Rubrics A **holistic rubric** requires the teacher to score the overall process or product as a whole, without judging the component parts separately (Nitko 2001). Figure 4.5 presents a "generic" framework for developing a holistic scoring rubric based on a five-point scale.

Figure 4.5 Generic framework for a holistic scoring rubric.

Score	Description
5	Performance or product reflects complete understanding of the assessment task or problem. The performance or product reflects all requirements of the task or problem.
4	Performance or product reflects considerable understanding of the assessment task or problem. The performance or product reflects all requirements of the task or problem.
3	Performance or product reflects partial understanding of the assessment task or problem. The performance or product reflects nearly all requirements of the task or problem.
2	Performance or product reflects little understanding of the assessment task or problem. Many requirement of the task or problem are missing.
1	Performance or product reflects no understanding of the assessment task or problem.
0	Task or problem not undertaken.

As an illustration, a high school English teacher might use the framework presented in Figure 4.5 for a holistic assessment of students' ability to write a clear, well-organized essay. A score of 5 would mean the essay reflected characteristics such as clear organization, accurate and precise use of words, adequately developed ideas, insightful analysis of the topic, and effective transitions from paragraph to paragraph. An essay with a score of 3 might have grammatical errors, problems with logic, confusing sentences, and a lack of transitions from paragraph to paragraph. And an essay with a score of 1 might be very confusing and contain only a few sentences that are clear and understandable.

Analytic Rubrics   Unlike the holistic scoring rubric, an **analytic rubric** requires that the teacher score separate, individual parts of the product or performance according to prespecified criteria and then add the individual scores to obtain a total score (Moskal 2000; Nitko 2001). Figure 4.6 on page 162 presents a "generic" framework for developing an analytic scoring rubric based on a five-point scale.

Continuing with the example that focuses on teaching essay writing at the high school level, a teacher might evaluate students' essays with reference to the following four criteria, each of which would be evaluated according to Figure 4.6's description of performances at the "beginning," "developing," "accomplished," and "highly accomplished" levels:

Figure 4.6 Generic framework for an analytic rubric.

	Beginning	Developing	Accomplished	Highly Accomplished	Score
Criteria #1	Performance or product reflects beginning level of performance.	Performance or product reflects emerging performance at the mastery level.	Performance or product reflects performance at the mastery level.	Performance or product reflects performance at the highest level of mastery.	
Criteria #2	Performance or product reflects beginning level of performance.	Performance or product reflects emerging performance at the mastery level.	Performance or product reflects performance at the mastery level.	Performance or product reflects performance at the highest level of mastery.	
Criteria #3	Performance or product reflects beginning level of performance.	Performance or product reflects emerging performance at the mastery level.	Performance or product reflects performance at the mastery level.	Performance or product reflects performance at the highest level of mastery.	
Criteria #4	Performance or product reflects beginning level of performance.	Performance or product reflects emerging performance at the mastery level.	Performance or product reflects performance at the mastery level.	Performance or product reflects performance at the highest level of mastery.	

- *Criteria 1*: The essay is organized clearly—the introduction "sets the stage" for what follows and the conclusion summarizes key ideas.
- *Criteria 2*: The essay is free of grammatical errors.
- *Criteria 3*: The essay has a unifying idea that is clear and easy to follow.
- *Criteria 4*: Effective paragraphing and transitions from one paragraph to the next provide an organizing structure and facilitate movement from one idea to the next.

To help you develop scoring rubrics for eventual use in your classroom, Figure 4.7 presents a step-by-step process for designing holistic and analytic scoring rubrics.

Multiple Measures of Student Learning

There is no single "right way" to assess student learning. Clearly, it will be important for you to provide your students with multiple opportunities to demonstrate what they know and are able to do. If your students know that they have different ways to demonstrate their success, they will develop more positive views of themselves as learners. They will find learning to be an enjoyable experience.

Students who previously might have disliked a subject because they associated assessments of learning in that area with failure can develop positive views about a subject if they know they have different ways to demonstrate their learning. They know that they have multiple opportunities to be successful. As assessment expert

Figure 4.7   Designing scoring rubrics: a step-by-step procedure.

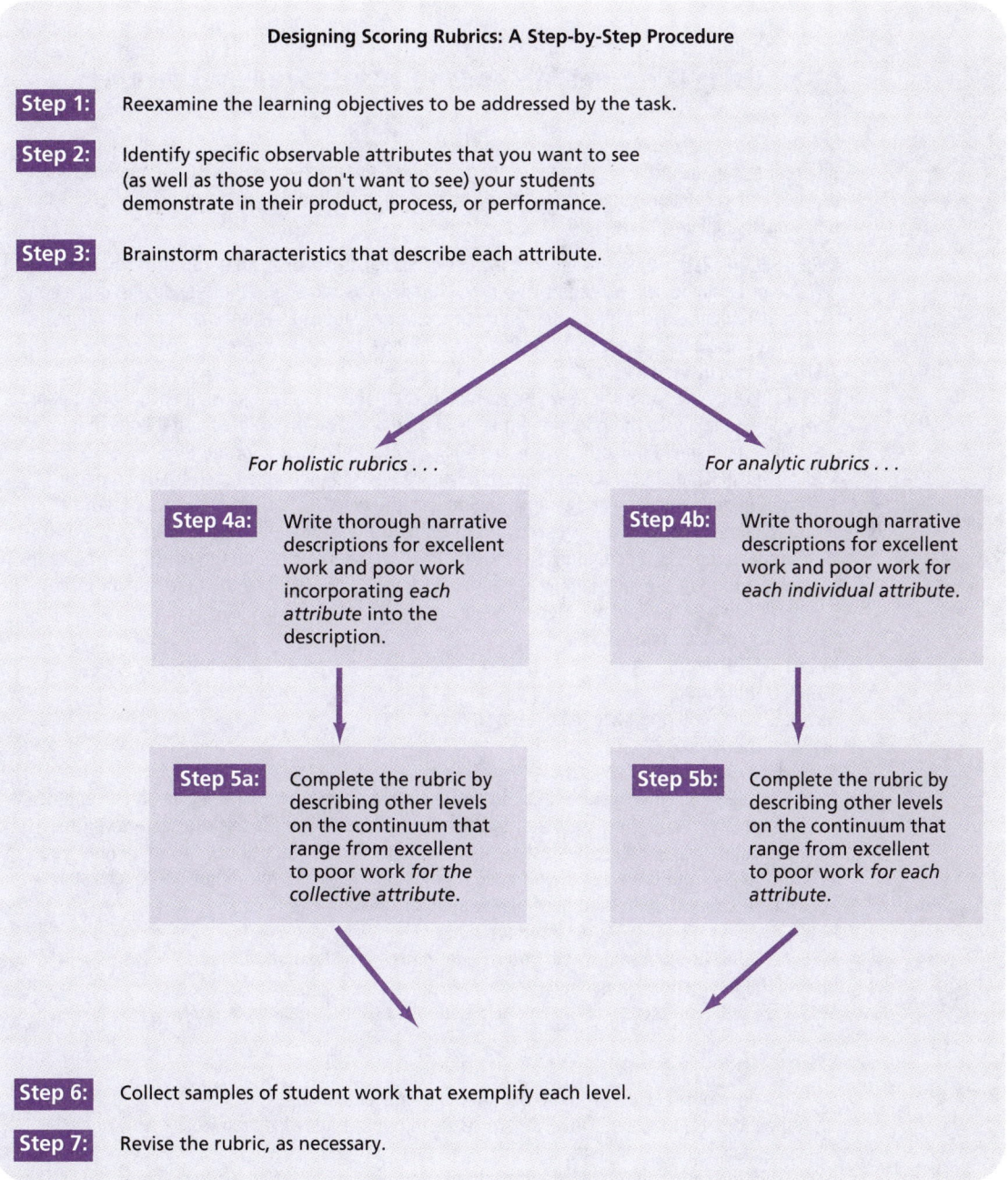

Designing Scoring Rubrics: A Step-by-Step Procedure

Step 1:   Reexamine the learning objectives to be addressed by the task.

Step 2:   Identify specific observable attributes that you want to see (as well as those you don't want to see) your students demonstrate in their product, process, or performance.

Step 3:   Brainstorm characteristics that describe each attribute.

For holistic rubrics . . .

Step 4a: Write thorough narrative descriptions for excellent work and poor work incorporating *each attribute* into the description.

Step 5a: Complete the rubric by describing other levels on the continuum that range from excellent to poor work *for the collective attribute.*

For analytic rubrics . . .

Step 4b: Write thorough narrative descriptions for excellent work and poor work for *each individual attribute.*

Step 5b: Complete the rubric by describing other levels on the continuum that range from excellent to poor work *for each attribute.*

Step 6:   Collect samples of student work that exemplify each level.

Step 7:   Revise the rubric, as necessary.

Source: Craig A. Mertler, "Designing Scoring Rubrics for Your Classroom," *Practical Assessment, Research & Evaluation, 2001, 7*(25). Used with permission.

Case for
Reflection

Using Different Methods to Assess Student Learning

The following transcription from an actual classroom session shows how a teacher skillfully uses different techniques to assess students' learning. First, the teacher focuses on the memorization of rules and vocabulary; then she turns to completion and fill-in exercises; and last, she has students practice their oral delivery.

MRS. LEFLUIR: Today we will study the gender of nouns. In Spanish, all nouns are either masculine or feminine. Nouns ending in *o* are generally masculine, and those ending in *a* are generally feminine. Tisha, can you identify the following nouns as either masculine or feminine? (writes on board) *libro pluma cuaderno gramatica*

TISHA: (Correctly identifies each.)

MRS. LEFLUIR: Now, let's see how you identified each of the words and what each word means.

TISHA: Well, I followed the rule that if it ends in an *o* it will be masculine but if it ends in an *a* it will be feminine. I think the words are *book, pen, notebook,* and *grammar.*

MRS. LEFLUIR: Good. Now for the next step, you've all used indefinite articles *a* or *an* many times in your speaking and writing. In Spanish, the word *un* is used for *a* or *an* before a masculine noun, and *una* is used for *a* or *an* before a feminine noun. In Spanish, the article is repeated before *each* noun. Now, using the vocabulary words on the board, let's place the correct form of the indefinite article in front of each word (shifting the task demand). Why don't you take the first one, Ted?

TED: It would be *un libro.*

MRS. LEFLUIR: Mary.

MARY: *Una pluma.*

MRS. LEFLUIR: Bob and Mike, take the next two.

BOB: *Un cuaderno.*

MIKE: *Una gramatica.*

MRS. LEFLUIR: OK. Now, we are ready to put our knowledge to work. I will give you a sentence in English and you translate it into Spanish, being sure to include the correct form of the indefinite article (shifting the task demand again). For this you will need to remember your vocabulary from last week. If you need to, look up the words you forgot. Mark, let's start with you. Come up to the board and write: Do you want a book?

MARK: (writes on board) *Desea usted un libro?*

MRS. LEFLUIR: Good. And how did you decide to use *un* instead of *una?*

MARK: The noun ended in *o.*

MRS. LEFLUIR: (continues with three other examples) (Borich 1996, 406–407).

Questions

1. How does Mrs. LeFluir promote her students' critical thinking?
2. When Mrs. LeFluir says "Now, we are ready to put our knowledge to work," how does this statement facilitate students' learning?
3. Within the short time covered by this transcription, why does Mrs. LeFluir change the "task demand" so frequently?

Rick Stiggins puts it, "We [now] understand how to use classroom assessment to keep students confident that the achievement target is within reach. . . . We must build classroom environments in which students use assessments to understand what success looks like and how to do better next time. . . . If teachers assess accurately and use the results effectively, then students prosper" (Stiggins 2004, 24–26).

Summary

What Is the Role of Assessment in Teaching?

- Effective schools frequently and systematically assess student learning.

- Classroom assessments of student learning enable teachers to make judgments about the performance of students and about their own performance as teachers.

- Assessment is the process of gathering data to determine students' knowledge, skills, and attitudes within a certain area of the school curriculum.

- Formal assessments—such as final exams, tests, and critiques of performances—are developed prior to having students complete the assessments.

- Informal assessments occur during teaching, and they are made spontaneously.

- Teachers use classroom assessments for four purposes: (1) to determine how well students have learned, (2) to identify feedback that will enhance student learning, (3) to develop strategies to improve their teaching effectiveness, and (4) to determine if students have reached a certain level of performance.

What Methods Can You Use to Assess Student Learning?

- To assess student learning, teachers use quantitative and qualitative approaches, measurement and evaluation techniques, and formative and summative evaluation.

- Standardized assessments (or standardized tests) are pencil-and-paper tests taken by large groups of students and are scored in a uniform manner.

- Norm-referenced assessments compare students' scores with scores of other students who are similar.

- Criterion-referenced assessments compare students' learning with clearly defined criteria or standards.

What Are Emerging Trends in Classroom Assessment?

- Among the emerging trends in classroom assessment are authentic assessments, portfolio assessments, peer assessments, self-assessments, performance-based assessments, alternate assessments, and project-based learning.

How Can You Develop High-Quality Classroom Assessments?

- Validity and reliability are two qualities of high-quality classroom assessments.

- Scoring rubrics are rating scales that consist of preestablished performance criteria.

- Holistic rubrics are used to evaluate student performances or products related to a performance task.

- Analytic rubrics are used to score separate, individual parts of a performance or product.

- There is no single "right way" to assess student learning, and students' views of themselves as learners improve if they know that they have different ways to demonstrate their learning.

Key Terms and Concepts

alternate assessments, 155
alternative assessments, 148
analytic rubric, 161
assessment, 138
authentic assessment, 149
criterion-referenced
   assessments, 147
evaluation, 141
formal assessments, 138
formative evaluation, 141

holistic rubric, 160
informal assessments, 138
International Assessment of Educational Progress (IAEP), 143
measurement, 141
norm-referenced assessments, 146
peer assessment, 151
performance-based assessment, 152
portfolio assessment, 150
project-based learning (PBL), 156

qualitative assessments, 140
quantitative assessments, 139
reliability, 158
scoring rubrics, 160
self-assessment, 152
standardized assessments, 142
summative evaluation, 141
Third International Mathematics and
   Science Study (TIMSS), 143
validity, 158

Reflective Application Activities

Discussion Questions

1. How much emphasis do you think teachers should place on using alternative assessments in the classroom?
2. What are the advantages of peer assessment? Disadvantages? To what extent do you plan to use peer assessment in your classroom?

Professional Journal

1. Reflecting on the K–12 schools you attended, how often did you take norm-referenced assessments? How did you feel about taking those assessments of your learning?
2. Again, reflect on your K–12 school experiences. To what extent did you practice self-assessment of your own learning? What effect(s) did this have on your motivation to succeed?

Online Assignments

1. Using your favorite search engine, gather online information and resources about authentic assessments that you will use in your classroom.
2. With classmates, join in an online discussion on one or more of the following topics presented in this chapter:

criterion-referenced assessments

norm-referenced assessments

peer assessment

performance-based assessment

portfolio assessment

project-based learning (PBL)

scoring rubrics

standardized assessments

Observations and Interviews

1. Interview one or more teachers to find out how they assess students' learning. To what extent do they use the alternative forms of assessment discussed in this chapter?
2. Interview a group of students in the subject area and at the grade level you plan to teach to find out how they assess their own learning. What are the effects of self-assessment on their motivation to succeed?

Professional Portfolio

Using the " 'Generic' Lesson Plan for a Unit of Study" presented in Appendix 4.1, prepare a lesson plan at the grade level and in the subject area for which you are preparing to teach. Include at least one authentic classroom assessment of students' learning in your plan.

Appendix 4.1
"Generic" Lesson Plan for a Unit of Study

Teacher _____ Grade Level _____ Subject _____

Unit Topic_____ Length of Time _____

1. **Introduction**: What is the nature and scope of the unit? How will the unit benefit students? Briefly, what skills, concepts, issues, and activities will the unit address?

2. **Objectives**: (expected learning outcomes—i.e., what will students be expected to be able to do? Objectives can cover the cognitive, psychomotor, and affective domains).
    a. What do I expect students to be able to do?
    b. What changes in students' behavior do I wish to see?
    c. What should each be able to do to demonstrate that he/she has mastered each objective in the unit?

3. **Content of Unit**:
    a. What topics will I cover in my teaching? When will I teach those topics?
    b. Skills, topics, subtopics, concepts, issues, information, etc., covered in unit.
    c. List of activities and time for each (e.g., one week, two class sessions).

4. **Methods and Activities**:
    a. How am I going to teach the unit?
    b. What methods will I use: large group discussions, cooperative learning groups, discovery learning, mastery learning, etc.?
    c. In what activities will students participate: e.g., preparing oral and/or written reports, working in small committees, going on field trips, playing educational games, listening to guest speakers, etc.?

5. **Teaching Materials and/or Resources**:
    a. What materials and/or resources will you need to teach the unit?
    b. What materials will students need?
    c. What textbooks, software, or reference materials will be used?

6. **Assessment of Student Learning**:
    a. How will I measure and evaluate students' progress or achievement?
    b. How will I know if I have achieved the objectives for the unit?
    c. What assessments will I use to measure students' learning: quizzes, tests, observations of classroom behavior, portfolios, projects, performances, etc.?

5 Teaching and Technology

The ways that we use technologies in schools should change from technology-as-teacher to technology-as-partner in the learning process. Students do not learn from technology, they learn from thinking. Technologies can engage and support thinking when students learn with technology.

—David H. Jonassen and Jane Howland,
Learning to Solve Problems with Technology: A Constructivist Perspective, 2003

In media class, Tony, who is also a mentor for the [Marin School of the Arts and Technology] teachers in art and technology, taught students skills such as digital photography, movie production, and multimedia presentations. Using the information gathered during science class, students created computer presentations about watersheds. Small groups also created a news show that was for a broadcast simulation; the students were responsible for everything from conducting interviews and writing scripts to filming and editing.

Throughout the six-week project, students made several trips to the watershed. Using probes and handheld computers, they measured pH levels in local water sources, and, back in the classroom, the students analyzed the data they had collected.

On several occasions, the fieldwork analysis was halted so classroom time could be devoted to digging deeper into a subject or concept. For example, when the students were reviewing topographic maps of the area, it became clear that many had never seen this type of map before and were unable to read them. [Another teacher at the school] immediately taught a lesson about the form and function of topographic maps, explaining what a contour line is and what it represents. With this foundation, the students were then able to continue with their learning.

"The most important role for the teacher in any project-based learning environment is not just to be an active facilitator, but to be the general manager," said Tony. "You have to be in there with the kids every day to some extent, checking in on what they are working on and what they are doing."

Tony . . . saw that the students were bringing their new knowledge from science class into his class. In their slide-show presentations, for example, the students integrated maps they studied, data they analyzed, and charts they created. Their scripts for the news broadcasts demonstrated the students' ability to synthesize the information and share it with an audience (Furger and Shaffner 2004).

Guiding Questions

1. How is technology transforming teaching and learning?

2. What technologies can teachers use?

3. How are teachers using computers and the Internet?

4. Does computer technology enhance student learning?

5. Should technology lead the way in improving U.S. schools?

6. What challenges must be met to integrate technology into schools?

Since the early 1980s, teachers have used computers as an *instructional delivery system* to present information to students. Today, teachers use computers not only for highly structured drill-and-practice exercises, but also as a *catalyst for group investigation and inquiry*. In the opening scenario, for example, Tony is using up-to-date technology to stimulate his students' higher-order thinking, creativity, and problem solving. For Tony, technology is a tool to create a rich, stimulating environment that fosters collaboration, inquiry, and decision making.

How Is Technology Transforming Teaching and Learning?

Technology has transformed teaching and learning in our nation's schools. Each day, students communicate via the Internet with other students around the world. They use child-oriented search engines such as Yahooligans! and KIDLINK to search the World Wide Web for information about whales, the Brazilian rain forest, or the planet Mars. They go to chat rooms or newsgroups for children, where they can chat with children in other countries or participate in global networking projects for children.

Tony's classroom at the Marin School of the Arts and Technology is representative of how new technologies have transformed the learning environments in today's schools. Moreover, the pace of change shows no signs of letting up—as Bill Gates, chairman of the Microsoft Corporation, stated: "In the next few years—a time I call the 'digital decade'—we'll see computing become a much more significant and indispensable part of all our lives" (Gates 2002, i). Similarly, Rod Paige, U.S. Secretary of Education under the George W. Bush administration, stated in his introduction to a federal report titled *Visions 2020: Transforming Education and Training Through Advanced Technologies* that "technology can not only *improve* instruction, but also *transform* what we think of as education" (U.S. Department of Commerce 2002a, 1).

Technology and the Challenge to Schools

The Internet, the World Wide Web, and related telecommunications technologies can further transform teaching and learning. However, we must ask the following question: "How committed are teachers, administrators, policymakers, parents, and the general public to enabling students to realize the full impact that technology can have on their learning?" As the following statement suggests, the future of schools may depend on educators' response to this question:

> The doubling of technological power through the 1990s morphed us into a high-speed, high-tech society. As a result, we are all experiencing accelerated change at a pace never before experienced in human history. Most of us involved in education are simply unprepared for this, and consequently, we have not been able to respond to it as quickly as the world outside of education has. We must quickly catch up or face the unenviable prospect of becoming irrelevant (McCain and Jukes 2001, 58–59).

Additionally, educators must develop new assessment techniques to evaluate students' learning through their use of advanced telecommunications such as the Internet and the World Wide Web. The number of correct responses on homework, quizzes, and examinations will no longer suffice to measure students' learning. "If teachers want students to be able to use ditto masters, then they shouldn't spend thousands of dollars on systems that support computer-assisted instruction. If teachers want to reinforce their didactic role and their role as information providers, then they should also leave computers alone" (Morton 1996, 419).

The CEO Forum on Education and Technology (2001) has called on teachers to use technologies to help students develop the following "21st century skills" they will need for life and work in the digital age:

Digital Age Literacy

1. Basic, scientific, and technological literacy
2. Visual and information literacy
3. Cultural literacy and global awareness

Inventive Thinking

4. Adaptability/managing complexity
5. Curiosity, creativity, and risk taking
6. Higher-order thinking and sound reasoning

Effective Communication

7. Teaming, collaboration, and interpersonal skills
8. Personal and social responsibility
9. Interactive communication

High Productivity

10. Prioritizing, planning, and managing for results
11. Effective use of real-world tools
12. Relevant, high-quality products

When you think about your future as a teacher who will be expected to help students develop "21st century skills," you may find that future at once exciting and intimidating, enticing and threatening. You may ask, will I be ready to meet the challenge of integrating technologies into my teaching? In a very real sense, it is in the hands of people like you to develop new ways to use new technologies in the classrooms of tomorrow.

E-Learning and Virtual Schools

At Hudson High School in Hudson, Massachusetts, ten students are working at computers in a small room marked "VHS Lab." One of the students is working on an assignment for an online media studies course taught by a teacher in Malaysia. Another student is studying technology and multimedia in a course taught by a teacher in Georgia. Their classmates include students from throughout the nation, Asia, Europe, and South America.

Hudson High School is one of a growing number of high schools in the nation that are using **e-learning**, or online education, to supplement the school curriculum. A small school with an enrollment of 880, Hudson has access to 128 courses online, most of which would not be included in the traditional curriculum. E-learning "broadens the curriculum way beyond what we'd normally be able to offer," says the principal (Trotter 2002).

Hudson High receives its online courses through the Virtual High School (VHS), a consortium of high schools run by VHS Inc., a nonprofit foundation. The Hudson School District cofounded the program in 1995, along with the Concord Consortium, a nonprofit research and development organization, under a five-year grant from the federal government. The VHS has two hundred member schools in twenty-eight states and eight countries. Each member school must contribute a teacher to teach at least one online class of twenty students.

The VHS was one of the nation's first two online programs for high schools—the other was the e-school run by the Hawaii Department of Education. Since then, Apex Learning in Bellevue, Washington, the Florida Virtual School, and several colleges and universities have offered online courses to high school students. In fact, by the end of the 2001–02 school year, between forty and fifty thousand K–12 students had enrolled in an online course (WestEd 2001). Figure 5.1 shows that twelve states had established **virtual schools** by the end of the 2001–02 school year. Five states—Idaho, Maryland, Mississippi, Oklahoma, and Texas—were developing or piloting virtual schools. Also, twenty-five of the thirty-seven states and the District of Columbia that allowed charter schools also permitted cyber charter schools. Sixty-seven virtual charter schools in seventeen states served 21,000 students in 2002 (Le 2003).

With the spread of virtual schools and courses, some educators, policymakers, and researchers have expressed concern about exaggerated claims for online learning. In addition, they are worried about what is lost when students do not meet face-to-face with their classmates and teachers. As Alan Warhaftig, a Los Angeles high school English teacher who earned certification from the National Board for Professional Teaching Standards (NBPTS), said, there is an "overall weakness to that notion that online schools can replace the school environment." He doubts that online classrooms can provide the "looking-in-the-eyes" factor that teachers use to monitor students' understanding of a lesson or how they might be feeling (Trotter 2002). Similarly, the 2001 Phi Delta Kappan/Gallup Poll (Rose & Gallup 2001, 46) revealed that the public disapproves, by 67 percent to 30 percent, of allowing students to earn high school credits over the Internet without attending a regular school. Of the 30 percent who approve of virtual courses, only 49 percent would be willing to have their own child "go through high school taking mostly courses online over the Internet at home instead of attending a regular high school."

Figure 5.1   Virtual schools, 2001–02.

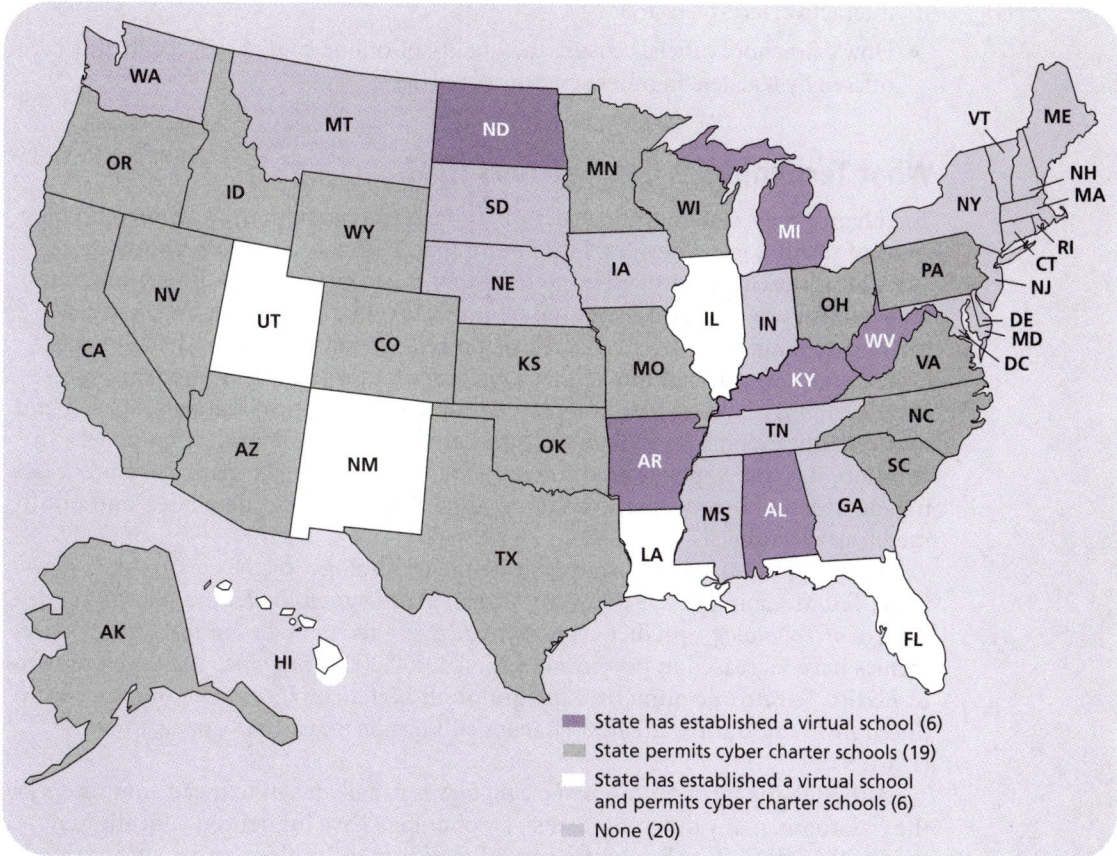

State has established a virtual school (6)

State permits cyber charter schools (19)

State has established a virtual school and permits cyber charter schools (6)

None (20)

Source: Technology Counts 2002: E-Defining Education (2002) *Education Week.* May 2002. Retrieved at www.edweek.org/sreports/tc02. Used with permission.

The trend toward e-learning and virtual schools no doubt will continue. Meanwhile, several questions need to be addressed to ensure that virtual students have quality online learning experiences:

- Although online learning may be appropriate for high school students, should online learning be made available to elementary and middle school students?

- Should online courses be aligned with state academic standards?

- Who should provide for students' technological needs when they take an online course?

- Are online teachers trained effectively to teach via the Internet?

- Should parent approval be required before a child enrolls in an online course?

- Should students receive the same credit for an online course as they would for an interactive, face-to-face class?
- How can school officials ensure the quality of online courses, especially those offered by teachers in other states or countries?

What Technologies Can Teachers Use?

To enhance their classroom instruction, today's teachers can draw from a dazzling array of technological devices. Little more than a decade ago, the technology available to teachers who wished to use more than the chalkboard was limited to an overhead projector, a 16-mm movie projector, a tape recorder, and, in a few forward-looking school districts, television sets. Today, teachers and students use ever-more-powerful desktop and laptop computers with built-in modems, faxes, and CD-ROM players; videodisc players; camcorders; optical scanners; speech and music synthesizers; laser printers; digital cameras; and LCD projection panels. In addition, they use sophisticated software for web browsing, e-mail, word processing, desktop publishing, presentation graphics, spreadsheets, databases, and multimedia applications.

Although the array of currently available technology for the classroom is dazzling, Ted McCain and Ian Jukes, authors of *Windows on the Future: Education in the Age of Technology*, predict even more dazzling technologies in the future: "Electronics have increased in power more than 1,000,000 times since the development of ENIRC [electronic numerical integrator and calculator, an early computer introduced in 1946], but the greatest changes still lie ahead. Fasten your seat belts!" (2001, 9).

Although the term *educational technology* is usually taken to mean computers in the classroom, many different forms of technology have influenced education in the United States. If we broadly define **educational technology** as inventions that enable teachers to reach their goals more effectively, it is clear that for some time teachers have been integrating into their classrooms many forms of educational technology, from the humble chalkboard to the overhead projector. One technology that has had a long and perhaps controversial history in education is television.

The Television Revolution

The television revolution in the United States began with great optimism. David Sarnoff, who founded NBC and introduced the first color television at the New York World's Fair in 1939, confidently predicted that television was "destined to provide greater knowledge to larger numbers of people, truer perception of the meaning of current events, more accurate appraisal of men in public life, and a broader understanding of the needs and aspirations of our fellow human beings" (Sarnoff 1940). Since that time, television has become an omnipresent feature of life in the United States, and its effects—both positive and negative—on all facets of American life are still being studied and debated, and for good cause. Children spend an estimated equivalent of two months of the year watching television. The typical child between six and eleven years of age watches about twenty-seven hours a week; and, by the time they graduate from high school, young people have watched an average of 22,000 hours of television (Shenk 1998).

Critics of television point out that it encourages passivity in the young, may be linked to increases in violence and crime, often reinforces sexual and ethnic stereotypes, retards growth and development, and may be linked to learning disorders. Psychologist Jerome Singers contends that "most [heavy-viewing] kids show lower information, lower reading recognition or readiness to reading, [and] lower reading levels; [and they] tend to show lower imaginativeness and less complex language usage" (quoted in Shenk 1998, 61). Some say that television robs children of the time they need to do homework, to read and reflect, and to build bonds with family members and others through interaction.

However, television can enhance students' learning. Excellent educational programs are aired by the Public Broadcasting Service and by some cable and other commercial networks. Television has also had a positive impact on how students are taught in schools. With the increased availability of video equipment, many schools have begun to have students produce their own television documentaries, news programs, oral histories, and dramas. Many schools have closed-circuit television systems that teachers use to prepare instructional materials for students in the district, and many districts have **distance learning networks** that use two-way, interactive telecommunications to provide enrichment instruction to students in remote areas or staff development to teachers.

Channel One One of the most controversial uses of television in the schools is Channel One, started by Christopher Whittle in 1990. Watched daily by about eight million teenagers in more than 12,000 public and private schools in nearly every state, **Channel One** is a twelve-minute news broadcast, with two minutes of commercials for which advertisers pay as much as $200,000 per thirty-second time slot (Walsh 1999a).

On agreeing to show Channel One programs to most students on 90 percent of school days (students may opt out of viewing), schools receive the program free as well as $25,000 worth of equipment (a satellite dish, two videocassette recorders, nineteen-inch color monitors mounted throughout the school, and internal wiring) that is regularly serviced at no charge. According to the Channel One Network, 99 percent of schools choose to renew their three-year contract to carry Channel One, and the Network has received numerous awards and aired more than $70 million worth of public service announcements. Moreover, the Network points out, schools are encouraged to use the equipment for other educational purposes, such as viewing programs on the Learning Channel, CNN, the Discovery Channel, and C-Span; producing student news shows; conducting teacher in-service programs; and making daily announcements.

The Channel One contributions to education notwithstanding, professional associations such as the National Education Association, educational leaders, and politicians have maintained that advertisements have no place in the classroom. At a 1999 Senate committee hearing, consumer advocate Ralph Nader labeled Channel One "the most brazen marketing ploy in the history of the United States" and cited "parental neglect and the delinquency of school boards" as key reasons for the network's popularity (Walsh 1999b). According to William Hoynes (1998), a sociology professor at Vassar College, the primary goal of Channel One is not to inform students but to assemble a vast "teen market" and then sell high-priced advertising slots. His analysis of Channel One programs led him to conclude that they were "fundamentally commercial" and their educational value "highly questionable." Another critic of Channel One made the following observation: "Of the 10 minutes of 'news,' only two to three minutes is breaking news . . . the remainder is a hodgepodge of contests, self-promotion, light features and profiles, music intros, and pop quizzes" (Baker 2002, 39).

The Computer Revolution

At Consolidated High School District (CHSD) 230 in suburban Chicago, students are using handheld computers—wallet-sized computers many people use to keep track of appointments, e-mail, and the current news on the Internet. The district equipped its three high schools with 2,200 Palm IIIxe's in the form of both classroom sets and individual handhelds that could be bought or rented by students. Students conduct science experiments outdoors with computerized probes and create graphs on the spot as they enter spreadsheet data. Teachers no longer need to

These students are broadcasting a live program from their school's television studio. How have the television revolution and the computer revolution changed education for the better? For the worse?

write assignments on the blackboard because they can "beam" instructions to students' handhelds, often called *personal digital assistants*, or PDAs. Students' written reports now include animated pictures, and flash cards to memorize important information have become a fun computer game. According to science teacher Laurie Ritchey, "For once I think education is keeping up with what's going on in the real world and not sitting there chiseling something into a rock" (Curtis 2002).

Although personal computers may not have transformed all schools so that all students have learning experiences like those at CHSD 230, computers have had a significant impact on education. Like the dawn of the television era over sixty years earlier, the widespread availability of personal computers has been heralded as a technological innovation that will change the teaching–learning process. As Bill Gates predicted in *The Road Ahead* (Gates, Myhrvold, and Rinearson 1996), "I expect education of all kinds to improve significantly within the next decade . . . information technology will empower people of all ages, both inside and outside the classroom, to learn more easily, enjoyably, and successfully than ever before."

Computers and Instruction   Since the early 1980s, the use of computers to enhance instruction has grown steadily. Two of the more common approaches are computer-assisted instruction (CAI) (sometimes called computer-*aided* instruction) and computer-managed instruction (CMI). **Computer-assisted instruction (CAI)** relies on computer programs that provide students with highly structured drill-and-practice exercises or tutorials. CAI is effective with at-risk students and students with disabilities, because it accommodates their special needs and instruction is appropriately paced (Bialo 1989; Jones 1994; Kozma et al. 1992; Norris 1994; Signer 1991). Moreover, CAI can provide students with a more positive, supportive environment for learning. Students can avoid embarrassment, because their inevitable mistakes while learning are not exposed to peers. Figure 5.2 on page 179 presents several additional student-centered and technology-centered advantages of CAI.

Computer-managed instruction (CMI) relies on programs that evaluate and diagnose students' needs and then, based on that assessment, guide them through the next steps in their learning. CMI also records students' progress for teachers to monitor. CAI and CMI can result in reduced teacher–student interactions, if the teacher interprets his or her role as primarily that of record keeper or manager. On the other hand, CAI and CMI can enhance teacher–student interactions: "Freed from the necessity of conducting routine drills and performing many management duties, the teacher has more time to be the vital human link between student and knowledge. The computer does not supplant teachers; it supports them" (Bitter and Pierson 1999, 249).

An increasingly popular approach to computer-based instruction is computer-enhanced instruction (CEI). Unlike CAI and CMI, **computer-enhanced instruction (CEI)** is less structured and more inquiry oriented. The following example illustrates how CEI was used at Richmond Academy in New York City to involve students in archeological inquires.

Case for Reflection

The Role of Technology in the Life of a High School Student— A 2020 Scenario

Eddy's day starts when his Internet earring goes off at 6:30 A.M. with his favorite music playing. He wakes up, and sees his schedule for the day on his wall screen. He notices that he has early lunch today so he makes sure to bring a snack along with him. After getting ready, Eddy returns to grab his learning tablet and notices that he has received a bus alert with an exact GPS location. His bus is running 15 minutes late so he has some extra time to get ready. He tells his virtual mentor to identify his daily learning packet that he has received from school which contains all of his work projects, meetings, and notes for the day. They are read to Eddy via voice in his earring.

Eddy has team deliverables due to be presented in his first class period. He will review the presentation with his team through his two-way video tablet on the way to school. He compares his schedule to his teacher's schedule and picks a time he can log in for the remote meeting for a one on one. His calendar is automatically updated with the new appointment and a message is sent to all the team members, including the teacher. Eddy's virtual mentor checks the bus online and announces to Eddy that it is just turning down his street. He gathers his tablet and his gym bag and heads out the door.

Upon entering the bus, Eddy's clothes scan his student number and the school is immediately notified that he has made the bus and will be conferencing in en route. Eddy arrives to school fifteen minutes late, but has been in constant communication with his team going over last minute details for the presentation, and they're good to go. His music comes up and he listens to his favorite song as he walks across campus. He arrives and joins the project team who are reviewing details about the Persian Gulf War that are relevant to Eddy's schoolmates in Egypt on this project. Eddy reviews a vision of the history of the discussion and watches as personalized information puts the discussion into context for him. A set of questions are automatically configured for him to review, and a green light goes on indicating it's his turn to engage.

An alert appears on his tablet right before the end of the period, reminding him that he is to meet his science team outside today. Today in science, Eddy is completing his personalized learning project. This project was designed especially for Eddy's learning style and allows him to use an observation-based instructional process. While outside, Eddy works on the effects of light on plants, using his virtual biosphere to experiment. He collects real-time data from various laboratories throughout the world, helping him manage his unique ecosystem.

Eddy heads to the cafeteria where he picks up his pre-ordered lunch and debits his student account. After lunch, Eddy has three more projects to check in on and then a free period. During his free period, Eddy has signed up to learn Chinese from a school in Beijing. Eddy signs in to the course and begins talking to his classmates via embedded cameras and a virtual interface for picking objects up. (Hinrichs 2002, 6–7).

Questions

1. How realistic is this scenario for a typical day in the life of a high school student in 2020?
2. Technology obviously plays a significant role in Eddy's life—how do you think technology shapes the life of Eddy's teachers?
3. Based on this scenario, how will the work life of teachers change between now and 2020?

Figure 5.2 Advantages of computer-assisted instruction (CAI).

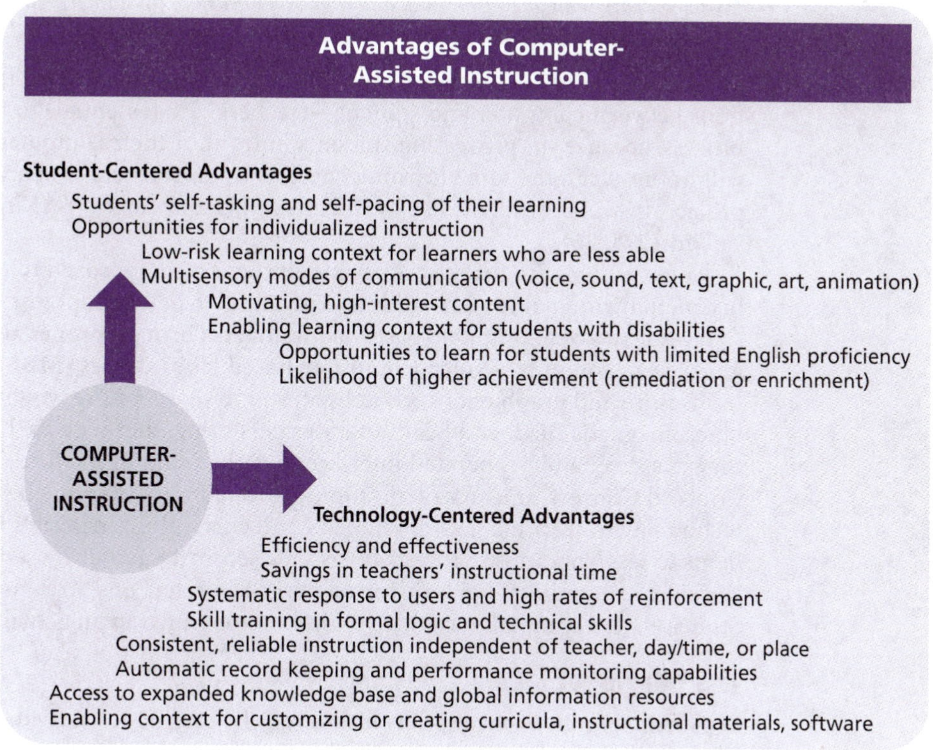

Advantages of Computer-Assisted Instruction

Student-Centered Advantages

Students' self-tasking and self-pacing of their learning
Opportunities for individualized instruction
Low-risk learning context for learners who are less able
Multisensory modes of communication (voice, sound, text, graphic, art, animation)
Motivating, high-interest content
Enabling learning context for students with disabilities
Opportunities to learn for students with limited English proficiency
Likelihood of higher achievement (remediation or enrichment)

COMPUTER-ASSISTED INSTRUCTION

Technology-Centered Advantages

Efficiency and effectiveness
Savings in teachers' instructional time
Systematic response to users and high rates of reinforcement
Skill training in formal logic and technical skills
Consistent, reliable instruction independent of teacher, day/time, or place
Automatic record keeping and performance monitoring capabilities
Access to expanded knowledge base and global information resources
Enabling context for customizing or creating curricula, instructional materials, software

Ninth-graders file into their social studies classroom and, before class begins, log on to one of six workstations at tables against the walls. They argue noisily about what they are finding as they unearth an archaeological site in ancient Greece. The students have been working on the computer-based archaeology simulation for about three weeks, and teams of students are each responsible for excavating one of four separate quadrants of the site. It is a welcome break for the ninth-graders, who in their other classes spend much of their time taking lecture notes and learning to parse sophisticated texts as part of their college-prep curriculum. Here they are "digging up" pottery shards, fragments of weapons, pieces of masonry, and bits of ancient texts, and trying to identify and interpret each artifact in order to fit it into their emerging picture of the site as a whole. In their research the students visit local museums, consult reference works on Greek history, art, and architecture, and ask other teachers in the school to help translate texts. Cleverly, the students' teachers have filled the site with ambiguous evidence, so that some teams find a preponderance of data suggesting the site was a temple, while others find artifacts mostly suggesting it was a battlefield. In weekly meetings the teams present their latest findings to the rest of the class, and a hot debate ensues as the amateur archaeologists struggle to reconcile the fragmentary and ambiguous data. On this day the classroom is active and noisy, yet controlled, as students take turns at the computer, graph their findings on large wall-charts, call across the room to ask if anyone has a spearhead to compare with one just found, and argue about whose final interpretation of the site will best explain the bulk of the evidence (Brunner and Tally 1999, 24–25).

Unlike CAI or CMI, teachers in CEI play a critical role in facilitating interactions between computer and student—teachers "are [essential] to the learning process, because simply seating students in front of their computers to surf the Net will not result in the same learning curve as when teachers assign well-designed projects in which students use the Net to gather information" (Kirkpatrick and Cuban 1998, 26).

Some schools are using another inquiry-oriented approach to enhancing instruction with computers—the microcomputer-based laboratory (MBL), sometimes called CBL (computer-based laboratory). Through probes and sensors attached to computers, **microcomputer-based laboratories (MBL)** enable students to measure and graph data such as light, sound temperature, voltage, skin resistance, magnetic field, and heat flow. Students can gather data in the school laboratory or use a battery-operated interface to gather data in the field. For example, Concord Consortium, an organization dedicated to developing new ways to use technology in teaching, has developed MBL curriculum materials that enable students to learn about rain forests by using a sensor to gather local data for such variables as humidity, light, dissolved oxygen in rivers and streams, and acid rain. Students then compare local data with those obtained in an actual rain forest.

The "Magic" of Media

Personal computers have so revolutionized the instructional media available to teachers that today it is no exaggeration to refer to the "magic" of media. Carol Gilkerson, a Christa McAuliffe Educator, describes how instructional media have transformed her teaching:

One of the chief strengths of using technology in the classroom is that it enables me to adapt my instruction to the individual needs and learning styles of the students. As computer activities can be tailored to student needs, the class becomes more student-centered. CD-ROM, videodisc, and captioned instructional television present information visually and allow students to learn complex material more easily.

Some of the most exciting forms of media magic involve CD-ROMs, videodiscs, and interactive multimedia. Recent advances in computer technology have made it possible for students to become much more active in shaping their learning experiences. On a four-inch **CD-ROM**, they can access the equivalent of about 270,000 pages of text, about nine hundred 300-page books; or on a twelve-inch **videodisc** they can access the equivalent of about 54,000 photographic slides. Computer-supported **interactive multimedia** allow students to integrate information from huge text, audio, and video libraries.

Hypermedia   Systems consisting of computer, CD-ROM drive, videodisc player, video monitor, and speakers now allow students to control and present sound, video images, text, and graphics with an almost limitless array of possibilities. Students who use such hypermedia systems, the most familiar of which is the World Wide Web, can follow their curiosity, browse through enormous amounts of information, and develop creative solutions for multidimensional, real-life problem situations. Online databases in many fields are changing the way students conduct library research, as more computerized reference works—such as directories, dictionaries, and encyclopedias—become available.

The term **hypermedia** refers to documents composed of text, audio, and visual information stored in a computer and accessed by the user in a nonlinear fashion. "Rather than reading an information space sequentially in a predetermined order, a user of [hypermedia] explores the information space in his or her own order, usually based on his or her interests" (Schwartz and Beichner 1999, 56), with the computer used to "link" related segments of information into larger "webs" or networks. A hypermedia system is an effective learning tool because it allows students to actively construct their own learning experiences based on their interests, preferences, and learning styles.

Computer Simulations   For students, computer simulations can be engaging and very motivational. Simulations model complex, multidimensional events in the real world and can range from the lemonade stand that elementary school students plan and run vicariously, practicing basic arithmetic and problem-solving skills, to a mock trial, which Harvard Law students can participate in via videodisc and computer. As learners work their way through a simulation, they make decisions at critical points, enter their decisions into the computer, and then receive feedback on the consequences of those decisions.

Currently available **computer-based simulations** provide students with contextually rich learning experiences, from visiting the great museums of the world to exploring the bottom of the Pacific Ocean to experiencing what it was like to be a pioneer setting out in a wagon train from St. Louis to the coast of Oregon. Figure 5.3 on page 182, for example, shows a household water use simulator from *Exploring the Nardoo*, a CD-ROM program that focuses on a range of water management investigations related to the Nardoo, an imaginary river in Australia. The Nardoo program, developed by the Interactive Multimedia Learning Laboratory at the University of Wollongong in Australia, requires students to solve problems, measure, synthesize data, and communicate findings as they "conduct" research at the Water Research Centre. After students enter the number of baths, showers, toilet flushes, dish washings, car washes, and so on a hypothetical family uses per day, the simulator calculates the family's water usage and compares it with national averages. Students then implement various water-saving strategies throughout the household and rerun the simulation to determine the amount of water saved.

Home–School Communication Systems   Computer-based home–school communication systems such as the Phone Master Notification System are helping busy teachers and parents exchange information. By interfacing a computer program with its

Figure 5.3 Household water use simulator from *Exploring the Nardoo.*

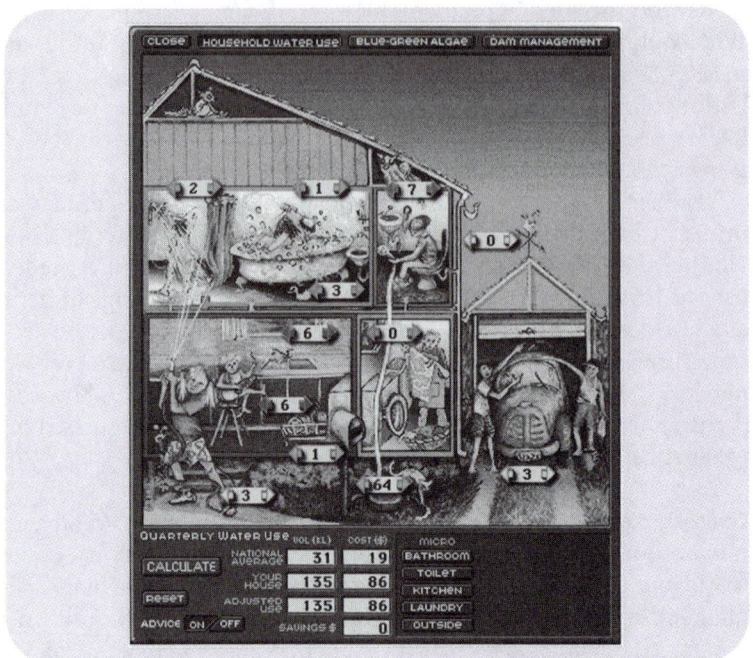

Source: Interactive Multimedia Learning Laboratory, Faculty of Education, University of Wollongong, Wollongong, New South Wales, Australia. Used with permission.

computer-based student records, Georgetown Middle School in Georgetown, Kentucky, enables teachers to use a "Talking Gradebook" to communicate students' progress to parents. Or, by using a touchtone phone and entering a teacher's room number, Georgetown students and parents can access homework assignments, test scores, and current grades.

Increasingly, schools are using sophisticated **home–school communication systems** to strengthen their educational programs. Some communication systems even include a "tip line" that uses voice disguising to provide students with an anonymous, safe way to provide tips to help reduce school violence. Schools are also using home–school communication systems to disseminate the following kinds of information:

Absence and tardy parent notification
Bus schedules
Club information
Congratulatory calls
Invitations to school events
Lunch menus

PTA/PTO information
Reminders to vote on bond issues
School cancellations, early dismissals
Teacher reminders for assignments/activities

The Internet

Observers estimate that the amount of information in the world doubles every nine hundred days (Bitter and Pierson 2002). The Internet, consisting of thousands of interconnected computers around the globe, and the **World Wide Web** (the most popular "entrance" to the Internet) make available to teachers and students much of this information. As Table 5.1 shows, the size of the World Wide Web has increased exponentially since 1995. In addition, newsgroups and chat rooms on the Internet enable teachers and students to communicate with people around the world.

Newsgroups   Through **newsgroups**, students can create electronic bulletin boards of their own and discuss topics of mutual interest with students at other schools, in the same community, or around the world. Messages are "posted" on the bulletin board for others to read at their convenience. When students "surf" into a news-group, they will find messages arranged by subject and author, with responses listed beneath the original message.

Chat Rooms   Students can also participate in "live" discussions held in a **chat room**. Chat rooms use Internet Relay Chat (IRC) technology and allow users to

Table 5.1 Growth of the Internet and the World Wide Web (WWW)

	1995	1996	1997	1998	1999	2002
Number of people online (worldwide)*	26,000,000	55,000,000	101,000,000	150,000,000	179,000,000	580,780,000
Number of WWW sites (worldwide)	23,500	299,403	1,681,868	3,689,227	4,389,131	38,000,000
Number of hosts (computers connected to Internet worldwide)	6,642,000	12,881,000	19,540,000	36,739,000	43,230,000	162,128,000

*Figures include both adults and children.
Note: Numbers are estimates.

Source: Data compiled from Nua Ltd., Internet Surveys, 2002; Internet Software Consortium (ISC), 2002; and Robert H. Zakon, Hobbes' Internet Time-line, 2002.

participate in live, online, typed discussions. In some chat rooms, students can talk to online experts in a wide array of fields and receive immediate responses to their questions.

KIDLINK, a well-known chat room for children ages ten to fifteen, is carefully monitored and open only to registered users. The goal of KIDLINK is to promote global dialogue among young people, and students must answer four questions when they register: (1) "Who am I?" (2) "What do I want to be when I grow up?" (3) "How do I want the world to be better when I grow up?" and (4) "What can I do now to make this happen?" Teacher-leaders of KIDLINK organize and monitor numerous projects; for example, the "Draw a Story for Me" project for kindergarten and first-grade students around the world has the following objectives.

Students will:

1. Communicate with other kids by means of artwork
2. Learn some easy English words and sentences
3. Learn some computer skills
   - Draw with graphics software
   - Use a scanner to import drawings into a computer
   - Upload pictures to KidSpace
   - Send pictures as attachments by e-mail to the project moderator
4. Learn some habits and customs of other people
5. Enjoy new friends all over the world (KIDLINK 2002)

Videoconferencing Videoconferences can be held over the Internet if users have video cameras connected to their computers and C-U SeeMe, PictureTel, or similar software installed. As with any educational technology, care must be taken that **videoconferencing** is more than a "high tech" way for teachers to lecture to passive students at other locations. "Videoconferencing best supports meaningful learning by helping diverse learners to collaborate and converse with each other in order to solve problems and construct meaning" (Jonassen, Peck, and Wilson 1999, 82).

How Are Teachers Using Computers and the Internet?

As the preceding section illustrates, a dazzling array of technologies is available for teachers to use in the classroom. However, the availability and use of these tools for teaching and learning are two different matters. To what extent and how are teachers actually using new technologies? How useful do they find them? To answer these questions, the U.S. Department of Education sponsored the Teaching, Learning, and Computing (TLC) survey, which gathered data from three groups: (1) a nationally representative sample of approximately 2,250 fourth- through twelfth-grade teachers at public and private schools throughout the country, (2) 1,800 teachers at "high-end" technology schools and schools participating in national or regional educational reform programs, and (3) 1,700 principals and school-level technology coordinators (Anderson and Ronnkvist 1999; Becker 1999, 2001; Ravitz, Wong, and Becker 1999).

Preparing Lessons

The Internet has been termed "the world's largest library," and, as such, it can be a remarkable resource for planning lessons. According to the TLC survey, 28 percent of teachers use the Internet weekly or more often to gather information and resources on the Internet for their teaching, and 40 percent do so occasionally. Among teachers who have access to the Internet at school as well as at home, 46 percent report weekly or more frequent use. In Washington State's Kent School District, for instance, teachers learn to use the district's Staff Toolbox website (see Figure 5.4 on page 186) where they share lesson plans and gather information on students' progress in other classes. Kent teachers also use the Toolbox to complete previously onerous paperwork online and to sign up for in-service training.

Communicating with Other Educators

Compared to their use of the Internet to prepare lessons and gather resources, teachers use the Internet less often to communicate with other educators, according to the TLC survey. Only 16 percent of teachers used e-mail to communicate with teachers in other schools, and 23 percent did so occasionally. However, "by far the most important variable in predicting teachers' Internet use is the teacher's level of classroom connectivity" (Becker 1999, 29). For example, a comparison of e-mail use between teachers who had Internet access at home and at school with teachers who had access only at home revealed that teachers with classroom access were *three times as likely* to e-mail teachers at other schools. Not surprisingly, if teachers don't have ready access to the Internet during their daily professional lives, their use of e-mail is less frequent.

Although efforts to integrate technology into schools require information about the extent of teachers' access to and use of the Internet, it is important to ask whether teachers believe the Internet is a valuable tool for teaching. In response to this question, TLC survey data revealed that 49 percent of teachers believe that having a computer with e-mail capabilities on their own desk is "essential," and, similarly, 47 percent believe having web access in the classroom is "essential." In addition, another 38 percent believe e-mail access is "valuable," and 41 percent believe Web access is "valuable." These results seem to counter the observation that "a lot of teachers say, '[Technology] is one more thing on my plate and I don't know how it will help me' " (Ortiz 1999).

Posting Information and Student Work on the Web

In addition to using e-mail to communicate with other educators, 18 percent of teachers posted information, professional opinions, or student work at least once

Figure 5.4   Staff Toolbox, Kent School District.

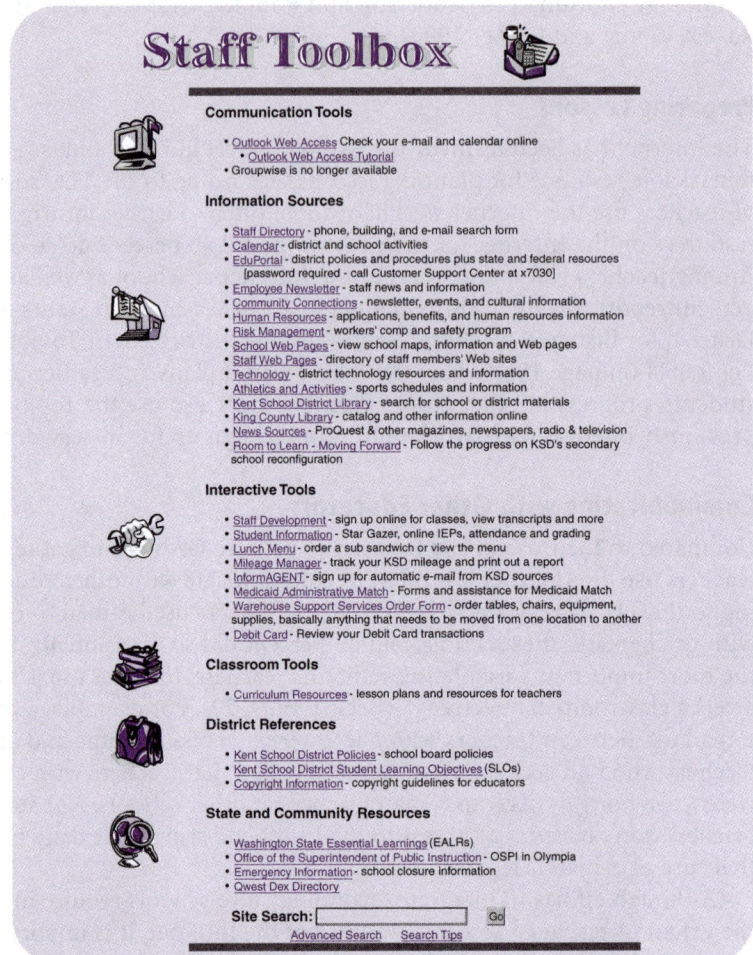

Source: Kent School District, Kent, Washington. Copyright © 1995–2005 by the Kent School District. Used with permission.

on the Web. For instance, as with the use of e-mail, the likelihood of teachers posting information, opinions, or student work was strongly related to connectivity in the classroom. As classroom access to the Internet continues to increase, teachers' use of the Internet to communicate with other educators and to post material will also increase.

Many school districts have taken steps to increase teacher professional communications via the Internet. As part of a "Reinventing Education" grant program, teachers in the San Jose Unified School District keep journals of their progress at integrating technology into instruction, and they share these with other teachers online. To ensure that teachers use their training in technology, the principal of Philadelphia's Hill-Freedman Middle School accepts lesson plans only by e-mail and posts daily announcements exclusively on the Internet (CEO Forum on Education and Technology 1999).

Facilitating Students' Learning via Computers and Cyberspace

In previous sections of this chapter, we have seen several examples of how teachers are using computers and the Internet to enhance students' learning. Figure 5.5,

Figure 5.5   Software use by frequent computer-using teachers.

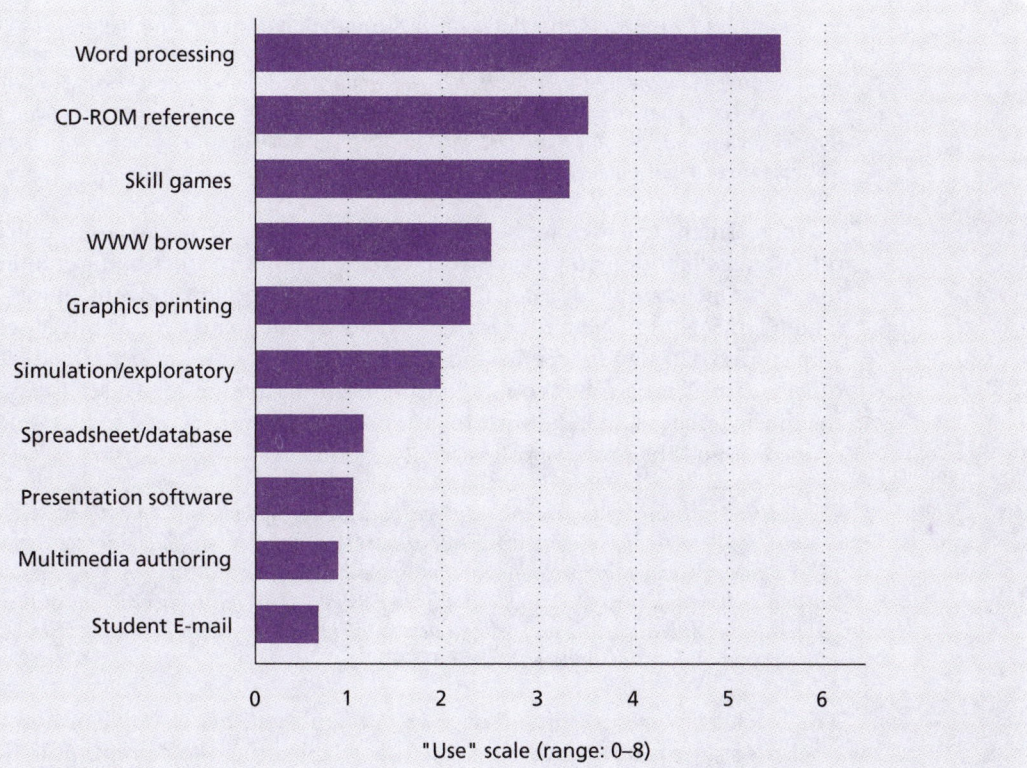

*Use is defined as teachers reporting that a typical student in one of their classes used computers more than 20 times during the school year. Percentage of teachers (by subject taught) who report "frequent computer use": computer, 80%; business, 70%; elementary self-contained, 43%; vocational, 42%; English, 24%; science, 17%; social studies, 12%; math, 11%; fine arts, 9%.

Source: Adapted from Henry Jay Becker, *How Are Teachers Using Computers in Education?* Paper presented at the Annual Meeting of the American Educational Research Association, Seattle, April 2001, pp. 4, 12.

based on TLC survey data, documents the extent of this usage among teachers whose students typically use a computer more than twenty times during a school year. After word processing, the use of CD-ROM references, and games to build skills, using a Web browser is the most common teacher-directed use of computers by students. As with teachers' use of the Internet, student use is directly related to classroom connectivity. Among teachers with modems in the classroom, almost half had students use web search engines on at least three occasions. Moreover, teachers whose classrooms had direct high-speed connections instead of modem connections were 25 percent more likely to have students search the Web ten or more times. In the following, a science teacher comments on the benefits of having students search for information on the Internet:

> I think it [the Internet] provides more opportunities for the kids than relying primarily on a textbook. I think that the Web allows them to go out and see things that the book just can't show them. If they want they can go out and see excellent schematics of the human cell. They can go out and see excellent photographs of cells. They can spend all day looking underneath a microscope and never see a cell as nice as they can find on line because they put the best ones out there (Wallace 2004, 462).

Increasingly, teachers are having students use the Internet to communicate with others, to collaborate on projects with classes at other schools, and to publish on the Web. One example of a collaborative web-based project is ThinkQuest at Lakeland High School in New York State. As their winning entry for a college scholarship contest, Lakeland students and a faculty sponsor developed a website to help others learn. Though she thought a computer teacher should oversee the project, the music teacher and band director who had reluctantly agreed to be the faculty sponsor found the project professionally energizing:

> At first I just wanted to give the team feedback. Then the kids' excitement and motivation got to me—they were doing extraordinary academic work and loving it. I discovered a whole new way to research, learn, and use technology. The kids taught me so much and as they did, they grew intellectually and socially. This has truly been one of the most rewarding and authentic professional development experiences of my career (CEO Forum on Education and Technology 1999).

The Teachers' Voices feature on page 189 presents another example of how one teacher's students developed a website that enabled them to communicate with people around the world.

Does Computer Technology Enhance Student Learning?

The use of computers and other technologies in schools has grown enormously since the early 1980s. Now, as a director of the North Central Regional Education Laboratory noted, "For policymakers, the honeymoon for technology is over. They

Teachers' Voices

Putting Research and Theory into Practice

Inside, Looking Out

Mark Gross

When I first walked into my new classroom, I noticed something very odd: There were no windows. This, I thought, is not going to be fun. But my classes turned that liability into an adventurous global project that has touched thousands of lives.

I teach international relations in a public high school on the east side of San Jose, California. To understand how countries relate, students must understand how people relate, and the first step in getting along is seeing the world through the eyes of others. With that principle in mind, a project was born: Outside My Window.

My students decided to make a virtual window consisting of photographs taken through the real windows of other people. We hoped these images would come from all over the world, giving distant people a chance to connect and create understanding. There were many challenges, however: We had to build a website that captured the idea and provided a way to post submitted images. We had to promote the idea to people overseas. We had to excite other schools. Plus, I had to prepare and teach a class every day.

The solution was to allow the students to organize their own nonprofit "company." They elected an executive team and then worked together. Also, each student sent an e-mail to at least five people to solicit participation in the project and asked each one of them to forward the e-mail to others. We designed and built the website using an online toolset available at www.godaddy.com, and we contacted international organizations.

It took months, but the photos came in. We now have more than one hundred from all over the world, and more than three thousand people have visited the site. We use a wireless network to download the

photos . . . and a color printer to create the images, which we post on our walls. Some photos are haunting, like the one taken at a concentration camp in Poland. Some are artful and colorful. Others are funny, like the one from Maine of a large bug on a window. Many simply show plain views from people's windows, because that's what life mostly is—plain.

Through this activity, we learned what works and what doesn't. For instance, projects must be bounded by reasonable time frames. Also, open-ended ideas can make group participation difficult. It has nevertheless been a rewarding experience. Students discovered the power of the Internet, and they learned about the difficulty of executing good ideas. They also figured out that, in a small way, they can touch the world. All from a room with no windows.

Questions

1. As a result of their participation in the "Outside My Window" project, what did Gross's students learn?
2. In the subject area and at the grade level you are preparing to teach, how could you use the Internet to develop a group project similar to the one Gross developed with his students?
3. Regarding the project described in your response to the preceding question, what problems might you encounter in facilitating the project? How would you overcome those problems?

Mark Gross teaches international relations at Evergreen Valley High School in San Jose, California. His article appeared in *Edutopia: The New World of Learning*, September/October 2004, pp. 18–19. Copyright © 2004 The George Lucas Educational Foundation (www.edutopia.org). All rights reserved. Reprinted with permission.

are starting to say, 'Show us the results' " (Williams 1999). Regarding the effects of technology on learning, research results are just now beginning to appear.

Apple Classrooms of Tomorrow Project (ACOT)

One of the most informative research studies is based on the Apple Classrooms of Tomorrow (ACOT) project launched in seven K–12 classrooms in 1986. Participating students and teachers each received two computers—one for school and one for home. Eight years later, study results indicated that all ACOT students performed as well as they were expected without computers, and some performed better. More important, perhaps, "the ACOT students routinely and without prompting employed inquiry, collaboration, and technological and problem-solving skills" (Mehlinger 1996, 405). Also, 90 percent of ACOT students went on to college after graduating from high school, while only 15 percent of non-ACOT students did. Furthermore, the behavior of ACOT teachers also changed—they worked "more as mentors and less as presenters of information" (Mehlinger 1996, 404).

An additional positive finding of the ACOT study was how teachers gradually began to use the computers in new ways in the classroom. "When [ACOT] teachers were able to move past that pervasive teacher-centered view of education, students and teachers, as communities of learners, were able to benefit from the range of individual areas of expertise represented by the entire group" (Bitter and Pierson 1999, 43). Teachers rearranged their classrooms to enable students to work collaboratively on projects, and they frequently made arrangements for students who wished to stay after school to work on multimedia projects. Frequently, "students and teachers collaborated together, with the students often in the role of expert or resource person" (Schwartz and Beichner 1999, 33–34).

Integrating Technology   Teacher participants in the ACOT study were volunteers, many of whom had little experience with educational technology. As with teachers learning any new instructional strategy, the ACOT teachers frequently struggled to adjust to their new computer-filled rooms. Researchers found that the teachers progressed through five distinct stages as they integrated the technology into their teaching (Sandholtz, Ringstaff, and Dwyer 1997).

1. *Entry stage*—For many teachers, this was a period of painful growth and discomfort; learning to use computers presented challenges similar to those faced by beginning teachers.
2. *Adoption stage*—Becoming more proactive toward the challenge of integrating computers, teachers began to teach students how to use the computers and software.
3. *Adaptation stage*—Teachers turned from teaching the technology to using the technology as a tool to teach content.

4. *Appropriation stage*—Teachers moved from merely accommodating computers in their daily routines to personally exploring new teaching possibilities afforded by the technology.

5. *Invention stage*—Eager to move beyond teacher-centered instruction, teachers began to collaborate with peers in developing authentic, inquiry-oriented learning activities.

As informative as the ACOT study has been, it is important to remember that the project was funded by a computer manufacturer. Perhaps the outcomes were influenced by commercial bias and/or the expectation that computers *could not* have had anything other than a significant positive influence on teaching and learning. In fact, Schwartz and Beichner (1999, 34) suggest that the ACOT project "epitomizes what might be termed the 'Emperor's New Clothes' perspective on technology in education. [To] take the ACOT reports at face value would be to accept the notion that technology is the panacea that education has been searching for for ages."

Findings from Other Research Studies

A powerful way to determine whether certain educational practices actually influence students' learning is to conduct *meta-analyses*, that is, to "take the findings from single studies and calculate a way to compare them with each other. The goal is to synthesize the findings statistically and determine what the studies reveal when examined all together" (Kirkpatrick and Cuban 1998, 27). One such meta-analysis reviewed the results of 133 research studies on educational technology from 1990 through 1994. The results of that study follow:

- Educational technology has a significant positive impact on achievement in all subject areas, across all levels of school, and in regular classrooms as well as those for special-needs students.
- Educational technology has positive effects on student attitudes.
- The degree of effectiveness is influenced by the student population, the instructional design, the teacher's role, how students are grouped, and the levels of student access to technology.
- Technology makes instruction more student-centered, encourages cooperative learning, and stimulates increased teacher–student interaction.
- Positive changes in the learning environment evolve over time and do not occur quickly (Mehlinger 1996, 405).

Another meta-analysis conducted by Heather Kirkpatrick and Larry Cuban (1998) at Stanford University also addressed the complications and difficulties involved in determining the effects of computers on learning, particularly when much of the research in that area is methodologically flawed. Research studies, they pointed out, "are of little use unless they elaborate the children's ages, the subject, the software used, the kinds of outcomes that were sought, and how the study was done (31)." With these limitations in mind, the following is a brief summary of Kirkpatrick and Cuban's findings:

1. Seven of the single studies of elementary and secondary students yielded positive findings related to achievement and attitude change, whereas seven studies yielded negative or mixed findings.

2. Ten of the single studies on the effectiveness of computers to teach in core areas such as mathematics, reading, science, and social studies yielded results ranging from very positive to "cautiously negative."

3. Ten meta-analyses found higher levels of student achievement in computer-using classrooms.

4. Five meta-analyses found that student attitudes improved and students learned more in less time in computer-using classrooms.

On the basis of their meta-analysis of the research, much of it considered methodologically flawed due to a lack of scientific controls, Kirkpatrick and Cuban conclude that "we are unable to ascertain whether computers in classrooms have in fact been or will be the boon they have promised to be (31)."

The ambiguities of research on computer-based instruction aside, it is clear that educational technology *can* have positive effects on learning and teaching, and indications are that technology will influence all aspects of education even more in the future. Thus the question to be asked about the effectiveness of educational technology is not, "Is it effective?" Instead, the question should be, "How and under what circumstances does educational technology enhance students' learning?" As more funds are made available to purchase hardware and software, train teachers, and provide technical support, the benefits of classroom media magic will become even more widespread.

Should Technology Lead the Way In Improving U.S. Schools?

Daily, the mass media feature stories on schools and classrooms that have been transformed through the use of computer-based modes of teaching and learning. Additional reports appear regularly describing the development of new technologies that hold further promise for the improvement of education in the United States. The advantages outlined in these reports include:

- Systematic, well-structured, and consistent lessons
- The ability of students to pace their learning
- The ability of teachers to accommodate their students' varied learning styles and preferred paces of learning
- Opportunities for students in rural and remote areas to interact with students and teachers in diversely populated urban and suburban areas

- Increased record-keeping efficiency, which allows teachers to spend more time with students
- Immediate feedback and reinforcement for students
- Improved student engagement and motivation that result from learning materials with color, music, video, and animated graphics
- More effective assessment of students' learning
- Cost-effectiveness
- The acquisition of computer literacy skills needed for the twenty-first century workplace

For several years, some people have been questioning the role of technology in improving schools in the United States. An *Atlantic Monthly* cover story titled "The Computer Delusion" even suggested that spending money on computers in the classroom was a form of "malpractice" (Oppenheimer 1997). Some critics, like Stanford professor Larry Cuban, believe it is misguided to assume that teaching will benefit from the use of computers, as have other forms of work:

> *The essence of teaching is a knowledgeable, caring adult building a relationship with one or more students to help them learn what the teacher, community, and parents believe to be important. It is an intertwining of emotional and intellectual bonds that gives a tone and texture to teaching and learning unlike what occurs in other work environments. The lure of higher productivity in teaching and learning via computer technologies, however, has seduced reformers to treat teaching like other forms of labor that gained productivity after automation (Cuban 1999a, 53).*

Elsewhere, Cuban (1999b) suggests several seldom-considered factors that might account for why the increase in available educational technologies is not reflected in more effective use of technology in the classroom:

- *Contradictory advice from experts*—Cuban points out that teachers have been presented with an "ever-shifting menu of advice" about what computer skills to teach students, ranging from how to program computers in the 1980s to how to do hypertext programming or HTML in the 1990s.
- *Intractable working conditions*—Although technology has transformed most workplaces, teaching conditions have changed little. Teachers are "people for whom rollerblades would be in order to meet the day's obligations," Cuban says, and they are hard pressed to find time and energy to integrate new technologies into their teaching.
- *The inherent unreliability of the technology*—Software malfunctions, servers that crash, and the continual need for computers with more memory and speed are among the problems Cuban notes.
- *Policymakers' disrespect for teachers' opinions*—Teachers are seldom consulted about which machines and software are most appropriate and reliable for their teaching.

These students receive immediate feedback and reinforcement, are more engaged and motivated, and are acquiring important twenty-first-century workplace skills by using computers at school. Should computers and other technology be at the forefront of efforts to improve schools?

Other critics, like *Chicago Tribune* columnist Bob Greene, are clear about the place of computers in the classroom: "The key to helping the next generation of American children be bright, literate, intellectually self-sufficient, steeped in the most important areas of knowledge? It all comes down to computers in the classroom. Get rid of them" (Greene 1999, 1). Critics like Greene believe that computers can have a dampening effect on the intellectual development of children, not unlike television, and should not be used extensively in the classroom until the high school level. As Greene puts it: "We are not doing [children] any favors by plopping them in front of yet another set of screens and programming them to tap and stare away."

Lastly, many critics are concerned about what they view as tremendous pressure, much of it coming from technology-oriented corporations, for schools to "go online." Moreover, "As technology products change and evolve at lightning speed, there is a decided tendency toward throwing out older teaching methods with the older machines. Sometimes this is a good idea; sometimes it would be a shame" (Roblyer 2003, i).

As our lives are increasingly shaped by technology and as shrill messages from politicians, business leaders, parents, and others continue to proclaim that the United States is falling behind other countries in educational attainment, technology is mistakenly touted as the "magic bullet"—the panacea to turn the schools around.

Are schools falling prey to computer-oriented "hype" encouraged by technology corporations, big business, ambitious superintendents who want their districts to be ahead in the race for the latest technology, and politicians promoting the latest "quick fix" for education? What will be the consequences for schools that have cut art, music, and physical education classes to purchase computers? Will computer technology help the United States develop the kind of students and citizens the nation needs? Is there a "fit" between the power of computers and the educational goals we seek? Are there more cost-effective ways to achieve these educational goals? These are among the difficult questions being addressed as the role of technology in education reform is being debated.

The Opposition: Computers *Will Not* Improve Education

Among the first to question the role of technology in the classroom was Clifford Stoll, one of the pioneers of the Internet and author of *Silicon Snake Oil: Second Thoughts on the Information Highway* (1996). In *High-Tech Heretic: Why Computers Don't Belong in the Classroom and Other Reflections by a Computer Contrarian*, Stoll (1999, xiv) points out that "I believe that a good school needs no computers. And a bad school won't be much improved by even the fastest Internet links. That a good teacher can handle her subject without any multimedia support. . . . That it's unnecessary—and misleading—to push children's work onto the Internet. That students, justifiably, recognize computer assignments primarily as entertainment, rather than education." Similarly, David Shenk concludes his book, *Data Smog: Surviving the Information Glut* (1998, 220), with eight "Principles of Technorealism" endorsed by several of the nation's leading experts on technology; Principle 5 states:

Wiring the Schools Will Not Save Them

The problems with America's public schools—disparate funding, social promotion, bloated class size, crumbling infrastructure, lack of standards—have almost nothing to do with technology. Consequently, no amount of technology will lead to the educational revolution prophesized by President Clinton and others. The art of teaching cannot be replicated by computers, the Net, or by "distance learning." These tools can, of course, augment an already high quality educational experience. But to rely on them as any sort of panacea would be a costly mistake.

Similarly, other critics have cautioned the public against pushing schools into the computer revolution. A sampling of their comments follow:

Too often, what computers actually connect children to are trivial games, inappropriate adult material, and aggressive advertising. They can also isolate children, emotionally and physically, from direct experience of the natural world. The "distance" education they promote is the opposite of what all children, and especially children at risk need most—close relationships with caring adults (Alliance for Childhood 2000, 4).

So far, the most that can be said about computer-based instruction is that vast sums have been lavished on a technology whose educational potential has yet to be proven. We can only guess the long-term effects of computer use on young children's development (Armstrong and Casement 2000, xii).

"Optimistic" is probably the kindest word to describe the current status of educational computing in the United States. The good examples [aren't] always easy to find and [are] far outnumbered by the bad ones (Healy 1998, 78).

Policymakers, administrators, and parents have, essentially, demanded that teachers use the Internet. That demand has not been accompanied by serious efforts to understand what it takes for teachers to be able to use the Internet effectively in teaching. In fact, when schools respond to the mantra "Train the teachers," they almost always neglect to answer the question, "To do what?" (Wallace 2004, 482).

Perhaps the strongest argument that computers will not improve education is the fact that computers can distract educators from what should be their focus—students, their learning, and their lives. Computers can depersonalize education, distancing students from each other and from their teachers. Computers are not sensitive to students' needs, nor do they notice when a student's work habits, communication, demeanor, grooming, or dress change abruptly, signaling trouble. Computers don't know when a student is discouraged, sad, lonely, fearful, or "stuck" in his or her learning. Also, computers are poor substitutes for true companions—they do not laugh, commiserate, or share warmly with their users. Clearly, they cannot provide the human dimension that is needed so greatly in today's schools.

The Advocates: Computers *Will* Improve Education

Despite media stories and articles critical of the call for more computers in schools, enthusiasm for technology in schools remains strong. For example, in an MCI nationwide poll in 1998, almost 60 percent of the public answered "a great amount" when asked, "How much do you think computers have helped improve student learning?" (Trotter 1998, 6). Following are a few representative comments that rebut arguments against computers in the schools.

The answer to the poor use of computers or incomplete research about their effect on educational outcomes is not to ignore the machines or banish them from the classroom. . . . The challenge for twenty-first-century educators is to find balanced, sensible, and pedagogically sound ways of using these remarkable new tools (Gordon 2003, 4–5).

It has become fashionable to say that computers in education are a bust. [However,] the new media can positively change the role of the teacher and student, shifting education from broadcast to interactive learning. When done effectively, [the] results are dramatic (Tapscott 1999).

There are real dangers in looking to technology to be the savior of education. But it won't survive without the technology (Jane David, Apple consultant, quoted in Oppenheimer 1997).

As long as educators remember that computers are not an end in themselves but a tool for enhancing the educational experiences of students, computers have great potential to improve education. To avoid using computers, whatever the reason, is to limit learning possibilities. Motion pictures, videos, and television, once viewed as threats to education, have become generally accepted in classrooms. Further development of today's educational technology will do the same.

What Challenges Must Be Met to Integrate Technology into Schools?

Clearly, educational technology *does* have positive effects on learning and teaching, and indications are that technology will influence all aspects of education even more in the future. However, Figure 5.6 illustrates four challenges that must be met so that all students attend "high-end technology schools": (1) providing broadband Internet access for all schools, (2) providing access to technology for all students, (3) obtaining quality educational software, and (4) providing high-quality, continuous training in technology for teachers. To fail to meet these challenges will short-change students and prevent them from participating fully in the digital age.

Broadband Internet Access for All Schools

Internet access is a vital part of a school's capacity to benefit from the vast resources found in cyberspace. Through the Internet, teachers and students can

Figure 5.6   Creating "high-end technology schools": four key challenges.

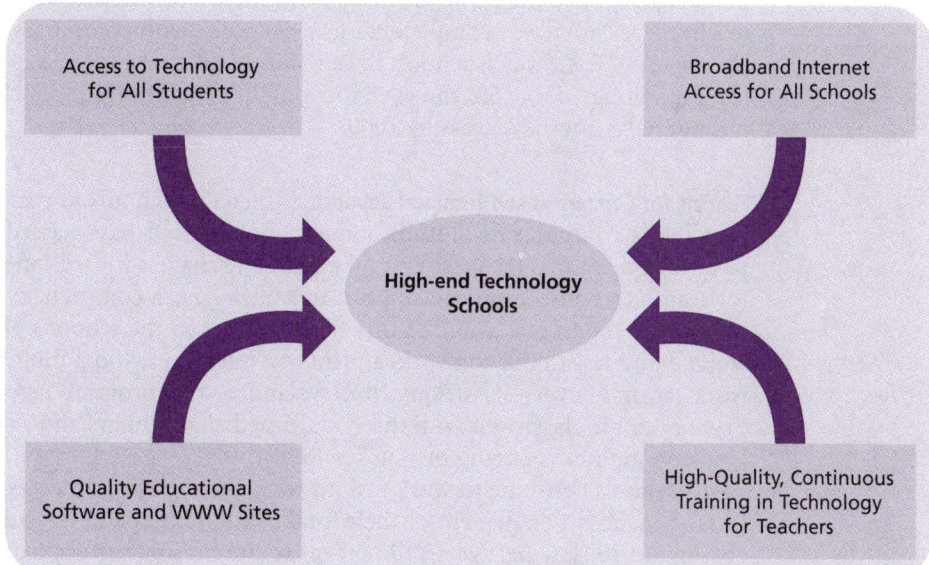

draw from the world's best libraries, museums, and cultural resources. In 1995, President Bill Clinton created the **National Information Infrastructure (NII)** to encourage all schools, libraries, hospitals, and law enforcement agencies to become connected to the "information superhighway." A year later, the Education rate (E-rate) program was established to help schools and libraries connect to the Internet. The **E-rate** program provides schools with Internet access at discounted rates based on the income levels of students' families and whether their location is urban or rural (rural communities receive up to a 10 percent discount). Schools with more poor students get higher subsidies. With increased purchasing power from the E-rate program, schools can purchase improved telephone service and greater bandwidth, thus allowing more data to travel across wires for Internet and e-mail use.

The percentage of the nation's public schools with Internet access has risen dramatically since the mid-1990s. Thirty-five percent of public schools had access to the Internet in 1994; by the fall of 2000, 98 percent were connected. In addition, by fall 2000, there were no differences in school access to the Internet by school characteristics such as poverty level or metropolitan status (National Center for Education Statistics 2001).

Before the E-rate program, the richest schools had almost 50 percent more Internet-linked classrooms per teacher. This difference disappeared after the E-rate program began. By 2000, some poorer districts had more Internet connections than wealthier districts (Goolsbee and Guryan 2002). However, a study of technology usage in all schools in California from 1996 to 2000 found that increased Internet access did not lead to better student scores on the math, reading, or the science sections of the Stanford Achievement Test. Study results did point out that it may be too early to see the positive effects from increased Internet access because most teachers are "novice or completely inexperienced" with computers (Goolsbee and Guryan 2002). Although schools have made significant progress in their technological capabilities, Table 5.2 shows that about 25 percent of public school classrooms did not have Internet access by 2000.

Funding for Computers and Technical Support   To enable schools to participate more fully in the computer revolution, some school districts have passed bond measures to fund educational technology, and a few states have adopted long-term budgets for computers and technical support. In Milwaukee, a comprehensive technology plan called for all one hundred fifty-six buildings in the school system to be networked and for a mini-network, a printer, a television, and a multimedia teacher workstation in every classroom. In Cleveland, a state program has provided every primary grade classroom with three multimedia computers and each teacher with a laptop computer (Harrington-Lueker 1999).

As schools continue to work toward the goal of having Internet access in every classroom, about 66 percent of their total technology spending is devoted to purchasing up-to-date hardware, 19 percent to purchasing software, and 15 percent to providing staff development (Market Data Retrieval 2002).

Table 5.2 **Percent of instructional rooms with Internet access in public schools, by school characteristics: 1994–2000**

Instructional Rooms with Internet Access

School Characteristic	1994	1995	1996	1997	1998	1999	2000
All public schools	3	8	14	27	51	64	77
Instructional level[1]							
Elementary	3	8	13	24	51	62	76
Secondary	4	8	16	32	52	67	79
School size							
Less than 300	3	9	15	27	54	71	83
300 to 999	3	8	13	28	53	64	78
1,000 or more	3	4	16	25	45	58	70
Metropolitan status							
City	4	6	12	20	47	52	66
Urban fringe	4	8	16	29	50	67	78
Town	3	8	14	34	55	72	87
Rural	3	8	14	30	57	71	85
Percent minority enrollment[2]							
Less than 6 percent	4	9	18	37	57	74	85
6 to 20 percent	4	10	18	35	59	78	83
21 to 49 percent	4	9	12	22	52	64	79
50 percent or more	2	3	5	13	37	43	64
Percent of students eligible for free or reduced-price school lunch[3]							
Less than 35 percent	3	9	17	33	57	73	82
35 to 49 percent	2	6	12	33	60	69	81
50 to 74 percent	4	6	11	20	41	61	77
75 percent or more	2	3	5	14	38	38	60

1Data for combined schools are included in the totals and in analyses by other school characteristics but are not shown separately.

2Percent minority enrollment was not available for some cases. In 1994, this information was missing for 100 schools. In subsequent years, the missing information ranged from 46 schools (1995) to 6 (1997).

3The breakouts for the percentage of students eligible for free or reduced-price school lunch have been revised this year and therefore are different from the ones reported in previous Internet access reports.

Note: All of the estimates in this report were recalculated from the raw data files using the same computational algorithms. Consequently, the estimates presented here may differ trivially (i.e., 1 percent) from previously published results.

Source: Taken from National Center for Education Statistics. (May 2001). *Internet Access in U.S. Public Schools and Classrooms: 1994–2000.* Washington, DC: National Center for Education Statistics, p. 4.

Although schools are getting more computer hardware, most cannot afford to hire sufficient support staff for technology. About 30 percent of schools employ a full-time coordinator of technology, about 40 percent employ a part-time coordinator, and about 30 percent have no on-site technical support personnel (Furger 1999). As a result, most schools rely on central district personnel or computer-savvy teachers for support.

At urban schools, the ability to narrow what has been termed the **digital divide** between poor and more affluent schools is often limited by enormous obstacles, including "limited resources, low expectations, overwhelming poverty, teacher contracts, entrenched bureaucracies, political infighting, and the sheer size of these districts" (Williams 1999). *Barriers and Breakthroughs: Technology in Urban Schools*, a study by the Education Writers Association (1999), revealed that, while most urban districts have "lighthouse" schools in which sophisticated technologies are fully integrated into the curriculum, they also have schools with woefully limited technologies.

Commercial Computer Labs   Confronted with limited budgets to purchase computers, about two thousand public and private schools during the late 1990s accepted "free" computer labs (complete with software, training, and maintenance) from companies such as California-based ZapMe. In exchange, schools agreed that classes would use the labs at least four hours a day and that students would be exposed to onscreen advertisements that ran continuously in a $2'' \times 4''$ box in a bottom corner of the screen, changing every fifteen seconds. In addition, schools agreed to allow ZapMe and its for-profit partners to use the labs for computer training and related activities.

However, free, commercially oriented computer labs like ZapMe led critics such as Ralph Nader to compare the labs to the controversial Channel One. Eventually, ZapMe bowed to pressure from critics and ceased providing free labs to schools. On the demise of ZapMe, its founder pointed out that school districts and parents were mostly enthusiastic about the labs and stated that "if you're not going to charge more taxes or bond issues, what options do the schools have?" (Tweney 2000)

Access to Technology for All Students   The nation's schools have made significant strides toward reducing the student–computer ratio. In 1999, a survey by Quality Education Data revealed that only 25 percent of K–12 schools could be characterized as "high-end technology schools" with a student–computer ratio of 6:1 or less (Anderson and Ronnkvist 1999). By 2002, however, the average ratio was less than 4:1 per computer used for instruction and less than 6:1 per multimedia computer, according to a survey of 87,100 schools (Market Data Retrieval 2002).

Although schools have reduced the number of students per computer, there is evidence of a digital divide if computer use at school and at home is compared to family income and minority-group status. In *A Nation Online: How Americans Are Expanding Their Use of the Internet*, the U.S. Department of Commerce (2002b) reported that only 33.1 percent of children (ages ten to seventeen) in the lowest income category use computers at home, compared with 91.7 percent of children in the highest income category. However, schools do help equalize the disparity in computer use among children from various income categories; according to *A Nation Online*, 80.7 percent of children in the lowest income category use computers at school, compared with 88.7 percent of children in the highest income category.

Figure 5.7 shows that Hispanic and African American children—who have lower computer use rates at home—have computer use rates at school that result in their having overall use rates that are comparable to white and Asian American and Pacific Islander children. The overall computer use rate for Hispanic children is 84.4 percent; 88.8 percent for African American children; 94 percent for Asian and Pacific Islander children; and 95.4 percent for white children.

Quality Educational Software and Websites

For students and teachers to benefit from Digital Age technology, high-quality software and websites, not just the latest hardware, must be readily available. Since computers first began to be used extensively in education in the 1980s, inadequacy of software has been a common criticism. By the turn of the century, the situation had not changed much: "Though schools have increased their outlays for software, their choices are few and far between when it comes to superior programs designed specially for classroom use" (Furger 1999). Some programs tend to deemphasize humanistic, holistic, and open-ended fields of knowledge, which are not easily

Figure 5.7 Computer use among ten- to seventeen-year-olds by race and location, 2001.

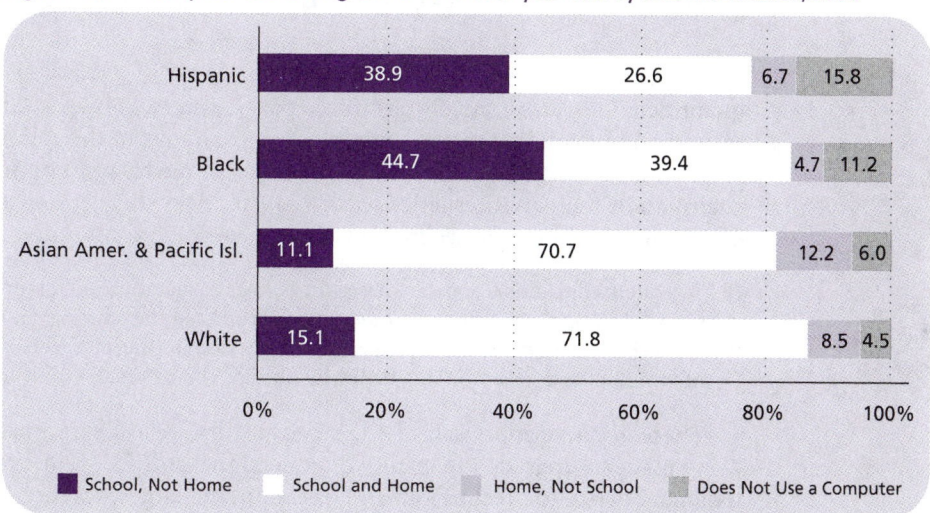

Source: NITA and ESA, U.S. Department of Commerce, using U.S. Census Bureau Current Population Survey Supplements. *A Nation Online: How Americans Are Expanding Their Use of the Internet.* February, 2002, p. 48. Washington, DC: U.S. Department of Commerce.

What are the potential repercussions for schools that cannot afford to provide students with up-to-date technology?

quantified. Others are merely electronic page-turners, known as "drill-and-kill" software, that simply transfer textbooks or workbooks to the computer monitor. As William J. Bennett, the U.S. Secretary of Education who went on to become the chairman of K12, an Internet-based school, and David Gelernter, a Yale professor of computer science and technology advisor for K12, point out:

> Too often, educational software has promoted glitz, glamour, and graphics instead of serious learning. Too often, the Internet has promoted the "surfing culture" where users click their way across an ocean of information, feeling overwhelmed by the vastness of it all and never dipping below the surface (Bennett and Gelernter 2001).

These negative appraisals of educational software aside, promising efforts are being made to upgrade the quality of educational software. For example, the International Society for Technology in Education, the largest teacher-based organization devoted to disseminating effective methods for using educational technology and developer of national "Technology Foundation Standards" for preK–12 students, is working with teachers around the country to identify high-quality software to meet their curriculum goals. Steadily, new, more powerful hypermedia learning software programs are appearing that present students with problems to solve that are interesting, multifaceted, and embedded in real-world contexts. To help you evaluate computer-based instructional materials, Appendix 5.1 presents "Criteria for Evaluating Software Programs," and Appendix 5.2 presents "Criteria for Evaluating World Wide Web Sites."

High-Quality, Continuous Training in Technology for Teachers

Using technology to enhance students' learning requires more than investing in the latest hardware, software, and connectivity to the Internet. In the words of *The Technology Literacy Challenge (U.S. Department of Education 1996), "Upgrading teacher training is key to integrating technology into the classroom and to increasing student learning"* (italics in original). E-mailing students, parents, and peers; conducting classroom demonstrations augmented with multimedia; using presentation graphics to address students' varied learning styles; and designing lessons that require students to use the Internet as a resource for inquiry should be second nature for teachers.

Just as new technological skills are needed in the workplace, a high degree of technological literacy is needed in the classroom. Thus acquiring proficiency in the ever-evolving array of technologies should be an important part of professional development for new and veteran teachers. However, teachers frequently complain of a lack of training in how to use technology to reach their curriculum goals. Only 20 percent of teachers believe they are well prepared to integrate educational technology into the curriculum, and among the teachers who seek training in technology, 50 percent pay for their training with their own money (CEO Forum on Education and Technology 1999). On average, only 9 percent of a school district's technology budget is spent on teacher training, less than one-third of the U.S. Department of Education's recommendations (Furger 1999).

Technical Support for Teachers   Although survey data indicate that about half of teachers have participated in technology-related staff development, those training sessions often tend to emphasize the basics of computer use rather than how to integrate technology with instruction in their subject matter (Ravitz, Wong, and Becker 1999). Moreover, 38 percent of teachers reported that at least once a month they needed help integrating computers into their lessons, but only 15 percent reported that they "always" get that help, and only 12 percent more say that such help is "mostly" available. In the absence of high-quality, continuous training in how to integrate technology into teaching, some students will continue to make observations like the following two high school students quoted in a 2002 report titled *The Digital Disconnect: The Widening Gap Between Internet-Savvy Students and Their Schools*:

> "Our teachers usually . . . don't really know what to do with [the Internet]." "I never really got an assignment that specifically said you have to use the Internet" (Levin and Arafeh 2002, 16).

In addition, teachers have similar experiences related to technical support to keep computers working and software programs functioning properly. Forty-six percent of teachers say they need technical help at least once a month, and only 31 percent of these teachers say that such help is "always" or "mostly" available when they need it. After technical help is given, about one-third of teachers say the help was "excellent" or "very good," one-third say it was "good," and the remaining third say it was "fair" or "poor." Not surprisingly, 54 percent of school leaders who responded to a survey by the National School Boards Association (2002) reported that they rely on students to provide assistance with computers and advice about using the Internet.

Integrating Technology into Teaching   In response to the uneven quality of professional development and technical support, several state departments of education, school districts, and individual schools are taking steps to ensure that teachers have the help they need to fully integrate technology into their teaching. In North Carolina, for example, all new teachers must take an examination to demonstrate their mastery of basic technology competencies in the following nine areas:

1. Computer operation skills
2. Setup, maintenance, and troubleshooting
3. Word processing/introductory desktop publishing
4. Spreadsheet/graphing
5. Databases
6. Networking
7. Telecommunications
8. Media communications (including image and audio processing)
9. Multimedia integration

In addition, North Carolina is one of two states (along with Vermont) that require new teachers to develop a portfolio demonstrating mastery of "advanced" technology competencies, which is evaluated by public school and university faculty chosen by the new teacher's preservice program. The advanced competencies reflect the ability to use multiple forms of technology as they relate to the following four dimensions of learning:

1. Curriculum
2. Subject-specific knowledge
3. Design and management of learning environments/resources
4. Child development, learning, and diversity

In addition, teachers applying for five-year license renewal in North Carolina must have thirty to fifty hours of technology training. This chapter's Relevant Standards feature stresses the importance of developing skills in using advanced technologies to enhance student learning.

Relevant Standards

Skills in Using Advanced Technologies

As the following standards indicate, highly accomplished teachers integrate advanced technologies into their teaching to create environments that enhance student learning. They are skilled in using technology in a variety of ways—from drill-and-practice sessions to group investigation and project-based learning.

- "[Teacher candidates] present content to students in challenging, clear, and compelling ways and integrate technology appropriately." (National Council for Accreditation of Teacher Education [NCATE], 2002, 15. Standard 1: Candidate Knowledge, Skills, and Dispositions, "target" level of knowledge.)

- "[Accomplished] teachers know about the breadth of options available to them, such as innovative instructional formats that involve discovery learning, conceptual mapping, brainstorming, working with computers. . . . " (National Board for Professional Teaching Standards [NBPTS], 2002, 13. "Supporting statements" for Proposition #3: "Teachers are responsible for managing and monitoring student learning.")

- "The teacher knows how to enhance learning through the use of a wide variety of materials as well as human and technological resources (e.g., computers, audio-visual technologies, videotapes and discs, local experts, primary documents and artifacts, texts, reference books, literature, and other print resources." (Interstate New Teacher Assessment and Support Consortium, [INTASC], 1992, 20. "Knowledge" statement for Principle #4: "The teacher understands and uses a variety of instructional strategies to encourage students' development of critical thinking, problem solving, and performance skills.")

- "Instructional materials and resources are suitable to the instructional goals and engage students mentally." (Praxis Series, "distinguished" level of performance for Domain 3: Instruction, Component 3c: Engaging Students in Learning.) (Danielson 1996, 99)

At the school-district level, creative approaches are extending teachers' technological literacy. For example, the board of education in Baldwin Park, California, leased nine hundred notebook computers and gave them to teachers and administrators in all of the district's twenty-one schools (Caterinicchia 1999).

Teacher Education and Technological Literacy Teacher-education programs also will play a key role in preparing technologically competent teachers to fill the roughly two million teaching vacancies the National Center for Education Statistics has projected between 1998 and 2008. However, as the CEO Forum on Education and Technology stated in its *School Technology and Readiness Report* released in 1999: "America's schools of education have only just begun to focus on preparing their students [to] understand, access, and bring technology-based experiences into the learning process (8)." For example, according to the Milken Exchange on Education Technology's report *Will New Teachers Be Prepared to Teach in a Digital Age?* less than half of student teachers routinely use technology during their field

Technology in Teaching

How is technology changing the roles of teachers and students?

Educational technology enables students to experience events or study phenomena that they could not witness firsthand. By integrating educational technology into various learning tasks and across subject areas, teachers can provide students with learning experiences that would have been impossible just a few years ago. Most important, careful and purposeful use of educational technology changes the roles of teachers and students and enhances students' higher order and problem-solving skills.

As you read the following two vignettes, consider how the use of educational technology changes the roles of teachers and students.

Vignette #1

At first, it may look like they're taking part in a graduation ceremony, but the students who march across the stage at Maine's Falmouth Audubon Society to shake hands with their principal and teachers aren't walking away with diplomas. They're walking away with tangible results of their learning.

In this particular case, the eighty-five seventh-graders from Helen King Middle School in Portland each received a copy of "Fading Footprints,"

a CD-ROM they produced about Maine's endangered species. During the ceremony, which included thank-yous to teachers and experts who had helped on the project, some students explained the process. "I made sure all the links worked." Others talked a little about what they learned. "You can ask me anything about the Harlequin duck." Then they all repaired to a courtyard for cake and punch.

"The state's web site probably doesn't have as good information as what's in here," says Mark McCollough, a U.S. Fish and Wildlife Service expert on endangered species who had advised the students. "I want to share this with our regional office."

The students are heady with the knowledge that outsiders appreciate their work, and that it may be used by professionals. "The hard work that went into it–people are noticing it," beams Amelia, the Harlequin duck expert. "I know I worked a little harder because I knew it was going to be seen," says Miranda, another seventh-grader.

Celebrations with everyone from parents to community members are an important part of the learning process at King, which has adopted the Expeditionary Learning Outward Bound model of

experience, and less than half of field experience supervisors or cooperating teachers can advise them on how to integrate technology into the curriculum (Milken Exchange on Education Technology 1999).

To ensure that preservice teachers possess the ability to integrate technology into the classroom, the National Council for the Accreditation of Teacher Education (NCATE) has developed technology-related guidelines that teacher-education programs must meet as a criterion for accreditation (National Council for the Accreditation of Teacher Education 2002). Also, many teacher-education programs have taken innovative steps such as the following to ensure that their graduates possess the ability to integrate technology into the classroom.

personalized, project-based learning. At least twice a year, students, who stay with the same group of teachers for two years—a practice called "looping"—undertake four- to twelve-week interdisciplinary projects. Besides incorporating such subjects as art, science, and language arts, the projects include well-considered use of computer technology, which has been enhanced by the decision of the state to provide all Maine seventh- and eighth-graders with iBook laptop computers ("Laptops on Expedition," The George Lucas Educational Foundation, January 19, 2004; retrieved from www.glef.org/php/article.php?id=Art_1127&key=137).

Vignette #2

There's no shortage of vivid description in stories from Linda Mitchell's third-grade language arts students at Nuuanu Elementary School in Honolulu. And Mitchell thinks that happy circumstance may have something to do with giving her students a number of ways to come to the writing, including through technology.

Before Tamlyn and Quinn did their descriptive writing, they created storyboards about the action they wanted to represent in an assignment on "expanding the moment"—making the story more intense by describing a fleeting instant in great detail. From their story board, they each created a

computer animation of the action. Frame by frame, the animation in turn sparked their imaginations and helped them create word pictures. "It gives you ideas about what you see," says Quinn. HyperStudio® and Kid Pix® were among the computer programs they used.

"What the animation does is it assists the children in visualizing the action," explains Mitchell, who teaches language arts enrichment classes. "The animation is a way of them developing the picture so they relate that to the writing, to what they hear, what they see, what they feel. Technology, she adds, "gives you one more way of teaching something." In the library, first-graders are following the progress of Miss Junie 2, an endangered sea turtle they adopted (for 85 cents each) from the Caribbean Conservation Corporation (CCC). Miss Junie 2 started her trip in Tortuguero, Costa Rica, and students regularly click onto the CCC site to check her movements as tracked by satellite and then write about her travels and ocean life in journals. Teacher Erin Okata integrated social studies, language arts, science, math, fine arts, and technology into the project as a way to help students develop an awareness of ocean life and to meet specific Hawaii state curriculum standards ("From Hula to High Tech," The George Lucas Educational Foundation, February 9, 2004; retrieved from www.glef.org/php/article.php?id=Art_1126&key=137).

- At Washington State University, students develop an online portfolio of literacy strategies that are critiqued by teachers around the state.
- At the University of Virginia, students use the Internet to link with students at eleven other universities to analyze case studies based on commonly occurring problems in classrooms; students also write their own cases and post them on the Web.
- At San Diego State University, student teachers, along with classroom teachers and school administrators, participate in a weekly "Multimedia Academy" taught by university staff and former student teachers.

- At the University of Northern Iowa, students learn from television-mediated observations of "live" classrooms at a P–12 laboratory school and conduct question–answer sessions with the laboratory school teachers.
- At Indiana University, students, as well as visitors from around the world, learn about educational technology at the Center for Excellence in Education, a new state-of-the-art facility with seven hundred computers, an "enhanced technology suite," a building-wide video distribution system, and a two-way video distance-learning classroom.
- At Boise State University, students complete a fifteen-hour technology fieldwork internship in a public school classroom with a teacher who effectively integrates technology into the curriculum.

The Technology in Teaching feature on pages 206 and 207 illustrates further how the integration of technology into schools is changing the roles of teachers and students.

Despite progress in integrating technology into schools, the following observation by the Web-Based Education Commission accurately sums up the work that remains: "The Internet is perhaps the most transformative technology in history, reshaping business, media, entertainment, and society in astonishing ways. But for all its power, it is just now being tapped to transform education" (Web-Based Education Commission 2001, 1). Schools will need extensive support as they continue striving to meet the four challenges outlined in this section. Teachers, professional associations, the private sector, state and federal governments, and local communities must continue to work together to enable classroom "media magic" to enhance every student's learning.

Fortunately, teachers, along with others who have an interest in education, are becoming more sophisticated in understanding the strengths and limitations of technology as a tool to promote learning. They know full well that like another educational tool—the book—the computer *can* be a powerful, almost unlimited medium for instruction and learning, if they carefully reflect on *how* it will further the attainment of the goals and aspirations they have for their students.

Summary

How Is Technology Transforming Teaching and Learning?

- Technology is a tool teachers can use to achieve educational goals and to create particular kinds of learning environments.

- Technology can provide students with a structured, efficient instructional delivery system, or it can spark their interest in open-ended, inquiry-oriented learning.

- In many schools and classrooms, technology has already transformed teaching and learning; however, teachers, administrators, policymakers, and parents must realize that advanced telecommunications will require new approaches to teaching and assessing students' learning.

What Technologies Can Teachers Use?

- Through technologies such as two-way interactive telecommunications, CD-ROM players, interactive multimedia, handheld computers, computer simulations, and hypermedia, teachers are creating learning environments that allow students to become more active in shaping their learning experiences.

- If *educational technology* is broadly defined as inventions that enable teachers to reach their goals more effectively, then it is clear that for some time all teachers have been using various forms of educational "technology."

- Though considerable evidence suggests that television retards children's growth and development, the medium, if properly used, can enhance students' learning.

- Channel One is a controversial use of commercial-based television in the schools, and many critics question its educational value.

- Three common uses of computers in instruction are computer-assisted instruction (CAI), computer-managed instruction (CMI), and computer-enhanced instruction (CEI).

- Some schools have microcomputer-based laboratories (MBLs) that students use to gather and analyze various kinds of data.

- Newsgroups, chat rooms, and videoconferencing on the Internet enable teachers and students to communicate with people around the world.

How Are Teachers Using Computers and the Internet?

- Teachers most frequently use the Internet to gather information and resources for teaching.

- Teachers who have classroom access to the Internet are more likely than those without access to communicate via e-mail and to post information and student work on the World Wide Web.

- After word processing and using CD-ROM references, performing "research" on the Web is the most common teacher-directed use of computers by students.

Does Computer Technology Enhance Student Learning?

- Although how and to what extent computers and other technologies are being used in schools is not known, research indicates that technology has a positive impact on students' achievement and attitudes.

- The Apple Classrooms of Tomorrow (ACOT) project showed that teachers progress through five stages as they integrate technology into teaching: entry, adoption, adaptation, appropriation, and invention.

- Single research studies and meta-analyses of large numbers of single studies indicate that the effects of computers on students' learning are varied—some report learning gains, some don't, and others report "mixed" outcomes.

- Despite the ambiguities of research on computer-based instruction, it is clear that technology *can* have positive effects on learning.

Should Technology Lead the Way in Improving U.S. Schools?

- From the need to acquire computer literacy skills for the twenty-first century to the importance of allowing students to pace their learning, the role that technology should play in improving schools has been widely publicized.

- Some critics believe that schools are under tremendous pressure, much of it coming from technology-oriented corporations, to integrate technology.

- According to some critics, technology has little to add to the art of teaching, and it will not help schools face critical problems such as overcrowding, limited funds, and school violence.

- Despite criticisms of technology in the schools, the public believes that computers have increased students' learning.

What Challenges Must Be Met to Integrate Technology into Schools?

- Four challenges must be met so that all students can attend "high-end technology schools": (1) providing broadband Internet access for all schools, (2) providing access to technology for all students, (3) obtaining quality educational software, and (4) providing high-quality, continuous training in technology for teachers.

- Many schools report inadequate funding for computers and technical support.

- A "digital divide" is evident when access to computers is compared to minority-group status and family income.

- Since the National Information Infrastructure (NII) was developed to encourage all schools to use advanced telecommunications, nearly all schools and 75 percent of classrooms have access to the Internet.

- Though the quality of many software programs is low, new hypermedia programs are being introduced that present students with multifaceted, engaging, and authentic learning experiences.

- Only 20 percent of teachers believe they are well prepared to integrate technology into the curriculum.

- Though school district spending on technology training for teachers is often inadequate and the quality of that training uneven, state departments of education, school districts, and individual schools are developing new approaches to providing teachers with support as they integrate technology.

- Many teacher-education programs have developed innovative approaches to preparing technologically competent teachers.

Key Terms and Concepts

CD-ROM, 180
Channel One, 175
chat room, 183
computer-assisted instruction (CAI), 177
computer-based simulations, 181
computer-enhanced instruction (CEI), 177
computer-managed instruction (CMI), 177

digital divide, 200
distance learning networks, 175
educational technology, 174
e-learning, 172
E-rate, 198
home–school communication systems, 182
hypermedia, 181
interactive multimedia, 180

microcomputer-based laboratories (MBL), 180
National Information Infrastructure (NII), 198
newsgroups, 183
videoconferencing, 184
videodisc, 180
virtual schools, 172
World Wide Web, 183

Reflective Application Activities

Discussion Questions

1. In addition to the content and processes students learn through the use of educational technology, what "lessons" might they learn through the "hidden curriculum" created by educational technology?

2. With regard to the subject area and grade level for which you are preparing to teach, what are the advantages and disadvantages of teaching concepts with and without educational technology?

Professional Journal

1. Based on your experiences, is the classroom use of educational technology educationally sound? To what extent does educational technology merely entertain students?

2. With regard to the subject area and grade level for which you are preparing to teach, what educational technologies do you plan to use?

Online Assignments

1. With classmates, join or start an online discussion on one or more of the following topics or another topic presented in the chapter.

   computer simulations

   computer-assisted instruction (CAI)

   computer-managed instruction (CMI)

   computer-enhanced instruction (CEI)

   educational software

   educational technology

   hypermedia

   interactive multimedia

2. Find out more about educational newsgroups and distance learning networks. How might you use newsgroups or distance learning networks in your preparation as a teacher? As a teacher, how might you and your students use these two forms of educational technology? What knowledge and skills do you need to start or participate in an educational newsgroup or distance learning network? Using the Internet, develop a list of resources for both.

Observations and Interviews

1. Survey a local school district to determine the educational technologies used by teachers. How and how often are these technologies used for instruction? What is the availability of computers and software for student use?

2. Find an online chat room frequented by teachers and enter (or initiate) a discussion on educational technology. What are the teachers' views of integrating technology into the classroom? What technologies, software, and instructional activities have they found most effective?

Professional Portfolio

Prepare a catalog of interactive multimedia resources and materials that you will use as a teacher. For each entry, include an annotation that briefly describes the item, how you will use it, and where it may be obtained. As with the selection of any curriculum materials, try to find evidence of effectiveness, such as results of field tests, published reviews of educational software, awards, or testimonials from educators. View and report on at least one program you have included in your personal catalog. Explain in your report how you will integrate this multimedia resource into your curriculum.

Appendix 5.1
Criteria for Evaluating Software Programs

	Poor	Fair	Excellent
User friendliness			
How easy is it to start the program?	❑	❑	❑
Is there an overview or site map for the program?	❑	❑	❑
Can students easily control the pace of the program?	❑	❑	❑
Can students exit the program easily?	❑	❑	❑
Can students create their own paths through the program and develop their own links among elements?	❑	❑	❑
After first-time use, can students bypass introductory or orientation material?	❑	❑	❑
Does the program include useful hotlinks to Internet sites?	❑	❑	❑
Inclusiveness			
Can students with hearing or visual impairments make full use of the program?	❑	❑	❑
Can students navigate the program by making simple keystrokes with one hand?	❑	❑	❑
Does the material avoid stereotypes and reflect sensitivity to racial, cultural, and gender differences?	❑	❑	❑
Textual Material			
How accurate and thorough is the content?	❑	❑	❑
Is the content well organized and clearly presented?	❑	❑	❑
Is the textual content searchable?	❑	❑	❑
Can the content be integrated into the curriculum?	❑	❑	❑
Images			
Is the image resolution high quality?	❑	❑	❑
Is the layout attractive, "user friendly," and uncluttered?	❑	❑	❑
Do the graphics and colors enhance instruction?	❑	❑	❑
How true are the colors of the images?	❑	❑	❑
Are the images large enough?	❑	❑	❑
Does the program have a zoom feature that indicates the power of magnification?	❑	❑	❑
Does the program make effective use of video and animation?	❑	❑	❑
Audio			
Are the audio clips high quality?	❑	❑	❑
Does the audio enhance instruction?	❑	❑	❑
Technical			
Is installation of the program easy and trouble-free?	❑	❑	❑
Are instructions clear and easy to follow?	❑	❑	❑
Is user-friendly online help available?	❑	❑	❑
Are technical support people easy to reach, helpful, and courteous?	❑	❑	❑
Motivational			
Does the program capture and hold students' interest?	❑	❑	❑
Are students eager to use the program again?	❑	❑	❑
Does the program give appropriate, motivational feedback?	❑	❑	❑
Does the program provide prompts or cues to promote students' learning?	❑	❑	❑

Appendix 5.2
Criteria for Evaluating World Wide Web Sites

Authoritativeness	Poor	Fair	Excellent
The author(s) are respected authorities in the field.	❏	❏	❏
The author(s) are knowledgeable.	❏	❏	❏
The author(s) provide a list of credentials and/or educational background.	❏	❏	❏
The author(s) represent respected, credible institutions or organizations.	❏	❏	❏
Complete information on references (or sources) is provided.	❏	❏	❏
Information for contacting the author(s) and webmaster is provided.	❏	❏	❏

Comprehensiveness			
All facets of the subject are covered.	❏	❏	❏
Sufficient detail is provided at the site.	❏	❏	❏
Information provided is accurate.	❏	❏	❏
Political, ideological, and other biases are not evident.	❏	❏	❏

Presentation			
Graphics serve an educational, rather than decorative, purpose.	❏	❏	❏
Links are provided to related sites.	❏	❏	❏
What icons stand for is clear and unambiguous.	❏	❏	❏
The website loads quickly.	❏	❏	❏
The website is stable and seldom, if ever, nonfunctional.	❏	❏	❏

Timeliness			
The original website was produced recently.	❏	❏	❏
The website is updated and/or revised regularly.	❏	❏	❏
Links given at the website are up-to-date and reliable.	❏	❏	❏

6 Your Induction into Teaching

From the beginning, I welcome students into a classroom that has high standards and is peaceful, productive and safe. Creating an atmosphere where they can be themselves validates who they are, where they have come from, and how much they can accomplish.

Kathy Mellor, 2004 National Teacher of the Year

Your student teaching seminar just ended. Now, you and three other students are seated in the faculty–student lounge, enjoying sodas and talking about finding a job.

"What was the interview like?" you ask one of your classmates, upon learning that he interviewed yesterday for a position at an urban school.

"Yeah, tell us," another student adds. "I'm really anxious about interviewing. I don't know what to expect. There're so many things they could ask."

"Well, I was interviewed by the principal and two people from the district office—I think they were in personnel. At first, they asked questions like the ones we used in our seminar role plays: 'Why do you want to teach? What are your weaknesses? Use five adjectives to describe yourself.' "

"What else?" you ask, anxious to complete a mental image of the interview process so you'll be ready for your first interview next week.

"They asked me to describe a student teaching lesson that went well," he continues. "After I did that, one of them asked 'How could the lesson have been better—either for the entire class or for a certain student?' That one took some thinking."

As he goes on to reconstruct his response, you imagine how you would answer the same question.

Moments later, he says, "Then, one that really surprised me came when I was asked 'What would you do if your principal told you to stop a classroom activity because it was too noisy and left a mess for the custodians to clean up? But, the activity really involved the kids and they learned a lot.' "

He pauses for a sip of soda and then continues, "Another one was, 'Give us an example of a principle that guides your teaching.' "

Impressed with the district's ability to pose challenging questions, you again imagine how you would respond.

A few minutes later, another student asks, "What about portfolios? Did they spend much time looking at yours?"

"Did they ever!" your classmate exclaims. "With my application materials I included a portfolio on CD-ROM, plus I gave them the web address for my portfolio. They were pretty impressed. It was obvious that they had looked at just about everything in the portfolio. They asked all kinds of questions. Half the questions were about how to make a digital portfolio. But they also really wanted to see things that were related to how much my students learned while I was student teaching."

With the mention of portfolios, you're reminded of tomorrow's workshop on creating electronic portfolios. You plan to have a portfolio on CD-ROM that you can take to your first job interview next week. In addition, you wonder what else you should do to prepare for the interview and what steps you can follow to increase your chances of finding the best possible teaching position.

Guiding Questions

1. Why is your induction into teaching important?
2. How will you become certified?
3. Will you have difficulty getting a teaching job?
4. How will you find your first teaching job?
5. What can you expect as a beginning teacher?
6. How can you become a member of a learning community?
7. How can you collaborate with other teachers?
8. How will your teaching performance be evaluated?

Near the end of your teacher education program, you will begin thinking about making the transition from being a student to being a teacher. It is natural for you to feel both excited and a bit fearful when thinking about that transition. As a teacher, you will assume an entirely new role—a role that requires some time before it becomes comfortable.

You will need to take several steps before securing your first teaching position. Preparing well for these steps will go a long way toward helping to make your entry into teaching professionally rewarding and personally satisfying. The first section of this chapter discusses the most critical phase of learning to become a teacher— your induction into the profession. The remaining sections discuss how to obtain your first teaching position, how to make the first days and weeks of teaching productive and satisfying, and how to become part of a professional, collaborative learning community.

Why Is Your Induction into Teaching Important?

The retention of public school teachers has become a major problem throughout the United States. Each year, scores of beginning teachers enter classrooms with vigor and determination; regrettably, however, many soon leave the profession. Up to 50 percent of new teachers in the United States leave the profession within the first five years (National Commission on Teaching and America's Future 2003).

Clearly, beginning teachers need support, guidance, and encouragement to become confident, skilled professionals.

Some beginning teachers eventually give up their chosen profession because their problems and concerns go unattended. Veteran teachers, who recall their own early struggles as beginning teachers, often have a "sink-or-swim" attitude toward the difficulties encountered by those just entering the profession (Glickman, Gordon, and Ross-Gordon 2004). "Since I had to learn to cope with the challenges of beginning teaching on my own, today's teachers either have to sink or swim," they reason. In addition, beginning teachers may believe that they should appear as skilled as master teachers on the faculty. Interviews with new teachers suggest that they want to talk about the problems they encounter in their work. They want assistance to help them to be successful during the first few years of teaching. Instead, however, they may experience isolation and have few opportunities to share their experiences with colleagues.

Problems and Concerns of Beginning Teachers

The problems and concerns of beginning teachers can be extensive. The following problems cause some beginning teachers to think about leaving the profession: maintaining classroom discipline, motivating students, responding to individual differences, assessing students' work, maintaining positive relationships with parents, organizing classroom activities, securing adequate teaching materials and supplies, and dealing with the problems of individual students.

In some cases, teachers experience frustration related to lack of preparation time, conflicts with principals, difficulties with student misconduct, and undesirable teaching assignments (e.g., larger class sizes than experienced teachers). Additionally, Glickman, Gordon, and Ross-Gordon (2004) found that a lack of dialogue about instruction, minimal involvement in schoolwide decisions about curriculum and instruction, and the absence of a shared technical culture are among the reasons why teachers leave the profession.

Induction into the Profession

One solution to the problem of teacher attrition is to provide beginning teachers with induction programs that provide them with support during their first years in the profession. Many states and local school districts, often in collaboration with colleges and universities, have begun teacher induction and/or internship programs. Among the programs that have received national attention are the Florida Beginning Teacher Program, the California Mentor Teacher Program, the Virginia Beginning Teacher Assistance Program, and the Kentucky Beginning Teacher Internship Program.

Induction programs provide beginning teachers with continued assistance at least during the first year. Most induction programs serve the following purposes:

- Improving teaching performance
- Increasing the retention of promising beginning teachers during the induction years

- Promoting the personal and professional well-being of beginning teachers by improving teachers' attitudes toward themselves and the profession
- Satisfying mandated requirements related to induction and certification
- Transmitting the culture of the school system to beginning teachers

To accomplish these purposes, induction programs offer such resources as workshops based on teacher-identified needs, observations by and follow-up conferences with individuals not in a supervisory role, support from mentor (or buddy) teachers, and support group meetings for beginning teachers.

Teacher Induction in Other Countries

Beginning teachers in many other countries are provided extensive support, guidance, and encouragement that enable them to become confident, skilled professionals. Increasingly, U.S. school districts are replicating induction practices that have provided much-needed support for beginning teachers in other countries (Parkay and Oaks 1998). The following sections describe five features of effective teacher induction programs in other countries. These features are based on a cross-national study of teacher induction practices co-sponsored by the U.S. Department of Education and the Education Forum of APEC (Asia-Pacific Economic Cooperation), and are reported in *From Students of Teaching to Teachers of Students* (U.S. Department of Education, 1997).

1. *New teachers are viewed as professionals on a continuum, with increasing levels of experience and responsibility; novice teachers are not expected to do the same job as experienced teachers without significant support.* According to the APEC Teacher Induction Study, beginning teachers in Japan and New Zealand are given lighter teaching loads than other teachers. New teachers are also assigned to classes school officials perceive as less difficult. This practice differs from the widespread U.S. practice of assigning beginning teachers to the most difficult classes. As a New Zealand principal put it, "I assign new teachers to classes where I expect fewer discipline problems and parents who are easier to deal with" (U.S. Department of Education, 1997, April 18, 1).

2. *New teachers are nurtured and not left to "flounder on their own"; interaction with other teachers is maximized.* In many Asian countries, for example, beginning teachers are typically assigned by the government to a school where they are considered novices and inducted into the profession by master teachers. In New Zealand, the isolation of beginning teachers is lessened by assigning them to classrooms next door to a "buddy teacher" or among other teachers of the same grade level.

It is not unusual for new and experienced teachers in these countries to move back and forth between one another's classrooms to observe and to exchange materials and strategies. In Japan, beginning teachers have at least two periods per week to be observed or to observe other teachers, and at least three periods for consultation with master teachers. These practices are in sharp contrast to those found in the United States, where, "isolated behind classroom doors with little feedback or help, [teachers] learn merely to cope rather than to teach well" (National Commission on Teaching and America's Future, 1996, 5).

3. *Teacher induction is a purposive and valued activity.* In Japan, for example, master teachers receive one-year leaves of absence to supervise new teachers. The master teachers' supervisory responsibilities include observing new teachers and providing comments and suggestions for improvement. In New Zealand, schools with a beginning teacher receive 20 percent more funding for that teacher's position, so release time can be provided for that teacher to observe and consult with other teachers and take part in inservice training.

4. *Schools possess a culture of shared responsibility and support, in which all or most of the school's staff contributes to the development and nurturing of the new teacher.* To communicate to the new teacher that he or she will be nurtured in an environment that fosters professional success, one of the responsibilities of Japanese principals is to ensure that all teachers in the building assist the first-year teacher. On the other hand, beginning teachers in the United States are often quite aware that they are "on their own" during their first years of teaching.

5. *Assessment of new teachers is downplayed.* Lastly, a critical difference between the experiences of beginning teachers in the United States and those in many other countries is that U.S. teachers experience an induction process that is more assessment and performance oriented. Many states, for example, have established professional standards boards to regulate and improve the professional practice of teachers. In many other countries, however, beginning teachers experience an induction process designed to help them improve rather than to evaluate their effectiveness. "In Australia/Northern Territory, for example, the administration asks schools to focus less on administering assessments of teacher competency, and more on helping teachers prepare for assessment. A teacher's failure is seen as a failure on the part of the administration" (U.S. Department of Education, 1997, April 18, 3). The APEC Induction Study noted that downplaying assessment contributes to a nonthreatening environment in which it is easier for new teachers to ask for assistance and support. "Teachers do not seem to feel threatened or even uncomfortable about being observed, or about asking questions they fear will reveal professional inadequacies" (U.S. Department of Education, 1997, April 18, 3).

How Will You Become Certified?

Successful completion of a college or university teacher preparation program will not automatically enable you to teach. State certification is required for teaching in the public schools, and in many private schools as well. In some cases, large cities (e.g., Chicago, New York, Buffalo) have their own certification requirements that must be met. And certain local school districts have additional requirements, such as a written examination, before one can teach in those districts.

A **teaching certificate** is actually a license to teach. The department of education for each of the fifty states and the District of Columbia sets the requirements for certification. A certificate usually indicates at what level and in what content areas one may teach. One might, for example, be certified for all-level (K–12) physical education or art, secondary English, elementary education, or middle-level education. Currently, about two-thirds of the states offer certification for teaching at the middle school or junior high level—an increase from 1987 when about half of the states offered such certification. In addition, a certificate may list other areas of specialization, such as driver's training, coaching, or journalism. If you plan to go into nonteaching areas such as counseling, librarianship, or administration, special certificates usually are required.

State Certification Requirements

For a person to receive a teaching certificate, all states require successful completion of an approved teacher education program that culminates with at least a bachelor's degree. To be approved, programs must pass a review by the state department of education approximately every five years. In addition to approval at the state level, most of the nearly 1,300 programs in the nation have regional accreditation, and more than 525 voluntarily seek accreditation by the National Council for Accreditation of Teacher Education (NCATE) (2002). Currently, all states require an average of six to eight semester credits of supervised student teaching. Alabama, Colorado, Idaho, Indiana, Nevada, New York, and Virginia require a master's degree for advanced certification; Arizona, Maryland, Montana, Oregon, and Washington require either a master's degree or a specified number of semester credits after certification (Kaye 2001). Additional requirements may also include U.S. citizenship, an oath of loyalty, fingerprinting, or a health examination.

A few states, including Iowa, New Mexico, North Carolina, and Oklahoma, waive state licensing requirements for teachers certified by the National Board for Professional Teaching Standards (NBPTS). About half of the states will issue a license to a person from another state who holds a valid NBPTS certificate. For a current listing of state and local action supporting NBPTS certification, call the NBPTS at 800-22TEACH.

Nearly all states now require testing of teachers for initial certification. States use either a standardized test (usually the National Teacher Examination [NTE] or Praxis) or a test developed by outside consultants. Areas covered by the states' tests usually include basic skills, professional knowledge, and general knowledge. Many states also require an on-the-job performance evaluation for certification (see Table 6.1 on pages 222–223).

There is a trend away from granting teaching certificates for life. Some states, for example, issue three- to five-year certificates, which may be renewed only with proof of coursework completed beyond the bachelor's degree. And, amid considerable controversy, several states, including Connecticut, Maryland, Massachusetts, New Hampshire, Rhode Island, South Carolina, and Wisconsin, have enacted testing for **recertification** of experienced teachers. Though each state's policy differs, all have moved away from allowing teachers to take any education-related classes to renew their certification. New Hampshire and South Carolina, for instance, require that teachers pursue professional development in their subject areas, as well as in technology, to become recertified (Boser 2000).

Certification requirements differ from state to state, and they are frequently modified. To remain up-to-date on the requirements for the state in which you plan to teach, it is important that you keep in touch with your teacher placement office or certification officer at your college or university. You may also wish to refer to *Requirements for Certification for Elementary and Secondary Schools* (The University of Chicago Press), an annual publication that lists state-by-state certification requirements for teachers, counselors, librarians, and administrators. Or, you may contact the teacher certification office in the state where you plan to teach (see Appendix 6.1, "Directory of State Teacher Certification Offices in the United States" at the end of this chapter).

Currently, forty-seven states and the District of Columbia are members of the **Interstate Certification Agreement Contract**, a reciprocity agreement whereby a certificate obtained in one state will be honored in another. If you plan to teach in a state other than the one in which you are currently studying, you should find out whether both states share a reciprocity agreement.

About 404,000 teachers, many of whom are noncertified, teach in the United States' growing system of private, parochial, for-profit, and charter schools (National Center for Education Statistics 2002a). Private and parochial schools supported largely by tuition and gifts and for-profit schools operated by private educational corporations usually have no certification requirements for teachers. Also, teacher-created and teacher-operated charter schools, though they are public, are often free of state certification requirements. A school's **charter** (an agreement between the school's founders and its sponsor—usually a local school board) may waive certification requirements if the school guarantees that students will attain a specified level of achievement.

Alternative Certification

Despite the national movement to make certification requirements more stringent, concern about meeting the demand for two million new public school teachers by the year 2008–09 (American Federation of Teachers 2001) and attracting minority-group members into the teaching profession has resulted in increasing use of alter-

Table 6.1 Assessment requirements for the initial teaching certificate

State	Basic Skills Exam					Subject Matter Exam	General Knowledge Exam	Knowledge of Teaching Exam	Assessment of Teaching Performance	Footnotes
	Reading 1	Math 2	Writing 3	Spelling 4	Other 5	6	7	8	9	
Alabama	(1)	(1)	(1)	(1)		(2)		(2)	X	(1) For admission to program (2) Institution's exit exam
Alaska	X	X	X							
Arizona						X		X	X	
Arkansas	X	X	X			X		X		
California	X	X	X			(1)				(1) Or completion of an approved subject matter program
Colorado						X				
Connecticut	X	X	X			X				Praxis I—CBT and Praxis II
Delaware	X	X	X							Praxis I Pre-Professional Skills Test
District of Columbia	X	X	X			X			X	Praxis I Pre-Professional Skills Test
Florida	X	X	X			X	X	X	X	
Georgia	(1)	(1)	(1)			X				(1) Praxis I required in Georgia approved programs, eff. 3/1/99
Hawaii	X	X	X			X		X		
Idaho										
Illinois	X	X	X		(1)	X				(1) Grammar
Indiana	X		X		(1)	X	X	X		(1) Listening
Iowa										
Kansas	X	X	X					X		
Kentucky	(1)	(1)	(1)	X		(2)		(2)	X	(1) Required for admission to teacher education (2) Fingerprint check is required for employment
Louisiana	X	X	X		(1)	X	X	X	X	(1) Communication skills
Maine					(1)		X	X		(1) Communication skills
Maryland	X	X	X			X		X	X	
Massachusetts (1)										(1) Two-part exam covering communication and literacy skills and the subject matter knoweldge for the certificate
Michigan	X	X	X			X	(1)			(1) Elementary Certificate exam (subject-area exam)
Minnesota	X	X	X		(1)					(1) PPST required
Mississippi						X		X		

State	1	2	3	4	5	6	7	8	Notes
Missouri	(1)	(1)	(1)	(1)		X		(2)		(1) For entry into teacher education (2) If no subject knowledge test is designated
Montana	X	X	X							
Nebraska	X	X	X							
Nevada	X	X	X			X		X		
New Hampshire	(1)	(1)	(1)			X				Praxis I and Praxis II
New Jersey						X	(1)		X	(1) For elementary education
New Mexico	X	X	X				X	X		
New York							X	X		
North Carolina	(1)	(1)	(1)			X				(1) Prior to entry into teacher education
North Dakota	(1)	(1)	(1)	(1)		X		X		(1) Prior to entry into teacher education
Ohio	X	X	X			X		X	(1)	(1) Entry year Perf. Assess-2002
Oklahoma	X	X	X			X	X	X	X	
Oregon	X	X	X			X			(1)	(1) For Oregon graduates
Pennsylvania	X	X	X		(1)	X	(2)	X		(1) Listening (2) Includes Math
Rhode Island (1)							X			(1) Principles of Learning Teaching Test
South Carolina	X	X	X			X		X	X	
South Dakota (1)	X	X	X			X			X	(1) Required within the institutional program requirements
Tennessee (1)						X		X		(1) Basic skills exams in reading, math, and writing are covered in PPST.
Texas (1)						X		X		(1) Screening for admission to a teacher preparation progam includes college level skills in reading, oral and written communication, critical thinking, and mathematics
Utah								(1)		(1) Entry year requirement
Vermont	X	X	X			(1)				(1) See Emerging Trends
Virginia	X	X	X			X				
Washington	(1)	(1)	(1)							(1) Required prior to entering teacher education
West Virginia	X	X	X			X		X	X	
Wisconsin	X	X	X							
Wyoming										

Source: *The NASDTEC Manual 2001: Manual on the Preparation and Certificate of Educational Personnel*. Mashpee, MA: National Association of State Directors of Teacher Education & Certification, pp. B-6–B-7. Used with permission.

native teacher certification programs. In 1983, only eight states offered alternatives; by 2002, forty-five states had alternative routes to certification (Feistritzer 2002; Roach and Cohen 2002).

Alternative certification programs are designed for people who already have at least a bachelor's degree in a field other than education and want to become licensed to teach. It is estimated that about 175,000 people have been licensed through alternative certification programs since 1983 (Feistritzer 2002). Most alternative certification programs are collaborative efforts among state departments of education, teacher education programs in colleges and universities, and school districts. For example, Washington State University, in collaboration with area school districts, has a federally funded program to prepare paraprofessional educators (e.g., teachers' aides) in southwest Washington to become bilingual/ESL teachers. Compared with recent college graduates who enter teaching directly from a traditional college-based teacher preparation program, those who enter teaching through alternate routes tend to

- Have degrees with majors in subjects other than education
- Be more likely to have work experience in occupations other than education
- Be older
- More likely be people of color
- More likely be men (Feistritzer 2002)

All but two states may grant certification to those who do not meet current requirements. About half of the states may even give a substandard credential to those who hold less than a bachelor's degree. In response to occasional shortages of teachers in particular subject and grade-level areas, many state systems approve temporary measures, such as **emergency certification**. Nationwide, more than 12 percent of newly hired teachers enter the profession without any training at all, and another 15 percent enter without having fully met state standards, according to the National Commission on Teaching and America's Future.

Emergency certification is strongly resisted by professional teacher organizations and several state departments of education. Though strongly resisted by professional teacher organizations, alternative certification is likely to become even more widespread in the event of a teacher shortage.

The Praxis Series

Thirty-five of the forty-three states that include tests as part of their certification process require completion of the **Praxis Series: Professional Assessments for Beginning Teachers** developed by Educational Testing Service (ETS) in consultation with teachers, educational researchers, the National Education Association, and the American Federation of Teachers. The Praxis Series (*praxis* means putting theory into practice) enables states to create a system of tests that meet their specific licensing requirements.

What are some alternatives for becoming certified or licensed to teach? What are some current trends in certification and what conditions might account for those trends?

The Praxis Series, which replaced the National Teacher Examination in the mid-1990s, consists of three components:

- *Praxis I: Academic skills assessments*—Praxis I covers the "enabling skills" in reading, writing, and mathematics that all teachers need, regardless of grade or subject taught. Two formats, computer-based and pencil-and-paper, are available for the Praxis I assessment, which is given early in a student's teacher education program. To help students pass Praxis I, ETS offers online practice test items and, for students who need help in improving basic academic skills, LearningPlus, an interactive computer software program that provides instruction and diagnostic placement tests in reading, writing, and mathematics.

- *Praxis II: Subject assessments*—Praxis II measures teacher education students' knowledge of the subjects they will teach. In most cases, Praxis II tests are taken on completion of an undergraduate program. The tests, available in more than seventy subject areas, have a core content module required by every state, with the remaining modules selected on an individual basis by the states. Each state can base its assessment on multiple-choice items or on candidate-constructed-response modules. In addition, Praxis II includes the Principles of Learning and Teaching (PLT) test and the Professional Knowledge test; each is a two-hour test to assess teachers' professional knowledge. The PLT is available in three versions: K–6, 5–9, and 7–12.

- *Praxis III: Classroom performance assessments*—Praxis III is a performance-based assessment system, not a test. Developed after extensive job analyses, reviews of research, and input from educators, Praxis III involves the assessment of actual teaching skills of the beginning teacher. The assessments focus on the four domains of the Praxis Framework for Teaching, as presented in Figure 1.1 on page 6): planning and preparation, the classroom environment, instruction, and professional responsibilities. In addition, Praxis III assesses the teacher's sensitivity to developmental levels and cultural differences among students. In-class assessments and pre- and post-observation interviews conducted by trained state and local personnel are the main components of Praxis III. The observations are supplemented by work samples—for example, lesson plans. Following Praxis III assessments, which normally are completed by the end of the first year of teaching, the state makes a decision about whether to grant a license to teach.

Will You Have Difficulty Getting a Teaching Job?

When you think ahead to a career in teaching, a question you are likely to ask yourself is, "How hard will it be to find a job?" From time to time, **teacher supply and demand** figures have painted a rather bleak picture for those entering the teaching profession. At other times, such as now, finding a position has not been difficult.

In 2002, the U.S. Department of Education announced that approximately 2.4 million teachers would be needed during the next eleven years because of teacher attrition and retirement and increased student enrollment (National Center for Education Statistics 2002b). This projection jumped as high as 2.7 million if declining student–teacher ratios based on nationwide class size reduction efforts were considered (National Center for Education Statistics 2002c).

Even during times of teacher surplus, talented, qualified teachers are able to find jobs. Teaching is one of the largest professions in the United States; out of a national population of about 288 million, about 47.4 million children attended public elementary and secondary schools in fall 2002, where they were taught by approximately 3.2 million teachers (National Center for Education Statistics 2002d). Within such a large profession, annual openings resulting from retirements and career changes alone are sizable.

Demand by Geographic Region and Specialty Area

Although public elementary and secondary school enrollments are projected to rise less than 1 percent between 1999 and 2011, growth will vary widely across the nation. Enrollment will increase in the West and South by 8 percent and 1 percent, respectively. In contrast, a decrease of 4 percent is projected for the Northeast, and a decrease of 3 percent is expected in the Midwest. Figure 6.1 shows the percent change in public K–8 and 9–12 enrollment by region.

The ease with which you will find your first teaching position is also related to your area of specialization. In 2004, for example, job seekers able to teach bilingual education, special education, English as a second language (ESL), mathematics, chemistry, or physics were in an especially favorable position. For current employment opportunities according to specialty area and geographic region and for

Figure 6.1   Percent change in grades K–12 enrollment in public schools, by state: Fall 1999 to Fall 2011.

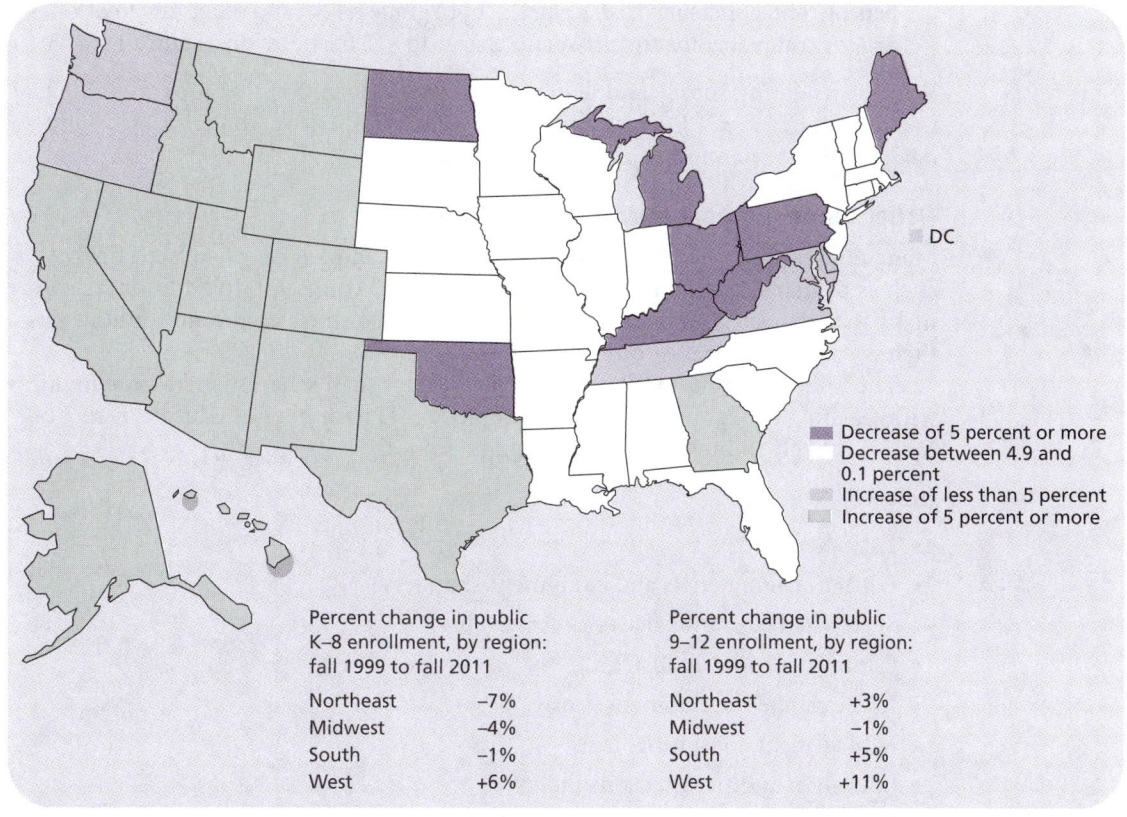

Decrease of 5 percent or more
Decrease between 4.9 and 0.1 percent
Increase of less than 5 percent
Increase of 5 percent or more

Percent change in public K–8 enrollment, by region: fall 1999 to fall 2011		Percent change in public 9–12 enrollment, by region: fall 1999 to fall 2011	
Northeast	–7%	Northeast	+3%
Midwest	–4%	Midwest	–1%
South	–1%	South	+5%
West	+6%	West	+11%

Source: U.S. Department of Education, National Center for Education Statistics, Common Core of Data Surveys, and State Public Elementary and Secondary Enrollment Model. Adapted from *Projections of Education Statistics to 2011.* Washington, DC: National Center for Education Statistics, 2001.

other job-search resources, check the following publications by the American Association for Employment in Education, Inc. (AAEE) (3040 Riverside Drive, Suite 125, Columbus, OH 43221-2550, (614) 485-1111, fax (614) 485-9609, www.aaee.org, aaee@osu.edu). Be aware, however, that the AAEE does not provide placement services or maintain lists of vacancies.

- *The Job Search Handbook for Educators*—Supply–demand data, interview techniques, résumé advice, and other job-search suggestions, $8
- *The Job Hunter's Guide: Services and Career Fairs for Educators*—Includes job fairs across the nation (dates, times, locations, contact information), listing of colleges and universities that offer services to students who are not their own graduates, teacher certification reciprocity among states, subscriptions to vacancy listings or websites, computer referral systems, and other resources, $15

- *Directory of Public School Systems in the U.S.*—Names, addresses, and phone numbers of contact persons, district size, school grade levels, and other information, $80 for complete directory; from no charge to $12 for individual state directories

When considering supply and demand estimates, remember that jobs are to be had in oversupplied areas. Job hunting will be more competitive, though, and you may have to relocate to another region of the country.

Other Career Opportunities for Teachers

Many nonteaching jobs are available in education and education-related fields, such as principal, assistant principal, librarian, and counselor. In addition, there are many jobs that, although removed from the world of the classroom, would nevertheless enable you to use your teaching skills.

The following outline lists several places other than schools where individuals with teaching backgrounds are often employed. The number of education-related careers is likely to increase in the coming decades.

Industry

- Publishers
- Educational materials and equipment suppliers
- Specialized educational service firms
- Communications industries
- Research and development firms
- Management consulting firms
- Education and training consultants
- Educational divisions of large corporations—Xerox, IBM, CBS, General Electric, Westinghouse, etc.

Government

- Federal agencies—U.S. Office of Education, Bureau of Prisons, Department of Labor, Office of Economic Opportunity, Department of Justice, Department of Health, Education and Welfare, etc.
- Federal programs—Bureau of Indian Affairs Schools, Bureau of Prisons Schools, Job Corps, Overseas Dependent Schools, Peace Corps, Teacher Corps, Upward Bound, VISTA, etc.
- Regional educational networks—Research and development centers, regional educational laboratories, sixteen clearinghouses of the Educational Resources Information Center (ERIC), etc.
- Jobs in state departments of education

Education-Related Associations

- Research centers and foundations

- Professional associations—National Council of Teachers of English, National Association of Mathematics Teachers, National Education Association, American Federation of Teachers, Phi Delta Kappa, Kappa Delta Pi, Educational Testing Service, etc.

Community Organizations

- Community action programs—Upward Bound, neighborhood health centers, legal services, aid to migrant workers, etc.
- Social service agencies—United Fund agencies, Boy Scouts, Girl Scouts, YMCAs and YWCAs, settlement houses, boys' and girls' clubs, etc.
- Adult education centers
- Museums
- Hospitals

How Will You Find Your First Teaching Job?

Near the end of your teacher education program, you will probably become increasingly concerned about finding a teaching position. The "Job Search Timetable Checklist" presented in Appendix 6.2 may help you plan your job search. Also, Figure 6.2 presents the factors more than two hundred school-hiring officials think are most important when they are considering first-time teachers for employment. The remainder of this section discusses five critical steps in that sequence: finding out about teaching vacancies, preparing a résumé, writing letters of inquiry and letters of application, being interviewed, and selecting a position.

Finding Out About Teaching Vacancies

Your college or university probably has a placement service designed to help graduates find jobs. On a regular basis, placement offices usually publish lists of vacancies, which are posted and, in many cases, mailed to students who have registered with the office and set up a credentials file. In addition, you can use the Internet to connect with other universities that have accessible online placement services.

A **credentials file** (known as placement papers at some institutions) usually includes the following: background information on the applicant, the type of position sought, a list of courses taken, performance evaluations by the applicant's cooperative teacher, and three or more letters of recommendation. With each job application, the candidate requests that his or her credentials be sent to the appropriate person at the school district, or the school district itself may request the applicant's papers. Placement offices usually charge a small fee for each time a candidate's papers are sent out.

A job announcement describes the position and its requirements and provides the name and address of the individual to contact at the school district. For each position you are interested in, send a letter of application to the appropriate person along with your résumé. In addition, you may have your placement office send

Figure 6.2 Moving from "candidate" to "teacher".

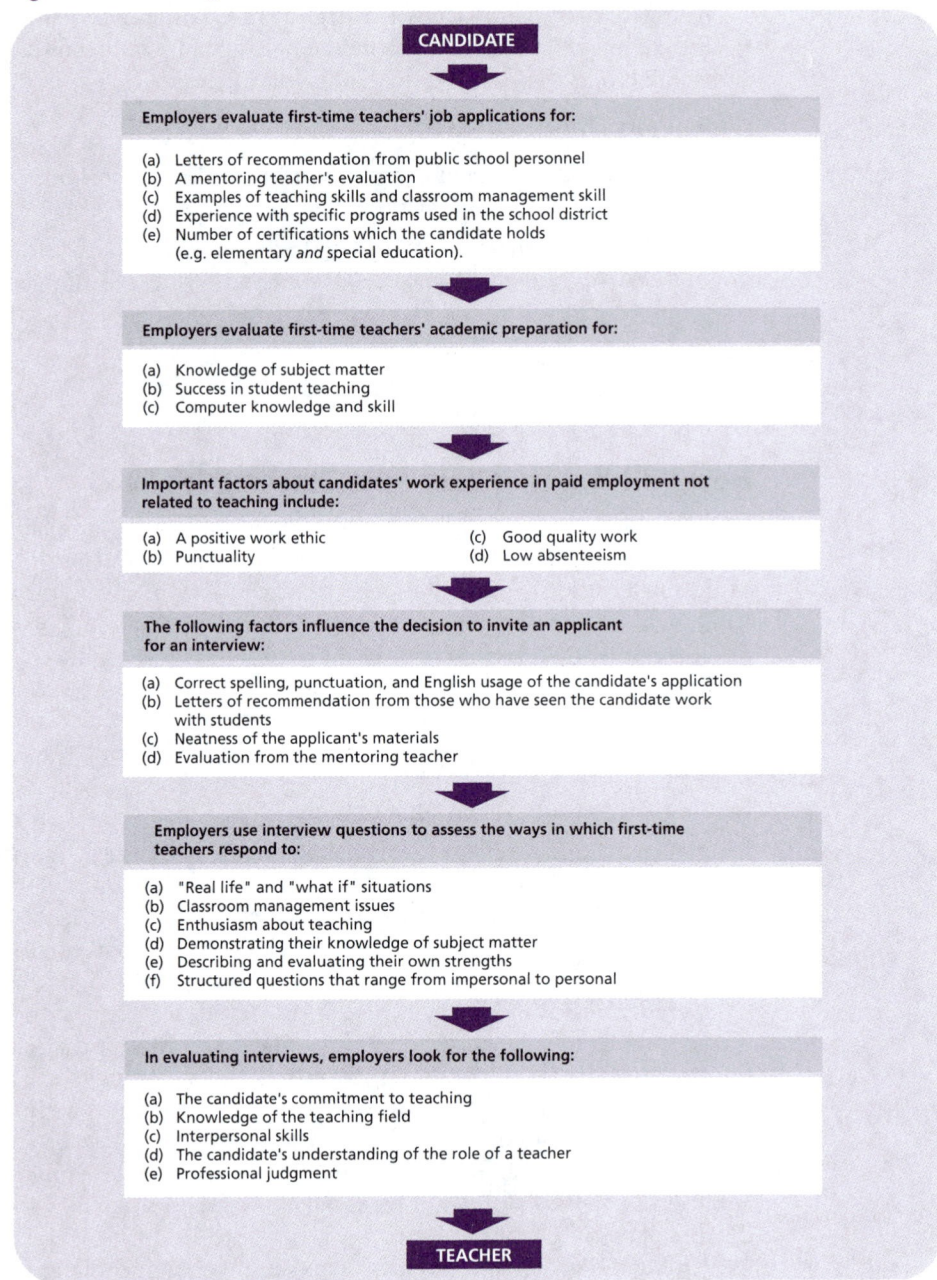

Note: Items arranged in order of importance.
Source: Adapted from Judy McEnany and Patricia Reuss, "Fascinating Facts for First-Time Teachers," *2001 Job Search Handbook for Educators,* American Association for Employment in Education, p. 30. Used with permission.

your credentials file. Placement offices also frequently set up on-campus interviews between candidates and representatives of school district personnel departments.

State department of education employment offices help teachers locate positions. Like college and university placement offices, states publish lists of job openings, which are then distributed to registered candidates. Because most of these states will assist out-of-state candidates, you can register in more than one state.

Personal networking will play an important role in landing the right job. Let people know you are looking for a job—friends, teachers at schools you have attended, faculty at the school where you student teach, and people you meet at workshops and conferences. Also, with access to the Internet, you can conduct a global job search and even make your résumé available to millions of people. The following noncommercial Internet sites can be helpful in your job search efforts:

- School district websites
- State departments of education websites
- *Project Connect*—After obtaining a free user name and password, you can search teaching vacancies on the Web and post information about yourself, sponsored in part by the AAEE
- *America's Job Bank*—A comprehensive, free job-search service linked to two thousand state employment offices

Preparing Your Résumé

A **résumé** presents a concise summary of an individual's professional experiences, education, and skills. Résumés must be typed and preferably no longer than one page, two pages at most. Although there is no right way to prepare a résumé, it should present—in a neat, systematic way—key information that will help an employer determine your suitability for a particular position. Because your résumé will most likely be your first contact with an employer, it must make a good impression.

Ordinarily, a résumé contains the following information:

- Personal data
- Education
- Certificates held
- Experience
- Activities and interests
- Honors and offices held
- Professional memberships
- References

Figure 6.3 on page 232 is a résumé prepared by Linda M. Rodriguez that you can use as a model. To prepare an effective résumé, read "Résumé Advice for Educators" in Appendix 6.3.

Figure 6.3 Résumé.

Linda M. Rodriguez

Personal Data

Born: October 16, 1983

Address and Phone: 948 W. Third
Spokane, WA 99206
(509) 924-1234
lmrodrig@abc.com

Education

B.A., Elementary Education, Washington State University, June 2004.

Certificates Held

Major Area: Elementary Education, K–8

Minor Area: Bilingual Education

Experience

Student Teaching, Garden Springs Elementary, W. 5116 Garden Springs Road, Spokane, WA 99204, Spring 2004. Cooperating teacher: Mrs. Becky Jones. Observed, assisted, and taught regular and accelerated 3rd grade classes in a multilingual setting. Organized after-school tutoring program and developed a unit on using the World Wide Web in the classroom. Attended site-based council meetings with Mrs. Jones and assisted in the development of community-based partnerships.

Camp Counselor and Recreation Director, YWCA Summer Camp, Spokane, WA.
Directed summer recreation program comprised of 10 counselors and 140 elementary aged girls.

Volunteer Telephone Counselor, Spokane County Crisis Hotline, June 2002–June 2004.

Activities and Interests

Spokane County Historical Society, Secretary, 2004.

Member, Washington State University Community Service Learning Center.

Hobbies: Jogging, Aerobics, Piano, Water Skiing.

Honors

B.A. with Honors, Washington State University, June 2004.

Washington State Scholarship, 2002–2004.

Professional Memberships

Washington Association for Supervision and Curriculum Development.

Kappa Delta Pi.

Instructional Technology Skills

Word processing, Internet and World Wide Web, optical scanner, interactive electronic whiteboard,

LCD computer projection panel, NovaNET (computer-based learning system).

Career Objective

Seeking K–8 position in multicultural/multilingual setting.

References

References and credentials file available upon request.

Writing Letters of Inquiry and Application

As a job seeker, you will most likely have occasion to write two kinds of letters: letters of inquiry and letters of application. A **letter of inquiry** is used to determine if a school district has, or anticipates, any teaching vacancies. This type of letter states your general qualifications and requests procedures to be followed in making a formal application (see Figure 6.4 on page 234). A letter of inquiry should also include your résumé as well as a self-addressed, stamped envelope for the school district's convenience. Be prepared not to receive a reply for each letter of inquiry you send out. Many school districts are unable to respond to all inquiries.

A **letter of application** (often called a cover letter) indicates your interest in a particular position and outlines your qualifications for that job. Because most districts have several vacancies at any given time, it is important that the first sentence of your letter refer to the specific position for which you are applying. The body of the letter should then highlight why you would be an excellent choice to fill that position. Also, inform the reader that your credentials file will be sent on request or is being sent by your placement office. Close the letter by expressing your availability for an interview (see Figure 6.5 on page 235).

Participating in a Job Interview

The interview is one of the most important steps in your search for an appropriate position. As the dialogue in the scenario at the beginning of this chapter suggests, school district representatives may ask a wide range of questions, both structured and open ended.

What questions might you be asked in an interview for a teaching position? What questions should you have about the teaching position? About the school?

Figure 6.4 Letter of inquiry.

Linda M. Rodriguez
948 W. Third
Spokane, Washington 99206

April 5, 2006

Dr. Lawrence Walker
Office of Personnel Services
City School District
100 Post Oak Boulevard
Houston, Texas 77056

Dear Dr. Walker:

This letter is to express my interest in a teaching position in the Houston City School District. Specifically, I would like to know if you anticipate any vacancies at the elementary level for fall of 2004. This June I will receive my B.A. (with honors) in elementary education from Washington State University. My supporting endorsement will be in bilingual education.

As a student teacher this spring semester, I taught regular and accelerated 3rd grade classes at Garden Springs Elementary School in Spokane, Washington. One class had 25 students, 3 of whom were diagnosed as having learning disabilities. At Garden Springs, I introduced students to science resources on the World Wide Web, and each student learned how to send e-mail messages to students in other countries.

My education at Washington State University, I believe, has prepared me well to teach in today's classrooms. I have had a course that focuses on meeting the needs of at-risk learners, and my supporting endorsement in bilingual education has prepared me to meet the challenges of working with students from diverse linguistic backgrounds. If possible, I would like a position that would allow me to develop programs for students with non–English backgrounds.

Enclosed you will find my résumé, which provides additional information about my experiences and activities. If there are any positions for which you think I might be suited, please send application materials in the enclosed stamped, self-addressed envelope. I appreciate your consideration, and I look forward to hearing from you.

Sincerely,

Linda M. Rodriguez

Linda M. Rodriguez

In some districts, you might be interviewed by the principal only; in others, the superintendent, the principal, and the department chairperson might interview you; and in still others, classroom teachers might interview you. Regardless of format, the interview enables the district to obtain more specific information regarding your probable success as an employee, and it gives you an opportunity to ask

Figure 6.5   Letter of application.

Linda M. Rodriguez
948 W. Third
Spokane, Washington 99206

May 5, 2006

Dr. Mary Lamb
Associate Superintendent for Personnel
Metropolitan School District
Wacker Office Building
773 Ranier Avenue
Seattle, Washington 98504

Dear Dr. Lamb:

This letter is in support of my application for the position of 4th grade teacher at City Elementary School. This June I will receive my B.A. (with honors) in elementary education from Washington State University. My supporting endorsement will be in bilingual education.

As my enclosed résumé indicates, I just completed my student teaching at Garden Springs Elementary School in Spokane. During that 16-week period, I taught regular and accelerated 3rd grade classes. One class had 25 students, 3 of whom were diagnosed as having learning disabilities. I also organized an after-school tutoring program and assisted my cooperating teacher in developing community-based partnerships.

A major interest of mine is using technology in the classroom. I am familiar with various hypermedia programs and NovaNET, a computer-based learning system. At Garden Springs, I introduced students to science resources on the World Wide Web, and each student learned how to send e-mail messages to students in other countries.

As a result of my rewarding experiences at Garden Springs Elementary and in light of my preparation in bilingual education, I believe I could make a significant contribution to the educational program at City Elementary.

I have arranged for my credentials to be forwarded from Washington State University's placement office. If you require additional information of any sort, please feel free to contact me. At your convenience, I am available for an interview in Seattle. I thank you in advance for your consideration.

Sincerely,

Linda M. Rodriguez

Linda M. Rodriguez

questions about what it is like to teach in the district. By asking questions yourself, you demonstrate your interest in working in the district. Appendix 6.4 "Sample Interview Questions for Candidates to Ask" presents seventeen questions you can ask. In addition, at some point in the interview process you may wish to present brief highlights from your professional portfolio. Or, if you have created Internet and/or CD-ROM versions of your portfolio, you could give the hiring official(s) the URL for the portfolio or a copy of the CD-ROM itself.

Accepting an Offer

One day you are notified that a school district would like to hire you. Your job search efforts have paid off! In the competition for positions, you have been successful. However, accepting your first teaching position is a major personal and professional step. Before signing a contract with a district, you should carefully consider job-related questions such as the following:

- In regard to my abilities and education, am I suited to this position?
- Would I like to work with this school's students, administrative staff, and teachers?
- Is the salary I am being offered sufficient?
- Will this position likely be permanent?
- Would I like to live in or near this community?
- Would the cost of living in this community enable me to live comfortably?
- Are opportunities for continuing education readily available?

In addition, you should reflect on the workplace conditions that are essential for your job satisfaction. For example, how would you complete the following statements?

- Ideally, my first position would be teaching students who have the following backgrounds and characteristics . . .
- For me, an ideal work setting would be a school that . . .
- My fellow teachers would help me during my first year of teaching by . . .
- When not in school, my colleagues and I would enjoy . . .
- My principal and/or supervisor would appreciate the way I . . .
- In his or her feedback on my teaching, my principal and/or supervisor would be most impressed with . . .
- During my first year at the school I would volunteer to . . .
- Five years after I began teaching at this school, I would like to be . . .

If you accept the offer, you will need to return a signed contract to the district along with a short letter confirming your acceptance. As a professional courtesy, you should notify other districts to which you have applied that you have accepted a position elsewhere.

What Can You Expect as a Beginning Teacher?

Once you accept the professional challenge of teaching, it is important to prepare well in advance of the first day of school. In addition to reviewing the material you will teach, you should use this time to find out all you can about the school's students, the surrounding community, and the way the school operates. You should also reflect on your expectations.

The First Day

The first day of school can be frightening, as the following beginning teacher admits:

> *My first day of teaching in the classroom—alone! All of the other teachers look calm and are even smiling. I'm so nervous about fitting in at this school, making friends with my colleagues, and being respected by my students. What if the students misbehave and I don't handle it properly? Or what if the principal walks in unannounced? (Hauser and Rauch 2002, 35)*

Veteran teachers can also feel anxious on the first day of school; however, anxiety can be used to set a positive tone for the rest of the school year, as the following experienced teacher points out:

> *The anxiety level for both teachers and students about [the] first day is high. Taking advantage of these feelings can make for a good beginning.*
>
> *Students like to have guidelines on how the class will be run as well as what is expected of them academically. I always begin by welcoming the students into my class and immediately giving them something to do. I hand them their textbook and an index card. On the card, they write their name, address, telephone number, and book number.*
>
> *While the students are filling out their cards and looking at the textbook, I set up my seating chart and verify attendance. Within ten minutes of meeting the students, I begin my first lesson. By keeping clerical chores to a minimum, I try to have more time on task. After a closure activity, somewhere in the middle of the class period I take a few minutes to explain how their grade will be determined, the rules of the class, and when extra help sessions are available.*
>
> *Next, we deal with some curriculum content, and then I make a homework assignment. I tell the students that any homework assignment will be written on the chalkboard every day in the same location.*
>
> *Setting high standards on the first day makes the following days easier. We will always need to monitor and adjust, but this will be within the framework set on the first day (Burden and Byrd 1999, 177).*

Creating a pleasant, learning-oriented climate on the first day—as Kathy Mellor, the 2004 National Teacher of the Year who provides the epigraph for this chapter, does—will contribute greatly to your success during the first year. On the first day, students are eager to learn and are hopeful that the year will be a productive one. In addition, nearly all students will be naturally receptive to what you have to say. To them, you are a new, unknown quantity, and one of their initial concerns is to find out what kind of a teacher you will be. It is therefore critical that you be well organized and ready to take charge.

Case for
Reflection
My First Day of Teaching

Today is your first day of teaching. In a few minutes the bell will ring, signaling to students out on the playground and the adjacent grassy playing field that they should enter the building and report to their first-period class.

The school is in a multi-ethnic area of a large city. The surrounding neighborhood consists primarily of run-down multiple-family dwellings and small businesses. More than half of the students are from families on some form of public assistance.

You glance at the twenty-seven names on your class roster. Several names are from ethnic backgrounds that are different from yours.

Right after the bell rings, you step out into the hallway. As you do so, five children appear at the top of the stairs. They enter your room, talking loudly and breathlessly in Spanish about their plans for recess.

"Yo se que puedo cotter mas rapido que el," a tall thin boy exclaims.

"¡Claro, vamos a tener otra carrera y ahi les ensenaremos quien es mas rapido!" another boy says, his small right fist jabbing the air for emphasis.

"Ja, Jose se va a llevar una sorpresa cuando pierda," a short girl giggles.

As you wait for the remaining students to enter your room, you think about your first day of teaching. "How will I meet the needs of students from different cultural and linguistic backgrounds?" "How will students react to my rules regarding classroom discipline?" "Do I have enough activities to keep students engaged for the entire class period?" "Will I find an experienced teacher to whom I can turn for advice?" "How can I get the parents of my students involved?" "Will I enjoy teaching?" "Will my students enjoy having me as their teacher?"

Questions

1. Imagine that you are almost ready to experience your first day as a teacher. What questions would you have, in addition to those contained in the preceding case?
2. On your first day of teaching, what will be your primary goals? How will you know that you have achieved those goals?
3. What words and phrases best describe the classroom environment you will create during your first few months of teaching?

Advice from Experienced Teachers

Experienced K–12 teachers in urban, suburban, and rural schools have several recommendations on preparing for the first day of school. Like the teachers who recommended first-day-of-school classroom management strategies in Chapter 2, their recommendations focus on planning, establishing effective management practices, and following through on decisions.

There are little things you can do, such as having a personal note attached to a pencil welcoming each child. You may want to do a few little tricks in science class or read them your favorite children's story. But, don't put all your energy into the first day and have that day be the highlight of the year. Be well prepared and have plenty of things to do. Don't worry if you don't get everything done. Remember, you have all year.

—Middle school science teacher

On the first day, have plenty of activities to keep students engaged. Don't worry about having too many activities. If you don't get to some activities, you can use those the following day. With experience, you will learn how many activities to prepare.

—Fifth-grade teacher

On the first day, I review classroom rules and procedures. I am very clear and specific about my expectations for classroom behavior.

—Seventh-grade teacher

From the first day, kids know I'm there to teach. I always teach something on the first day, or review material they learned last year. That way, they know I'm in charge and I expect them to learn. Kids expect the teacher to take charge from the beginning. Teachers who do that seldom have problems.

—High school math teacher

How Can You Become a Part of Your Learning Community?

Success in your first year of teaching will be determined by the relationships you develop with students, their families, your colleagues, school administrators, and other members of the school community. All of these groups contribute to your effectiveness as a teacher, but the relationships you establish with students will be the most important (and complex) you will have as a teacher.

Relationships with Students

The quality of your relationships with students will depend in large measure on your knowledge of students and commitment to improving your interactions with them. As a first-year teacher put it:

It is amazing when every student is involved and enjoying the lesson. At moments like these, I realize that I'm educating real people and making a difference in their futures.

I really connected with my students because they saw that learning can be fun. They realized that I, too, am a person who cares about them and wants them to succeed. It makes my job feel complete and I know I'm in the right profession (Hauser and Rauch 2002, 36).

Your relationships with students will have many dimensions. Principally, you must see that each student learns as much as possible; this is your primary responsibility as a professional teacher. You will need to establish relationships with a great diversity of students based on mutual respect, caring, and concern. Without attention to this personal realm, your effectiveness as a teacher will be limited. In addition, teachers are significant models for students' attitudes and behaviors.

Relationships with Colleagues and Staff

Each working day, you will be in close contact with other teachers and staff members. As the experience of the following teacher suggests, it will definitely be to your advantage to establish friendly, professional relationships with your colleagues:

> I was on a staff with a group of teachers who really supported me. They made it a part of their day to come into my room and see how I was doing and to share things. They made it easy to ask questions and work with them. They started me on the track of cooperating with other teachers and sharing my successes and failures with them.
>
> They did such a good job of taking care of each other that my needs were always met. I had plenty of supplies, counseling help, administrative help. The school was a community. Anything I needed to be successful was provided.

During your first few months of teaching, it is wise to communicate to colleagues that you are willing to learn all you can about your new job and to be a team player. As mentioned earlier, beginning teachers frequently are given less desirable assignments, and experienced faculty more desirable ones. Your willingness to take on a difficult assignment with good humor and to give it your best effort will establish you as a valuable faculty member.

Your colleagues may also appreciate learning from you about new approaches and materials—if you share in a manner that does not make others feel inferior. The following comments by a high school department chair, for example, illustrate a first-year Spanish teacher's positive influence on others:

> She won the respect of all her colleagues in the school who have dealt with her almost immediately, not because she's so competent in Spanish and not because she's so competent as a teacher, but because she handles everything with such sensitivity and sensibleness.
>
> Because of the way she operates—which is quietly but effectively—she has raised the whole tenor of expectations in the department. We have some very fine faculty in Spanish, but I would speculate they don't see their group self-image as intellectuals but rather as "people people." Because of what Elizabeth has brought to the school: the knowledge about how to use computers, her knowledge of foreign language oral proficiency, her knowledge of Spanish film and Spanish authors, she has kind of lifted everybody up and helped her colleagues see themselves in a little bit different light and to improve professionally (Dollase 1992, 49).

It is important that you get along with your colleagues and contribute to a spirit of cooperation and **collegiality** in the school. Some teachers you will enjoy being around; others you may wish to avoid. Some will express obvious enthusiasm for teaching; others may be bitter and pessimistic about their work. Be pleasant and friendly with both types. Accept their advice with a smile, and then act on what you believe is worthwhile.

Relationships with Administrators

Pay particular attention to the relationships you develop with administrators, department heads, and supervisors. Though your contacts with them will not be as frequent as with other teachers, they can do much to ensure your initial success. The following comments illustrate the information new teachers often desire from their school principals:

- *"I would like affirmation from my principal that I am doing things OK. If not, I would like to know about it so I can address and correct the situation."*

- *"I would like to meet monthly with my principal to discuss things like 'hidden agendas,' culture and traditions of the school, expectations, regular events, and what to expect, as well as an opportunity to bitch and gripe a bit."*

- *"The principal should express the expectations that he has for students in the school. I needed to know about the parameters of the grading system. I needed to know expectations for lesson plans"* (Brock and Grady 2001, 18–19).

Principals are well aware of the difficulties you might encounter as a first-year teacher, and they are there to help you succeed. However, because the demands on their time are intense, you should not hesitate to be proactive about meeting with them to discuss issues of concern.

The principal of your new school will, most likely, be the one to introduce you to other teachers, members of the administrative team, and staff. He or she should inform you if there are assistant principals or department heads who can help you enforce school rules, keep accurate records, and obtain supplies, for example. The principal may also assign an experienced teacher to serve as a mentor during your first year.

Relationships with Parents

Developing positive connections with your students' parents can contribute significantly to students' success and to your success as a teacher. In reality, teachers and parents are partners—both are concerned with the learning and growth of the children in their care. As U.S. Secretary of Education Rod Paige pointed out, "We need to build a bridge between powerful scientific research, homes, and pre-schools and make sure that adults know how vital it is that children have strong cognitive development, even before they enter school. Teachers and parents around the country [must work together] to ensure that no child is left behind" (U.S. Department of Education 2001). Figure 6.6 shows the percentage of students in grades K–12 whose parents reported involvement in activities at their child's school.

It is important that you become acquainted with parents at school functions, at meetings of the Parent Teacher Association or Organization (PTA or PTO), at various community events, and in other social situations. To develop good communication with parents, you will need to be sensitive to their needs, such as their work schedules and the language spoken at home. The following additional general strategies will help you develop good communication with the families of your students:

- Listen. Don't assume you know what the parent wants or needs.

- Try to have empathy. All families face challenges at times.

- Look for the strengths of the family members.

Figure 6.6 Parental involvement: percentage of students in grades K–12 whose parents reported involvement in specific activities in their child's school, 1999.

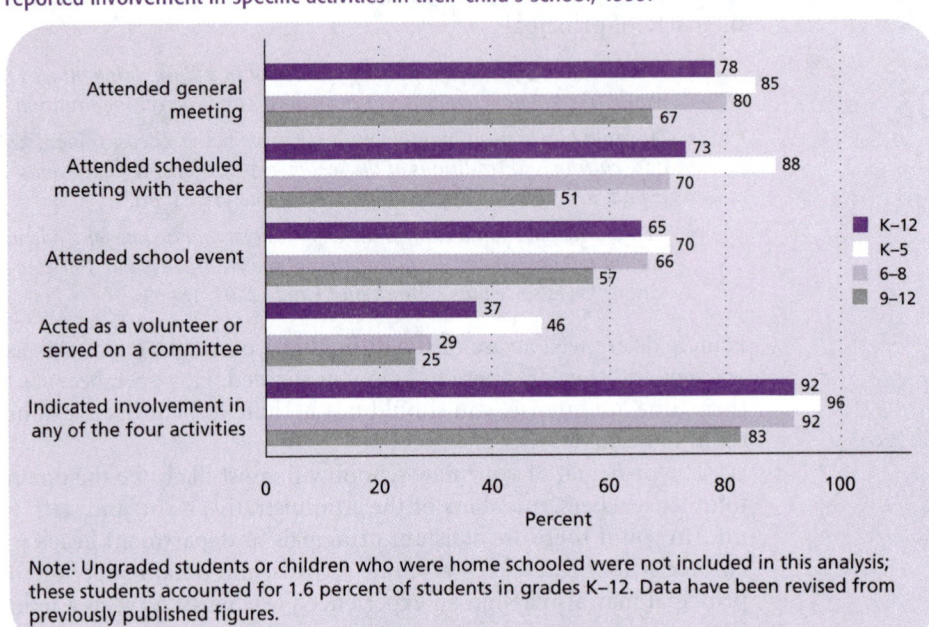

Note: Ungraded students or children who were home schooled were not included in this analysis; these students accounted for 1.6 percent of students in grades K–12. Data have been revised from previously published figures.

Source: U.S. Department of Education, NCES. National Household Education Surveys Program (NHES), 1999 (Parent Interview Survey). Taken from *The Condition of Education 2001–Societal Support for Learning: Family Support.* Washington, DC: Department of Education.

- Look at the child within his or her family, not in isolation.
- Give clear, understandable information.
- Establish positive contact with parents early in the year.
- Take care in presenting bad news to parents. Don't wait, focus on the issue, avoid being judgmental, and counterbalance it by mentioning the student's strengths.
- Make an effort to understand the family's background. Some parents have very different expectations and customs concerning their children, parent involvement, communication with the school, and so on.
- Encourage parents to ask good questions about their children. Understand that you may have to teach some parents these skills (Dryfoos and Maguire 2002, 127).

Maintaining contact with parents and encouraging them to become involved in their children's education will significantly enhance the achievement of your students. One research study, based on interviews with the parents and guardians of almost 17,000 K–12 students, showed that parental involvement results in higher levels of student achievement, more positive attitudes toward school, greater participation in extracurricular activities, fewer suspensions and expulsions, and fewer grade repetitions (Nord and West 2001). In light of these findings, it is important that you be willing to take the extra time and energy to pursue strategies such as the following for involving parents:

- Ask parents to read aloud to the child, to listen to the child read, and to sign homework papers.
- Encourage parents to drill students on math and spelling and to help with homework lessons.
- Encourage parents to discuss school activities with their children and suggest ways parents can help teach their children at home. For example, a simple home activity might be alphabetizing books; a more complex one would be using kitchen supplies in an elementary science experiment.
- Send home suggestions for games or group activities related to the child's schoolwork that parent and child can play together.
- Encourage parents to participate in school activities such as a sports booster club, career day, and music and drama events.
- Involve parents in their children's learning by having them co-sign learning contracts and serve as guest speakers.

The Goals 2000: Educate America Act funded parent resource centers in each state plus the District of Columbia (see Appendix 6.5, "Parent Information and Resource Centers"). To help families get involved in their children's learning, these centers offer training for parents, hotlines, mobile training teams, resource and lending libraries, support groups, and referral networks. The U.S. Department of Education also sponsors the Partnership for Family Involvement in Education, designed to help students act as a link between their teachers and schools and their families and communities. (For information, call (800) USA-LEARN.)

Family involvement resources are also available on the Internet through the National Parent Information Network (NPIN), a project sponsored by the ERIC system. (For information, call (800) 583-4135.) NPIN resources include information for parents on child development, testing, working with teachers, and home-learning activities.

Community Relations

Communities provide significant support for the education of their young people and determine the character of their schools. In addition, communities often help their schools by recruiting volunteers, providing financial support for special projects, and operating homework hotline programs. For example, school–community partnerships have been formed through "The Employer's Promise," a national effort to involve communities in supporting the family's central role in children's learning:

Parents can be a teacher's greatest partners in determining the success of his or her students. What are some ways you can reach out to know your students' parents and gain their support?

- John Hancock Financial Services sponsors "Kids-to-Go," a program of day-long supervised activities for employees' school-age children during school holidays in Boston.

- Southern California Edison supports the Parent Institute for Quality Education, which has trained 7,500 parents from East Los Angeles to participate actively in their children's education.

- Hewlett-Packard staggers start times for employees who volunteer at the corporation's on-site elementary school and accommodates the schedules of employees with school-age children.

- American College Testing's "Realize the Dream" program provides workshops and resources to involve parents in their children's education.

How Can You Participate in Teacher Collaboration?

The relationships that build a learning community involve **collaboration**—people working together, sharing decision making, and solving problems. As a member of a dynamic, changing profession, your efforts to collaborate will result in greater understanding of the teaching–learning process and improved learning for all students. By working with others on school governance, curriculum development, school–community partnerships, and educational reform, you will play an important role in enhancing the professional status of teachers. In the following Technology in Teaching feature, Bill Gates, chairman of the Microsoft Corporation,

Technology in Teaching

How can teachers help to find new ways to use technology in education?

Bill Gates believes that technology will play an even greater role in education in the future. In the following excerpt from his introduction to the U.S. Department of Commerce's report titled *Visions 2020: Transforming Education and Training Through Advanced Technologies*, Gates stresses the important role teachers can play in collaborating with others to find new ways to use technology in education.

The pace of innovation is accelerating in all the core technologies of computing—from processing power to storage to network bandwidth—making it possible for computers to become better connected, easier and more intuitive to use, even less costly, and capable of handling all kinds of information. While this will create countless opportunities for business, entertainment and communication, the application of these technologies to the way people learn is the most important—and exciting.

By giving students access to a new world of information, sparking creativity, and facilitating rich communication and collaboration across vast distances, computers have long been a powerful tool for education. At the same time, the Internet has brought an unprecedented level of great educational content to a wide audience, encouraging teachers to share curriculums and resources worldwide. E-mail has facilitated improved communication among administrators, teachers, students, parents and educational researchers, and emerging Web services technologies will create further opportunities for collaborative learning.

Increased industry and government funding in learning science promises to vastly improve the ways technology is applied to learning. And in the years ahead, a whole generation of kids will leave college and enter the workforce with a broad understanding of the ways they can use technology effectively in their jobs.

But we've still got a long way to go before we see how much technology can really do—particularly in education. Solving business problems with computers looks easy when compared to the often complex and little-understood process of learning. And technology is only part of the solution. All the computers in the world won't make a difference without enthusiastic students, skilled and committed teachers, involved and informed parents, and a society that underscores the value of lifelong learning.

Finding effective ways to use technology to enhance learning is a challenge that educators, academics, policymakers and the technology industry must work together to solve . . . technology can help everyone—from preschoolers to lifelong learners—to realize their full potential.

Bill Gates

Bill Gates
Chairman and Chief Software Architect
Microsoft Corporation

Source: 2020 Visions: Transforming Education and Training Through Advanced Technologies, Washington, DC: U.S. Department of Commerce, 2002, p. i.

---

stresses the importance of teachers collaborating with others to develop new ways to use technology in education.

The heart of collaboration is meaningful, authentic relationships among professionals. Such relationships, of course, do not occur naturally; they require commitment and hard work. Friend and Bursuck (2002, 76–77) have identified seven characteristics of collaboration, which are summarized in the following:

- Collaboration is voluntary; teachers make a personal choice to collaborate.
- Collaboration is based on parity; all individuals' contributions are valued equally.
- Collaboration requires a shared goal.
- Collaboration includes shared responsibility for key decisions.
- Collaboration includes shared accountability for outcomes.
- Collaboration is based on shared resources; each teacher contributes something—time, expertise, space, equipment, or other resource.
- Collaboration is emergent; as teachers work together, the degree of shared decision making, trust, and respect increases.

Schools that support the essential elements of collaboration are collegial schools "characterized by purposeful adult interactions about improving schoolwide teaching and learning" (Glickman, Gordon, and Ross-Gordon 2004, 6). The following sections examine four expressions of teacher collaboration: peer coaching, staff development, team teaching, and co-teaching.

Peer Coaching

Experienced teachers traditionally help novice teachers, but more formal peer coaching programs extend the benefits of collaboration to more teachers. **Peer coaching** is an arrangement whereby teachers grow professionally by observing one another's teaching and providing constructive feedback. The practice encourages teachers to learn together in an emotionally safe environment. According to Bruce Joyce and Marsha Weil, peer coaching is an effective way to create communities of professional educators, and all teachers should be members of coaching teams:

> If we had our way, *all* school faculties would be divided into coaching teams—that is, teams who regularly observe one another's teaching and learn from watching one another and the students. In short, we recommend the development of a "coaching environment" in which all personnel see themselves as coaches (Joyce, Weil, and Calhoun 2000, 440).

Through teacher-to-teacher support and collaboration, peer coaching programs improve teacher morale and teaching effectiveness.

Staff Development

Today, teachers often contribute to the design of staff development programs that encourage collaboration, risk taking, and experimentation. In some programs, teachers at similar grade levels or in similar content areas meet to share ideas, strategies, and solutions to problems. Teachers are frequently given released time from regular duties to visit other schools and to observe exemplary programs in action. This chapter's Relevant Standards feature stresses the importance of teachers collaborating with other educators as they design staff development programs aimed at enhancing student learning.

Relevant Standards

Contributing to Staff Development

As the following standards indicate, highly accomplished teachers value collaboration. They go beyond their classrooms to design and implement staff development programs with their colleagues. They understand that they have a responsibility to participate in staff development activities that contribute to overall school improvement and student learning.

- "[Teacher candidates] are able to foster relationships with school colleagues, parents and families, and agencies in the larger community to support students' learning and well being." (National Council for Accreditation of Teacher Education [NCATE], 2002, 18. Supporting statement for Standard 1: Candidate Knowledge, Skills, and Dispositions.)

- "Proficient teachers collaborate in planning the instructional program of the school to assure continuity of learning experiences for students. They possess the interpersonal skills needed to work on teams and a willingness to work together in the interest of the school community. Their understanding of the technical requirements of a well-coordinated curriculum enables them to participate in planning and decision-making within teams, departments or other educational units outside the classroom, laboratory or studio." (National Board for Professional Teaching Standards [NBPTS], 2002, 18. "Supporting statements" for Proposition #5: Teachers are members of learning communities.")

- "The teacher participates in collegial activities designed to make the entire school a productive learning environment." (Interstate New Teacher Assessment and Support Consortium [INTASC], 1992, 34. "Performance" statement for Principle #10: "The teacher fosters relationships with school colleagues, parents, and agencies in the larger community to support students' learning and well-being.")

- "Support and cooperation characterize relationships with colleagues. Teacher takes initiative in assuming leadership among the faculty." (Praxis Series, "distinguished" level of performance for Domain 4: Professional Responsibilities, Component 4d: Contributing to the School and District.) (Danielson 1996, 114)

One example of a collaborative staff development program is at Sherman Oaks Community Charter School in San Jose, California. Every school day between 11:30 a.m. and 1 p.m., Sherman Oaks teachers meet for ninety minutes of professional development. The teachers discuss and debate instructional theory and practice, try to solve problems that have come up or are likely to come up in their classrooms, discuss curriculum, seek advice, offer encouragement, or quietly reflect. As one teacher put it, "It's always wonderful stuff—things that get your brain stretched. I feel like a professional" (Curtis 2000).

Another collaborative program is the Maryland Electronic Learning Community (MELC), a teacher development and support group that provides formal training in technology integration followed by ongoing collaboration and support. Funded in part by the U.S. Department of Education, the MELC project is a coalition of partners who form an electronic learning community using technologies such as digitized video, Internet resources, two-way video and audio for distance

These teachers are collaborating on the design of a staff development program for their school. What are some forms of professional collaboration in which you will participate as a teacher?

learning, and e-mail to support and enhance middle school curriculum and professional development (Fulton and Riel 1999).

Team Teaching

In **team teaching** arrangements, teachers share the responsibility for two or more classes. They divide the subject areas between them, with one preparing lessons in mathematics, science, and health, for instance, while the other plans instruction in reading and language arts. Team-teaching arrangements may also be made according to the performance levels of the children. For example, one teacher may teach the lowest- and highest-ability reading groups and the middle math group, while the other teaches the middle-ability reading groups and the lowest and highest mathematics group.

In many schools, team-teaching arrangements are so extensive that children move from classroom to classroom for 40- to 50-minute periods just as students do at the high school level. In the following Teachers' Voices feature, three teachers at a science and technology high school explain how they team teach a cluster of three courses in an integrated program.

Teachers' *Voices*   Putting Research and Theory into Practice

Redesigning the Model: A Successfully Integrated Approach to Teaching and Learning

Dennis M. McFaden, Barbara A. Nelson, and Chip M. Randall

By making integrated project work an important and equal component of our curriculum and restructuring our schedule within a clustered time block, we have fundamentally shifted the paradigm of how we teach and what is taught. It makes us teach what the students need to know when they need to know it, resequencing fundamental concepts to fit the project requirements. It minimizes the content-driven mindset so that needed skills can be taught and reinforced within the context of a legitimate application. These skills can then be transferred from one subject area to another through work on the project itself. This model also allows us to do projects that none of us could do separately or completely without sacrificing the essentials of our individual subject areas.

Critical to the implementation of our integrated program is the realization that we are partners in teaching a single integrated course and are not just trying to combine three separate ones. This does not mean that *each* of us is expected to be expert in all three disciplines or that the content of the individual courses should be watered down or homogenized.

In fact, we do a better job in teaching the content-specific concepts and skills in our individual courses because we constantly reinforce them, providing a contextual framework. This model requires a transformation in mindset from three separate courses, each vying for its share of time, resources, and importance, to one in which each is integrated naturally into a fabric of instruction and learning that values the contribution each discipline brings to our understanding of the world.

It is the interdisciplinary strand that directs and focuses this integrated approach. In fact, it provides the fundamental framework of how we connect topics, present ideas, and sequence units throughout the school year. . . .

Our project model is collegial for both teachers and students. This approach gives us the opportunity to

support and learn from each other and serves as a vehicle to model the collaborative team effort we are trying to teach. Students see their teachers collaborating, making decisions, scheduling, and assigning responsibilities as we design and revise *our* project—the course itself. We are modeling the skills we hope to develop in our students. . . .

The advantage of this model is not just for the students. The advantages of risk taking, being actively involved in learning, and working and planning with colleagues, all of which we stress as critical with the students, also apply to us. The collegial sharing and support inherent in this model provides a dimension of professional development that is rare in the current educational reality of closed doors and required meetings.

Questions

1. With reference to the grade level and subject area for which you are preparing to teach, describe a team-teaching arrangement. Who would be members of the team, and what would be the role of each person on the team?
2. What are the advantages and disadvantages of team-teaching arrangements?
3. How might your participation in a team teaching arrangement enhance students' learning and your relationships with them?

Dennis M. McFaden is a science teacher and winner of the 1995 National Science Foundation State Award for Excellence in the Teaching of Secondary Science. *Barbara A. Nelson* is an English teacher. *Chip M. Randall* is a technology education teacher. All three teach at the Thomas Jefferson High School for Science and Technology in Alexandria, Virginia. The preceding is excerpted from their article in the *NASSP Bulletin 80*, no. 577 (February 1996), pp. 1–6. Copyright © 1996 National Association of Secondary School Principals. www.principals.org. Reprinted with permission.

The practice of team teaching is often limited by student enrollments and budget constraints. As integrated curricula and the need for special knowledge and skills increase, however, the use of collegial support teams (CSTs) will become more common. A **collegial support team (CST)** provides teachers with a "safe zone" for professional growth, as one teacher commented:

> *[The CST] allows me much discretion as to the areas I'd like to strengthen. Therefore, I am truly growing with no fear of being labeled or singled out as the "teacher who is having problems." I am aware of problem spheres and I work to correct these with the aid of my colleagues (Johnson and Brown 1998, 89).*

The members of a team make wide-ranging decisions about the instruction of students assigned to the team, such as when to use large-group instruction or small-group instruction, how teaching tasks will be divided, and how time, materials, and other resources will be allocated.

Co-Teaching

In **co-teaching** arrangements, two or more teachers, such as a classroom teacher and a special education teacher or other specialist, teach together in the same classroom. Co-teaching builds on the strengths of two teachers and provides increased learning opportunities for all students (Friend and Bursuck 2002). Typically, co-teaching arrangements occur during a set period of time each day or on certain days of the week. Among the several possible co-teaching variations, Friend and Bursuck (2002) have identified the following:

- *One teach, one support*—One teacher leads the lesson; the other assists.
- *Station teaching*—The lesson is divided into two parts; one teacher teaches one part to half of the students, while the other teaches the other part to the rest. The groups then switch and the teachers repeat their part of the lesson. If students can work independently, a third group may be formed or a volunteer may teach at a third station.
- *Parallel teaching*—A class is divided in half, and each teacher instructs half the class individually.
- *Alternative teaching*—A class is divided into one large group and one small group. For example, one teacher may provide remediation or enrichment to the small group, while the other teacher instructs the large group.

How Will Your Teaching Performance Be Evaluated?

Most teachers are evaluated on a regular basis to determine if they are able to create and sustain effective learning environments for students. Performance criteria vary and are usually determined by the school principal, district office, the school board, or a state education agency. In most schools, the principal or a member of the leadership team evaluates teachers.

Teacher evaluations serve many purposes, such as determining whether teachers should be retained, receive tenure, or be given merit pay. Evaluations also help teachers assess their effectiveness and develop strategies for self-improvement. In fact, "teachers who receive the most classroom feedback are also most satisfied with teaching" (Glickman, Gordon, and Ross-Gordon 2004, 323).

Quantitative and Qualitative Evaluation

Typically, supervisors use quantitative or qualitative approaches (or a combination) to evaluate teachers' classroom performance. **Quantitative evaluation** includes pencil-and-paper rating forms the supervisor uses to record classroom events and behaviors objectively in terms of their number or frequency. For example, a supervisor might focus on the teacher's verbal behaviors—questioning, answering, praising, giving directions, and critiquing.

Qualitative evaluation, in contrast, includes written, open-ended narrative descriptions of classroom events. These more subjective measures are equally valuable in identifying teachers' weaknesses and strengths. In addition, qualitative evaluation can capture the complexities and subtleties of classroom life that might not be reflected in a quantitative approach to evaluation.

Clinical Supervision

Many supervisors follow the four-step **clinical supervision** model in which the supervisor first holds a preconference with the teacher, then observes in the classroom, analyzes and interprets observation data, and finally holds a postconference with the teacher (Glickman 2002; Acheson and Gall 1997; Goldhammer, Anderson, and Krajewski 1993; Pajak 1999; Smyth 1995; Snyder and Anderson 1996). During the preconference, the teacher and supervisor schedule a classroom observation and determine its purpose and focus and the method of observation to be used. At the postconference, the teacher and supervisor discuss the analysis of observation data and jointly develop a plan for instructional improvement.

Fulfilling the clinical supervision model is difficult and time-consuming, and time-pressed administrators must often modify the approach. For example, when Kim Marshall was a principal at a Boston elementary school with thirty-nine teachers, he made four random, unannounced five-minute visits to classrooms each day. This schedule allowed him to observe every teacher during a two-week period, and each teacher about nineteen times during a year. According to Marshall,

> . . . a regular cycle of five-minute classroom visits with a follow-up conversation after each one is the most efficient way for a principal to monitor classrooms and find the answers to [the following] key questions:
>
> - Are teachers on track with the curriculum?
> - Are the students learning?
> - Are teachers "happy campers" in terms of their jobs and their lives?
> - Do some teachers deserve special praise?
> - Do some teachers need redirection, emergency support, or a negative evaluation? (Marshall 2003, 703).

Regardless of the approach used to evaluate your teaching performance, remember that evaluation will enhance your growth and development as a teacher. Experienced teachers report that periodic feedback and assistance from knowledgeable, sensitive supervisors is very beneficial. Evaluation results in "improved teacher reflection and higher-order thought, more collegiality, openness, and communication, greater teacher retention, less anxiety and burnout, greater teacher autonomy and efficacy, improved attitudes, improved teaching behaviors, and better student achievement and attitudes" (Glickman, Gordon, and Ross-Gordon 2001, 329).

Summary

Why Is Your Induction into Teaching Important?

- Annually, up to one-third of beginning teachers in the United States leave the profession within the first few years.

- Beginning teachers may experience isolation and receive little support.

- Among the problems that cause some beginning teachers to think about leaving the profession are maintaining classroom discipline, motivating students, responding to individual differences, assessing students' work, maintaining positive relationships with parents, organizing classroom activities, securing adequate teaching materials and supplies, and dealing with the problems of individual students.

- Induction programs provide beginning teachers with support during their first years in the profession.

- Beginning teachers in many other countries participate in induction programs that provide them with extensive support, guidance, and encouragement.

How Will You Become Certified?

- State certification is required for teaching in public schools and in many private schools. Some large cities and local school districts have additional criteria for certification. Certification requirements for teachers vary from state to state and are frequently modified. Some states waive licensing requirements for teachers certified by the National Board for Professional Teaching Standards (NBPTS).

- Most states require testing of teachers for initial certification, and some require recertification after a three- to five-year period.

- States that are members of the Interstate Certification Agreement Contract honor teaching certificates granted by certain other states.

- Private, parochial, for-profit, and charter schools employ about 404,000 noncertified teachers. Many states offer alternative and emergency certification programs.

- The Praxis Series: Professional Assessments for Beginning Teachers is required in most states for initial certification. The Praxis Series includes assessments of academic (basic) skills, subject matter knowledge, and classroom performance.

Will You Have Difficulty Getting a Teaching Job?

- Teacher supply and demand in content areas and geographic regions influences finding a teaching position.

- Teaching is a large profession, involving more than 47 million students in public K–12 schools and more than 3 million teachers.

- Job vacancies result from retirements, relocation, and career changes. Elementary and secondary enrollments and the demand for new teachers will increase through 2011.
- Education-related career opportunities for teachers include principal, assistant principal, librarian, counselor, and teaching roles in government and the private sector.

How Will You Find Your First Teaching Job?

- Information about teaching vacancies may be obtained through placement services, state departments of education, and personal networking on the Internet.
- A résumé is a concise summary of an individual's experiences, education, and skills. A letter of inquiry is used to find out if a school district has any teaching vacancies. A letter of application (or cover letter) indicates an individual's interest in and qualifications for a teaching position.

What Can You Expect as a Beginning Teacher?

- Beginning teachers should prepare instructional strategies and materials and learn about their students and the community well in advance of the first day of school.
- Experienced teachers' recommendations for beginning teachers focus on planning, organizing, and following through.

How Can You Become a Member of a Learning Community?

- The learning community includes students, their families, colleagues, and members of the community.
- Research indicates that parental involvement is a key factor in children's academic achievement.
- Training programs, hotlines, referral networks, and partnership programs are among the resources teachers can use to involve parents and members of the community.

How Can You Collaborate with Other Teachers?

- Teachers collaborate through participation in school governance, curriculum development, school–community partnerships, and educational reform.
- Four approaches to teacher collaboration are peer coaching, staff development, team teaching, and co-teaching.

How Will Your Teaching Performance Be Evaluated?

- Performance criteria for evaluating teachers are developed by school principals, districts, school boards, or states.
- Quantitative approaches to teacher evaluation focus on the incidence, frequency, or amount of teacher or student behavior in various categories.
- Qualitative approaches to teacher evaluation are usually written narratives focusing on the qualities of classrooms and events, such as classroom climate and teaching style.

Key Terms and Concepts

alternative certification, 224
charter, 221
clinical supervision, 251
collaboration, 244
collegial support team (CST), 250
collegiality, 240
co-teaching, 250
credentials file, 229
emergency certification, 224

induction programs, 217
Interstate Certification Agreement Contract, 221
letter of application, 233
letter of inquiry, 233
peer coaching, 246
Praxis Series: Professional Assessments for Beginning Teachers, 224

qualitative evaluation, 251
quantitative evaluation, 251
recertification, 221
résumé, 231
teacher supply and demand, 226
teaching certificate, 220
team teaching, 248

Reflective Application Activities

Discussion Questions

1. Do you think there are any limitations regarding the extent to which a teacher should become involved in community affairs? As a teacher, what community activities might you become involved in?

2. Looking ahead to your first teaching assignment, do you anticipate any conflict in on-the-job relationships? Explain. How do you plan to handle these conflicts?

Professional Journal

1. When you become a teacher, in what collaborations and partnerships will you participate? How might these activities contribute to your effectiveness as a teacher? How might your involvement enhance students' learning and your relationships with them?

2. Imagine your first day as a teacher. Describe what you see.

Online Assignments

1. Explore and compare teacher proficiencies and teaching standards according to state boards of education, national standards organizations, and teacher and subject area organizations. Begin by locating the following organizations online and information about your school's education program in relation to state and national standards.

   National Association for State Boards of Education (NASBE)

   National Association of State Directors for Teacher Education and Certification (NASDTEC)

   National Board for Professional Teaching Standards (NBPTS)

   National Council for Accreditation of Teacher Education (NCATE)

   Continue your search by accessing the government or education department of a locality, region, or state where you plan to teach and gathering information about becoming a teacher there.

2. Formulate a research question concerning demographic aspects of teachers and schools in the United States. Then go online to gather current national and state sta-

tistics on your question. For example, your question might relate to one or more of the following topics.

- teacher recruitment
- teacher shortages
- teaching salaries and benefits
- characteristics of the teaching force
- attitudes of teachers
- information about school districts
- public schools compared to private schools
- independent and private schools
- characteristics of parochial schools

Begin your data search in the U.S. Department of Education's National Center for Education Statistics (NCES).

Observations and Interviews

1. Interview a few experienced teachers for their recollections about the "high points" and "low points" they experienced as beginning teachers. What lessons are evident in their responses? Are there common themes that characterize the "high points" they recall? The "low points"?

2. Interview a few teachers and administrators about their experiences with professional collaboration and parental involvement. What examples do they provide, and how do these reflect the seven characteristics of collaboration presented in this chapter? How do students benefit from collaboration and parental involvement? What suggestions do the teachers and administrators have for improving collaboration and parental involvement?

Professional Portfolio

Draft a preliminary professional résumé. Review the section in this chapter titled "Preparing Your Resume" and "Resume Advice for Educators" in Appendix 6.3. In addition, examine the resume prepared by Linda M. Rodriguez (Figure 6.3).

In your resume, under "Personal Data," provide a current address and a permanent address. Also, under "Education," specify an anticipated graduation date. Under "Experience," include work experience that indicates your ability to work with people. Begin with your most recent experiences and present information in reverse chronological order.

Appendix 6.1

Directory of State Teacher Certification Offices in the United States

Alabama
Teacher Education and Certification
P.O. Box 302101
Montgomery, AL 36130-2101
(334) 242-9560
Fax: (334) 242-0498

Alaska
Department of Education
Teacher Education & Certification
801 West 10th Street, Suite 200
Juneau, AK 99801-1894
(907) 465-2831 or 2026

Arizona
Arizona Dept. of Education
Certification Unit
P.O. Box 6490
Phoenix, AZ 85005-6490
(602) 542-4367

Arkansas
Teacher Education & Licensure
State Dept. of Education
4 State Capitol Mall
Little Rock, AR 72201-1071
(501) 682-4342
(501) 682-4898

California
Commission on Teacher
   Credentialing
Box 944270
Sacramento, CA 94244-2700
(916) 445-7254
Fax: (916) 327-3166
credentials@ctc.ca.gov

Colorado
Educator Licensing
State Dept. of Education
201 E. Colfax Avenue

Denver, CO 80203
(303) 866-6628

Connecticut
Bureau of Certification and
   Teacher Preparation
State Dept. of Education
P.O. Box 150471
Hartford, CT 06115-0471
(860) 566-5201
Fax: (860) 566-8929

Delaware
Teacher Certification
Dept. of Public Instruction
P.O. Box 1402
Dover, DE 19903
(302) 739-4686

District of Columbia
Educational Credentialing &
   Standards
825 N. Capitol Street, N.E.
6th Floor Washington, DC 20002
(202) 442-5377
Fax: (202) 442-5311

Florida
Bureau of Teacher Certification
Florida Education Center
325 W Gaines, Rm. 201
Tallahassee, FL 32399-0400
(850) 488-2317 (out of state)
(800) 445-6739 (in state)

Georgia
Professional Standards Commission
Certification Section
1454 Twin Towers East
Atlanta, GA 30334
(404) 657-9000
mail@gapsc.com

Hawaii
Office of Personnel Services
Teacher Recruitment Unit
P.O. Box 2360
Honolulu, HI 96804
(808) 586-3420
(800) 305-5104
Fax: (808) 586-3419

Idaho
Teacher Certification
State Dept. of Education
P.O. Box 83720
Boise, ID 83720-0027
(208) 332-6880

Illinois
Illinois State Board of Education
Certification & Placement Section
100 N. First Street
Springfield, IL 62777-0001
(217) 782-4321

Indiana
Indiana Professional Standards
   Board
Teacher Licensing
251 East Ohio Street, Suite 201
Indianapolis, IN 46204-2133
(317) 232-9010
Fax: (317) 232-9023

Iowa
Board of Educational Examiners
Grimes State Office Building
Des Moines, IA 50319-0147
(515) 281-3245

Kansas
Certification Section
Kansas State Dept. of Education
Kansas State Education Building

Note: Many state offices have websites; use a search engine to determine whether an office has a website and its current URL.

120 SE 10th Ave.
Topeka, KS 66612-1182
(785) 296-2288

Kentucky
Kentucky Dept. of Education
Division of Certification
1024 Capital Center Drive
Frankfort, KY 40601-1972
(502) 573-4606

Louisiana
Louisiana Dept. of Education
Teacher Certification, Room 700
P.O. Box 94064
Baton Rouge, LA 70804-9064
(225) 342-3490
(225) 342-3499

Maine
Division of Certification
Department of Education
State House Station 23
Augusta, ME 04333
(207) 287-5944

Maryland
Division of Certification 18100
State Dept. of Education
200 West Baltimore St.
Baltimore, MD 21201
(410) 767-0412

Massachusetts
Massachusetts Dept. of Education
Office of Teacher Certification and
Credentialing
350 Main Street
Malden, MA 02148
(781) 388-3300, X665
Fax: (781) 388-3475

Michigan
Office of Professional Preparation
& Certification
Michigan Dept. of Education
P.O. Box 30008
Lansing, MI 48909
(517) 373-3310

Minnesota
Teacher Licensing

State Dept. of Children, Families
and Learning
1500 Highway 36 West
Roseville MN 55113
(651) 582-8691

Mississippi
Teacher Certification
State Dept. of Education
Box 771
Jackson, MS 39205-0771
(601) 359-3483
Fax: (601) 359-2778

Missouri
Teacher Certification
Dept. of Elementary and
Secondary Education
P.O. Box 480
Jefferson City, MO 65102
(573) 751-3486

Montana
Teacher Certification
Office of Public Instruction
P.O. Box 202501
Helena, MT 59620-2501
(406) 444-3150

Nebraska
Teacher Certification
State Dept. of Education
301 Centennial Mall South
Box 94987
Lincoln, NE 68509-4987
(800) 371-4642

Nevada
Licensure and Certification
Nevada Dept. of Education
700 East 5th St.
Carson City, NV 89701
(702) 687-3115

New Hampshire
Bureau of Credentialing
State Dept. of Education
101 Pleasant St.
Concord, NH 03301
(603) 271-2407
Fax: (603) 271-4134

New Jersey
Office of Licensing and Credentials
P.O. Box 500
Trenton, NJ 08625-0500
(609) 292-2070

New Mexico
Director
Professional Licensure Unit
Education Building
300 Don Gaspar
Santa Fe, NM 87501-2786
(505) 827-6587

New York
Office of Teaching
State Education Department
Albany, NY 12234
(518) 474-3901/2/3/4

North Carolina
North Carolina Dept. of Public
Instruction
Licensure Section
301 N. Wilmington Street
Raleigh, NC 27601-2825
(919) 733-4125
(800) 577-7994

North Dakota
Education Standards and Practice
Board
Teacher Certification
600 E. Boulevard Ave.
Bismarck, ND 58505-0880
(701) 328-2264

Ohio
Professional Development and
Licensure
State Dept. of Education
65 South Front St., Rm. 412
Columbus, OH 43215-4183
(614) 466-3593
Fax: (614) 466-1999

Oklahoma
Professional Standards
State Dept. of Education
2500 N. Lincoln Blvd.
Rm. 211

Oklahoma City, OK 73105-4599
(405) 521-3301
Fax: (405) 521-6205

Oregon
Teacher Standards and Practices
    Commission
Public Service Bldg.
255 Capitol Street, N.E.
Suite 105
Salem, OR 97310-1332
(503) 378-3586

Pennsylvania
Bureau of Teacher Certification &
    Preparation
Dept. of Education
333 Market Street
Harrisburg, PA 17126-0333
(717) 787-3356
00certifica@psupen.psu.edu

Rhode Island
Office of Teacher Certification
State Dept. of Education
Shepard Building
255 Westminster St.
Providence, RI 02903-3400
(401) 222-4600

South Carolina
Office of Teacher Education,
    Certification, & Evaluation
1600 Gervais St.
Columbia, SC 29201
(803) 734-8466
Fax: (803) 734-2873
licensure@sde.state.sc.us

South Dakota
Teacher Certification
Office of Policy and Accountability

700 Governors Drive
Pierre, SD 57501-2291
(605) 773-3553
Fax: (605) 773-6139

Tennessee
Office of Teacher Licensing
State Dept. of Education
5th Floor, Andrew Johnson Tower
710 James Robertson Parkway
Nashville, TN 37243-0377
(615) 533-4885
Fax: (615) 532-7860

Texas
State Board for Educator
    Certification
1001 Trinity
Austin, TX 78701
(512) 469-3001

Utah
Certification and Professional
    Development Section
State Board of Education
250 East 500 South Street
Salt Lake City, UT 84111
(801) 538-7740
Fax: (801) 538-7973

Vermont
Licensing Office
Dept. of Education
120 State Street
Montpelier, VT 05620-2501
(802) 828-2445
Fax: (802) 828-3140

Virginia
Office of Professional Licensure
Department of Education
P.O. Box 2120

Richmond, VA 23216-2120
(804) 225-2022

Washington
Office of Professional Education
Superintendent of Public
    Instruction
Old Capitol Building
P.O. Box 47200
Olympia, WA 98504-7200
(360) 753-6773

West Virginia
State Dept. of Education
Building 6, Room 337
1900 Kanawha Blvd., East
Charleston, WV 25305-0330
(800) 982-2378

Wisconsin
Teacher Education, Licensing and
    Placement
Box 7841
Madison, WI 53707-7841
(608) 266-1028 (direct line)
(608) 266-1027 (voice mail)
Fax: (608) 264-9558

Wyoming
Professional Teaching Standards
    Board
2300 Capitol Avenue
Hathaway Building, 2nd Floor
Cheyenne, WY 82002
Fax: (307) 777-6234
PTSB@www.k12.wy.us

Appendix 6.2
Job Search
Timetable Checklist

This checklist is designed to help you make good use of your time as you conduct your job search. We encourage you to use this checklist in conjunction with the services and resources available from your college or university career services office.

August/September
(12 months prior to employment)

_____ Review your career services' Web site for information relating to your field.

_____ Register with your career services office and become oriented to their programs.

_____ Begin to define the type and size of school systems in which you have an interest.

October
(11 months prior to employment)

_____ Begin to identify references and consider where you want to deposit letters of recommendation, résumés, etc. (e.g., your career services office, a commercial service).

_____ Meet with a counselor in your career services office to discuss your job-search plan.

November/December
(8–10 months prior to employment)

_____ Begin developing résumés which can be scanned, used for online applications, e-mailed, and mailed. You will need cover letters for résumés which you mail.

_____ Begin networking by contacting friends, faculty members, past teachers, etc., to inform them of your career plans.

_____ Finalize your résumé(s) and have them critiqued in your career services office. For those to be mailed, check out reproduction processes.

_____ Attend appropriate career planning workshops.

_____ Begin developing a list of school systems in which you are interested.

_____ Check out school system Web sites and contact to obtain necessary application materials.

_____ If relocating away from your geographic area, contact a career services office in the area to which you are moving and request reciprocity of services.

Source: Checklist prepared by Bruce Brewer, State University of West Georgia, for American Association for Employment in Education (AAEE), *2002 Job Search Handbook for Educators.* Columbus, OH: American Association for Employment in Education, p. 6. The *Handbook* is available for $8.00 from AAEE.

_____ Determine certification requirements. Make sure you have completed testing requirements for your field(s). If you are applying to out-of-state school systems, contact the appropriate State Department of Education or Professional Standards to determine requirements.

January
(8 months prior to employment)

_____ Complete online or paper applications for school systems and send with appropriate résumés and cover letters.

_____ Inquire about school systems that will be recruiting at your institution, or at regional job fairs, or virtual career fairs. Inquire about the processes for interviewing with these systems.

_____ Research school systems with which you will be applying and interviewing.

February/March/April
(5–7 months prior to employment)

_____ Participate in on-campus interviews and career fairs (virtual or otherwise) related to education. Send thank you letters as appropriate.

_____ Register with online job search systems.

_____ Monitor the job vacancy listings available on the Internet in your state, in your career services office, etc.

April–August
(1–5 months prior to employment)

_____ Stay up-to-date with job openings through online systems and your career services office.

_____ Maintain communication with your network of contacts.

_____ Contact school systems by phone or e-mail to stay in touch with potential job openings.

_____ Aggressively network with educational contacts. Keep them up to date on your progress.

_____ Accept an offer that is appropriate to your particular situation.

_____ Inform those associated with your search once you have accepted a position. This includes those systems in which your application is still active. Then celebrate!

Appendix 6.3
Résumé Advice for Educators

A modern-day résumé is a written advertisement focused toward a prospective employer. In a résumé, however, the "product" being advertised is you, the candidate.

Many job applicants become confused about what to include on a résumé. This article covers the most common informational categories, but you should strive to include any information that you feel will enhance your chances of being selected for an interview.

SEEKING THE "PERFECT" RÉSUMÉ

Just as every individual is different, each résumé presents a distinct combination of skills, abilities, and qualifications about its author. This is why it is impossible to find a perfect sample résumé and simply copy it. Your background is unique, and cannot be found in a book. However, reviewing other résumés will certainly be helpful because they will provide a rich supply of ideas and perspectives for your document.

While the perfect résumé may be an elusive concept, excellent résumés have many characteristics in common. An excellent résumé is one to two pages in length. It is free of typographical errors, produced on high-quality bond paper, accentuates your most salient qualities and qualifications, is organized and easy to read, and conveys a sense of who you are to the reader. This is easier said than done!

You need to remember that in today's job market, school principals are inundated with résumés. One or two pages is about the maximum they are willing to read about each candidate. As a prospective teacher, a résumé with any typographical error is a signal that you are poorly prepared to instruct others, so be sure to have your final document read by others, until all errors are eliminated.

Résumés for teaching and résumés for business have both similarities and differences. Organization, style, appearance, neatness, and punctuation issues apply to both. (If you need help with these issues, you will find useful books on the topic in your institution's career planning and placement office or at local bookstores.) However, educators' résumés typically include additional categories: student teaching, clinical experience, and certification information.

As you work to write the "perfect" résumé you will undoubtedly receive a variety of well-intentioned advice, and some of it will be conflicting. Everyone will have an opinion to offer. One of your most difficult tasks will be to evaluate what you hear. Pursue different opinions, and then decide what makes sense for you.

STATEMENT OF TEACHING OBJECTIVE

It is appropriate to include a "Career Objective" or "Teaching Objective" statement on your résumé. While optional, this statement is highly recommended because it helps identify the specific areas in which you wish to teach. Consider the advantages and disadvantages of the following three sample objectives, then develop your own to fit your requirements.

1. Elementary Teaching Position, K–6.
2. Seeking a classroom position in the upper elementary grades that provides an opportunity to facilitate academic, social, and personal growth of students.
3. Secondary or middle school position in science/math, in a suburban location. Qualified and interested in coaching track, volleyball, or swimming.

Source: Lorn B. Coleman, *2001 Job Search Handbook for Educators.* Columbus, OH: American Association for Employment Education, pp. 15–16. Used with permission.

Objective 1 is descriptive and to the point. However, additional elements are incorporated into examples 2 and 3. Objective 3 is well thought out and developed, although unless you intend to decline all offers other than those in suburban locations, you should avoid using a phrase which defines location too tightly. The reader will assume that you mean what you say.

STUDENT TEACHING INFORMATION

It is important that beginning teachers provide information about their student teaching experiences. Do not assume that all student teaching experiences are alike, and therefore need not be described. Some principals remain interested in your student teaching experience even after you have several years of professional experience.

Review the following two examples, and then develop a section that accurately portrays your own experience.

1. Northwestern High School
   Rolling Hills, Illinois
   Student Teacher
   Taught 11th-grade chemistry and math courses in an open classroom format. Coordinated field study trips, and a "Careers in Science" day.
2. MacKenzie Elementary School
   Chicago, Illinois
   Student Teacher
   September–December, 1995
   Observed, assisted, and taught regular and accelerated classes. Developed daily lesson and unit plans. Assisted in after-school tutoring program. Coordinated a revised parent conference format that increased teacher–parent interaction. Refined an existing computer database for classroom record keeping.

Note how the examples include pertinent details of student teaching experiences beyond the routine aspects, it is this information that demonstrates ways in which you made yourself valuable. In your narrative, try to focus on how your presence made something better to make your experience stand out from those who merely developed lesson plans and assisted teachers.

PAST EMPLOYMENT INFORMATION

Normally, an employer wants to know about your last ten years of professional experience. As a prospective teacher, you should include any experiences in which you worked with K–12-age individuals. Examples of pertinent positions would include camp counselor, teacher's aide, tutor, Scout troop leader, and so forth.

Many candidates dismiss nonteaching experiences as unrelated, and fail to include them on their résumés. However, principals and school administrators can draw valuable inferences regarding your work habits from this information. Dependability, responsibility, and leadership potential are just a few of the desirable traits you can document with information about jobs you have held.

RELATED ACTIVITIES AND INTERESTS

Information about activities and interests helps you present the image of a well-rounded and versatile teacher. The following categories represent just a few of the areas you may want to include.

- Volunteer activities
- Professional memberships
- Special interests
- Honors and awards
- Committee work
- Training
- Study abroad
- Community involvement
- Fluency in languages other than English
- Computer skills
- Leadership activities
- Professional development activities
- Class projects
- Scholarships

Remember, the more areas of knowledge and expertise that you demonstrate, the more likely you are to become a desirable candidate in the eyes of school administrators. School districts actively seek candidates who are flexible and willing to take on a variety of tasks in the school.

A FEW FINAL DO'S AND DON'T'S

Make sure that your résumé is not a jigsaw puzzle of unrelated odds and ends, expecting that the principal will be able to piece them together. If those who receive your résumé have to work hard to figure it out, it is likely that they will just move on to the next résumé!

When your résumé is complete, print your final copy on a laser-jet printer, and have copies made at a printing service on high-quality, bond paper. Conservative paper—white, off-white, or ivory—is always suitable. Your printing service can help you select a paper which has matching envelopes to enhance your presentation. Be sure to purchase blank paper that matches your résumé so your cover letters will also match your presentation package.

Writing your résumé should be an introspective, exhilarating, positive, pat-yourself-on-the-back experience. If you approach it with this spirit, your résumé will be one of which you are justifiably proud.

Appendix 6.4

Sample Interview Questions for Candidates to Ask

If you are serious about teaching in the district where you are interviewing, there are many questions to which you need to know the answers before you accept an offer. Your interviewer will surely cover some of your questions, but by asking pertinent questions you will show your interviewer that you understand fundamental issues relating to teaching. You should have several questions in mind before you arrive for your interview. The following seventeen questions should give you a good start.

1. What is the teacher/student ratio in your district?
2. Do you encourage teachers to earn advanced degrees?
3. How many classes a day will I be expected to teach?
4. Do you have teachers serving in areas for which they do not have full certification?
5. What are the school's students like?
6. What textbooks does the district use in this subject area?
7. Do teachers participate in curriculum review and change?
8. What support staff members are available to help students and teachers?
9. How does the teaching staff feel about new teachers?
10. What discipline procedures does the district use?
11. Do parents support the schools? Does the community?
12. Do your schools use teacher aides or parent volunteers?
13. What allowances are provided for supplies and materials?
14. Does the administration encourage field trips for students?
15. How are teachers assigned to extracurricular activities? Is compensation provided?
16. Does the district have a statement of educational philosophy or mission?
17. What are prospects for future growth in this community and its schools?

Source: American Association for Employment in Education (AAEE), *1997 Job Search Handbook for Educators*. Evanston, IL: Association for School, College and University Staffing, Inc., p. 23. Used with permission.

Appendix 6.5
Parent Information and Resource Centers

Alabama
Special Education Action Committee, Inc. (Alabama)
P.O. Box 161274
Mobile, AL 36616-2274
Phone: (251) 478-1208
Toll-Free: (800) 222-7322
Toll-Free Restrictions: AL residents only
Fax: (251) 473-7877

E-mail: seacofmobile@zebra.net
Website: www.
seacparentassistancecenter.com/

Alaska
Parents as Teachers Program
Fairbanks Native Association
552 Third Street
Fairbanks, AK 99701
Phone: (907) 451-1005
Fax: (907) 451-6296

E-mail: jerickson@alaskafamily.org
Website: www.alaskafamily.org/

Arizona
Chandler Education Foundation, Inc. (Arizona)
1525 West Frye Road
Chandler, AZ 85224-2006
Phone: (480) 812-7632
Fax: (480) 812-7020

E-mail:
cefgroup@chandler.k12.az.us
Website:
www.chandleredfoundation.org/

Arkansas
Center for Effective Parenting (Arkansas)
Suite 113

614 East Emma
Springdale, AR 72764
Phone: (479) 751-6166
Toll-Free: (800) PARENTO (727-3680)
Toll-Free Restrictions: AR residents only
Fax: (479) 751-1110

E-mail: longnicholas@uams.edu
Website: www.parenting-ed.org

California
Native American Parental Assistance Program (California)
Ahmium Education, Inc.
P.O. Box 366
San Jacinto, CA 92581-0366
Phone: (951) 654-2781
Toll-Free: (800) 924-8744
Fax: (951) 654-3089

E-mail: ernie@ivic.net

Colorado
Colorado Parent Information and Resource Center
Clayton Foundation
3607 Martin Luther King Boulevard
Denver, CO 80205
Phone: (303) 355-5387
Fax: (303) 321-2959

E-mail: jkaufman@gwclayton.org
Website: www.cpirc.org/

Connecticut
CT Parents Plus (Connecticut)
United Way of Connecticut
1344 Silas Deane Highway
Rocky Hill, CT 06067
Phone: (860) 571-6052

Fax: (860) 571-6530
E-mail:
evie.herrmann@ctunitedway.org
Website: www.ctparentsplus.org/

Delaware
No records found.

District of Columbia
Greater Washington Urban League (District of Columbia)
Parent Center
3501 14th Street, NW
Washington, DC 20010
Phone: (202) 265-8200
Fax: (202) 387-7019

E-mail: epperson@primanet.com
Website:
www.gwulparentcenter.org/

Florida
No records found.

Georgia
Albany/Dougherty Community Partnership for Education (Georgia)
P.O. Box 1726
1001 Highland Avenue
Albany, GA 31702-1726
Phone: (229) 888-0999
Fax: (229) 888-2664

E-mail:
partners@adpartnership.org

Hawaii
Pacific Resources for Education and Learning (Hawaii)
Suite 300

900 Fort Street Mall
Honolulu, HI 96813
Phone: (808) 441-1300
Fax: (808) 441-1385

E-mail: askprel@prel.org
Website: www.prel.org/programs/
pirc/pirc.asp
States Served: Federated States of
Micronesia, Hawaii, Common-
wealth of the Northern Mariana
Islands

Parental Information and Resource
Centers (Hawaii)
Parents and Children Together
Suite 103
1485 Linapuni Street
Honolulu, HI 96819
Phone: (808) 841-6177
Toll-Free: (877) 994-7472
Fax: (808) 841-1779

E-mail: fc@pacthawaii.org
Website: www.hawaiipirc.org/

Idaho
Family Advocate Program, Inc.
(Idaho)
Suite 10
3010 West State Street
Boise, ID 83703
Phone: (208) 345-3344,
Ext. 119
Fax: (208) 345-3700

E-mail: information@
familyadvocate.org
Website: www.ifep.net/

Illinois
Family Matters PTIC (Illinois)
2502 S. Veterans Drive
Effingham, IL 62401
Phone: (217) 347-5428
Toll-Free: (866) 436-7842
Fax: (217) 347-5119
TTY: (866) 436-7842

E-mail: info@fmptic.org
Website: www.fmptic.org/

Indiana
Indiana Center for Family, School,
and Community Partnerships
(The)
Suite 100
4755 Kingsway Drive
Indianapolis, IN 46205
Phone: (317) 205-2595
Toll-Free: (866) 391-1039
Toll-Free Restrictions: IN residents
only
Fax: (317) 205-9790

E-mail: info@fscp.org
Website: www.fscp.org/

Iowa
Iowa Parent Information Resource
Center
School Administrators of Iowa
12199 Stratford Drive
Clive, IA 50325
Phone: (515) 267-1115
Fax: (515) 267-1066

Website: www.higherplain.org/

Kansas
Keys For Networking, Inc. (Kansas)
1301 SW Topeka Boulevard
Topeka, KS 66612
Phone: (785) 233-8732
Toll-Free: (800) 499-8732
Toll-Free Restrictions: KS residents
only
Fax: (785) 235-6659

E-mail: jadams@keys.org
Website: www.keys.org/

Kentucky
Kentucky Parent Information
Center
Licking Valley Community Action
Program
203 High Street
Flemingsburg, KY 41041
Phone: (606) 845-0081
Toll-Free: (800) 327-5196
Fax: (606) 845-0418

E-mail: ahendrix@lvcap.com or
jplanck@lvcap.com
Website: www.kyparentinfo.org/

Louisiana
YWCA of Greater Baton Rouge,
Inc. (Louisiana)
East Baton Rouge Parish
Suite 7
3955 Government Street
Baton Rouge, LA 70806
Phone: (225) 383-0681
Fax: (225) 383-5733

E-mail: mhmac@aol.com or
ywcaprgm@aol.com
Website: www.ywca-br.org/

Maine
Maine Parent Federation
P.O. Box 2067
Augusta, ME 04338-2067
Phone: (207) 623-2144
Toll-Free: (800) 870-7746
Toll-Free Restrictions: ME residents
only
Fax: (207) 623-2148
TTY: (207) 623-2144

E-mail: parentconnect@mpf.org
Website: www.mpf.org/

Maryland
Family Works (The) (Maryland)
The Family Services Agency
Suite 100
610 East Diamond Avenue
Gaithersburg, MD 20877
Phone: (301) 840-3192
Toll-Free: (877) WERFMLY
(937-3639)
Toll-Free Restrictions: MD resi-
dents only
Fax: (240) 631-6949

E-mail: webmaster@
thefamilyworks.org
Website: www.thefamilyworks.org/

Massachusetts
Parents PLACE (Massachusetts)

Suite 420
1135 Tremont Street
Boston, MA 02120
Phone: (617) 236-7210
Toll-Free: (877) 471-0980
Fax: (617) 572-2094
TTY: (800) 331-0688

E-mail: jvohs@fcsn.org
Website: www.pplace.org/

Michigan
Families United for Success
   (Michigan)
Life Services System of Ottawa
   County, Inc.
11172 Adams
Holland, MI 49423
Phone: (616) 396-7566
Toll-Free: (800) 577-7661
Toll-Free Restrictions: MI residents
   only
Fax: (616) 396-6893

E-mail:
   mail@lifeservicessystems.org

Minnesota
Parent Advocacy Center for Educa-
   tion Rights
8161 Normandale Boulevard
Minneapolis, MN 55437
Phone: (952) 838-9000
Toll-Free: (800) 537-2237
Fax: (952) 838-0199
TTY: (952) 838-0190

E-mail: kthomas@pacer.org
Website:
   www.pacer.org/mpc/index.htm

Mississippi
Mississippi Forum on Children and
   Families
737 North President Street
Jackson, MS 39202
Phone: (601) 355-4911
Fax: (601) 355-4813

E-mail: jane.boykin@mfcf.org
Website: www.mfcf.org/

Missouri
Literacy Investment for Tomorrow
   (Missouri)
Suite 601
500 Northwest Plaza
Saint Ann, MO 63074-2221
Phone: (314) 291-4443
Toll-Free: (800) 729-4443
Fax: (314) 291-7385

E-mail: today@webster.edu or
   sschnell@webster.edu
Website: www.lift-missouri.org/

Montana
Montana Parent Information
   Resource Center
127 North Higgins
Missoula, MT 59802
Phone: (406) 543-3550
Toll-Free: (800) 914-1927
Toll-Free Restrictions: MT resi-
   dents only
Fax: (406) 721-4584

E-mail: mpirc@montana.com
Website: www.montanapirc.org/

Nebraska
Family Resource Center Coalition
   of Nebraska, Inc.
Suite 410
5109 West Scott Road
Beatrice, NE 68310
Phone: (402) 223-6040
Fax: (402) 223-6043

E-mail: ptimm@bvca.org
Website: www.frccn.org/

Nevada
Sunrise Children's Foundation—
   Parent Information and
   Resource Center (Nevada)
Sunrise Children's Hospital
   Foundation
Suite 148
3376 South Eastern Avenue
Las Vegas, NV 89109
Phone: (702) 648-1885

Toll-Free: (866) 638-7472
Toll-Free Restrictions: NV residents
   only
Fax: (702) 638-2258

E-mail: nvpirc@sunrisechildren.org
   or abtriche@sunrisechildren.org
Website:
   www.sunrisechildren.org/pirc.html

New Hampshire
Parents Involved in Education
   (New Hampshire)
Parent Information Center
P.O. Box 2405
Concord, NH 03302-2405
Phone: (603) 224-7005
Toll-Free: (800) 232-0986
Toll-Free Restrictions: NH resi-
   dents only
Fax: (603) 224-4365
TTY: (603) 224-7005

E-mail:
   info@parentinformationcenter.org
Website:
   www.parentinformationcenter.
   org/

New Jersey
Statewide Parent Advocacy Net-
   work of New Jersey, Inc.
Fourth Floor
35 Halsey Street
Newark, NJ 07102
Phone: (973) 642-8100
Toll-Free: (800) 654-7726
Toll-Free Restrictions: NJ residents
   only
Fax: (973) 642-8080

E-mail: span@spannj.org
Website: www.spannj.org/

New Mexico
Parents Reaching Out (New
   Mexico)
1920 B Columbia Drive, SE
Albuquerque, NM 87106
Phone: (505) 247-0192

Toll-Free: (800) 524-5176
Fax: (505) 247-1345

E-mail: nmproth@aol.com
Website:
www.parentsreachingout.org/

New York
No records found.

North Carolina
Parent Partners (North Carolina)
Exceptional Children's Assistance
  Center
Suite 102–103
907 Barra Row
Davidson, NC 28036
Phone: (704) 892-1321
Toll-Free: (800) 962-6817
Toll-Free Restrictions: NC residents
  only
Fax: (704) 892-5028

E-mail: ecac@ecacmail.org
Website: www.ecac-parentcenter.
  org/

North Dakota
North Dakota Parent Assistance
  and Supportive Schools Project
Pathfinder Family Center
Suite 18
1600 Second Avenue, SW
Minot, ND 58701-3459
Phone: (701) 837-7510
Toll-Free: (800) 7ND-PASS (763-
  7277)
Toll-Free Restrictions: ND resi-
  dents only
Fax: (701) 837-7540

E-mail: ndpass@minot.com
Website:
  www.pathfinder.minot.com

Ohio
Ohio Parent Information and
  Resource Center
788 Mt. Vernon Avenue
Cincinnati, OH 45219
Phone: (614) 257-6300 x108

Toll-Free: (866) 253-1829
Fax: (614) 257-6327

E-mail: emiller@cul.org

Oklahoma
Parents as Partners in Education
  (Oklahoma)
Suite 212
4801 Classen Boulevard
Oklahoma City, OK 73118-4622
Phone: (405) 478-4078
Toll-Free: (877) 706-7472
Fax: (405) 478-4077

E-mail: info@parentsaspartners.org
or
ksfrancisco@parentsaspartners.org

Oregon
No records found.

Pennsylvania
No records found.

Rhode Island
Rhode Island Parent Information
  Network, Inc.
175 Main Street
Pawtucket, RI 02860
Phone: (401) 727-4144
Toll-Free: (800) 464-3399
Toll-Free Restrictions: RI residents
  only
Fax: (401) 724-0867

E-mail: collins@ripin.org or
  ripin@ripin.org
Website: www.ripin.org/

South Carolina
Parentwise (South Carolina)
Voices for South Carolina's
  Children
P.O. Box 11644
Columbia, SC 29211
Phone: (803) 256-4670
Toll-Free: (877) 256-5374
Fax: (803) 256-8093

E-mail: nford@scparentwise.org
Website: www.scparentwise.org/

South Dakota
South Dakota Parent Resource
  Network
West River Foundation
P.O. Box 218
Sturgis, SD 57785
Phone: (605) 347-6260
Toll-Free: (800) 219-6247
Toll-Free Restrictions: SD residents
  only
Fax: (605) 347-5223

E-mail: Maryb@bhssc.tie.net or
  llaughlin@bhssc.tie.net

Tennessee
Tennessee Parents First Center
1000 Sevier Street
Nashville, TN 37208
Phone: (615) 255-4982
Toll-Free: (877) TNREADS
  (862-3237)
Fax: (615) 255-4783

E-mail: marshap@nashvilleread.org
Website: www.nashvilleread.org/

Texas
Parents As Teachers Project (Texas)
Mental Health Association in Texas
8401 Shoal Creek Boulevard
Austin, TX 78757
Phone: (214) 363-8661
Fax: (512) 454-3725

E-mail: menudd@mhatexas.org
Website: www.txpat.org/pat1.htm

Utah
Utah Family Center
5192 South Greenpine Drive
Salt Lake City, UT 84123
Phone: (801) 266-6166
Fax: (801) 293-0670

E-mail: info@utahfamilycenter.org
Website: www.utahfamilycenter.
  org/main.htm

Vermont
Vermont Parent Child Network
P.O. Box 646

Middlebury, VT 05753
Phone: (802) 388-3171
Toll-Free: (800) 639-1577
Toll-Free Restrictions: VT residents
 only
Fax: (802) 388-1590

Virginia
Virginia Parent Information
 Resource Center
Park Place Neighborhood and
 Leisure Center
606 West 29th Street
Norfolk, VA 23508
Phone: (757) 640-1116
Fax: (757) 683-9171

E-mail: sgoranson@vpirc.net
Website: www.vpirc.net/

Washington
Children's Home Society of
 Washington
P.O. Box 15190
3300 Northeast 65th Street
Seattle, WA 98115
Phone: (206) 695-3200, Ext. 286
Toll-Free: (800) 456-3339
Fax: (206) 695-3201
TTY: (206) 695-3202

E-mail: dulceh@chs-wa.org or
 mikef@chs-wa.org
Website:
 www.childrenshomesociety.org/

West Virginia
Family Connection (West Virginia)
P.O. Box 1118
Morgantown, WV 26507-1118
Phone: (304) 296-1655
Toll-Free: (800) 814-5534
Fax: (304) 296-2291

E-mail: Jfshafwv@aol.com
Website:
 www.wvfamilyconnections.net/

Wisconsin
Parents Plus (Wisconsin)
P.O. Box 452
Menasha, WI 54952-0452
Phone: (920) 729-1787
Toll-Free: (877) 384-1769
Toll-Free Restrictions: WI residents
 only
Fax: (920) 729-1137

E-mail:
susan.werley@parentspluswi.org
Website: www.parentspluswi.org/

Wyoming
Parent Education Network
 (Wyoming)
5 North Lobban
Buffalo, WY 82834
Phone: (307) 684-7441
Toll-Free: (877) 900-9736
Toll-Free Restrictions: WY resi-
 dents only
Fax: (307) 684-5314

E-mail: tdawson@wpic.org
Website: www.wpen.net

TERRITORIES

American Samoa
American Samoa Parent Network
P.O. Box 3432
Pago Pago, AS 96799
Phone: (684) 699-6946
Fax: (684) 699-6952

E-mail:
 SAMPAVE@samoatelco.com
Website:
 taalliance.org/ptis/amsamoa/

**Commonwealth of the Northern
Mariana Islands**
Ayuda Network, Inc. (Northern
 Mariana Islands)
Government Building No. 1253

Capital Hill
P.O. Box 503019
Saipan, MP 96950-3019
Phone: (670) 322-7469
Fax: (670) 322-7468

E-mail: ayudanet@gtepacifica.net
Website:
 www.gtepacifica.net/community/
 ayudanet/

Pacific Resources for Education
 and Learning (Hawaii)
Suite 300
900 Fort Street Mall
Honolulu, HI 96813
Phone: (808) 441-1300
Fax: (808) 441-1385

E-mail: askprel@prel.org
Website: www.prel.org/programs/
 pirc/pirc.asp
States Served: Federated States of
 Micronesia, Hawaii, Common-
 wealth of the Northern Mariana
 Islands

Federated States of Micronesia
Pacific Resources for Education
 and Learning (Hawaii)
Suite 300
900 Fort Street Mall
Honolulu, HI 96813
Phone: (808) 441-1300
Fax: (808) 441-1385

E-mail: askprel@prel.org
Website: www.prel.org/programs/
 pirc/pirc.asp
States Served: Federated States of
 Micronesia, Hawaii, Common-
 wealth of the Northern Mariana
 Islands

Guam
Sanctuary, Inc. (Guam)
P.O. Box 21030, GMF

Barrigada, GU 96921
Phone: (671) 475-7103
Fax: (671) 477-3117

E-mail: sanctuar@ite.net

Puerto Rico
APNI, Inc.
P.O. Box 21280
San Juan, PR 00928-1280
Phone: (787) 763-4665
Toll-Free: (800) 981-8393

Toll-Free Restrictions: PR residents
  only
Fax: (787) 765-0345
TTY: (787) 753-7185

E-mail: centroinfo@apnipr.org
Website: www.apnipr.org/

Republic of Palau
Palau Community Action Agency
P.O. Box 3000
Koror, PW 96940

Phone: (680) 488-3022
Fax: (680) 488-1169

Republic of the Marshall Islands
No records found.

Virgin Islands
Village-Virgin Island Partners In
  Recovery (The)
5105 Sunny Isles
St. Croix, VI 00823-5105
Phone: (340) 719-9800

Glossary

A

Academic learning time (p. 59): the amount of time students spend working on academic tasks with a high level of success (80 percent or higher).

Allocated time (p. 59): the amount of time teachers allocate for instruction in various areas of the curriculum.

Alternate assessments (p. 155): alternative ways of measuring the performance of students who are unable to participate in "traditional" approaches to assessment.

Alternative assessments (p. 148): approaches that assess students' ability to complete "real-life" tasks rather than merely regurgitate facts.

Alternative certification (p. 224): a provision allowing people who have completed college but not a teacher education program to become certified teachers.

Amendments to the Individuals with Disabilities Education Act (IDEA 97) (p. 119): amendments to IDEA that emphasize educational outcomes for students with disabilities and provide greater access through changes in eligibility requirements, IEP guidelines, public and private placements, student discipline guidelines, and procedural safeguards.

Analytic rubric (p. 161): a rating scale, or scoring guide, for evaluating part of a student's product or performance.

Assertive discipline (p. 70): an approach to classroom discipline requiring that teachers establish firm, clear guidelines for student behavior and follow through with consequences for misbehavior.

Assessment (p. 138): the process of gathering information related to how much students have learned.

Assistive technology (p. 122): technological advances (usually computer based) that help exceptional students learn and communicate.

Attention deficit disorder (ADD) (p. 113): a learning disability characterized by difficulty in concentrating on learning.

Attention deficit hyperactivity disorder (ADHD) (p. 113): a learning disability characterized by difficulty in remaining still so that one can concentrate on learning.

Authentic assessment (p. 149): an approach to assessing students' learning that requires them to solve problems or work on tasks that approximate as much as possible those they will encounter beyond the classroom.

Authentic learning tasks (p. 59): learning activities that enable students to see the connections between classroom learning and the world beyond the classroom.

B

Between-class ability grouping (p. 57): the practice of grouping students at the middle and high school levels for instruction on the basis of ability or achievement, often called *tracking*.

Bicultural (p. 36): the ability to function effectively in two or more linguistic and cultural groups.

Block scheduling (p. 61): a high school scheduling arrangement that provides longer blocks of time each class period, with fewer periods each day.

C

Caring classroom (p. 54): a classroom in which the teacher communicates clearly an attitude of caring about students' learning and their overall well-being.

CD-ROM (p. 180): a small plastic disk (usually 4.72 or 5.25 inches in diameter) that holds 600 or more megabytes of information that can be read by a computer.

Channel One (p. 175): a controversial twelve-minute news broadcast, including two minutes of commercials, aired daily in more than 12,000 public and private schools; schools receive Channel One programs, equipment, and service free of charge on agreeing to show the programs to students.

Character education (p. 99): an approach to education that emphasizes the teaching of values, moral reasoning, and the development of "good" character.

Charter (p. 221): an agreement between a charter school's founders and its sponsors specifying how the school will operate and what learning outcomes students will master.

Chat room (p. 183): an Internet site where students can participate in online discussions by typing in their comments and questions.

Choice theory (p. 65): an approach to classroom management, developed by psychiatrist William Glasser, based on a belief that students will usually make good choices (i.e., behave in an acceptable manner) if they experience success in the classroom and know that teachers care about them.

Classroom climate (p. 48): the atmosphere or quality of life in a classroom, determined by how individuals interact with one another.

Classroom culture (p. 48): the "way of life" characteristic of a classroom group; determined by the social dimensions of the group and the physical characteristics of the setting.

Classroom management (p. 61): day-to-day teacher control of student behavior and learning, including discipline.

Classroom organization (p. 57): how teachers and students in a school are grouped for instruction and how time is allocated in classrooms.

Clinical supervision (p. 251): a four-step model supervisors follow in making teacher performance evaluations.

Cognitive development (p. 93): the process of acquiring the intellectual ability to learn from interaction with one's environment.

Collaboration (p. 244): the practice of working together, sharing decision making, and solving problems among professionals.

Collaborative consultation (p. 124): an approach in which a classroom teacher meets with one or more other professionals (such as a special educator, school psychologist, or resource teacher) to focus on the learning needs of one or more students.

Collegial support team (CST) (p. 250): a team of teachers—created according to subject area, grade level, or teacher interests and expertise—who support one another's professional growth.

Collegiality (p. 240): a spirit of cooperation and mutual helpfulness among professionals.

Computer-assisted instruction (CAI) (p. 177): the use of computers to provide individualized drill-and-practice exercises or tutorials to students.

Computer-based simulations (p. 181): computer programs that present the user with multifaceted problem situations similar to those they will encounter in real life.

Computer-enhanced instruction (CEI) (p. 177): the use of computers to provide students with inquiry-oriented learning experiences such as simulations and problem-solving activities.

Computer-managed instruction (CMI) (p. 177): the use of computers to evaluate and diagnose students' learning needs and record students' progress for teachers to monitor.

Concrete operations stage (p. 93): the stage of cognitive development (seven to eleven years of age) proposed by Jean Piaget in which the individual develops the ability to use logical thought to solve concrete problems.

Constructivist teaching (p. 76): a method of teaching based on students' prior knowledge of the topic and the processes they use to construct meaning.

Contextual teaching and learning (CTL) (p. 78): an approach to teaching based on the theory that students learn best when they are involved in hands-on activities and have opportunities for personal discovery within the context of relationships that are familiar to them.

Cooperative learning (p. 58): an approach to education in which students work in small groups, or teams, sharing the work and helping one another complete assignments.

Co-teaching (p. 250): an arrangement whereby two or more teachers teach together in the same classroom.

Credentials file (p. 229): a file set up for students registered in a teacher placement office at a college or university that includes background information on the applicant, the type of position desired, transcripts, performance evaluations, and letters of recommendation.

Criterion-referenced assessments (p. 147): assessments in which student learning is compared with clearly defined criteria or standards, rather than the performance of other students.

Cross-age tutoring (p. 79): a tutoring arrangement in which older students tutor younger students; evidence indicates that cross-age tutoring has positive effects on the attitudes and achievement of tutee and tutor.

Curriculum (p. 24): the school experiences, both planned and unplanned, that enhance (and sometimes impede) the education and growth of students.

D

Digital divide (p. 200): inequities in access to computer technology that are related to minority-group status, family income, and gender.

Direct instruction (p. 73): a systematic instructional method focusing on the transmission of knowledge and skills from the teacher to the students.

Discovery learning (p. 77): an approach to teaching that gives students opportunities to inquire into subjects so that they "discover" knowledge for themselves.

Distance learning (p. 15): the use of technology such as video transmissions that enables students to receive instruction at multiple, often remote, sites.

Distance learning networks (p. 175): two-way, interactive telecommunications systems used to deliver instruction to students at various locations.

E

Education for All Handicapped Children Act (Public Law 94-142) (p. 119): a 1975 federal act that guarantees a free and appropriate education to all handicapped children (often referred to as the *mainstreaming law* or *Public Law 94-142*).

Educational technology (p. 174): computers, software, multimedia systems, and advanced telecommunica-

tions systems used to enhance the teaching–learning process.

E-learning (p. 172): education that is delivered via the Internet, satellite broadcast, interactive TV, or CD-ROM.

Emergency certification (p. 224): temporary, substandard certification requirements set by a state in response to a shortage of teachers.

E-rate (p. 198): a controversial program that uses fees from telecommunications companies to provide discounts on telecommunications services and wiring to schools and libraries.

Evaluation (p. 141): making judgments about, or assigning a value to, measurements of students' learning.

Exceptional learners (p. 110): students whose growth and development deviate from the norm to the extent that their educational needs can be met more effectively through a modification of regular school programs.

Explicit curriculum (p. 25): the behavior, attitudes, and knowledge that a school intends to teach students.

Extracurricular/cocurricular programs (p. 27): activities perceived as additions to the academic curriculum.

F

Field experiences (p. 14): opportunities for teachers-in-training to experience firsthand the world of the teacher, by observing, tutoring, and instructing small groups.

Formal assessments (p. 138): assessments of student learning developed prior to having students complete the assessment—tests, quizzes, homework, and critiques of performances, for example.

Formal operations stage (p. 93): the stage of cognitive development (eleven to fifteen years of age) proposed by Jean Piaget in which cognitive abilities reach their highest level of development.

Formative evaluation (p. 141): an assessment, or diagnosis, of students' learning for the purpose of planning instruction.

Full inclusion (p. 122): the policy and process of including exceptional learners in general education classrooms.

G

Gender bias (p. 36): subtle bias or discrimination on the basis of gender; reduces the likelihood that the target of the bias will develop to the full extent of his or her capabilities.

Gender-fair classroom (p. 36): education that is free of bias or discrimination on the basis of gender.

Gifted and talented (p. 114): exceptional learners who demonstrate high intelligence, high creativity, high achievement, or special talents.

Group investigation (p. 79): an approach to teaching in which the teacher facilitates learning by creating an environment that allows students to determine what they will study and how.

H

Hidden curriculum (p. 25): the behaviors, attitudes, and knowledge the school culture unintentionally teaches students.

Hierarchy of needs (p. 99): a set of seven needs, from the basic needs for survival and safety to the need for self-actualization, that motivate human behavior as identified by Abraham Maslow.

Holistic rubric (p. 160): a rating scale, or scoring guide, for evaluating a student's overall product or performance.

Home–school communication systems (p. 182): computer-based systems that allow schools to disseminate information to parents and, in turn, enable parents to communicate directly with school personnel.

Hypermedia (p. 181): an interactive instructional system consisting of a computer, CD-ROM drive, videodisc player, video monitor, and speakers. Hypermedia systems allow students to control and present sound, video images, text, and graphics in an almost limitless array of possibilities.

I

Inclusion (p. 122): the practice of integrating all students with disabilities into general education classes.

Individualized education plan (IEP) (p. 119): a plan for meeting an exceptional learner's educational needs, specifying goals, objectives, services, and procedures for evaluating progress.

Individuals with Disabilities Education Act (IDEA) (p. 119): a 1990 federal act providing a free, appropriate education to youth with disabilities between three and twenty-one years of age. IDEA superseded the earlier Education for All Handicapped Children Act (Public Law 94-142).

Induction programs (p. 217): programs of support for beginning teachers, usually during their first year of teaching.

Informal assessments (p. 138): spontaneous assessments of student learning that teachers make while teaching—noting students' facial expressions, asking questions to gauge students' understanding, and listening to students' explanations of how they solved problems, for example.

Information processing (p. 76): a branch of cognitive science concerned with how individuals use long- and short-term memory to acquire information and solve problems.

Inquiry learning (p. 77): an approach to teaching that gives students opportunities to explore, or inquire into, subjects so that they develop their own answers to problem situations.

Instructional goals (p. 81): broad, general statements of purpose that may apply to students in a school district, school, or individual classroom—for example, "students will understand biological concepts and principles."

Integrated curriculum (p. 30): a school curriculum that draws from two or more subject areas and focuses on a theme or concept rather than on a single subject.

Intelligence (p. 105): the ability to learn; the cognitive capacity for thinking.

Interactive multimedia (p. 180): computer-supported media that allow the user to interact with a vast, nonlinear, multimedia database to combine textual, audio, and video information.

International Assessment of Educational Progress (IAEP) (p. 143): a program established in 1991 for comparing the achievement of students in the United States with that of students from other countries.

Interstate Certification Agreement Contract (p. 221): a reciprocity agreement among approximately thirty states whereby a teaching certificate obtained in one state will be honored in another.

Interstate New Teacher Assessment and Support Consortium (INTASC) (p. 5): an organization of states established in 1987 to develop performance-based standards for what beginning teachers should know and be able to do.

K

Knowledge base (p. 7): the body of knowledge that represents what teachers need to know and be able to do.

L

Language-minority students (p. 36): students whose first language is not English.

Learning disability (LD) (p. 113): a limitation in one's ability to take in, organize, remember, and express information.

Learning objectives (p. 81): specific, measurable outcomes of learning that students are to demonstrate—for example, "students will identify the structural elements of cells and explain their functions."

Learning styles (p. 109): cognitive, affective, and physiological behaviors through which an individual learns most effectively; determined by a combination of hereditary and environmental influences.

Least restrictive environment (p. 119): an educational program that meets a disabled student's special needs in a manner that is identical, insofar as possible, to that provided to students in general education classrooms.

Letter of application (p. 233): a letter written in application for a specific teaching vacancy in a school district.

Letter of inquiry (p. 233): a letter written to a school district inquiring about teaching vacancies.

M

Mainstreaming (p. 121): the policy and process of integrating disabled or otherwise exceptional learners into regular classrooms with nonexceptional students.

Mastery learning (p. 75): an approach to instruction based on the assumptions that (1) virtually all students can learn material if given enough time and taught appropriately and (2) learning is enhanced if students can progress in small, sequenced steps.

Measurement (p. 141): the gathering of data that indicate how much students have learned.

Microcomputer-based laboratories (MBL) (p. 180): the use of computers to gather and then analyze data that students have collected in a school laboratory or in the field.

Microteaching (p. 17): a brief, single-concept lesson taught by a teacher education student to a small group of students; usually designed to give the education student an opportunity to practice a specific teaching skill.

Modeling (p. 75): the process of "thinking out loud" that teachers use to make students aware of the reasoning involved in learning new material.

Moral reasoning (p. 93): the reasoning process people follow to decide what is right or wrong.

Multicultural curriculum (p. 34): a school curriculum that addresses the needs and backgrounds of all students regardless of their cultural identity and includes the cultural perspectives, or "voices," of people who have previously been silent or marginalized.

Multicultural education (p. 32): education that provides equal educational opportunities to all students—regardless of socioeconomic status; gender; or ethnic, racial, or cultural backgrounds—and is dedicated to reducing prejudice and celebrating the rich diversity of U.S. life.

Multiple intelligences (p. 107): a perspective on intellectual ability, proposed by Howard Gardner, suggesting that there are at least seven types of human intelligence.

N

National Board for Professional Teaching Standards (NBPTS) (p. 5): a board established in 1987 that began issuing professional certificates in 1994–95 to teachers who possess extensive professional knowledge and the ability to perform at a high level.

National Council for Accreditation of Teacher Education (NCATE) (p. 5): an agency that accredits, on a voluntary basis, almost half of the nation's teacher education programs.

National Information Infrastructure (p. 198): a federal plan to create a telecommunications infrastructure linking all schools, libraries, hospitals, and law enforcement agencies to the Internet and the World Wide Web.

Newsgroups (p. 183): Internet sites where students can post and exchange information on electronic "bulletin boards."

Norm-referenced assessments (p. 146): assessments that compare a student's performance to the "typical" performance of other students at the same age and grade level; the comparison group of students is called the *norm group.*

Null curriculum (p. 26): the intellectual processes and subject content that schools do not teach.

O

Observations (p. 15): field experiences wherein a teacher education student observes a specific aspect of classroom life such as the students, the teacher, the interactions between the two, the structure of the lesson, or the setting.

Opportunity to learn (OTL) (p. 59): the time during which a teacher provides students with challenging content and appropriate instructional strategies to learn that content.

P

Pedagogical content knowledge (p. 9): the knowledge accomplished teachers possess regarding how to present subject matter to students through the use of analogies, metaphors, experiments, demonstrations, illustrations, and other instructional strategies.

Peer assessment (p. 151): an arrangement whereby students assess one another's work.

Peer coaching (p. 246): an arrangement whereby teachers grow professionally by observing one another's teaching and providing constructive feedback.

Peer-mediated instruction (p. 79): approaches to teaching, such as cooperative learning and group investigation, that utilize the social relationships among students to promote their learning.

Peer-tutoring (p. 79): an arrangement whereby students tutor other students in the same classroom or at the same grade level.

Performance-based assessment (p. 152): the process of determining students' ability to apply knowledge, skills, and work habits to the performance of specific

learning tasks; determining what students can do as well as what they know.

Portfolio assessment (p. 150): the process of determining how much students have learned by examining collections of work that document their learning over time.

Practicum (p. 18): a short field-based experience during which teacher education students spend time observing and assisting in classrooms.

Praxis Series: Professional Assessments for Beginning Teachers (p. 5, 224): a battery of tests available to states for the initial certification of teachers. Consists of assessments in three areas: academic skills, knowledge of subject, and classroom performance.

Preoperational stage (p. 93): the stage of cognitive development (two to seven years of age) proposed by Jean Piaget in which the individual begins to use language and symbols to think of objects and people outside of the immediate environment.

Problem-solving orientation (p. 14): an approach to teaching that places primary emphasis on the teacher's role as a decision maker and problem solver.

Project-based learning (PBL) (p. 156): an approach to learning in which students work in teams on complex, "real-world" projects that allow them to develop and apply skills and knowledge.

Psychosocial crisis (p. 96): a life crisis at one of eight different stages of growth and development. According to psychologist Erik Erikson, individuals must resolve each crisis to reach the next stage.

Psychosocial development (p. 93): the progression of an individual through various stages of psychological and social development.

Q

Qualitative assessments (p. 140): subjective assessments of student learning—for example, formal and informal observations of students' performance on learning tasks and/or the manner in which they approach those tasks.

Qualitative evaluation (p. 251): the appraisal of teacher performance through the use of written, open-ended descriptions of classroom events in terms of their qualities.

Quantitative assessments (p. 139): assessments of student learning that yield numerical scores that teachers use to evaluate student learning as well as the effectiveness of their teaching.

Quantitative evaluation (p. 251): the appraisal of teacher performance by recording classroom events in terms of their number or frequency—for example, teacher verbal behaviors such as questioning, praising, or critiquing.

R

Recertification (p. 221) the practice in some states of requiring experienced teachers to undergo periodic testing to maintain their teaching certificates.

Reflection (p. 14): the process of thinking carefully and deliberately about the outcomes of one's teaching.

Reflective teaching log (p. 21): a journal of classroom observations in which the teacher education student systematically analyzes specific episodes of teaching.

Reliability (p. 158): the degree to which an assessment provides results that are consistent over time.

résumé (p. 231): a concise summary of an individual's professional experiences and education.

S

Scaffolding (p. 76): an approach to teaching based on the student's current level of understanding and ability; the teacher varies the amount of help given (e.g., clues, encouragement, or suggestions) to students based on their moment-to-moment understanding of the material being learned.

Scoring rubrics (p. 160): rating scales that consist of pre-established criteria for evaluating student performance on learning tasks.

Self-assessment (p. 152): the process of measuring one's growth in regard to the knowledge, skills, and attitudes possessed by professional teachers.

Special education (p. 118): a teaching specialty for meeting the special educational needs of exceptional learners.

Stages of development (p. 92): predictable stages through which individuals pass as they progress through life.

Standardized assessments (p. 142): pencil-and-paper tests taken by large numbers of students and scored in a uniform manner (often called *standardized tests*). The test items, conditions under which students take the test, how the test is scored, and how the scores are interpreted are "standardized" for all who take the test.

Student-centered curriculum (p. 30): curricula that are organized around students' needs and interests.

Students with disabilities (p. 111): students who need special education services because they possess one or more of the following disabilities: learning disabilities, speech or language impairments, mental retardation, serious emotional disturbance, hearing impairments, orthopedic impairments, visual impairments, or other health impairments.

Subject-centered curriculum (p. 30): a curriculum that emphasizes learning an academic discipline.

Summative evaluation (p. 141): an assessment of student learning made for the purpose of assigning grades at the end of a unit, semester, or year and deciding whether students are ready to proceed to the next phase of their education.

T

Teacher supply and demand (p. 226): the number of school-age students compared to the number of available teachers; may also be projected based on estimated numbers of students and teachers.

Teachers' craft knowledge (p. 11): the knowledge teachers develop about teaching that derives from their experiences in the classroom, particularly the actions they have taken to solve specific problems of practice.

Teaching certificate (p. 220): a license to teach issued by a state or, in a few cases, a large city.

Teaching simulations (p. 17): an activity in which teacher education students participate in role-plays designed to create situations comparable to those actually encountered by teachers.

Team teaching (p. 248): an arrangement whereby a team of teachers teaches a group of students equal in number to what the teachers would have in their self-contained classrooms.

Third International Mathematics and Science Study (TIMSS) (p. 143): an international assessment of mathematics and science achievement among fourth-, eighth-, and twelfth-grade students in forty-one nations.

Time on task (p. 59): the amount of time students are actively and directly engaged in learning tasks.

Tyler rationale (p. 28): a four-step model for curriculum development in which teachers identify purposes, select learning experiences, organize experiences, and evaluate.

V

Validity (p. 158): the degree to which assessments measure what they are supposed to measure.

Videoconferencing (p. 184): the use of computer-mounted video cameras to conduct two-way interactive conferences over the Internet.

Videodisc (p. 180): a twelve-inch plastic disc, each side of which holds about thirty minutes of motion video, or 54,000 frames of video; each frame can be frozen with a high degree of clarity.

Virtual schools (p. 172): educational institutions that offer K–12 courses through the Internet or by means of web-based methods; an online learning space where teachers and students interact.

W

Within-class ability grouping (p. 57): the practice of creating small, homogeneous groups of students within a single classroom for the purpose of instruction, usually in reading or mathematics, at the elementary level.

World Wide Web (p. 183): the most popular connection to the Internet; composed of home pages that users access through browser programs such as Netscape Communicator, Microsoft Explorer, or America Online.

References

Acheson, A. A., and Gall, M. D. (1997). *Techniques in the clinical supervision of teachers: Preservice and inservice applications*, 4th ed. New York: Longman.

Alliance for Childhood. (2000). *Fools gold: A critical look at computers in childhood*. College Park, MD: Author.

American Federation of Teachers. (2001, September). *Educational issues policy brief*, No. 13. Washington, DC: Author.

Anderson, R. E., and Ronnkvist, A. (1999). *The presence of computers in American schools*. The University of California, Irvine, and the University of Minnesota: Center for Research on Information Technology and Organizations.

Appalachia Educational Laboratory. (1993). *Alternative assessment in math and science: Moving toward school a moving target*. Charleston, WV: Author.

Armstrong, A., and Casement, C. (2000). *The child and the machine: How computers put our children's education at risk*. Beltsville, MD: Robins Lane Press.

Avramidis, E., Bayliss, P., and Burden, R. (2000). A survey into mainstream teachers' attitudes towards the inclusion of children with special educational needs in the ordinary school in one local education authority. *Educational Psychology, 20*(2), 191–211.

Baker, R. (2002). Stealth TV. In A. Kohn and P. Shannon (Eds.), *Education, Inc.: Turning learning into a business*. Portsmouth, NH: Heinemann.

Banks, J. A. (2001). *Cultural diversity and education: Foundations, curriculum, and teaching*, 4th ed. Boston: Allyn and Bacon.

Banks, J. A. (2002). *An introduction to multicultural education*, 3rd ed. Boston: Allyn and Bacon.

Banks, J. A. (2003). *Teaching strategies for ethnic studies*, 7th ed. Boston: Allyn and Bacon.

Becker, H. J. (1999). *Internet use by teachers: Conditions of professional use and teacher-directed student use*. The University of California, Irvine, and The University of Minnesota: Center for Research on Information Technology and Organizations.

Becker, H. J. (2001, April). *How are teachers using computers in instruction?* Paper presented at the annual meeting of the American Educational Research Association, Seattle, WA.

Bennett, W. J., and Gelernter, D. (2001, March 14). Improving education with technology. *Education Week on the Web*.

Bensman, D. (2000). *Central Park East and its graduates: Learning by heart*. New York: Teachers College Press.

Berliner, D. C., and Biddle, B. J. (1995). *The manufactured crisis: Myths, fraud, and the attack on America's public schools*. Reading, MA: Addison Wesley.

Bialo, E. (1989). Computers and at-risk youth: A partial solution to a complex problem. *Classroom Computer Learning, 9*(4), 48–55.

Bitter, G. G., and Pierson, M. E. (1999). *Using technology in the classroom*, 4th ed. Boston: Allyn and Bacon.

Bitter, G. G., and Pierson, M. E. (2002). *Using technology in the classroom*, 5th ed. Boston: Allyn and Bacon.

Black, P., Harrison, C., Lee, C., Marshall, B., and Wiliam, D. (2004, September). Working inside the black box: Assessment for learning in the classroom. *Phi Delta Kappan*, 9–21.

Bloom, B. S. (1981). *All our children learning: A primer for parents, teachers, and other educators*. New York: McGraw-Hill.

Board of Education, Sacramento City Unified School District v. Holland, 786 F. Supp. 874 (E.D. Cal. 1992).

Borich, G. (1996). *Effective teaching methods*, 3rd ed. Upper Saddle River, NJ: Merrill.

Borich, G. D. (2000). *Effective teaching methods*, 4th ed. Upper Saddle River, NJ: Merrill.

Boser, U. (2000, May 3). States stiffening recertification for teachers. *Education Week on the Web*.

Boyer, E. (1995). *The basic school: A community for learning*. Princeton, NJ: The Carnegie Foundation for the Advancement of Teaching.

Brock, B. L., and Grady, M. L. (2001). *From first-year to first-rate: Principals guiding beginning teachers*. Thousand Oaks, CA: Corwin Press.

Brown, A. H. (1999). Simulated classrooms and artificial students: The potential effects of new technologies on teacher education. *Journal of Research on Computing in Education, 32*(2), 307–318.

Brown, F. B., Kohrs, D., and Lanzarro, C. (1991). *The academic costs and consequences of extracurricular participation in high school.* Paper presented at the Annual Meeting of Educational Research Association.

Brown, M. E. (1994). *Computer simulation: Improving case study methods for preservice and inservice teacher education.* ERIC Document Reproduction Services No. ED371 730.

Brunner, C., and Tally, W. (1999). *The new media literacy handbook: An educator's guide to bringing new media into the classroom.* New York: Anchor Books.

Burden, P. R., and Byrd, D. M. (1999). *Methods for effective teaching*, 2nd ed. Boston: Allyn and Bacon.

Cantor, L. (1989). Assertive discipline—more than names on the board and marbles in a jar. *Phi Delta Kappan, 71*(1), 57–61.

Carroll, J. (1963). A model of school learning. *Teachers College Record, 64.*

Caterinicchia, D. (1999, June 18). Teachers' limited tech know-how prompts laptop lease. *CNN Interative.*

CEO Forum on Education and Technology. (1999). *School technology and readiness report.* Washington, DC: Author.

Coladarci, T., and Cobb, C. D. (1996). Extracurricular participation, school size, and achievement and self-esteem among high school students: A national look. *Journal of Research in Rural Education, 12*(2), 92–103.

Colucci, K. (2000). Negative pedagogy. In J. L. Paul and K. Colucci (Eds.), *Stories out of school: Memories and reflections on care and cruelty in the classroom* (pp. 27–44). Stamford, CT: Ablex.

Commission on Student Learning (1993). *Essential Academic Learning Requirements.* Office of Superintendent of Public Instruction, Olympia, WA.

Costa, A. L. (1984). A reaction to Hunter's knowing, teaching, and supervising. In P. L. Hosford (Ed.), *Using what we know about teaching.* Alexandria, VA: Association for Supervision and Curriculum Development.

Cuban, L. (1999a, January). High-tech schools, low-tech teaching. *The Education Digest.*

Cuban, L. (1999b, August 4). The technology puzzle: Why is greater access not translating into better classroom use? *Education Week*, pp. 47, 68.

Curtis, D. (2002, March 12). Handhelds go to class. *Edutopia.* The George Lucas Educational Foundation.

Curwin, R., and Mendler, A. (1988). Packaged discipline programs: Let the buyer beware. *Educational Leadership, 46*(2), 68–71.

Curwin, R., and Mendler, A. (1989, March). We repeat, let the buyer beware: A response to Canter. *Educational Leadership, 46*(6), 83.

Danielson, C. (1996). *Enhancing professional practice: A framework for teaching.* Alexandria, VA: Association for Supervision and Curriculum Development.

Davis, G. A., and Rimm, S. B. (1998). *Education of the gifted and talented*, 4th ed. Boston: Allyn and Bacon.

Degnan, E., and Bozeman, W. (2001). An investigation of computer-based simulations for school crisis management. *Journal of School Leadership, 11*(4), 296–312.

DeRoche, E. F., and Williams, M. M. (2001). *Character education: A guide for school administrators.* Lanham, MD: Scarecrow Press.

Dewey, J. (1916). *Democracy and education: An introduction to the philosophy of education.* New York: Macmillan.

Dollase, R. H. (1992). *Voices of beginning teachers: Visions and realities.* New York: Teachers College Press.

Dryfoos, J., and Maguire, S. (2002). *Inside full-service community schools.* Thousand Oaks, CA: Corwin Press.

Duffy, G., and Roehler, L. (1989). The tension between information-giving and mediation: Perspectives on instructional explanation and teacher change. In J. Brophy (Ed.), *Advances in research on teaching*, vol. 1. Greenwich, CT: JAI Press.

Education Writers Association. (1999). *Barriers and breakthroughs: Technology in urban schools.* Washington, DC: Author.

Edyburn, D. L. (2003). *What every teacher should know about assistive technology.* Boston: Allyn and Bacon.

Eisner, E. W. (1998). *The kind of schools we need: Personal essays.* Portsmouth, NH: Heinemann.

Eisner, E. (2002). *The educational imagination: On the design and evaluation of school programs*, 3rd ed. New York: Macmillan College.

Ensign, G. (1998). *The Washington assessment of student learning: An update—May 1998.* Washington Commission on Student Learning. Available online at ospi.wednet.edu Directory: csl.wednet.edu/Web%20page/3%20assessment%20system/subdocuments/1.

Erikson, E. H. (1997). *The life cycle completed: Extended version with new chapters on the ninth stage of development by Joan M. Erikson.* New York: W. W. Norton.

Etzioni, A. (1999, June 9). The truths we must face to curb youth violence. *Education Week on the Web.*

Evertson, C. M., Emmer, E. T., and Worsham, M. E. (2003). *Classroom management for elementary teachers*, 6th ed. Boston: Allyn and Bacon.

Falk, B. (2002, April). Standards-based reforms: Problems and possibilities. *Phi Delta Kappan*, pp. 612–620.

Feistritzer, E. (2002). *Alternative teacher certification: A state-by-state analysis*. Washington, DC: National Center for Education Information.

Feldhusen, J. F. (1997). Educating teachers for work with talented youth. In N. Colangelo and G. A. Davis (Eds.), *Handbook of gifted education*. Boston: Allyn and Bacon.

Friend, M., and Bursuck, W. D. (2002). *Including students with special needs: A practical guide for classroom teachers*. Boston: Allyn and Bacon.

Fulton, K. P., and Riel, M. (1999, May 1). Professional development through learning communities. *Edutopia, 6*(2), 8–9. The George Lucas Educational Foundation.

Furger, R. (1999, September). Are wired schools failing our kids? *PC World*.

Furger, R., and Shaffner, M. (August 19, 2004). An incredible journey. *Edutopia online*. The George Lucas Educational Foundation. Retrieved from www.glef.org/1145

Gagné, R. M. (1974). *Essentials of learning for instruction*. Hinsdale, IL: Dryden.

Gardner, H. (1983). *Frames of mind*. New York: Basic Books.

Gardner, H. (September, 1997). Multiple intelligences as a partner in school improvement. *Educational Leadership*, pp. 20–21.

Gardner, H. (1999). *The disciplined mind: What all students should understand*. New York: Simon and Schuster.

Gates, B. (2002). Introduction. In Hinrichs, R., *A vision for lifelong learning—year 2020, 2020 visions: Transforming education and training through advanced technologies*. Washington, DC: U.S. Department of Commerce, 1–12.

Gates, B., Myhrvold, N., and Rinearson, P. M. (1996). *The road ahead*. New York: Penguin.

Gauld, L., and Gauld, M. (2002). *The biggest job we'll ever have: The Hyde School program for character-based education and parenting*. New York: Scribner.

George Lucas Educational Foundation. (2001, November). *Project-based learning research*. Retrieved from http://www.glef.org/index.html

Gerber, S. B. (1996). Extracurricular activities and academic achievement. *Journal of Research and Development in Education, 30*(1), 42–50.

Gilligan, C. (1993). *In a different voice: Psychological theory and women's development*. Cambridge, MA: Harvard University Press.

Glasser, W. R. (1997, April). A new look at school failure and school success. *Phi Delta Kappan*, pp. 596–602.

Glasser, W. R. (1998a). *Quality school*, 3rd ed. New York: Harper Perennial.

Glasser, W. R. (1998b). *The quality school teacher: Specific suggestions for teachers who are trying to implement the lead-management ideas of the quality school*. New York: Harper Perennial.

Glasser, W. R. (1998c). *Choice theory: A new psychology of personal freedom*. New York: HarperCollins.

Glasser, W. R., and Dotson, K. L. (1998). *Choice theory in the classroom*. New York: Harper Perennial.

Glickman, C. D. (2002). *Leadership for learning: How to help teachers succeed*. Alexandria, VA: Association for Supervision and Curriculum Development.

Glickman, C., Gordon, S. P., and Ross-Gordon, J. M. (2001). *SuperVision and instructional leadership*, 5th ed. Boston: Allyn and Bacon.

Glickman, C., Gordon, S. P., and Ross-Gordon, J. M. (2004). *SuperVision and instructional leadership*, 6th ed. Boston: Allyn and Bacon.

Goldhammer, R., Anderson, R. H., and Krajewski, R. J. (1993). *Clinical supervision: Special methods for the supervision of teachers*, 3rd ed. Fort Worth: Harcourt Brace Jovanovich.

Good, T. E., and Brophy, J. E. (2003). *Looking in classrooms*, 9th ed. Boston: Allyn and Bacon.

Good, T. E., and Grouws, D. (1979). The Missouri mathematics effectiveness project: An experimental study in fourth-grade classrooms. *Journal of Educational Psychology, 71*, 355–362.

Goolsbee, A., and Guryan, J. (2002). The impact of Internet subsidies in public schools. Working Paper 9090. Cambridge, MA: National Bureau of Economic Research.

Gordon, D. T. (Ed.). (2003). *Better teaching and learning in the digital classroom*. Cambridge, MA: Harvard Education Press.

Grant, C. A. (1994, Winter). Challenging the myths about multicultural education. *Multicultural Education*, pp. 4–9.

Grant, P. G., Richard, K. J., and Parkay, F. W. (1996, April). *Using video cases to promote reflection among preservice teachers: A qualitative inquiry*. Paper presented at the annual meeting of the American Educational Research Association, New York.

Greene, B. (1999, July 7). A 21st century idea for schools: Log off and learn. *Chicago Tribune*, sect. 2, p. 1.

Greenwood, G., Fillmer, H. T., and Parkay, F. W. (2002). *Educational psychology cases*, 2nd ed. Upper Saddle River, NJ: Merrill Prentice Hall.

Guenemoen, R. F., Thompson, S. J., Thurlow, M. L., and Lehr, C. A. (2001). *A self-study guide to implementation of inclusive assessment and accountability systems: A best practice approach*. Minneapolis, MN: University of Minnesota, National Center on Educational Outcomes.

Hallahan, D. P., and Kauffman, J. M. (2000). *Exceptional children: Introduction to special education*, 8th ed. Boston: Allyn and Bacon.

Hallahan, D. P., and Kauffman, J. M. (2003). *Exceptional children: Introduction to special education*, 9th ed. Boston: Allyn and Bacon.

Hansen, D. T. (1995). *The call to teach*. New York: Teachers College Press.

Hanson, J. R., & Silver, H. F. (2000). *Learning preference inventory*. Woodbridge, NJ: Thoughtful Education Press.

Hardman, M. L., Drew, C. J., and Egan, M. W. (2002). *Human exceptionality: Society, school, and family*, 7th ed. Boston: Allyn and Bacon.

Harrington-Lueker, D. (Ed.). (1999). *Barriers and breakthroughs: Technology in urban schools*. Washington, DC: Education Writers Association.

Harris Interactive, Inc. (2001). *The MetLife Survey of the American Teacher: Key Elements of Quality Schools*. New York: Author.

Hauser, M., and Rauch, S. (2002). New teacher! An exciting and scary time. *2002 Job search handbook for educators*. Columbus, OH: American Association for Employment in Education.

Healy, J. M. (1998). *Failure to connect: How computers affect our children's minds—for better and worse*. New York: Simon and Schuster.

Henriques, M. E. (1997, May). Increasing literacy among kindergartners through cross-age training. *Young Children*, pp. 42–47.

Henry, M. E. (1996). *Parent–school collaboration: Feminist organizational structures and school leadership*. Albany, NY: State University of New York Press.

Henry, E., Huntley, J., McKamey, C., and Harper, L. (1995). *To be a teacher: Voices from the classroom*. Thousand Oaks, CA: Corwin Press.

Hiebert, J., Gallimore, R., and Stigler, J. W. (2002). A knowledge base for the teaching profession: What would it look like and how can we get one? *Educational Researcher, 31*(5), 3–15.

Hinrichs, R. (2002). *A vision for lifelong learning—year 2020*. In *2020 visions: Transforming education and training through advanced technologies*. Washington, DC: U.S. Department of Commerce, 1–12.

Hole, S. (1998). Teacher as rain dancer. *Harvard Educational Review, 68*(3), 413–421.

Holland, A., and Andre, T. (1987, Winter). Participation in extracurricular activities in secondary schools. *Review of Educational Research*, pp. 437–466.

Holt-Reynolds, D. (1999). Good readers, good teachers? Subject matter expertise as a challenge in learning to teach. *Harvard Educational Review, 69*(1), 29–50.

Howard, V. E., Williams, B. F., Port, P. D., and Lepper, C. (2001). *Very young children with special needs*. Upper Saddle River, NJ: Merrill Prentice Hall.

Hoynes, W. (1998, Summer). News for a teen market: The lessons of Channel One. *Journal of Curriculum and Supervision*, pp. 339–356.

International Association for the Evaluation of Educational Achievement. (1997a). *Mathematics achievement in the primary school years: LEA's third international mathematics and science study*. Amsterdam, Netherlands: International Association for the Evaluation of Educational Achievement.

International Association for the Evaluation of Educational Achievement. (1997b). *Science achievement in the primary school years: LEA's third international mathematics and science study*. Amsterdam, Netherlands: Author International Association for the Evaluation of Educational Achievement.

Jersild, A. (1955). *When teachers face themselves*. New York: Teachers College Press.

Johnson, D. W., and Johnson, R. T. (1999). *Learning together and alone: Cooperative, competitive, and individualistic learning*, 5th ed. Boston: Allyn and Bacon.

Johnson, J., and Immerwahr, J. (1994). *First things first: What Americans expect from the public schools, a report from Public Agenda*. New York: Public Agenda.

Johnson, M. J., and Brown, L. (1998). Collegial support teams. In D. J. McIntyre and D. M. Byrd (Eds.), *Strategies for career-long teacher education: Teacher education yearbook VI*. Thousand Oaks, CA: Corwin Press.

Jonassen, D. H., Peck, K. L., and Wilson, B. G. (1999). *Learning with technology: A constructivist perspective*. Upper Saddle River, NJ: Merrill.

Jonassen, D. H., and Howland, J. (2003). *Learning to solve problems with technology: A constructivist perspective*. Upper Saddle River, NJ: Merrill Prentice Hall.

Jones, J. (1994). Integrated learning systems for diverse learners. *Media and Methods, 31*(3).

Jordan, W. J., and Nettles, S. M. (1999). *How students invest their time out of school: Effects on school engagement, perceptions of life chances, and achievement*. Baltimore: Center for Research on the Education of Students Placed at Risk.

Joyce, B., Weil, M., and Calhoun, E. (2000). *Models of teaching*, 6th ed. Boston: Allyn and Bacon.

Joyce, B., Weil, M., and Calhoun, E. (2004). *Models of teaching*, 7th ed. Boston: Allyn and Bacon.

Katz, Y. J. (1999). Kindergarten teacher training through virtual reality: Three-dimensional simulation methodology. *Educational Media International, 36*(2), 151–156.

Kaye, E. A. (Ed.). (2001). *Requirements for certification of teachers, counselors, librarians, administrators for elementary and secondary schools–66th edition, 2001–2002.* Chicago: The University of Chicago Press.

Kennedy, M. (1999). Ed schools and the problem of knowledge. In J. D. Raths and A. C. McAnich (Eds.), *Advances in teacher education*, vol. 5. *What counts as knowledge in teacher education?* (pp. 29–45). Stamford, CT: Ablex.

KIDLINK. (2002). Kidproj in KidSpace. KIDLINK Society. Retrieved from http://www.kidlink.org/KIDPROJ/projects.html

Kirkpatrick, H., and Cuban, L. (1998). Computers make kids smarter—right? *TECHNOS Quarterly, 7*(2), 26–31.

Kohlberg, L. (2000). The cognitive-developmental approach to moral education. In F. W. Parkay and G. Hass (Eds.), *Curriculum planning: A contemporary approach*, 7th ed. (pp. 136–148). Boston: Allyn and Bacon.

Kostelnik, M. J., Onaga, E., Rohde, B., and Whiren, A. (2002). *Children with special needs: Lessons for early childhood professionals.* New York: Teachers College Press.

Kounin, J. (1970). *Discipline and group management in classrooms.* New York: Holt, Rinehart and Winston.

Kozma, R., et al. (1992). Technology and the fate of at-risk students. *Education and Urban Society, 24*(4), 440–453.

Krogh, S. L. (2000). Weaving the web. In F. W. Parkay and G. Hass (Eds.), *Curriculum planning: A contemporary approach*, 7th ed. (pp. 338–341). Boston: Allyn and Bacon.

Larry P. v. Riles, 793 F.2d 969 (9th Cir. 1984).

Le, P. (2003, September 14). Students pick up pace with online classes. Associated Press.

Leinhardt, G. (1990). Capturing craft knowledge in teaching. *Educational Researcher, 19*(2), 18–25.

Levin, D., and Arafeh, S. (2002). *The digital disconnect: The widening gap between Internet-savvy students and their schools.* Washington, DC: The Pew Internet and American Life Project.

Lewis, R. B., and Doorlag, D. H. (1999). *Teaching special students in general education classrooms*, 5th ed. Upper Saddle River, NJ: Merrill.

Linn, R. L., and Gronlund, N. E. (2000). *Measurement and assessment in teaching*, 8th ed. Upper Saddle River, NJ: Merrill.

MacNaughton, R. H., and Johns, F. A. (1991, September). Developing a successful schoolwide discipline program. *NASSP Bulletin*, pp. 47–57.

Mahoney, J., and Cairns, R. B. (1997). Do extracurricular activities protect against early school dropout? *Developmental Psychology, 33*(2), 241–253.

Market Data Retrieval. (2002). *Technology in education 2002.* Shelton, CT: Author.

Marks, H. M., Newmann, F. M., and Gamoran, A. (1996). Does authentic pedagogy increase student achievement? In F. M. Newmann, et al. (Eds.), *Authentic achievement: Restructuring schools for intellectual quality* (pp. 49–76). San Francisco: Jossey-Bass.

Marshall, K. (2003, May). Recovering from HSPS (hyperactive superficial principal syndrome): A progress report. *Phi Delta Kappan*, 701–709.

McCain, T., and Jukes, I. (2001). *Windows on the future: Education in the age of technology.* Thousand Oaks, CA: Corwin Press.

McMillan, J. H. (2001). *Classroom assessment: Principles and practice for effective instruction*, 2nd ed. Boston: Allyn and Bacon.

Meek, C. (2003, April). Classroom crisis: It's about time. *Phi Delta Kappan*, 592–595.

Mehlinger, H. D. (1996, February). School reform in the Information Age. *Phi Delta Kappan*, pp. 400–407.

Michie, G. (1999). *Holler if you hear me: The education of a teacher and his students.* New York: Teachers College Press.

Milken Exchange on Education Technology. (1999). *Will new teachers be prepared to teach in a digital age? A national survey on information technology in teacher education.* Santa Monica, CA: Author.

Modi, M., Konstantopoulos, S., and Hedges, L. V. (1998). *Predictors of academic giftedness among U.S. high school students: Evidence from a nationally representative multivariate analysis.* Paper presented at the annual meeting of the American Educational Research Association, San Diego. Eric Document Number ED422 356.

Morton, C. (1996, February). The modern land of Laputa: Where computers are used in education. *Phi Delta Kappan*, pp. 416–419.

Moskal, B. M. (2000). Scoring rubrics: what, when, and how? *Practical Assessment, Research, & Evaluation, 7*(3).

National Board for Professional Teaching Standards. (2002). *What Teachers Should Know and Be Able to Do*. Arlington, VA: Author.

National Center for Education Statistics. (1995a). *Educational policy issues: Statistical perspectives: Extracurricular participation and student involvement*. Washington, DC: U.S. Department of Education: Author.

National Center for Education Statistics. (1995b). *A first look—findings from the National Assessment of Educational Progress*. Office of Educational Research and Improvement, U.S. Dept. of Education, Washington, DC.

National Center for Education Statistics. (1999). *Digest of education statistics 1998*. Washington, DC: U.S. Department of Education, Office of Educational Research and Improvement.

National Center for Education Statistics. (2001). *Projections of education statistics to 2011*. Washington, DC: U.S. Department of Education: Author.

National Center for Education Statistics. (2002a). *Special analysis—private schools: A brief portrait*. Washington, DC: U.S. Department of Education: Author.

National Center for Education Statistics. (2002b). *Predicting the need for newly hired teachers in the U.S. to 2008–09*. Washington, DC: U.S. Department of Education: Author.

National Center for Education Statistics. (2002c). *Projections of education statistics to 2008*. Washington, DC: U.S. Department of Education: Author.

National Center for Education Statistics. (2002d). *The digest of education statistics 2001*. Washington, DC: U.S. Department of Education: Author.

National Commission on Excellence in Education (1983). *A nation at risk: The imperative for educational reform*. Washington, DC: U.S. Government Printing Office.

National Commission on Teaching and America's Future. (2003a). *What matters most: Teaching for America's future*. New York: Author.

National Commission on Teaching and America's Future. (2003b). *No dream denied: A pledge to America's children*. Washington, DC: Author.

National Council for Accreditation of Teacher Education. (2002). *Professional standards for the accreditation of schools, colleges, and departments of education—2002 edition*. Washington, DC: Author.

National Joint Committee on Learning Disabilities. (1997). *Operationalizing the NJCLD definition of learning disabilities for ongoing assessment in schools*. Rockville, MD: Author.

National School Boards Association. (2002). *Are we there yet? Research and guidelines on school's use of the Internet*. Alexandria, VA: Author.

Newmann, F. M., and Wehlage, G. G. (1995). *Successful school restructuring: A report to the public and educators by the Center on Organization and Restructuring of Schools*. Madison, WI: University of Wisconsin, Center on Organization and Restructuring of Schools.

Newmann, F. M., et al. (Eds.). (1996). *Authentic achievement: Restructuring schools for intellectual quality*. San Francisco: Jossey-Bass.

Nitko, A. J. (2001). *Educational assessment of students*, 3rd ed. Upper Saddle River, NJ: Merrill.

Noddings, N. (2002). *Educating moral people: A caring alternative to character education*. New York: Teachers College Press.

Nord, C. W., and West, J. (2001). *National household education survey: Fathers' and mothers' involvement in their children's schools by family type and resident status*. Washington, DC: U.S. Department of Education, National Center for Education Statistics.

Norris, C. (1994). Computing in the classroom: Teaching the at-risk student. *Computing Teacher, 21*(5), 12, 14.

Oaks, M. M., Grantman, R., and Pedras, M. (2001). Technological literacy: A twenty-first century imperative. In F. W. Parkay and G. Hass (Eds.), *Curriculum planning: A contemporary approach*, 7th ed. (pp. 439–445). Boston: Allyn and Bacon.

Oberti v. Board of Education of the Borough of Clementon School District, 789 F. Supp. 1322 (D.N.J. 1992).

Olson, K. (2004). No hollow promise: Preparing teachers for their toughest assignment. *Washington State Magazine*, Fall 2004, 33–37.

Oosterhof, A. (2003). *Developing and using classroom assessments*. Upper Saddle River, NJ: Merrill Prentice Hall.

Oppenheimer, T. (1997, July). The computer delusion. *The Atlantic Monthly*, pp. 45–62.

Ortiz, M. G. (1999, April 19). Urban schools lag in technology. *Detroit Free Press*.

Pajak, E. (1999). *Approaches to clinical supervision: Alternatives for improving instruction*. Norwood, MA: Christopher-Gordon.

Pang, V. O. (1994, December). Why do we need this class: Multicultural education for teachers. *Phi Delta Kappan*, 289–292.

Parkay, F. W. (1983). *White teacher, black school: The professional growth of a ghetto teacher*. New York: Praeger.

Parkay, F. W., and Hass, G. (2000). *Curriculum planning: A contemporary approach*, 7th ed. Boston: Allyn and Bacon.

Parkay, F. W., and Oaks, M. M. (1998, April). *Promoting the professional development of teachers: What the U.S. can learn from other countries.* Paper presented at the Annual Meeting of the American Educational Research Association, San Diego.

Parnell, D. (2000). *Contextual teaching works.* Waco, TX: Center for Occupational Research and Development.

PASE (Parents in Action on Special Education) v. Hannon, 506 F. Supp. 831 (E.D. Ill. 1980).

Paul, J. L., and Colucci, K. (2000). Caring pedagogy. In J. L. Paul and T. J. Smith (Eds.), *Stories out of school: Memories and reflections on care and cruelty in the classroom* (pp. 45–63). Stamford, CT: Ablex.

Paul, J. L., Christensen, L., and Falk, G. (2000). Accessing the intimate spaces of life in the classroom through letters to former teachers: A protocol for uncovering hidden stories. In J. L. Paul and T. J. Smith (Eds.), *Stories out of school: Memories and reflections on care and cruelty in the classroom* (pp. 15–26). Stamford, CT: Ablex.

Piirto, J. (1999). *Talented children and adults: Their development and education.* Upper Saddle River, NJ: Merrill.

Pitton, D. E. (1998). *Stories of student teaching: A case approach to the student teaching experience.* Upper Saddle River, NJ: Merrill.

Posner, G. J. (2000). *Field experience: A guide to reflective teaching,* 5th ed. New York: Longman.

President's Commission on Excellence in Special Education. (2002). *A new era: Revitalizing special education for children and their families.* Washington, DC: Author.

Public Agenda. (1999). *Reality check: The status of standards reform.* New York: Author.

Rand, M. K., and Shelton-Colangelo, S. (1999). *Voices of student teachers: Cases from the field.* Upper Saddle River, NJ: Merrill.

Ravitz, J. L., Wong, Y. T., and Becker, H. J. (1999). Report to participants. The University of California, Irvine, and The University of Minnesota: Center for Research on Information Technology and Organizations.

Reilly, K. C. (2000). Using habits of mind to look "inside the text." In Costa, A. L. and Kallick, B. (Eds.). *Activating & engaging habits of mind* (pp. 98–102). Alexandria, VA: Association for Supervision and Curriculum Development.

Renzulli, J. S. (1998). The three-ring conception of giftedness. In S. M. Baum, S. M. Reis, and L. R. Maxfield, (Eds.), *Nurturing the gifts and talents of primary grade students.* Mansfield Center, CT: Creative Learning Press.

Ripple, R. E., and Rockcastle, V. E. (Eds.). (1964). *Piaget rediscovered: A report of the conference on cognitive studies and curriculum development.* Ithaca, NY: School of Education, Cornell University.

Roach, V., and Cohen, B. A. (2002). *Moving past the politics: How alternative certification can promote comprehensive teacher development reforms.* Alexandria, VA: National Association of State Boards of Education.

Roblyer, M. D. (2003). *Integrating educational technology into teaching,* 3rd ed. Upper Saddle River, N.J: Merrill/Prentice Hall.

Rogers, K. (1991). *The relationship of grouping practices to the education of the gifted and talented learner.* Storrs, CT: National Research Center on the Gifted and Talented, University of Connecticut.

Rose, L. C., and Gallup, A. M. (2004, September). The 36th Phi Delta Kappa/Gallup Poll of the public's attitudes toward the public schools. *Phi Delta Kappan,* 41–56.

Rosenshine, B. (1988). Explicit teaching. In D. Berliner and B. Rosenshine (Eds.), *Talks to teachers.* New York: Random House.

Rosenshine, B. (1995). Advances in research on instruction. *The Journal of Educational Research, 88*(5), 262–268.

Rosenshine, B., and Stevens, R. (1986). Teaching functions. In M. C. Wittrock (Ed.), *Handbook of research on teaching,* 3rd ed. (pp. 376–391). New York: Macmillan.

Rosenshine, B., Meister, C., and Chapman, S. (1996). Teaching students to generate questions: A review of the intervention studies. *Review of Educational Research, 66*(2), 181–221.

Sallie Mae Corporation. (1995). *A report from the 1994 Sallie Mae symposium on quality education.* Washington, DC: Author.

Salovey, P., and Feldman-Barrett, L. (Eds.). (2002). *The wisdom of feelings: Psychological processes in emotional intelligence.* New York: Guilford Press.

Salovey, P., and Sluyter, D. J. (Eds.). (1997). *Emotional development and emotional intelligence: Educational implications.* New York: Basic Books.

Salovey, P., Mayer, J. D., and Caruso, D. (2002). The positive psychology of emotional intelligence. In C. R. Snyder & S. J. Lopez (Eds.), *The handbook of positive psychology* (pp. 159–171). New York: Oxford University Press.

Sandholtz, J. J., Ringstaff, C., and Dwyer, D. C. (1997). *Teaching with technology: Creating student-centered classrooms*. New York: Teachers College Press.

Sarnoff, D. (1940). Foreword. In L. R. Lohr, *Television broadcasting*. New York: McGraw-Hill.

Scales, P. C. (2001). The public image of adolescents. *Society 38*(4), 64–70.

Schifter, D. (Ed.). (1996). *What's happening in math class? Envisioning new practices through teacher narratives*, vol. 1. New York: Teachers College Press.

Schneider, R. B., and Barone, D. (1997, Spring). Cross-age tutoring. *Childhood Education*, pp. 136–143.

Schmuck, R. A., and Schmuck, P. A. (2001). *Group processes in the classroom*, 8th ed. Boston: McGraw-Hill.

Schwartz, J. E., and Beichner, R. J. (1999). *Essentials of educational technology*. Boston: Allyn and Bacon.

Search Institute. (2002). *Help your youth grow up healthy*. Minneapolis, MN: Author.

Sharan, Y., and Sharan, S. (1989/90, December/January). Group investigation expands cooperative learning. *Educational Leadership*, pp. 17–21.

Shenk, D. (1998). *Data smog: Surviving the information glut*. New York: HarperEdge.

Signer, B. (1991). CAI and at-risk minority urban high school students. *Journal of Research on Computing in Education, 24*(2).

Singer, A. (1994, December). Reflections on multiculturalism. *Phi Delta Kappan*, pp. 284–288.

Slavin, R. E. (2000). *Educational psychology: Theory and practice*, 6th ed. Boston: Allyn and Bacon.

Slavin, R. E. (2003). *Educational psychology: Theory and practice*, 7th ed. Boston: Allyn and Bacon.

Smyth, J. W. (1995). *Clinical supervision: Collaborative learning about teaching*. New York: State Mutual Book and Periodical Service.

Snyder, K. J., and Anderson, R. H. (Eds.). (1996). *Clinical supervision: Coaching for higher performance*. Lanham, MD: Scarecrow Press.

Spring, J. (1998). *Conflict of interests: The politics of American education*, 3rd ed. Boston: McGraw-Hill.

St. Michel, T. (1995). *Effective substitute teachers: Myth, mayhem, or magic?* Thousand Oaks, CA: Corwin Press.

Stanford, B. H. (1992). Gender equity in the classroom. In D. A. Byrnes and G. Kiger (Eds.), *Common bonds: Anti-bias teaching in a diverse society*. Wheaton, MD: Association for Childhood Education International.

Steinberg, L., Dornbusch, S., and Brown, B. (1996). *Beyond the classroom: Why school reform has failed and what parents need to do*. New York: Simon and Schuster.

Sternberg, R. J. (2002). Beyond g: The theory of successful intelligence. In R. J. Sternberg and E. L. Grigorenko (Eds.), *The general factor of intelligence: How general is it?* (pp. 447–479). Mahwah, NJ: Lawrence Erlbaum.

Stiggins, R. J. (2001). *Student-involved classroom assessment*, 3rd ed. Upper Saddle River, NJ: Merrill Prentice Hall.

Stiggins, R. (2004, September). New assessment beliefs for a new school mission. *Phi Delta Kappan*, 22–27.

Stoll, C. (1996). *Silicon snake oil: Second thoughts on the information highway*. New York: Anchor.

Stoll, C. (1999). *High-tech heretic: Why computers don't belong in the classroom and other reflections by a computer contrarian*. New York: Doubleday.

Strong, R., Silver, H., and Perini, M. (2001). *Teaching what matters most: Standards and strategies for raising student achievement*. Alexandria, VA: Association for Supervision and Curriculum Development.

Substitute Teaching Institute. (2002). *Fact sheet*. Logan, UT: Utah State University, Substitute Teaching Institute.

Tapscott, D. (1999, July 6). Kids, technology and the schools. *Computerworld*.

Terman, L. M., Baldwin, B. T., and Bronson, E. (1925). Mental and physical traits of a thousand gifted children. In L. M. Terman (Ed.), *Genetic studies of genius*, vol. 1. Stanford, CA: Stanford University Press.

Terman, L. M., and Oden, M. H. (1947). The gifted child grows up. In L. M. Terman (Ed.), *Genetic studies of genius*, vol. 4. Stanford, CA: Stanford University Press.

Terman, L. M., and Oden, M. H. (1959). The gifted group in mid-life. In L. M. Terman (Ed.). *Genetic studies of genius*, vol. 5. Sanford, CA: Stanford University Press.

Thelen, H. A. (1960). *Education and the human quest*. New York: Harper and Row.

Thelen, H. A. (1981). *The classroom society: The construction of educational experience*. New York: Wiley.

Tileston, D. W. (2004). *What every teacher should know about student assessment*. Thousand Oaks, CA: Corwin Press.

Tombari, M. L., and Borich, G. D. (1999). *Authentic assessment in the classroom: Applications and practice*. Upper Saddle River, NJ: Merrill.

Trotter, A. (1998, October 1). A question of effectiveness. *Education Week on the Web*.

Trotter, A. (2002, May 9). E-learning goes to school. *Education Week on the Web*.

Tweney, D. (2000, December 7). *No more free ride*. Tampa, FL: Business 2.0 Media, Inc.

Tyler, R. (1949). *Basic principles of curriculum and instruction*. Chicago: University of Chicago.

The University of Memphis. (Winter 1994/95). Technology provides field experiences. *Perspectives*. Memphis: The University of Memphis, College of Education.

U.S. Department of Commerce. (2002a). *A vision for lifelong learning—year 2020*. In *2020 visions: Transforming education and training through advanced technologies*. Washington, DC: Author.

U.S. Department of Commerce. (2002b). *A nation online: How Americans are expanding their use of the Internet*. Washington, DC: Author.

U.S. Department of Education. (1996). The technology literacy challenge. Washington, DC: Author.

U.S. Department of Education. (1997, April 18). *From college to first-year teaching: How the United States compares to several other countries*. Retrieved from www.ed.gov/pubs/APEC/teachers.html

U.S. Department of Education. (1997). *From students of teaching to teachers of students*. Washington, DC: Author.

U.S. Department of Education. (1999). *Schools with IDEAs that work*. Washington, DC: Author.

U.S. Department of Education. (2001, July 27). *Ready to read, ready to learn* [news release]. Washington, DC: Author.

Utay, C., and Utay, J. (1997). Peer-assisted learning: The effects of cooperative learning and cross-age peer tutoring with word processing on writing skills of students with learning disabilities. *Journal of Computing in Childhood Education, 8*.

Van Reusen, A. K., Shoho, A. R., and Barker, K. S. (2000). High school teacher attitudes toward inclusion. *High School Journal, 84*(2), 7–20.

Vaughn, S., Bos, C. S., and Schumm, J. S. (1997). *Teaching mainstreamed, diverse, and at-risk students in the general education classroom*. Boston: Allyn and Bacon.

Vygotsky, L. S. (1978). *Mind in society: The development of higher mental process*. Cambridge, MA: Harvard University Press.

Vygotsky, L. S. (1986). *Thought and language*. Cambridge, MA: MIT Press.

Walberg, H. J., and Greenberg, R. C. (1997, May). Using the learning environment inventory. *Educational Leadership*, pp. 45–47.

Wallace, R. M. (2004). A framework for understanding teaching with the Internet. *American Educational Research Journal, 41*(2), 447–488.

Walsh, M. (1999a, April 2). Conservatives join effort to pull the plug on Channel One. *Education Week on the Web*.

Walsh, M. (1999b, May 26). Nader, Schlafly lambaste Channel One at Senate hearing. *Education Week on the Web*.

Wasserman, S. (1994, April). Using cases to study teaching. *Phi Delta Kappan*, pp. 602–611.

Web-Based Education Commission. (2001). *The power of the Internet for learning: Moving from promise to practice*. Washington, DC: Author.

Wechsler, D. (1958). *The measurement and appraisal of adult intelligence*, 4th ed. Baltimore: Williams and Wilkins.

Wentz, P. J. (2001). *The student teaching experience: Cases from the classroom*. Upper Saddle River, NJ: Merrill Prentice Hall.

Westbury, I. (1992). Comparing American and Japanese achievement: Is the United States really a low-achiever? *Educational Researcher, 2*(15), 18–24.

WestEd. (2001). *Virtual schools: Trends and issues, a study of virtual schools in the United States*. San Francisco: WestEd.

Williams, J. (1999, April 18). Urban schools' obstacles hindering technology. *Milwaukee Journal Sentinal*.

Wilson, B. L., and Corbett, H. D. (2001). *Listening to urban kids: School reform and the teachers they want*. Albany, NY: State University of New York Press.

Wolfgang, C. H. (2001). *Solving discipline problems: Methods and models for today's teachers*, 5th ed. Boston: Allyn and Bacon.

Woolfolk, A. E. (2001). *Educational psychology*, 8th ed. Boston: Allyn and Bacon.

Yamamoto, K., Davis, O. L., Jr., Dylak, S., Whittaker, J., Marsh, C., and van der Westhuizen, P. C. (1996, Spring). Across six nations: Stressful events in the lives of children. *Child Psychiatry and Human Development*, pp. 139–150.

Zhang, L., and Sternberg, R. J. (2001). Thinking styles across cultures: Their relationships with student learning. In R. J. Sternberg and L. Zhang (Eds.), *Perspectives on thinking, learning, and cognitive styles* (pp. 197–226). Mahwah, NJ: Lawrence Erlbaum.

Zukowski, V. (1997, Fall). Teeter-totters and tandem bikes: A glimpse into the world of cross-age tutors. *Teaching and Change*, pp. 71–91.

Index